LAW AN
LIABILITY

Tender offers, exchange offers, and consent solicitations in connection with debt securities are important instruments of corporate restructurings, corporate rescues, recapitalizations, and other types of liability management of public and private companies. Although tender offers for shares, stocks, and other equity securities are covered by a vast literature on public mergers, takeovers, and acquisitions, the literature on liability management transactions for debt securities is scarce.

Law and Practice of Liability Management rectifies this by providing a systematic treatise on the law relating to this significant aspect of the global capital market. It guides students and professionals through the complex legal and regulatory requirements applicable to these transactions, the increasing regulatory interest by the world's leading financial regulatory authorities, and recent innovations in the structuring, legal techniques, and execution of the relevant transactions in international capital markets.

APOSTOLOS ATH. GKOUTZINIS is a partner in the capital markets group of the London office of Shearman & Sterling, with a focus on US federal securities laws, high-yield debt offerings, and international capital markets transactions in general. He is recognized as one of the leading lawyers in the European debt capital markets in general and the high-yield market in particular, and has represented issuers, sponsors, and underwriters in a wide variety of corporate and leveraged buyout high-yield bond offerings, investment-grade debt offerings, equity offerings, and other transactions. He has also played a central role in several liability management transactions involving investment-grade and high-yield debt securities.

LAW AND PRACTICE OF LIABILITY MANAGEMENT

Debt Tender Offers, Exchange Offers, Bond Buybacks and Consent Solicitations in International Capital Markets

APOSTOLOS ATH. GKOUTZINIS

CAMBRIDGE
UNIVERSITY PRESS

University Printing House, Cambridge CB2 8BS, United Kingdom

Cambridge University Press is part of the University of Cambridge.

It furthers the University's mission by disseminating knowledge in the pursuit of education, learning and research at the highest international levels of excellence.

www.cambridge.org
Information on this title: www.cambridge.org/9781316601143

First published 2013
Reprinted 2014
First paperback edition 2015

A catalogue record for this publication is available from the British Library

Library of Congress Cataloguing in Publication data
Gkoutzinis, Apostolos Ath.
Law and practice of liability management : debt tender offers, exchange offers, bond buybacks and consent solicitations in international capital markets / Apostolos Ath. Gkoutzinis.
pages cm.
Includes bibliographical references and index.
ISBN 978-1-107-02034-4 (hardback)
1. Asset liability management – Law and legislation 2. Capital markets – Law and legislation. 3. Debt. 4. Securities. 5. Credit I. Title.
K1329.5.G56 2013
346.73′0922 – dc23 2013023227

ISBN 978-1-107-02034-4 Hardback
ISBN 978-1-316-60114-3 Paperback

CONTENTS

PREFACE

> ἐμοὶ δέ κε ταῦτα μελήσεται ὄφρα τελέσσω· εἰ δ᾽ ἄγε τοι κεφαλῇ κατανεύσομαι ὄφρα πεποίθῃς· τοῦτο γὰρ ἐξ ἐμέθεν γε μετ᾽ ἀθανάτοισι μέγιστον τέκμωρ· οὐ γὰρ ἐμὸν παλινάγρετον οὐδ᾽ ἀπατηλὸνοὐδ᾽ ἀτελεύτητον ὅ τί κεν κεφαλῇ κατανεύσω. *Ομήρου Ιλιάδα, Α, 520–525*
>
> I will consider the matter, and will bring it about as you wish. See, I incline my head that you believe me. This is the most solemn promise that I can give to any god. I never recall my word, or deceive, or fail to do what I say, when I have nodded my head. *Homer's Iliad, Book I, 520–525*

It was summer of 2012 when I promised I would write this book. I am not quite sure why I felt the need to make such a promise. I had written a book before (in 2006), with the same leading publishing house, and cannot credibly propose that I had no idea, when making the promise, that a considerable amount of effort would be required. In many respects, the timing of this effort could not have been worse. During the past 24 months, an exceptionally strong financial market has allowed most lawyers practicing in my field to try more late-night and weekend takeaway dinners in the office than ever before, executing all sorts of financings in the debt and equity markets along the way. Very promptly and predictably, the excitement of the ill-conceived promise faded away, and it became agonizingly difficult to dedicate even the most miserly amount of time to this book. I am not even sure that anybody remotely familiar with my working schedule thought I was being serious about it. In any event, the manuscript became a close personal companion on long business flights, in airport lounges, on holidays, long weekends, late office nights between conference calls – adding a few lines here or there, checking a case, reviewing one of the SEC No-Action Letters, revising an earlier draft.

There were really two things that motivated me to pursue this endeavor to the very end: the (rather selfish) desire to leave something behind, a very modest intellectual legacy of my contribution to this field of law that I call the law of international capital markets and finance; and to remind my younger colleagues at Shearman & Sterling and my students (in the various law faculties that still, rather unwisely, think I am someone worth inviting to lecture) that the practice of law in this fast-moving field can and should be based more on intellectual content and less on precedent or habitual repetition of deal-making rituals.

The list of people to whom I owe immense personal gratitude is very long indeed. It includes academic and professional mentors, colleagues and friends, loyal clients, close personal friends, partners, associates, and other staff at Shearman & Sterling, and the many great lawyers I worked opposite and learned a great deal from in some of the biggest financing transactions of our time. They have all shaped my personality and helped me in more ways than they can realize. I feel enormous gratitude to all of them.

Despite the distance, the bond with my parents and my brother is as strong as it has ever been, as is their unconditional love. I could not ask for more. It is difficult to complete this next sentence about my Despina and the children. My debt is enormous and I can say very little to them. There really is no excuse for the long absence. Maria, Athanasie, Konstantine, Ioanni, my children: thank you for putting up with me. Despina, you deserve all the credit, I have always known that.

This book is dedicated to Ioannis, Konstantinos, Athanasios and Maria (in reverse order as promised but with equal and unmitigated admiration and love).

London, May 2014

1

Liability management for issuers of debt securities:

Summary of options and legal framework

1 Introduction

As the issuer of debt securities in the capital markets and its advisors are preparing for the customary celebratory closing dinner following the issuance of the securities to investors and the successful completion of an intense and (probably) expensive capital markets project, a liability management transaction for those same securities is probably the last thing on their minds. It is entirely unromantic for any newly wedded couple to be discussing the advantages and disadvantages of a divorce or going through the provisions of a nuptial agreement as they are boarding a flight, holding hands, to their honeymoon destination. And yet, honeymoons never last forever and marriages often come to a sudden end as well. For the issuer of debt securities that had once been issued and celebrated with a lot of fanfare, the equivalent of a messy divorce from its hapless investors takes the form of a liability management transaction against the background of the issuer's or its controlling shareholders' new financing or strategic plans and, in the worst case, against the background of considerable financial stress and the risk or the reality of bankruptcy.

No issuer of debt securities is protected forever from competitive market forces and external economic shocks. The issuer's (hitherto seemingly robust) financial and business plan may become entirely fanciful or require substantial revision as a result of tougher economic and financial conditions, structural changes, limited financing options, poor profitability, rising costs, and/or volatile macroeconomic environments in the issuer's main markets.

Often, issuers with fundamentally sound businesses and operations may suffer from lack of liquidity, working capital, and/or long-term funding. They may also find that financial and non-financial covenants in their existing financing agreements are at risk of being violated as a result of weaker than expected economic performance, which may trigger, in turn, default clauses in the same financing agreements and cross-default or cross-acceleration clauses in other financing documents then in effect. As issuers of debt securities come under operational and financial stress, their creditors (including debt investors), suppliers, and customers become extremely uncomfortable and begin to demand additional legal protections. These protections include more-favorable payment or prepayment terms, higher-quality collateral and tighter contractual protections, and often accelerate rather than avert the issuer's ultimate demise in the absence of a radical restructuring plan.

Any company in that or a similar situation should carefully identify, together with its financial and legal advisors, all the options that may help the company to manage its liabilities and cash payments, turn the business around, and avoid bankruptcy and other terminal events. In addition to operational improvements, sales of assets, and injections of fresh equity (which are outside the scope of this work), one or more liability management transactions in relation to the issuer's outstanding debt securities will always be on the menu of alternative options.

Corporate and sovereign issuers of debt securities seeking to manage their financial liabilities represented by such debt securities have a range of options at their disposal:

- to repay the principal amount due under the debt securities on the contractually agreed maturity date or to redeem the debt securities early, in whole or in part, in accordance with the terms and conditions of the relevant securities (*optional redemption*);
- to purchase the relevant debt securities, either directly or through an affiliate of the issuer, in a privately negotiated transaction from the holder(s) of those securities or in the open market through the services of a broker or dealer (*repurchase*);
- to offer publicly to purchase the principal amount outstanding of the relevant debt securities, in whole or in part, from the holders of the relevant securities, at a price to be determined by the terms of the offer and through a structured tendering process (*cash tender offer*); or
- to exchange the relevant series of debt securities, in whole or in part, for newly issued securities (debt or equity) or other liabilities having different terms and conditions relating to the principal amount, interest rates, payment dates, covenants, events of default, or other structural or contractual features as more specifically set forth in the terms and conditions of the exchange offer (*debt for debt* or *debt for equity exchange offer*).

Which option or combination of options the issuer and its advisors will decide to pursue will depend on a number of different factors, including the following important legal, commercial, and structural factors:

- the commercial and financial objectives of the liability management transaction;
- prevailing market conditions;
- the commercial feasibility of the transaction in light of the interests and objectives of the holders of the relevant securities;
- the identity and number of the holders of the debt securities;
- whether or not the holders of the securities are widely dispersed and located in different jurisdictions;
- the time and effort required to finalize the necessary documentation;
- the manner in which the debt securities are held (registered or bearer securities), and the clearing and settlement system in which transactions in the relevant securities clear and settle;
- legal and regulatory considerations;
- tax considerations;
- accounting considerations;
- contractual limitations and restrictions in the underlying legal documentation relating to the relevant securities and other existing contractual agreements;
- the commercial and legal framework of the market or markets on which the relevant securities are listed and traded (if at all);
- the estimated cost of the relevant liability management transaction; and
- whether or not the issuer has cash resources available to it and is willing or not to use such cash resources in connection with the relevant transaction.

Some of the options may even be appropriate for healthier companies that are not distressed as new funding sources, hitherto unavailable or unattractive to them, suddenly become available and attractive.

Annex I contains a summary guide to the various transaction alternatives available to issuers of debt securities in structuring liability management transactions.

1.1 Commercial objectives

In pursuing a liability management transaction for debt securities, the issuer and its advisors will want to achieve one or more of the following commercial objectives:

- the extinguishment, in whole or in part, of the relevant debt obligation represented by the relevant debt securities;
- a reduction of interest expense attributable to the debt securities;
- the extension of the stated date of maturity of the relevant debt obligation;
- amendment or modification of other economic or payment terms and conditions of the relevant debt securities (including, without limitation, amendments or modifications changing the mechanics of payment of interest and/or principal, changes affecting redemption or change of control provisions, or changes affecting the location or manner of payment);
- the amendment, modification, or elimination of restrictive covenants in relevant debt securities and other changes in the legal structure advantageous to the issuer such as releases of guarantees or security, assignment of the relevant legal obligation to a different legal entity, and the elimination of restrictions on asset disposals, mergers, and other business combination transactions;
- improvement in certain financial ratios of the issuer that are directly or indirectly affected by the cost of financial debt on the issuer's balance sheet;
- recognition of accounting gains (per share or in total) through the extinguishment of debt obligations at less than face value;
- regulatory or credit rating advantages; and
- extended corporate and financial restructuring, the management of cash and cash equivalents, and/or, in relation to issuers under severe stress, the avoidance of bankruptcy, liquidation, and similar terminal events.

Corporate and sovereign issuers of debt securities embarking on a liability management transaction usually pursue a combination of commercial objectives, while at the same time seeking the best possible documentary, legal, regulatory, accounting, and tax treatment of the commercial result that they desire to accomplish. A careful analysis of the reasons for a particular restructuring, the commercial objectives, and the other transactions that are involved in the restructuring must be undertaken to determine which particular liability management technique is the most suitable in a given situation. For example, an issuer that is able to meet its payment obligations under existing debt securities but needs permanent or temporary relief from the effects of existing maintenance or incurrence covenants will simply need to solicit the consents of the holders of the relevant securities to waivers of or amendments to the relevant restrictive covenants without seeking to change the economic terms of the relevant securities.

1.2 Differences between debt securities and equity securities

Securities issued by corporate or sovereign issuers and traded in capital markets are either *equity* (or *equity-linked*) securities or *debt* securities.

Equity securities such as stocks, shares, partnership or participation interests, investment contracts, and other similar securities are securities representing an initial equity contribution into the issuer of the relevant security and a set of voting and economic rights stemming from that contribution, as more specifically prescribed in the relevant corporate law of the jurisdiction of incorporation or organization of the issuer of the security and its charter or articles of association or similar constitutional document of the issuer.[1]

The *economic rights* represent the residual economic interest in the issuer of such security, i.e., the claim to the assets left after all other claimants (including financial and trade creditors, employees, and the government) have been satisfied in full. The *voting rights* allow the holders of the equity securities to exercise control over the issuer of those securities through the election of the board of directors of the issuer (or similar governing body) and their power to block or determine the outcome of certain significant economic or organizational events in the life of the issuer.

Debt securities such as bonds, notes, debentures, commercial paper, and other types of debt securities represent the simplest form of legal obligation, i.e., an obligation to pay an amount of money sometime in the future. They are financial liabilities on the issuer's balance sheet without any voting rights or any economic rights in the profits and losses of the issuer (other than the contractual right to receive payment of a fixed or determinable sum of money as more specifically determined by and/or in accordance with the terms and conditions of the relevant security). Long-term debt securities represent the commitment of capital to an issuer for a relatively long period of time (five years or more), whereas short-term debt securities represent the commitment of capital for a short period of time (between ninety days and five years).

The difference between liability management transactions for debt securities (e.g., tender offers, privately negotiated or public repurchases, exchange offers, redemptions, or consent solicitations) and similar transactions in the issuer's equity securities is significant.

[1] For an excellent discussion of the attributes of equity securities and its differences from debt securities, see William A. Klein and John C. Coffee, Jr, *Business Organization and Finance, Legal and Economic Principles*, 9th edn (Foundation Press: New York, 2005), ch. 4.

Tender offers or purchases of equity securities (in the open market or in privately negotiated transactions) aim to transfer corporate control from the existing holders of the equity securities to the buyer or, in the case of purchases of shares in the issuer by the issuer itself, to return equity capital back to the issuer's shareholders. Tender offers or purchases of debt securities aim to manage the financial liabilities of the issuer to achieve one of the restructuring objectives set forth above but do not affect, or aim to affect, the exercise of voting and investment control in the issuer by the holders of the equity securities of the issuer. This fundamental difference between certain types of liability management transactions in debt securities, compared to similar transactions in equity securities, has profound effects on the legal and regulatory framework governing liability management transactions relating to debt securities.

1.3 Types of transactions in debt securities

1.3.1 Sales and purchases of debt securities in secondary markets

Following the initial offer, issuance, and sale of debt securities to investors (a *primary sale*), which results in cash proceeds to the issuer of the relevant securities in consideration for the issuance of the securities to the relevant investors, debt securities are sold and purchased among investors in the secondary markets (a *secondary sale*) like any other asset is bought and sold in any other market. Sales of debt securities by the holders of the securities to other investors or back to the issuer do not generate any proceeds for the issuer.

Sales, purchases, and other transactions in equity and debt securities are conducted on securities exchanges and other organizations that maintain or provide a marketplace or facilities for bringing together purchasers and sellers of securities. They are also conducted in the over-the-counter markets in large volumes by the public generally (including retail investors and sophisticated institutional and professional investors). The prices established and offered in such secondary transactions are generally disseminated and quoted publicly, and constitute the basis for determining and establishing the prices at which securities are bought and sold between investors and other market participants.[2] As the history of finance amply demonstrates, the prices of securities, and the volumes of securities

[2] See generally Section 2 of the Securities Exchange Act of 1934, as amended (the "Securities Exchange Act").

offered for sale or sold, are susceptible to manipulation and control, and the dissemination of prices and other relevant information often triggers excessive speculation, resulting in market distortions, unreasonable fluctuations in the prices of securities, and outright fraud.[3]

Most secondary transactions in securities are sales or purchases of securities between a willing buyer and a willing seller in the secondary market. Securities transactions in the secondary market include any offer or sale of any security by any holder thereof (other than the issuer) to any other person (including the issuer of such security or an affiliate of the issuer). The number and value of transactions in securities in the secondary market easily dwarfs the number and value of securities issued by issuers and offered to buyers in primary capital-raising transactions. The concept of a secondary transaction therefore encompasses a wide range of transactions, from isolated trades by a particular investor on a securities exchange to an underwritten offering by affiliates of the issuer of the security.

Secondary transactions also include trades in the relevant securities in the secondary market by the issuer of those securities or an affiliate of the issuer. They also include tender offers for issued securities by the issuer of the securities (or an affiliate of the issuer) or an unaffiliated third party, or repurchases of the issued securities in the open market by the issuer of those securities or an affiliate of the issuer.

1.3.2 Purchases of debt securities for cash

A purchase of debt securities for cash is a very simple capital markets transaction: a person purchases a debt security for cash from an existing holder of the subject security. The purchaser of the subject securities could be the issuer of the securities (or an affiliate of the issuer) or a non-affiliated third party that purchases the subject securities for investment purposes.

An issuer of debt securities (or an affiliate of the issuer) may repurchase the outstanding debt securities for cash either (i) through the redemption of the subject securities in accordance with their terms, or (ii) in a privately negotiated transaction with a willing seller in the secondary capital market, in a public tender offer, or in one or more transactions in the open market.

[3] This is, for example, the rationale for the introduction of federal regulation of securities markets in the United States as set forth in Section 2 of the Securities Exchange Act.

Issuers of debt securities repurchase or redeem their debt securities to change the composition of their debt liabilities on the balance sheet. An issuer whose outstanding debt securities are trading in the securities markets at prices below the principal amount of the relevant securities due on the date of maturity may desire to purchase those securities at such discounted prices to reduce the overall debt burden of the issuer. Redemptions and repurchases of debt securities are also effective methods of reducing the overall cost of the debt capital of the relevant issuer. For example, if interest rates on debt instruments fall and bond prices rise, the option to redeem or repurchase outstanding debt securities can be very appealing as the issuer, through the repurchase or the redemption, will retire a debt obligation with a low price and a high interest rate and replace it with a debt obligation issued at a higher price and a lower interest rate. Moreover, the rationale for the repurchase or redemption of the outstanding debt securities may also be the change of the maturity profile of the issuer's outstanding debt (for example, by financing a repurchase of short-term debt securities with the issuance of long-term debt securities or long-term bank borrowings). Sometimes, the motivation behind the repurchase or redemption is the need to change the currency or interest rate profile of the issuer's outstanding debt obligations.

2 Redemptions of debt securities in accordance with their terms

In the absence of special provisions in the documentation, holders of debt securities cannot be compelled to accept payment of the principal amount prior to the stated maturity date of the relevant debt security. Nevertheless, an issuer of debt securities may be able to *redeem* early (i.e., prior to the stated maturity date) the outstanding debt securities, in whole or in part, in accordance with their terms (assuming that the right of redemption is expressly granted to the issuer pursuant to the terms and conditions of the securities).[4] The issuer's *right of redemption* is exercised by the issuer by notice to the holders of the subject securities and, if applicable, the intermediary (the *trustee*) that may hold the subject securities in trust for the benefit of the bondholders.[5]

[4] Some types of securities (including securities with short-term maturities or zero-coupon securities) provide full call protection to maturity and are not redeemable at the option of the issuer.

[5] *Optional redemption* (i.e., redemption of the securities at the option of the issuer) leads to the extinguishment of the liabilities represented by the securities to be redeemed and, consequently, it is one of the options for managing financial liabilities. Optional redemption

From the perspective of the issuer of the debt securities, the right of redemption may be significant for a number of reasons: business developments may require modifications of the terms of the debt securities that will be unacceptable to the holders of the debt securities, and redemption of the debt securities may be the only viable alternative. Redemption may also be necessary for the completion of a merger, acquisition, or business combination; or a high interest rate debt security may become unduly burdensome and redemption may be the only viable alternative for the financial profile of the issuer.

If less than the whole principal amount of the debt securities is to be redeemed, the amount redeemed must usually be a multiple of the smallest denomination of the debt securities, which varies from as little as $1,000 to $200,000 or the equivalent in euros, sterling, or other international currencies (in debt securities that are designed to be exempt from the prospectus requirements of the Prospectus Directive).[6] Sometimes, the documentation will provide that any partial redemption must be of a prescribed minimum amount (especially in issues of debt securities held by a small number of sophisticated institutions).

The issuer may elect to exercise the right of redemption for the whole or a part of the outstanding principal amount of the subject securities. Payment of the redemption price (i.e., the price at which the issuer redeems the subject securities) is made on the date of redemption, usually between thirty and sixty days after notice of redemption is delivered to the holders

should be distinguished from *mandatory redemption*, which is the mandatory repayment of the relevant securities by the issuer (i.e., the acceleration of the stated maturity of the securities) upon the occurrence of certain events set forth in the relevant terms and conditions. Mandatory redemption is not a liability management transaction and will not be considered further. Optional redemption at the discretion of the issuer should also be distinguished from the repurchase of the debt securities by the issuer *at the option of the holders*. For example, indentures for corporate debt securities often specify that upon the occurrence of certain events (e.g., a change of control or a sale of assets), the issuer is obligated to make an offer to the holders to repurchase any principal amount of debt securities that the holders wish to "put back" to the issuer at their option. This type of repurchase is an option, not an obligation, of the holders and aims to protect holders from fundamental changes in the creditworthiness of the issuer. Any such offer made by the issuer can be rejected by the holders, in which case no further obligation arises. The triggering event causes a mandatory offer as far as the issuer is concerned and an optional tender of the securities to the issuer as far as the holders are concerned. It is not an optional or voluntary transaction of the issuer and cannot be used for liability management purposes.

[6] EU Directive 2003/71/EC on the prospectus to be published when securities are offered to the public or admitted to trading as amended or supplemented (including by Directive 2010/73/EU) (the "Prospectus Directive"), OJ L 345, 31.12.2003, p. 64.

and, if applicable, to the trustee, the fiscal agent, the paying agent, or such other financial intermediary that performs similar functions. As a contractual matter, the terms of the subject securities provide that, once the notice of redemption is mailed or published, all outstanding debt securities called by the issuer for redemption become due and payable on the date of redemption at the redemption price. Thus, the legal effect of the exercise of the right of redemption is the acceleration of the repayment of the redeemed subject securities on the redemption date; therefore, earlier than the initially contracted maturity date. Upon the payment of the redemption amount on the redemption date, the legal obligations represented by the securities to be redeemed are extinguished.

There are many different variations on the right of the issuer to redeem its outstanding debt securities. The terms of the subject securities may provide that the debt securities are not redeemable during an agreed initial period of time or at all. If the terms of the subject securities establish a right of redemption, they may provide that the right of redemption may be exercised only if the entire outstanding amount of debt securities is called for redemption; alternatively, they may provide for the right to redeem the subject securities in part without limitation or in part but subject to the condition that a partial redemption may only be exercised for an agreed minimum outstanding principal amount.

There is also a great variation on contractual terms calculating the redemption price of redeemable debt securities. The redemption price typically will reflect the expected yield to maturity on the redemption date if the objective is that bondholders will be made "whole." In that instance, the redemption price will be equal to the nominal principal amount of the subject securities, plus the present value of future interest payments, thus leading to the payment of a premium to bondholders over the nominal principal amount of the subject securities. It is common to start with a redemption premium equal to the initial issue price of the debt securities plus an amount equal to the annual interest rate on the securities, which then declines in each year in patterned steps to zero at some agreed date. In most cases, the premium is scaled down to zero one year before the stated maturity date; in other cases it could be set to zero two or even five years before maturity. One reason for allowing some time to redeem without premium is to give the issuer an opportunity to refund the remaining principal amount of the issue in better market conditions. Under some indentures, a permitted redemption may be made on any date while other indentures permit redemption only on an interest payment date.

Whether the issuer can redeem the subject securities or not must be checked for compliance not only with the terms of the subject securities but also with the terms of the issuer's other contractual agreements (including agreements governing debt financings such as credit facility agreements or indentures for other outstanding debt securities). Many credit facility agreements and similar instruments, as well as indentures for certain type of debt securities (such as high-yield debt securities) include covenants limiting the ability of the issuer to redeem, repurchase, replace, or refinance certain types of debt obligations (as more specifically defined in the relevant document). As a result, depending on the issuer's specific capital structure, the redemption of an outstanding issue of debt securities may be permitted under its own terms but restricted by the terms of another contractual agreement, credit facility agreement, or bond indenture. The usual contractual provisions to be checked include definitions of, and restrictions on, permitted indebtedness, restricted payments and redemptions of subordinated liabilities, permitted refinancings and debt repurchases, and permitted liens. Board approval is also usually required for the redemption of an issuer's securities prior to their stated maturity. Finally, the underlying documentation will also specify who can exercise the right of redemption. In addition to the issuer, the parent company of the issuer is often also entitled under the terms of the securities to redeem the securities.

The terms of certain debt securities do not allow the redemption thereof with the proceeds from offers and sales by the issuer or an affiliate of the issuer of lower-cost debt securities. The usual wording in the underlying documentation permits the issuer of the relevant securities to redeem the securities; provided, however, that the securities may not be redeemed pursuant to such option from the proceeds, or in anticipation, of the issuance of any indebtedness for money borrowed by or for the account of the issuer (or any subsidiary of the issuer) if the interest cost or interest factor applicable thereto (calculated in accordance with generally accepted financial practice) shall be less than a certain percentage per annum.

It has been argued that this limitation bars redemption during any period when the issuer is in the process of borrowing at a rate lower than that prescribed by the terms of the documentation, regardless of whether the direct source of the funds is the issuance of equity, the sale of assets or merely cash on hand. US courts have rejected this view and held that what determines the availability of the optional redemption is the direct source of funds used in the redemption.[7] Although cash is fungible, if the redemption is completed with the proceeds from any transaction other than the borrowing of funds at a rate lower than that prescribed by the terms of the documentation, the redemption can be effected. This view does not eliminate the protection of bondholders in those circumstances. An issuer contemplating redemption would still be required to fund such redemption from a source other than lower-cost borrowing, such as reserves, the sale of assets, or the proceeds of a common stock issue. Bondholders are thus protected against the type of continuous short-term refunding of debt in times of plummeting interest rates that the language is intended to prohibit.

Redemptions of debt securities are simple events, very lightly documented. A notice of redemption is disseminated in the prescribed manner and payment of the redemption amount is made on the set redemption date. There are no special documentary formalities or deliverables such as offering documents, legal opinions, comfort letters, and similar transaction documents that are required in other types of liability management transactions. There are no special regulatory requirements either. On the other hand, redemptions of debt securities have the obvious disadvantage of requiring cash resources (unlike exchange offers) and, even when the payment of a premium over the nominal principal amount is not required, the repayment of the principal amount to be redeemed is at par; thus the recovery of the holders of the debt securities is full and no debt relief is achieved (unlike, for example, purchases of debt securities at a discount or exchanges of debt securities with newly issued debt securities having a lower principal amount).

An optional redemption at par in accordance with the terms and conditions of the securities should be distinguished from an optional redemption *at a discount* following the amendment of the relevant terms and conditions with the consent of the holders of the relevant debt securities. Holders of debt securities may always give their consent to amendments or modifications of the redemption provisions to allow for a discounted redemption when the initial terms and conditions require redemption

7 See, e.g., *Morgan Stanley & Co., Inc.* v. *Archer Daniels Midland Co.*, 570 F. Supp. 1529 (D.C.N.Y., 1983) and cases cited; *Franklin Life Insurance Co.* v. *Commonwealth Edison Co.*, 451 F. Supp. 602 (S.D. Ill., 1978), aff'd *per curiam* on the opinion below, 598 F.2d 1109 (7th Cir.), rehearing and rehearing en banc denied, id., cert. denied, 444 U.S. 900, 100 S. Ct. 210, 62 L. Ed. 2d 136 (1979).

at par (or at par plus an applicable premium). Modification of the terms of an optional redemption requires, in most cases, the consent of each holder of the relevant series of securities or, more recently, the consent of holders representing at least 90 percent or 95 percent of the principal amount of the debt securities then outstanding. A simple majority is in most cases not sufficient.

In connection with an optional redemption of debt securities, the issuer must also insure that it has complied with the anti-fraud and market abuse provisions of the US federal securities laws and the EU capital markets directives (and implementing national legislation). The redemption of the debt securities itself will be a material event or development to be disclosed to the issuer's public security holders (to the extent the issuer has any class of securities listed or publicly traded on an organized securities market). In addition, if the offering document under which the securities to be redeemed were initially offered and sold to investors did not disclose the issuer's right or intention to redeem the securities, the issuer could be subject to liability for omitting to disclose a material fact relating to the redemption. Offering documents for redeemable securities at the option of the issuer should always include a general statement that the issuer may decide to redeem the relevant securities in accordance with their terms.

3 Repurchases of debt securities by the issuer or an affiliate of the issuer

If a corporate or sovereign issuer of outstanding debt securities (or, in the case of a corporate issuer, the broader consolidated corporate group of which the issuer is part) has excess cash from operating revenues, fresh borrowings, or the sale of assets and wishes to reduce the principal amount (and debt service obligations) of its outstanding indebtedness, it could purchase the subject debt securities from the holders thereof, either directly or through a subsidiary or affiliate. If at the time of the repurchase by the issuer (or its affiliate) the relevant debt securities are trading in the open market at a price lower than the nominal value of the principal amount of such securities, or if the privately negotiated price agreed with the seller of the securities is lower than the nominal value of the principal amount of the securities subject to the sale (*below par*), the repurchase of those securities at the then current market price would lead to a greater reduction of the issuer's consolidated indebtedness than the reduction that the issuer would otherwise achieve with the same amount of cash through the partial redemption of the relevant debt securities at their nominal par value. This type of debt repurchase by the issuers (or their affiliates) is a popular method of debt liability management by corporate groups and sovereign issuers at times of financial stress when the market price of the relevant subject securities has declined considerably due to concerns over the solvency or liquidity of the relevant issuer. The issuer may also wish to retire debt securities with inappropriate or problematic covenants.

There are four possible transaction structures available to issuers considering a repurchase of their own debt securities: (i) a repurchase of the subject securities by the issuer of those securities; (ii) a repurchase of the subject securities by a parent company of the issuer; (iii) a repurchase of the subject securities by a subsidiary of the issuer; and (iv) a repurchase of the subject securities by a person (other than a parent company or a subsidiary of the issuer) that is an *affiliate*[8] of the issuer.

3.1 Transaction alternatives

The repurchase of outstanding debt securities by the issuer (or an affiliate of the issuer), in whole or in part, can be effected in a single, privately negotiated transaction between the seller and the purchaser of the debt securities. Alternatively, the issuer (or an affiliate of the issuer) may initiate a series of repurchases of outstanding debt securities in the open market with the assistance of a broker or dealer that will solicit or procure interested sellers of the relevant securities. There are significant legal, regulatory, and disclosure issues relating to a series of related repurchases of debt securities in the open market (as opposed to a single, privately negotiated purchase of debt securities from a single holder of those debt securities).

The issuer or the purchasing affiliate may negotiate the purchase price directly with the selling security holder or it may purchase the securities

[8] An *affiliate* of, or a person affiliated with, the issuer of the securities, is a person who directly, or indirectly through one or more intermediaries controls or is controlled by, or is under common control with, the issuer. The term "control" (including the terms "controlling," "controlled by," and "under common control with") means the possession, direct or indirect, of the power to direct or cause the direction of the management and policies of a person, whether through the ownership of voting securities, by contract, or otherwise. See Rule 405 under the US Securities Act of 1933, as amended, 15 U.S.C., §§ 77a–77aa, as amended (the "Securities Act").

in the secondary market. The issuer may also engage a broker or dealer to identify potential sellers of the relevant securities, or the issuer may agree with the broker or dealer to purchase the debt securities from such broker or dealer.

3.2 Avoiding the application of the US Tender Offer Rules

The anti-fraud provisions of Section 14(e)[9] of the Securities Exchange Act, and Regulation 14E[10] thereunder are the principal provisions of the US federal securities laws governing tender offers for debt securities (the "US Tender Offer Rules"). If a series of related repurchases of debt securities in the open market are thought to be a *tender offer* within the meaning of the US Tender Offer Rules, the issuer (or an affiliate of the issuer) seeking to effect the repurchases will be subject to documentation, anti-fraud, timing, and other requirements when repurchasing the relevant debt securities, which are onerous and prescriptive. In addition, a bond repurchase program or a single repurchase of debt securities in the open market that is later held to have been a noncompliant tender offer subject to the US Tender Offer Rules will expose the purchaser of the debt securities to a variety of adverse consequences, including liability for violation of the US Tender Offer Rules, injunctive relief, and enforcement action by the Securities and Exchange Commission (the "SEC").

A tender offer is a publicly made offer to holders of debt securities to offer their debt securities for sale to the offeror at a specified or determinable price subject to specified general or transaction-specific conditions over a certain period of time which may be extended at the option of the offeror. The term "tender offer" is not, however, defined in the Securities Exchange Act or the US Tender Offer Rules; nevertheless, US courts have determined that an open market purchase or series of purchases may under certain circumstances constitute a *de facto* tender offer subject to the US Tender Offer Rules. The courts have articulated two tests to determine whether a tender offer has been made.

[9] The anti-fraud provisions and remedies of Section 14(e) of the Securities Exchange Act are discussed in more detail in Chapter 7.

[10] Regulation 14E, which comprises the rules and regulations of the SEC promulgated under Section 14(e) of the Securities Exchange Act ("Regulation 14E"), is discussed in more detail in Chapter 3.

The eight-factor test commonly known as the "Wellman test"[11] evaluates the following factors:

- whether there is active and widespread solicitation by an issuer of holders of its securities;
- whether solicitations are made for a substantial percentage of the issuer's securities;
- whether the offer is made at a premium over the prevailing market price. This is unlikely to be the case in an open market repurchase;
- whether the offer is firm rather than negotiable. Courts have looked to whether the terms of the offer are determined unilaterally by the offeror or whether they are subject to negotiation;
- whether the offer is contingent on the tender of a fixed number of securities and perhaps subject to a fixed maximum number of securities to be purchased. However, courts have generally ignored the presence of a maximum number of securities;
- whether the offer is open for only a limited period of time. This factor is related to the following factor, which concerns selling pressure;
- whether offerees are subjected to pressure to sell their securities. Courts have considered this to be the single most significant factor; and
- whether public announcements of a repurchase precede or accompany a rapid accumulation by the offeror of large amounts of its securities. Some courts have found that the "public announcement" may be satisfied by numerous activities, including the issuance of press releases outlining the details of the buying program. Other courts have refused to find a "public announcement" if the terms of the offer are publicized only to the extent required by law or stock exchange rules.

All of these factors need not be satisfied for an offer to be deemed to be a tender offer. The primary concern of the courts has been to prevent offers that put pressure on holders of securities, leading them to make uninformed, ill-considered decisions to sell. Offering a premium for a limited time can contribute to such pressure.

A separate totality test derived from the statutory purpose of the regulations (commonly referred to as the "Hanson test")[12] is based on the high sophistication level and knowledge of selling investors in privately negotiated transactions. The Hanson test turns on whether, unless the

[11] See *Wellman* v. *Dickinson*, 475 F. Supp. 783, 823–24 (S.D.N.Y. 1979), aff'd on other grounds, 682 F.2d 355 (2d Cir. 1982), cert. denied, 460 U.S. 1069 (1983).

[12] See *Hanson Trust PLC* v. *SCM Corp.*, 774 F.3d 47 (2d Cir. 1985) (hereinafter, "*Hanson*").

US Tender Offer Rules are followed, there will be a substantial risk that offerees will lack information needed to make a careful appraisal of the proposal put before them. Similarly, since the purpose of the US Tender Offer Rules is to protect the ill-informed solicitee in a tender offer, the question of whether a solicitation of offers to sell debt securities constitutes a "tender offer" within the meaning of the US Tender Offer Rules turns on whether, viewing the transaction in the light of the totality of circumstances, there appears to be a likelihood that unless the protection of the US Tender Offer Rules is followed there will be a substantial risk that solicitees will lack information needed to make a carefully considered appraisal of the proposal put before them.[13] In the *Hanson* case, the court held there was no tender offer, or any need for the plaintiffs to be protected, because, among other reasons, the plaintiffs were highly sophisticated, knowledgeable in the marketplace, and well aware of the essential facts needed to make an educated investment decision. Therefore, if there is a substantial risk that the offerees, although sophisticated, would lack necessary information, the transaction would fail the Hanson test and be deemed a tender offer.

As a result of both the Wellman and the Hanson tests, in order to reduce the risk of the purchase of debt securities in the open market being considered a tender offer, lawyers usually recommend that:

- the open market repurchases are only publicized to the extent required by law;
- the repurchase program should be completed over a meaningful period of time; the longer the period, the better; the offeror should not set a fixed deadline for the expression of interest in selling the securities;
- the solicitations should be made to a limited number of potential sellers; it is better to approach each potential seller and discuss the terms of the sale and purchase individually;
- the debt securities are purchased through brokers' transactions at or below prevailing market prices;

[13] Ibid. See also *Rand* v. *Anaconda-Ericsson, Inc.*, 794 F.2d 843, 848 (2d Cir. 1986) (finding case "directly controlled" by the standard set forth in *Hanson*). Other courts have continued to recognize the Wellman eight-factor test in determining whether an outsider's bid for the issuer's securities constitutes a tender offer. *Pin* v. *Texaco, Inc.*, 793 F.2d 1448, 1454 (5th Cir. 1986) (taking both tests into account); *Anago Inc.* v. *Tecnol Medical Products, Inc.*, 792 F. Supp. 514, 516–17 (N.D. Tex. 1992) (applying both the eight-factor test and the Hanson test); *Weeden* v. *Continental Health Affiliates, Inc.*, 713 F. Supp. 396 (N.D. Ga. 1989).

- each negotiation is independent of any other with varying prices and terms;
- each seller of the securities is sophisticated and knowledgeable;
- no attempt is made to impose the same terms on all sellers (a record of negotiation is helpful);
- the offerees should not be coerced (e.g., telling the holders of the debt securities that such debt securities will subsequently be illiquid to encourage sales);
- a ceiling is set on the percentage of the debt securities that the purchaser will repurchase that does not constitute a substantial percentage of the outstanding debt securities; a ceiling of between 10 percent to 15 percent is often used by experienced securities lawyers; or
- the purchaser avoids a rapid accumulation of the debt securities following any announcement of the plan to repurchase securities in the open market.

It goes without saying that all the facts and circumstances will be relevant in determining whether the repurchase of the debt securities will be a tender offer subject to the US Tender Offer Rules. We discuss the definition of a "tender offer" more fully in Chapter 2.

3.3 Anti-fraud remedies and disclosure considerations in debt repurchases

The purchase by the issuer (or an affiliate of the issuer) of the issuer's outstanding debt securities, in a privately negotiated transaction or in the open market (in a single transaction or in a program of a series of associated transactions) is subject to the anti-fraud provisions of the US federal securities laws and the anti-fraud, insider trading, and market abuse regulations of the EU securities laws and implementing national legislation.[14]

An issuer (or affiliate) purchasing its outstanding debt securities will be subject to the general anti-fraud provisions of Section 10(b) of the Securities Exchange Act and Rule 10b-5 promulgated thereunder ("Rule 10b-5"). Rule 10b-5 is by far the most important liability provision of the US federal securities laws and is designed to eliminate fraud and manipulation, and promote accurate disclosure in offering documents used in

[14] See Chapter 4 for a discussion of the EU regulatory framework relating to debt tender offers.

securities transactions in order to enable prospective investors to make informed investment decisions. Rule 10b-5, patterned closely after Section 17(a) of the Securities Act, prohibits the use of any means of interstate commerce to (i) employ any device, scheme, or artifice to defraud, (ii) make material misstatements or omissions, or (iii) engage in any course of business that operates as a fraud against any person, in connection with the purchase or sale of any security or securities-based swap agreement.

In general, to prevail on a Rule 10b-5 claim, a plaintiff must prove that the defendant (i) made a false statement or an omission of material fact, (ii) with "scienter," (iii) in connection with the purchase or sale of a security, (iv) upon which the plaintiff justifiably relied, and (v) which proximately caused (vi) the plaintiff's economic loss.[15] Rule 10b-5 makes clear that it is sufficient if the wrongful conduct occurred "in connection with" purchases or sales of securities. The "in connection with" requirement is satisfied if the defendant sold or purchased securities fraudulently regardless of whether the securities are purchased in a primary transaction or in the open market.

Rule 10b-5 limits liability to a material omission of facts or misrepresentation. The leading case on materiality is *TSC Industries, Inc.* v. *Northway, Inc.*,[16] which defined a "material" fact as one to which there is a substantial likelihood that a reasonable investor would attach importance in making an investment decision because the fact would significantly alter the "total mix" of available information. The omission of any such "material fact" in the context of a purchase of debt securities would expose the issuer purchasing those securities (and any controlling persons thereof) to the risk of liability under Rule 10b-5 (assuming that a plaintiff could establish scienter and the remaining conditions of Rule 10b-5 were met). In purchasing securities in the open market, the issuer (or an affiliate of the issuer) is under an affirmative duty under Rule 10b-5 to avoid omissions of a material fact (as "materiality" is defined for purposes of Rule 10b-5). Generally, a finding of materiality will be based on the total mix of information available to investors. This is a crucial concept. Relying on this "total mix" concept, for example, courts have held that

[15] See, from a long list of cases, *Ashland, Inc.* v.*Oppenheimer & Co.*, 648 F.3d 461, 468 (6th Cir. 2011); *Katyle* v. *Penn Nat'l Gaming, Inc.*, 637 F.3d 462, 480 (4th Cir.) cert. denied, 132 S. Ct. 115 (2011); *Desai* v. *Deutsche Bank Sec. Ltd.*, 573 F.3d 931, 939 (9th Cir. 2009); *Cent. Laborers' Pension Fund* v. *Integrated Elec. Servs. Inc.*, 497 F.3d 546, 550 (5th Cir. 2007); *Miss. Pub. Emps.' Ret. Sys.* v. *Bos. Scientific Corp.*, 649 F.3d 5, 20 (1st Cir. 2011); *Cardon* v. *TestOut! Corp.*, 244 F. App'x 908, 914–15 (10th Cir. 2007).

[16] 426 U.S. 438 (1976).

omissions of fact are not material as long as the market possessed the correct information from other sources; and cautionary language in documentation is sufficient to render alleged omissions not material. Information that is generally circulated through the media or other publicly available information will be considered in its entirety in assessing the total mix of information available to potential offerees in a repurchase program for debt securities. The test of materiality is whether a reasonable investor would have considered the matter significant; it is not sufficient to show that a bondholder has found the information to be of interest.

Furthermore, Rule 10b-5 places a duty upon the issuer of the securities (and any officer, director, or other affiliate of the issuer), when in possession of material non-public information, either to refrain from trading in the company's securities on the basis of that information or to disclose the information before trading.[17] "Disclosure" here means adequate public dissemination of the information so that it is fully reflected in the price of the security of the company before the insider engages in the trading.[18] Violation of the insider trading prohibition can lead to significant damages and penalties, as well as criminal charges, against the offending officer or director.

Whether an issuer (or an affiliate of the issuer) violates the anti-fraud and insider trading prohibitions in connection with the repurchase of the debt securities will depend on the facts and circumstances. There is no rule or case that specifies what must be disclosed prior to the repurchase of debt securities in these circumstances. Consequently, prior to making any purchases of its own debt securities, the issuer (or the purchasing affiliate of the issuer) must analyze whether it is in possession of material non-public information such as unreleased earnings results, material litigation, a prospective merger, or the sale of assets. If such material non-public information is in the possession of the issuer or the purchasing affiliate, the purchase of the debt securities cannot be initiated before the relevant information is disclosed to the public in all material respects.

Securities lawyers are often asked if the purchase of the debt securities by the issuer or an affiliate of the issuer, or the intention of the issuer or the purchasing affiliate to purchase the debt securities, is itself material non-public information that should be disclosed to the market in advance

[17] See *In the Matter of Cady, Roberts & Co.*, 40 SEC 907 (1961) (explaining that the duty arises whenever there is a relationship that gives access, directly or indirectly, to information in circumstances in which the information is intended to be available only for a reasonable corporate purpose and not for the personal use or benefit of any other person).

[18] See *SEC* v. *Texas Gulf Sulphur*, 401 F.2d 833 (2d Cir. 1968).

of the commencement of the purchases of the securities. It is difficult to answer this question in the abstract because the materiality or not of the issuer's intentions and purchases will depend on the specific facts and circumstances. In most cases and absent unusual circumstances, we do not believe the repurchases themselves to be material non-public information that must be disclosed to the market. If the likely impact of the repurchases on the financial condition and results of operations of the issuer or the affiliate is material, then additional disclosure should be considered. For example, a selling bondholder may argue that it would not have sold at the agreed price if it had known the totality of the consequences of the bond repurchase program, including the quantum of the relevant tax liability. Also, if the percentage of the outstanding debt securities sought in the repurchase program is such that, following the completion of the repurchase program, the principal amount of the outstanding securities held by non-affiliates of the issuer will be substantially reduced and illiquid, then additional disclosure may also be advisable.

If additional disclosure is advisable, it can be effected either through an ad hoc public announcement in advance of the repurchases or through the inclusion of a statement in the issuer's periodic reports to the effect that the issuer may, from time to time, seek to retire or purchase its outstanding debt securities through cash purchases in the open market or through privately negotiated transactions or otherwise, and any such transactions may involve material amounts.

Private negotiations between the issuer of the debt securities and potential sellers of the debt securities may also trigger disclosure obligations under Regulation FD promulgated by the SEC under the Securities Exchange Act ("Regulation FD").[19] Regulation FD provides, subject to certain exceptions, that whenever an issuer, or any person acting on its behalf, discloses any material non-public information regarding the issuer or its securities to market professionals or holders of the issuer's securities, the issuer is obligated to make public disclosure of that information either simultaneously (in the case of an intentional disclosure) or promptly (in the case of inadvertent disclosure).

3.4 Contractual limitations

The issuer of the debt securities (or the purchasing affiliate) should also consider the terms and conditions of the relevant securities and whether

[19] 17 C.F.R. §§ 243.100–243.103 (2011).

or not those terms and conditions limit the ability of the issuer or the purchasing affiliate to purchase the securities in the open market or in a privately negotiated transaction. The indenture for the relevant debt securities is unlikely to prohibit repurchases of bonds. However, if the issuer of the relevant securities has any outstanding bank or other debt, the relevant contracts governing the terms of that debt (such as credit agreements or other types of contractual arrangements evidencing indebtedness) may prohibit the repurchases or refinancings of other debt instruments (including debt securities) unless such redemptions, repurchases, or refinancings are permitted specifically by exemptions in the relevant agreements available for those purposes. Furthermore, high-yield bond indentures restrict the ability of high-yield issuers to repurchase debt securities that are junior in right of payment to the high-yield notes issued under the relevant indenture. All of these financing agreements (including any intercreditor agreements) must be reviewed before the repurchases can be initiated. Finally, indentures for debt securities usually prevent the issuer of the securities and all affiliates of the issuer from voting any debt securities held thereby and, consequently, repurchases of debt securities are not useful in influencing bondholder voting results when the issuer is seeking to make changes to the existing bond documentation.

3.5 Tax issues

A repurchase by an issuer of its debt securities at a discount to its face value will generally result in taxable income to the issuer resulting from the cancellation of the relevant indebtedness and the benefit generated by such cancellation. The amount of the taxable income is generally the difference between the principal amount of indebtedness represented by the debt securities that were the subject of the repurchase or redemption over the price paid by the issuer or purchasing affiliate in the relevant transaction. Expert tax advice should be sought prior to initiating the repurchase of the issuer's debt securities by the issuer or an affiliate of the issuer.

Chapter 6 examines the legal aspects of repurchases of debt securities in detail.

4 Cash tender offers

Depending on the facts and circumstances, a redemption or repurchase of the outstanding debt securities by the issuer or an affiliate of the issuer may not provide the issuer with the desired commercial benefits, particularly if the issuer seeks to retire all or substantially all of the outstanding debt securities. Purchasing the securities in the open market is usually not the right transaction alternative if the issuer is seeking to purchase the debt securities in whole or in substantial part, or the issuer is seeking to effect changes to the terms and conditions of the securities through a consent solicitation. In those circumstances, a tender offer for cash may be the most appropriate way to manage or restructure the issuer's financial liabilities.

A tender offer for issued securities is an offer by a person (the *tender offeror*) addressed to the existing holders (the *security holders*) of the issued securities (the *tender securities*) to purchase the tender securities (in whole or in part) for cash at a specified or at least determinable price over a specified period of time.

Cash tender offers for equity securities (*equity tender offers*) are an important method of acquiring control of a publicly held corporation. The tender offeror offers to purchase the publicly held equity securities of a company from the existing security holders for cash, usually at a price above the current market price of the subject securities. Those security holders accepting the offer are said to "tender" their securities for purchase. In a *friendly* equity tender offer, the tender offeror and the management of the issuer of the subject securities (the *target company*) are generally in agreement over the plan to effect a change of control transaction and work in concert to structure and present a tender offer to the existing security holders of the tender securities. In a *hostile* equity tender offer, the tender offeror launches a tender offer directed at the existing security holders of the tender securities of the target company but the management of the target company opposes, and actively defends against, the tender offer. Sometimes, a hostile equity tender offer becomes, with the passage of time and, often, adjustments to the terms of the tender offer, a friendly tender offer. *Debt tender offers* (i.e., tender offers for debt securities) are offers by the tender offeror to the security holders of the tender securities to purchase the outstanding debt securities (in whole or in part) for cash. Since debt securities do not carry voting rights and equity-like economic rights, debt tender offers do not seek to transfer corporate control from the current security holders of the target company to the tender offeror.

Cash tender offers for debt securities may be completed more quickly and with fewer transactional, regulatory, and documentation requirements than other types of tender offers, especially tender offers for equity or convertible debt securities. Cash tender offers for debt securities are subject to tender offer regulations (i.e., the anti-fraud provisions of Section 14(e) of the Securities Exchange Act and Regulation 14E thereunder) but are outside the more invasive requirements of the equity tender offer rules promulgated under Section 14(d) of the Securities Exchange Act.

In a cash tender offer for debt securities, the issuer (or an affiliate of the issuer) will mail tender offer materials to the holders of the debt securities describing the terms and conditions of the tender offer and providing them with all material information in connection therewith. The tender offeror usually commences the tender offer with the publication of a press release in one or more electronic and/or printed media.

A cash tender offer for debt securities is often accompanied by an exit consent solicitation that aims to effect certain changes to the debt securities that will not be tendered in the tender offer, often as a coercive strategy to induce as many holders of the tender securities as possible to tender their securities in the tender offer. Cash tender offers are not subject to the best-price rules applicable to tender offers for equity securities and, consequently, issuers commonly introduce an "early bird" premium payable to those holders that tender their securities during an initial "early tender" period (frequently ten business days).

The tender offer documentation will specify all the material terms and conditions of the tender offer, including the principal amount of securities sought to be purchased in the tender offer, the applicable tender offer price (or the method of calculating the purchase price), the tender offer period, the procedures for tendering the relevant securities, and other important terms and conditions. In some cases, the offeror will specify the principal amount of the tender securities sought to be purchased but will not specify the applicable tender offer price which shall be determined in accordance with a *Dutch auction* or a *modified Dutch auction* process. In a pure Dutch auction tender offer, the offeror solicits tenders of the relevant securities at a price offered by the tendering security holders (i.e., the price at which they are willing to tender). Since holders tender the securities at different prices, the offeror determines the securities to be purchased, starting with those being tendered at the lowest price, until the desired principal amount of securities has been accepted for purchase. A modified Dutch auction tender offer is very similar to a pure Dutch auction except that the offeror sets the minimum and maximum tender offer price, the acceptable range of prices at which the holders must tender; the range provides a ceiling and a floor, and the holders must choose their acceptable tender price from the prices within the specified range. Usually, the specified price range between the minimum and maximum consideration is relatively narrow. An issuer intending to commence a cash tender offer will usually appoint an experienced broker or dealer as financial and structuring advisor. The financial and structuring advisor will also manage the tender offer process and solicit tenders from the holders of the tender securities.

Chapters 2, 3 and 4 examine all aspects of tender offers for debt securities in detail.

5 Exchange offers

If the issuer of the debt securities does not have cash on hand, the liability management transaction must be structured as an exchange offer. In a debt exchange offer, the issuer of the debt securities offers to exchange a new debt or equity security for its outstanding debt securities. The holders of the existing securities tender the securities and, following the acceptance of the tender by the tender offeror, the tender offeror issues new debt or equity securities in consideration for the tender securities accepted for purchase. In other words, a debt exchange offer is the purchase of the issuer's debt securities by the issuer for non-cash consideration in the form of newly issued debt securities (in a debt-for-debt exchange offer) or equity securities (in a debt-for-equity exchange offer).

Exchange offers enable issuers to reduce the principal amount outstanding of their issued debt securities (by exchanging debt securities for newly issued debt securities having a lower principal amount or equity securities), reduce interest payments on the outstanding debt securities (by exchanging the outstanding debt securities for newly issued debt securities having lower interest payments), extend the maturity dates of outstanding debt securities, make changes to the non-financial terms of the existing debt securities, or effect any combination of the foregoing, in all cases through the issuance of new securities in consideration for the purchase of the outstanding debt securities by the issuer thereof.

An exchange offer is therefore a combination of two separate transactions: a tender offer by the issuer for the tender of the outstanding securities; and the offer and sale of new securities in consideration for the purchase of the tendered securities in the tender offer. Consequently, an exchange offer is subject to all the regulatory and legal requirements applicable to tender offers for the relevant securities, and the securities laws applicable to the offer and sale of the newly issued securities. For this reason, the documentation for an exchange offer will be more detailed than that for a cash tender offer to the extent that the offering memorandum must describe the business and financial condition of the issuer and the terms and conditions of the new securities (in addition to the terms and conditions of the tender offer). An exchange offer is also subject to the full application of the securities laws relating to the offer and sale of securities.

As a result, for purposes of the US federal securities laws, the new securities must be registered under the Securities Act or be exempt from registration thereunder. Thus, one can make a distinction between a *registered exchange offer*, in which the newly issued securities are registered under Section 5 of the Securities Act and subject to SEC review, and a *private* or *exempt exchange offer*, in which the newly issued securities are exempt from registration. The issuer and other offering participants will also be subject to securities laws liabilities, whereas the underwriters and other offering participants (other than the issuer) will need to conduct customary legal due diligence in connection with the offer and sale of the new securities.

In planning an exchange offer, the main issues considered by the issuer and its advisors are: (i) the terms of the newly issued securities offered to existing holders, including principal amount and coupon; (ii) registration and disclosure requirements under the Securities Act and the availability of exemptions; (iii) tax and accounting considerations; (iv) the likely impact of the exchange offer on the issuer's credit rating; and (v) the mechanics and documentation of the exchange offer, including timing and process, any exclusions of certain categories of holders from the scope of the exchange offer, required participation levels and withdrawal rights, the expiration time, and other pertinent procedural requirements.

Chapter 5 discusses the legal aspects of exchange offers in more detail.

6 Consent solicitations

The commercial objectives of the issuer of debt securities in a liability management transaction are often served through the solicitation of consents from the holders of the debt securities to waivers and/or modifications of the terms of the securities. The terms and conditions of the securities will specify that, with the consent of the holders of the debt securities representing a prescribed minimum percentage of the principal amount outstanding, the issuer may modify or amend, or waive an existing or pending default under, one or more terms and conditions of the relevant securities. The solicitation of consents may be conducted in connection with a tender offer or an exchange offer, or it could be initiated on a stand-alone basis.

A waiver is agreement by the holders of the debt securities to suspend the enforcement of one or more provisions of the bond indenture. It can be either temporary or permanent in nature. In a temporary waiver, the holders of the securities will provide their consent for the excuse of the issuer's breach of the relevant provision for a certain period of time. In a permanent waiver, the breach is excused permanently. An amendment, by contrast, modifies the terms and conditions of the relevant debt agreement (in this context, the bond indenture) in view of establishing more financial and non-financial terms with the consent of the holders.

6.1 Stand-alone consents

Consent solicitations not conducted in connection with a tender offer to purchase existing securities or an exchange offer in which new securities are offered in exchange for existing securities are subject to little regulation. Generally, a consent solicitation by itself does not involve the offer or sale of a security, and therefore does not require registration under the Securities Act or an exemption from the registration requirements of the Securities Act. A consent solicitation is also not subject to the anti-fraud provisions of the US federal securities laws and the equivalent anti-fraud and market abuse rules of the European regulatory framework. If, however, the amendments or waivers sought in a consent solicitation are so significant as to "substantially" affect the rights of the bondholders, the amendments to the bonds may be deemed to constitute the issuance of a new security, requiring registration under the Securities Act and qualification of the indenture under the US Trust Indenture Act of 1939 (the "Trust Indenture Act"), unless an exemption from each such statute is available. Traditionally, the "substantially affects" standard would be met, and a "new security" deemed to be created, if the modifications would alter the basic financial terms of the debt securities involved. Changes to restrictive covenants or other legal provisions would not, however, be deemed to constitute the issuance of a new security. Consent solicitations typically involve the payment of cash or other forms of consideration by the issuer to the bondholders in exchange for their waiver or consent. Payments may be structured to offer incentives to agree to consent early in the process, such as higher "early bird" consent fees payable to holders who tender within the first few days during which the consent solicitation is open.

Most indentures for debt securities provide that only a simple majority in principal amount of the debt securities issued and outstanding under such indenture would be required to amend or waive compliance with any provision of the indenture unless such provision is found in the short list of those provisions that require "super-majority" (e.g., 75 percent or 90 percent) or even unanimous consent (e.g., changes in the interest rate, the currency, the principal amount, the maturity or the ranking of the debt securities, and provisions of a similar fundamental nature).

As part of the consent solicitation process, the issuer will normally appoint one or more banks to act as solicitation agent. The primary role of the solicitation agent is to render financial advice to the issuer. The solicitation agent will generally also be available to answer questions from bondholders regarding the solicitation, although sometimes the issuer will also appoint a separate information agent to handle general questions from bondholders regarding the solicitation process. The issuer will also typically appoint a consent agent or tabulation agent responsible for purely administrative matters, such as collecting the consents and waivers.

In connection with the consent solicitation, the issuer's counsel usually prepares a consent solicitation statement to be distributed to bondholders. This document sets forth a description of the amendments and waivers sought by the issuer, the reasons behind the requested amendments and waivers, the consent payment offered to the bondholders, and the procedures for delivering a consent or waiver. In addition, counsel to the consent solicitation agent typically prepares a short consent solicitation agreement setting forth its fees and the other terms of its engagement as solicitation agent. The consent solicitation statement and consent solicitation agreement should take no more than two calendar weeks to prepare and finalize. The issuer's counsel would also prepare supplemental indentures reflecting the agreed amendments at the same time as the consent solicitation statement and consent solicitation agreement were being prepared. These would be executed once the consents were obtained. If the consent solicitation process is not conducted concurrently with a tender offer or an exchange offer there is no requirement to keep the offer open for at least twenty business days. A pure consent solicitation such as that being contemplated would typically be held open anywhere from five to twenty busines days.

6.2 *Exit consents in connection with tender or exchange offers*

Exit consents in connection with a tender or an exchange offer are different from stand-alone consents because the consenting security holder is giving consent to a waiver of a default under or modification of the terms and conditions of the tender securities as it tenders the relevant securities (thereby "exiting" the investment in the tender securities). As a result, the modified terms and conditions or the waived default or defaults (if the consents are given by the appropriate percentage of security holders) are binding on those security holders that have not tendered their securities in full. An exit consent is a mechanism that encourages security holders to tender their securities in the tender or exchange offer by threatening *holdouts* (i.e., security holders not tendering their securities) that, following the tender offer, the outstanding securities will have modified terms and conditions (usually offering fewer protections in terms of covenants, events of default, and similar provisions, if any). The consideration paid for the securities tendered and accepted for purchase in a cash tender offer with exit consents comprises a cash amount payable for the tendered securities and a cash fee payable for the granting of the exit consent, both of which can vary depending on market conditions. The amendments or waivers effected through the exit consents will not affect the tendering security holders because they will receive cash (in a cash tender offer), new securities (in an exchange offer), or a combination of cash and new securities. Accordingly, when an issuer of debt securities announces a tender offer, coupled with an exit consent solicitation, the holders of the debt securities must determine whether or not to participate in the tender offer or be left with a debt security that has little or no legal protection.

Consent solicitations are examined in detail in Chapter 8.

7 Regulatory framework

Redemptions of debt securities in accordance with their terms are not subject to any specific regulatory requirements. Repurchases of debt securities by the issuer of those securities (or an affiliate of the issuer), in privately negotiated transactions or in the open market, are subject to the generally applicable anti-fraud rules in connection with the sale or purchase of securities. Purchases of debt securities that are "tender offers" within the meaning of the US federal securities laws are subject to Section 14(e) of the Securities Exchange Act and the rules and regulations of the SEC promulgated thereunder. The anti-fraud provisions of Section 14(e) and the more specific rules and regulations promulgated by the SEC under the rule-making power given to the SEC by Section 14(e), as interpreted by judicial jurisprudence in numerous court cases and the interpretative releases and guidance of the SEC, have created a comprehensive system of federal regulation for debt tender offers and exchange offers in the United States.

In the European Union and the United Kingdom, there is no comprehensive system of regulation of debt tender offers and exchange offers. Issuers of debt securities and other transaction participants are, however, subject to the general anti-fraud and market abuse rules of the applicable securities laws, including the rules implementing the EU Market Abuse Directive, in connection with purchases of debt securities, tender offers, and exchange offers.

7.1 Rationale for regulating tender offers

The regulation of debt tender offers in the United States is part of the federal regulatory framework established by the amendments to the Securities Exchange Act that have become known as the "Williams Act"[20] in response to the risk of fraud and/or coercion of the investing public in connection with tender offers (primarily for equity securities).

The Williams Act was the Congressional response to the increased use of cash tender offers in corporate acquisitions, a device that had "removed a substantial number of corporate control contests from the reach of existing disclosure requirements of the federal securities laws." The Williams Act filled this regulatory gap.[21]

As the Supreme Court put it, there was no question that "Congress intended to protect investors" in enacting the Williams Act, which insures "that public shareholders who are confronted by a cash tender

[20] See 15 U.S.C. §§ 78m(d)–(e), 78n(d)–(f) (1982). The Williams Act amended the Securities Exchange Act by adding §§ 13(d)–(e) and §§ 14(d)–(f); see Pub. L. No. 90–439, 82 Stat. 454 (1968).

[21] See, e.g., *Edgar* v. *MITE Corp.*, 457 U.S. 624, 632, 102 S. Ct. 2629 (1982) (citing *Piper* v. *Chris-Craft Indus. Inc.*, 430 U.S. 1, 22, 97 S. Ct. 926, 939, 51 L. Ed. 2d 124 (1977) (hereinafter, "*Piper*")).

offer for their stock will not be required to respond without adequate information."[22] Adopted thirty-five years after the Securities Act, the Williams Act added the regulation of tender offers to the federal regulatory framework of securities markets in the United States. The Williams Act was designed to require the dissemination of material information about a tender offer and to provide sufficient procedural protections, by mandating disclosure of the tender offeror's identity and intention, regulating the offeror's acceptance of shares tendered and prohibiting any fraudulent activity in connection with a tender offer. The US Tender Offer Rules were addressed to a third-party tender offer for the securities of another issuer, as well as to a tender offer by an issuer for its own securities (including debt securities). It is noteworthy that those seeking to gain control of a company by offering an exchange of stock or by a proxy contest had already been required under the provisions of the Securities Act and the Securities Exchange Act to disclose certain important information. On the contrary, those attempting a takeover by means of the cash tender offer device were not required to reveal any information. The Williams Act was the legislative response to the regulatory gap.

The rules relating to tender offers for debt securities were established as anti-fraud protections within the scope of, and under the power given to the SEC by, Section 14(e) of the Securities Exchange Act. There is little doubt that the legislative motive behind the Williams Act was the concern that the market for corporate control through the acquisition of voting equity securities was becoming exposed to coercive or abusive practices. There is little, if any, reference in the legislative Congressional record that tender offers, repurchases, and similar transactions affecting debt securities were equally targeted by the legislative initiative. That said, there is no doubt today that the tender offer provisions of the Williams Act and the rules and regulations of the SEC promulgated thereunder apply to tender offers for debt securities, unless the relevant rules are by their terms expressly limited to equity securities.

7.2 Overview of the regulatory framework in the United States

The regulatory regime in the United States consists of six sections of the Securities Exchange Act, all adopted as part of the Williams Act reforms in 1968, in relation to tender offers and stock accumulations, and the rules,

[22] See *Piper*, fn 21 above, at 35 (quoting *Rondeau* v. *Mosinee Paper Corp.*, 422 U.S. 49, 58, 95 S. Ct. 2069 (1975)).

regulations, and forms adopted by the SEC thereunder. The six provisions are:

- Section 13(d) and Section 13(g) of the Securities Exchange Act, which require a person to file a form with the SEC once that person acquires beneficial ownership of more than 5 percent of a class of equity securities. The sections apply to any method of accumulation, including acquisitions that are not tender offers;
- Section 13(e) of the Securities Exchange Act, which applies to an issuer purchasing its own equity securities, whether or not by tender offer. Its most frequent application is in going-private transactions;
- Section 14(d) of the Securities Exchange Act, which requires compliance with specified disclosure, filing, dissemination, and substantive requirements in a tender offer where the tender offeror will own more than 5 percent of a class of equity securities after the tender offer. Unlike Section 13(d), stockholders receive information under Section 14(d) before they decide to sell;
- Section 14(e) of the Securities Exchange Act, which is the only provision introduced by the Williams Act that applies to all types of securities (including debt securities), providing that information disseminated in connection with a tender offer may not misrepresent or omit a material fact; and
- Section 14(f) of the Securities Exchange Act, which requires a mini-proxy statement regarding the election of a majority of the board of directors other than at a stockholders' meeting pursuant to an understanding with a person acquiring securities subject to Section 13(d) or Section 14(d) of the Securities Exchange Act.

In connection with debt tender offers and exchange offers, the regulatory framework consists of Section 14(e) of the Securities Exchange Act and the rules and regulations promulgated thereunder. Section 14(e) is a broad anti-fraud provision, very similar to Rule 10b-5. As we extensively discuss in the chapters that follow, the SEC has adopted the following substantive rules under the rule-making power of Section 14(e): Rule 14e-1(a) (offer must remain open for twenty business days); Rule 14e-1(b) (offer must remain open for ten business days after certain changes in the terms of the offer); Rule 14e-1(c) (payment must be made promptly); Rule 14e-1(d) (extensions must be publicly announced); Rule 14e-2 (position of target company with respect to a tender offer); Rule 14e-3 (transactions in securities on the basis of material, non-public information in the context of tender offers); Rule 14e-4 (prohibited transactions in connection with partial tender offers); Rule 14e-5 (prohibiting purchases outside a tender offer); Rule 14e-6 (repurchase offers by certain closed-end registered investment companies); Rule 14e-7 (unlawful tender offer practices in connection with roll-ups); and Rule 14e-8 (prohibited conduct in connection with pre-commencement communications). These rules, together with Section 14(e) and the associated case law in federal and state courts, SEC regulations, and SEC views reflected in SEC no-action letter relief or in telephonic interpretations create a comprehensive regulatory system for the regulation of debt tender offers and exchange offers in the United States. The philosophy of this regulatory system, which was established as part of the legislative reform introduced by the Williams Act, is deeply influenced by the policy objectives and rationale of the Williams Act. The entire regulatory apparatus applicable to tender offers and repurchases of debt securities aims to achieve the fair disclosure of all material information that enables holders of debt securities to make an informed decision without coercion, undue influence, pressure, or the effects of manipulative or coercive practices.

7.3 Differences in rules for equity and debt tender offers in the US Tender Offer Rules

Regulation 14E promulgated under the Securities Exchange Act and Section 14(e) of the Securities Exchange Act apply to all types of tender offers for equity and debt securities. Section 14(d) of the Securities Exchange Act and Regulation 14D promulgated by the SEC thereunder have established additional regulatory requirements that apply only to tender offers for equity securities that are registered pursuant to Section 12 of the Securities Exchange Act in which the tender offeror, as a result of the tender offer for such equity securities, is expected to hold more than 5 percent of the relevant class of equity securities.[23] Tender offers for equity securities made by the issuer of such securities (or an affiliate of the issuer) are not subject to Section 14(d) of the Securities Exchange Act but to the regulatory requirements of Rule 13e-4 under the Securities Exchange Act.

The regulatory framework for tender offers relating to equity or equity-linked securities is outside the scope of this book. It is, however, useful to

[23] Section 12(b) of the Securities Exchange Act requires the registration thereunder of any security that is listed on a national securities exchange and Section 12(g) of the Securities Exchange Act requires the registration under the Act of every security that is held by a certain number of holders.

summarize briefly the main regulatory requirements applicable to tender offers for equity securities and note their differences from Regulation 14E under the Securities Exchange Act, which is the rule of general application and applies to both equity and debt securities.

Regulation 14D and Rule 13e-4 under the Securities Exchange Act (collectively, the "equity tender offer rules") provide that a company (or its affiliate) making a tender offer for equity securities must file with the SEC, as soon as practicable on the date of the commencement of the tender offer, a tender offer statement on Schedule TO (the "Schedule TO"). The Schedule TO will include the offer to purchase and the letter of transmittal or similar acceptance forms that will be mailed to the holder of the target securities. The equity tender offer rules impose, among others, the following procedural, substantive, and disclosure requirements in connection with tender offers, which do not apply to tender offers for debt securities:

- *Filing requirement.* The offer and other communications relating thereto must be filed with the SEC[24];
- *Pre-commencement communications.* The equity tender offer rules set forth detailed requirements in relation to communications prior to the commencement of the tender offer[25];
- *Dissemination of materials.* The equity tender offer rules set forth detailed requirements about disclosure and dissemination of information to holders[26];
- *Information to be included.* The equity tender offer rules set forth detailed requirements about the content of the tender offer documentation[27];
- *Withdrawal rights.* Holders in equity tender offers must be able to withdraw tendered securities until the end of the offer period[28];
- *Proration rights.* In tender offers for less than the total outstanding amount of equity securities, if securities tendered exceed the amount

[24] Rules 14d-2 and 14d-3 (for third-party tender offers) and Rule 13e-4(c) (for issuer tender offers).

[25] Rule 14d-2(b) (for third-party tender offers) and Rule 13e-4(c)(1) (for issuer tender offers).

[26] Rules 14d-4 through 14d-6 (for third-party tender offers) and Rule 13e-4(d) through (e) (for issuer tender offers).

[27] Rule 14d-6(d) (for third-party tender offers) and Rule 13e-4(d) through (e) (for issuer tender offers).

[28] Rule 14d-7 (for third-party tender offers) and Rule 13e-4(f)(2) (for issuer tender offers).

of securities being sought, the offeror must purchase any tendered securities pro rata[29];

- *All holders.* Equity tender offers must be open to all holders of the target class[30]; and
- *Best price.* Consideration paid to any holder must be the highest consideration paid to any other holder during the offer.[31]

7.4 Overview of the regulatory framework in the European Union and the United Kingdom

Debt tender offers and exchange offers in the European Union, including the United Kingdom, are not subject to a regulatory system similar to that of the United States. Fraudulent or abusive practices in connection with tender offers of debt securities are regulated under the general anti-fraud and anti-abuse provisions of the Market Abuse Directive. Adopted in early 2003, the Market Abuse Directive introduced a comprehensive framework to address trading on the basis of material non-public information and market manipulation practices. The Directive aims to increase investor confidence and market integrity by prohibiting those who possess inside information from trading in related financial instruments, and by prohibiting the manipulation of markets through practices such as spreading false information or rumors and conducting trades which secure prices at abnormal levels.[32] In carrying out repurchases of debt securities in the market or a tender or exchange offer, the issuer of the securities (or an affiliate of the issuer) needs to insure that their conduct in relation to the transaction does not violate the applicable insider trading, market manipulation, and market abuse prohibitions. In the United Kingdom, these prohibitions take the form of statutory provisions in the Criminal Justice Act 1993 and the Financial Services and Markets Act 2000. In addition, certain listing rules for debt securities listed on the London Stock Exchange impose additional regulatory requirements for debt tender and exchange offers for listed securities.[33]

[29] Rule 14d-8 (for third-party tender offers) and Rule 13e-4(f)(3) (for issuer tender offers).
[30] Rule 14d-10(a)(1) (for third-party tender offers) and Rule 13e-4(f)(8)(i) (for issuer tender offers).
[31] Rule 14d-10(a)(2) (for third-party tender offers) and Rule 13e-4(f)(4) (for issuer tender offers).
[32] See the Market Abuse Directive, Recitals 1–14.
[33] See Chapter 4.

ANNEX I *Transaction alternatives for liability management of debt securities*

	Benefits	**Issues and disadvantages**
Redemptions	does not require changes to underlying documentation can be for the whole or part of the principal amount no special documentation requirements no registration with the SEC no liability under securities laws and no application of insider trading laws	requires cash does not lead to debt relief expensive liability management (premium over nominal amount may be payable) subject to notice subject to publication/ public dissemination
Repurchases of debt securities	no special documentation requirements no registration with the SEC purchase can be at a discount to nominal price; subject to market forces privately negotiated or over a securities market may hire financial advisor to assist	exposure to liability under the securities laws application of insider trading laws may trigger US Tender Offer Rules requires cash may only lead to retirement of a small percentage of total amount of securities outstanding
Debt tender offers	outside cumbersome US Tender Offer Rules applicable to equity securities no registration with the SEC purchase price can be at a discount to nominal price; subject to market forces can be for the whole or a part of the principal amount may hire financial advisor to assist can couple with consent solicitation	subject to Section 14(e) and debt US Tender Offer Rules requires offering documentation, legal opinions and other customary deliverables requires cash exposure to liability under the securities laws subject to procedural and substantive requirements of US Tender Offer Rules

	Benefits	Issues and disadvantages
Debt exchange offers (unregistered)	outside cumbersome US Tender Offer Rules applicable to equity securities no registration with the SEC purchase price can be at a discount to nominal price; subject to market forces can be for the whole or a part of the principal amount may hire financial advisor to assist can couple with consent solicitation does not require cash	subject to Section 14(e) and debt US Tender Offer Rules requires offering documentation, legal opinions, comfort letter, and other customary deliverables requires description of business and financial condition of issuer exposure to liability under the securities laws subject to procedural and substantive requirements of US Tender Offer Rules limited to qualified institutional buyers ("QIBs") or under the strict conditions of Section 3(a)(9) newly issued securities subject to resale restrictions
Debt exchange offers (registered)	outside cumbersome US Tender Offer Rules applicable to equity securities purchase price can be at a discount to nominal price; subject to market forces can be for the whole or a part of the principal amount may hire financial advisor to assist can couple with consent solicitation does not require cash new securities are freely transferable and not subject to resale restrictions	subject to Section 14(e) and debt US Tender Offer Rules requires offering documentation, legal opinions, comfort letter, and other customary deliverables subject to SEC registration requires description of business and financial condition of issuer exposure to liability under the securities laws subject to procedural and substantive requirements of US Tender Offer Rules

2

The definition of "tender offer" within the meaning of the US Tender Offer Rules

1 Introduction

The applicable legal and regulatory framework for a purchase of debt securities by the issuer (or an affiliate of the issuer) that is not a tender offer differs significantly from the legal and regulatory framework applicable to a purchase of debt securities that is a tender offer within the meaning of the US Tender Offer Rules.[34]

In 1968, in an attempt to deal with the proliferating use of cash tender offers as a means of acquiring control of public companies, the US Congress enacted Sections 13(d)–(f) and 14(d)–(f) of the Securities Exchange Act in a series of related amendments to the Securities Exchange Act that have since become widely known as the Williams Act. The Williams Act was enacted in response to the growing use of cash tender offers as a means of achieving corporate takeovers outside the reach of then-existing disclosure requirements of the US federal securities laws.[35]

A non-technical definition of a "tender offer for debt securities" is an offer by a person (the *tender offeror*) addressed to the existing holders (the *security holders*) of the issued securities (the *tender securities*) to purchase the tender securities (in whole or in part) for cash at a specified, or at least determinable, price over a specified period of time. The security holders are said to *tender* their securities for purchase.

[34] We use the term "US Tender Offer Rules" to describe Section 14(e) of the Securities Exchange Act and the rules and regulations adopted by the SEC thereunder, which are commonly referred to as "Regulation 14E under the Securities Exchange Act."

[35] See, e.g., *Piper*, 430 U.S. 1, 22, 97 S. Ct. 926, 939, 51 L. Ed. 2d 124 (1977). See also S. Rep. No. 550, 90th Cong., 1st Sess., 2–4 (1967); H. R. Rep. No. 1711, 90th Cong., 2d Sess., 2–4 (1968) (hereinafter, the "House Report"); U.S. Code Cong. & Admin. News 1968, 2811; 114 Cong. Rec. 21483–21484 (July 15, 1968) (Comments of Representatives Springer and Whalen); 113 Cong. Rec. 854–855 (January 18, 1967) (Comments of Senator Williams); id. at 24664 (August 30, 1967) (Comments of Senator Williams); id. at 24666 (Comments of Senator Javits).

The typical tender offer then, as described in the Congressional debates, hearings and reports leading to the adoption of the Williams Act, consists of a general, publicized bid by an individual or a group to buy publicly listed or traded securities at a price substantially above the then current market price of the relevant tender securities.[36] The typical tender offer is usually accompanied by newspaper and other publicity, a time limit for the tender of securities in response to the offer, and additional conditions fixing a quantity limit on the total number or amount of the tender securities that would be purchased in the tender offer by the tender offeror.

Cash tender offers for debt securities may be completed more quickly and with fewer transactional, regulatory, and documentation requirements than other types of tender offers, especially tender offers for equity or convertible debt securities, particularly those equity or convertible debt securities that are registered under Section 12 of the Securities Exchange Act or subject to the reporting obligations of Sections 13 and 15 of the Securities Exchange Act. Cash tender offers for debt securities are subject to tender offer regulations (i.e., the anti-fraud provisions[37] of Section 14(e) of the Securities Exchange Act and Regulation 14E thereunder) but are outside the more invasive requirements of the equity tender offer rules promulgated under Section 14(d) of the Securities Exchange Act.

Neither the Williams Act nor the rules and regulations adopted by the SEC thereunder define the term "tender offer" in connection with offers to purchase or solicitations of offers to sell equity or debt securities. While there have been three proposals by the SEC to formally define the term "tender offer,"[38] each time the SEC has declined to implement the

[36] See Senate Report; House Report; U.S. Code Cong. & Admin. News 1968, p. 2811; 113 Cong. Rec. at 855 (January 18, 1967) (Senator Williams); *Takeover Bids: Hearings on H.R. 14475, S. 510 before the Subcommittee on Commerce and Financing of the House Committee on Interstate and Foreign Commerce*, 90th Cong., 2d Sess., 10 (1968) (House Hearings) (Manuel Cohen, Chairman, SEC); id. at 44 (Donald Calvin, Vice-President, New York Stock Exchange); *Full Disclosure of Corporate Equity Ownership in Corporate Takeover Bids: Hearings on S. 510 Before the Subcommittee on Securities of the Senate Committee on Banking and Currency*, 90th Cong., 1st Sess. at 2 (1967) (Senate Hearings) (Senator Williams); id. at 17 (Manuel Cohen); id. at 42 (Senator Kuchel).

[37] For a discussion of the anti-fraud provisions of Section 14(e) of the Securities Exchange Act, see Chapter 7.

[38] The most recent proposal to define the term "tender offer" was made in the November 29, 1979 Proposed Amendments to Tender Offer Rules. See 1979 SEC LEXIS 218 (SEC Release No. 16385), pp. 8–16. The proposed definition was divided into two tiers which were intended to operate independently of each other. If an offer satisfied the criteria for either tier, it would be deemed a tender offer. Under the first tier, an offer was a "tender offer" if

proposed definition because it believed that, for purposes of the federal regulatory framework serving the policy objectives of the Williams Act, the term "tender offer" might well encompass transactions that have yet to be structured, having characteristics not typical of the transactions then identified in general custom and usage as tender offers. Thus, the question of what is understood under the term "tender offer" was intentionally left open in an effort to preserve the flexibility of both the SEC and the courts in making determinations on the applicability of the federal regulatory framework applicable to tender offers on a case-by-case basis.[39] Congress and the SEC were worried that any definition would be likely to allow market participants to evade the protections of the Williams Act in light of the almost infinite variety of terms and structures in the conduct of transactions that should be regulated as tender offers. The disadvantage of this approach is that market participants experience legal uncertainty when structuring transactions that could, under certain conditions, be regarded as "tender offers" within the meaning of the US Tender Offer Rules and, consequently, illegal tender offers when the transaction is completed without observing the requirements of the US Tender Offer Rules and turns out to have been a "tender offer" within the meaning of the US federal securities regulatory framework.

2 The conventional tender offer

A cash tender offer for debt securities, which is intended to be a tender offer and is regulated and structured as such, generally follows a simple pattern. The tender offeror offers a price, usually above the prevailing market price, to purchase the desired principal amount of the tender securities (either the entire outstanding principal amount of one or more series of tender securities or a specified percentage of the outstanding

all of the following four elements were present (unless an exception applied): "(1) one or more offers to purchase or solicitations of offers to sell securities of a single class; (2) during any 45-day period; (3) directed to more than 10 persons; and (4) seeking the acquisition of more than 5% of the class of securities." Under the second tier, an offer was a "tender offer" if all of the following three conditions were present: "First, the offers to purchase or the solicitation of offers to sell must be disseminated in a widespread manner. . . . Second, the price offered must represent a premium in excess of the greater of 5% of or $2 above the current market price of the securities being sought. The third condition of the second tier is that the offers do not provide for a meaningful opportunity to negotiate the price and terms." See SEC Release No. 16385, at pp. 14–16.

39 See, e.g., *Wellman* v. *Dickinson, et al.*, 475 F. Supp 783, 825 (S.D.N.Y. 1979) (hereinafter, the "*Wellman* case" or "*Wellman*").

principal amount of one or more series of tender securities). The tender offeror appoints a broker or dealer to advise on the structure of the tender offer and to manage the execution of the transaction. The tender offer is publicized to the market through the placement of newspaper notices and the distribution of press releases to traditional and electronic media. If the holders of the tender securities tender more than the principal amount of tender securities that the tender offeror is willing to purchase, the tender offeror may at his or her option purchase only the principal amount of the tender securities specified in the tender offer materials. A tender offer is different from an ordinary purchase transaction in the secondary market. The completion of the tender offer is often subject to conditions and the tender offeror reserves the option to accept for purchase a lesser or larger principal amount of tender securities than the amount indicated in the tender offer materials, to change the material terms and conditions of the tender offer, or to extend the expiration period for the tender offer.

3 Defining tender offers – the Wellman test

Although Congress and the SEC have been unwilling to adopt a formal definition of "tender offer" for purposes of the federal regulatory framework of the US Tender Offer Rules, the SEC has filed, from time to time starting in the late 1970s, *amicus briefs*[40] in several cases that considered whether or not a transaction or series of related transactions was a "tender offer" within the meaning of the Williams Act and the US Tender Offer Rules. In those cases, the SEC suggested, and the courts generally accepted, eight substantive elements as essential characteristics of tender offers. Over the years, the SEC has continued to endorse the same eight-factor test, which has been widely used by the courts.[41]

[40] An *amicus brief* is a legal opinion or legal statement filed with a court by an *amicus curiae* (literally, a friend of the court), someone, not a party to a case, who volunteers to offer information, testimony, or legal views on a matter that bears on the case litigated before the court. The decision on whether to admit the information lies at the discretion of the court.

[41] In addition to the eight-factor test, courts have considered two other tests to determine whether a particular transaction constitutes a tender offer. The first of these, developed in *S-G Securities, Inc.* v. *The Fuqua Investment Company*, states "where there is: 1) a publicly announced intention by the purchaser to acquire a substantial block of stock of the target company for purposes of acquiring control thereof, and 2) a subsequent rapid acquisition by the purchaser of large blocks of stock through open market and privately negotiated purchases, such actions constitute a tender offer." 466 F. Supp. 1114, 1126–27 (D. Mass. 1978) (hereinafter, "*S-G Securities*"). Since the eight-factor test was first adopted by the

Although originally adopted in the case *The Hoover Company* v. *Fuqua Industries, Inc.*,[42] the leading case on the SEC's eight-factor test is *Wellman*[43] and the eight-factor test is known as the "Wellman test."

In *Wellman*, a third-party bidder commenced a purchasing program pursuant to which thirty institutional investors and nine (presumably high-net worth) individuals holding large equity stakes in the target company were solicited over the phone. The solicitees were offered a premium for their shares but were only given hours to respond to the offer. Additionally, the offer was conditioned on the bidder obtaining 20 percent of the outstanding stock of the company, and the solicitees were given minimal information about the bid or the bidder, other than the price being offered. By the end of this purchase program, the bidder had accumulated approximately 34 percent of the target company's outstanding stock. On these facts, several of the target company's officers and shareholders commenced action, individually and derivatively, against the bidder for numerous federal securities laws violations, including violation of Section 14(d) of the Securities Exchange Act. The court agreed to apply the eight-factor test suggested by the SEC in its amicus brief and, on that basis, it concluded that the bidder's purchase program constituted a tender offer in violation of Section 14(d) of the Securities Exchange Act.

The eight-factor test adopted by the court in *Wellman* focused on the following factors or conditions: (i) an active and widespread solicitation of public security holders for the securities of an issuer; (ii) a solicitation made for a substantial percentage of the issuer's securities; (iii) an offer to purchase made at a premium over the prevailing market price; (iv) the terms of the offer are firm rather than negotiable; (v) the offer is contingent on the tender of a fixed number of securities, often subject to a fixed maximum number or amount of securities to be purchased; (vi) the offer

courts, the *S-G Securities* test has largely been rejected and criticized for being vague and subjective. See *SEC* v. *Carter Hawley Hale Stores, Inc.*, 760 F.2d 945, 953 (9th Cir. 1985) (hereinafter, the "*Carter Hawley*" or "*Carter Hawley* case"). A second alternative test was developed in *Hanson*. The *Hanson* test originated after the adoption of the eight-factor test, which the *Hanson* court characterized as "both unwise and unnecessary." 774 F. 2d 47, 57 (2d Cir. 1985). The *Hanson* test states: "since the purpose of Section 14(d) is to protect the ill-informed solicitee, the question of whether a solicitation constitutes a 'tender offer' within the meaning of Section 14(d) turns on whether, viewing the transaction in the light of the totality of circumstances, there appears to be a likelihood that unless the pre-acquisition filing strictures of that statute are followed there will be a substantial risk that solicitees will lack information needed to make a carefully considered appraisal of the proposal put before them." Id. While it criticizes the eight-factor test, the *Hanson* court relied on six of the eight factors to make a determination under its own totality of the circumstances test. See *Hanson* at pp. 57–8. *Hanson* is summarized below in section 2.4.

[42] 1979 U.S. Dist. LEXIS 11809 (hereinafter, "*Hoover*"). [43] See fn 39 above.

is open only for a limited time; (vii) the offeree being subject to pressure to sell the relevant securities; and (viii) whether the public announcements of a purchasing program concerning the target company precede or accompany the rapid accumulation of large amounts of the target company's securities.[44]

The courts have applied these eight factors flexibly, sometimes finding tender offers even if a number of factors are not satisfied, and giving greater or lesser weight to different factors, depending on the circumstances.[45] Additionally, while its absence from the Wellman test would suggest that the potential for shifts of control is not an essential element of a tender offer, all of the reported case law to date in this area has taken place in the corporate control context. We will examine each of the eight factors in turn.

3.1 *Active and widespread solicitation of public security holders*

To determine whether the first factor of the Wellman test has been satisfied, courts have looked at both the nature of the solicitation and those persons being solicited. Although the cases do not define the term "solicitation," in this context it means a request to holders of tender securities to tender or sell their securities.[46] Solicitation can be made in meetings in person or on the telephone, by mail, electronic mail or other means of communication, by radio, television or newspaper or other type of broad communication, and by the publication of tender offer materials (including a tender offer memorandum and other accompanying materials).

While the courts have never clearly explained what type of activity constitutes "active and widespread solicitation," they have provided guidance by the analysis of the facts before them.[47] For example, in *Wellman* the

[44] See *Wellman*, 475 F. Supp. at 823–4. Although the SEC's amicus brief in *Wellman* did not include the eighth factor (regarding publicity), the court noted that it was included in the SEC's amicus brief in *Hoover*, fn 42 above, and was most likely left out in this case because publicity was not a feature of the transaction at issue. Therefore, the court adopted the eighth factor as part of its test.

[45] See *Wellman*, at 824 (the *Wellman* court stated: "the absence of one particular factor . . . is not necessarily fatal to the Commission's argument because depending upon the circumstances involved in the particular case, one or more of the [eight Wellman factors] may be more compelling and determinative than the others.").

[46] See, e.g., Rule 14d-9 under the Securities Exchange Act.

[47] See *Cattleman's Investment Company* v. *Fears*, 343 F. Supp. 1248, 1251–52 (W.D. Okla. 1972) (active and widespread solicitation found where the defendant solicited public shareholders in person, over the telephone, and through the mail).

court focused on the percentage of stock held by the holders solicited (34 percent), the geographic dimensions of the effort (several states), and the number of holders solicited (thirty institutions and nine (apparently high-net worth) individuals) to conclude that "there was certainly 'active and widespread' solicitation involved."[48] Thus, a geographically diverse group of thirty institutional investors and nine sophisticated individuals who tendered 34 percent of the class of tender securities at a fixed price under selling pressure was "widespread solicitation."

Other courts have provided more complete analyses with respect to determining whether those being solicited are "public security holders." In *Hoover*,[49] through a series of three letters (and subsequent press releases explaining its solicitation and the terms of the bid), the bidder offered to purchase the stock from over 100 members of the Hoover family at a premium. When assessing the first factor, the court focused on the sophistication of the shareholders solicited, citing cases where solicitation limited to sophisticated investors had been found not to be a tender offer. The *Hoover* court distinguished those cases and concluded that there had been "active and widespread solicitation of public shareholders" because the solicitation of more than 100 members of an extended family with varying degrees of sophistication by the defendants was "the equivalent of a solicitation of all the public shareholders."[50] The court in *Brascan Limited* v. *Edper Equities Ltd.*[51] also considered the sophistication of the solicitees but concluded in that case that there was no widespread solicitation of public shareholders because "[t]he solicitations were directed to only approximately 50 of Brascan's 50,000 shareholders, each of the 50 being either an institution or a sophisticated individual holder of large blocks of Brascan shares."[52]

[48] See *Wellman*, 475 F. Supp. at 825.

[49] See fn 42 above.

[50] Ibid., at 15. The court in *Hoover* also appeared to imply that the determination that financial institutions and other institutional investors are sophisticated is not a foregone conclusion ("The Court will accept (at least for the purposes of discussion) the general consensus that financial institutions and other institutional investors are sophisticated.").

[51] 477 F. Supp. 773, 791 (S.D.N.Y. 1979) (hereinafter, "*Brascan*" or the "*Brascan* case").

[52] See the *Brascan* case. See also *Pin* v. *Texaco, Inc., et al.*, 793 F.2d 1448 (5th Cir. 1986) (holding that an issuer's purchase of 9.9 percent of the outstanding shares of its common stock from a group of sophisticated investors did not constitute a tender offer) (hereinafter, "*Pin* v. *Texaco*"); *Hanson*, 774 F.2d 47 (holding the direct purchase of 25 percent of the target company's stock from sophisticated investors did not constitute a tender offer); *Kennecott Copper Corporation* v. *Curtiss-Wright Corporation*, 584 F.2d 1195 (2d Cir. 1978) (off-the-market purchases made from largely sophisticated institutional shareholders was not a tender offer) (hereinafter, "*Kennecott Copper*"); *D-Z Investment Co.* v. *Holloway*, 1974 U.S. Dist. LEXIS 7027 (S.D.N.Y. 1974) (finding no tender offer when market purchases

Debt securities, especially high-yield debt securities, are commonly held by sophisticated institutional and other similarly qualified investors. Applying the law to repurchases of debt securities held by institutional investors or QIBs within the meaning of Rule 144A under the Securities Act, there is usually a strong argument that since the "qualified institutional buyers"[53] solicited in connection with a debt repurchase program are sophisticated investors, they are not the type of investors the Williams Act was designed to protect. Based on the cases enumerated above which make this distinction, it is arguable that a debt repurchase program for debt securities held by sophisticated institutional investors and/or QIBs does not involve the solicitation of public security holders as intended by the drafters of the Williams Act. While this position is strong and based on several cases, it is subject to critique. Since the *Wellman* court did not consider the sophistication of the solicitees, it can certainly be argued that *Wellman* supports the conclusion that "active and widespread solicitation" can be found even when the solicitation is addressed to QIBs or other institutional investors. Legal practitioners certainly take this conservative view when structuring offers to sophisticated holders of securities issued under Rule 144A and Regulation S under the Securities Act.

While limiting the number of solicitees in any offer for the purchase of debt securities may be helpful in terms of arguing the solicitation was not "widespread," the case law does not lend itself to hard and fast guidelines.[54] Nevertheless, under the first tier of the SEC's proposed two-tiered definition of "tender offer" in SEC Release No. 16385 (November 29, 1979), an offer had to be directed to more than ten persons to qualify as a tender offer. However, since the two tiers of the proposed definition were intended to operate independently, the fact that an offer was made to ten or fewer individuals would not necessarily mean that it was not a tender offer.[55] Additionally, it is important to consider that even though limiting the number of solicitees may be helpful for purposes of analyzing a

combined with four privately negotiated transactions with highly sophisticated financial institutions) (hereinafter, "*D-Z Investment Co.*").

[53] For the definition of "qualified institutional buyer," see Rule 144A(a)(i) of the Securities Act.

[54] Some investment banks have suggested an inverse relationship between the number of solicitees and the percentage of the aggregate amount of debt securities solicited, stating that they are comfortable repurchasing a higher percentage of the outstanding principal amount as the number of solicitees is reduced.

[55] See 1979 SEC LEXIS 218, at 9 ("SEC Release No. 16385").

potential cash offer for debt securities under the first factor of the Wellman test, it also inevitably results in a greater number of excluded security holders who may, in their frustration from being excluded, complain about the legality of the cash offer to purchase.

The vast majority of reported judicial cases relates to solicitations of tenders of the common stock of public companies. The definition of "tender offer" applies equally to offers to holders of common stock of private companies and offers to holders of debt securities of both public and private companies.

3.2 Solicitation of substantial percentage of outstanding principal amount

The second Wellman factor requires a "solicitation" of a "substantial percentage" of the relevant tender securities. Unlike the first Wellman factor, the solicitation need not be active and/or widespread. But there must be solicitation of some type even if it does not amount to a widespread or an active solicitation.

The second condition of the second Wellman factor is that the solicitation must be for a substantial percentage of the relevant class of securities. What matters is the percentage that is solicited, not the percentage that is ultimately sold. If a tender offeror solicits the entire class of the relevant target securities for the purchase, subject to certain conditions, of 10 percent of the solicited class, the solicitation is for the entire class, not for 10 percent of the class. On the other hand, if the tender offeror solicits persons holding 10 percent of the class and manages to purchase the entire 10 percent held by the persons solicited and, subsequently, purchases another 25 percent of the class in the open market without any form of solicitation preceding such purchase in the open market, the solicitation is for 10 percent of the relevant class of securities. The percentage solicited is easily calculated in the case of debt securities. The calculation is based on the principal amount of debt securities solicited divided by the total principal amount of the relevant series of debt securities outstanding.

The second Wellman factor is generally given short shrift by the courts due to its overlap with the first and eighth Wellman factors.[56] In fact, the

[56] See *Wellman*, 475 F. Supp. at 824 (stating: "the second characteristic, substantial percentage, does not move us very far"); *Hoover*, fn 42 above, at 11 (stating: "item 2 is also of limited value in analyzing Fuqua's offer").

court in *SEC* v. *Carter Hawley Hale Stores, Inc.*[57] all but dismissed this factor when it stated:

> it is unclear whether the proper focus of this factor is the solicitation or the percentage of stock solicited. . . . The solicitation and percentage of stock elements of the second factor will be addressed adequately in an evaluation of the first *Wellman* factor, which is concerned with solicitation, and the eighth *Wellman* factor, which focuses on the amount of securities accumulated.[58]

It also is noteworthy that the *Wellman* court when addressing this factor stated that Rule 14d under the Securities Exchange Act does not apply unless solicitation is for at least 5 percent of the outstanding shares, implying that a tender offer of less than that percentage could be a tender offer, but exempt from the US Tender Offer Rules. Similarly, in *Crane Co.* v. *Harsco Corporation*,[59] where Harsco repurchased a large block of shares of its common stock from arbitrageurs to prevent them from being tendered into a competing third-party tender offer, the court, doubting there had been any solicitation, stated that:

> even if Harsco's actions were deemed a solicitation for substantially all the Harsco stock traded since Crane's offer, less than 5% of Harsco's stock, it still would not be a solicitation for a substantial number of shares since the term "substantial" requires reference to the total number of Harsco shares.[60]

In other words, the court concluded that accumulations of less than 5 percent of the outstanding stock of a company are not per se "substantial" for purposes of the Wellman test.

While the *Crane* court's analysis would support the proposition that this factor is not satisfied if less than 5 percent of the outstanding principal amount of debt securities is purchased, a court applying the Wellman test to a purchase of debt securities will likely follow the majority of courts and give the second factor little independent weight. Of course, it is possible that a court reviewing a transaction under *Wellman* may conduct an analysis under the second factor. It is, however, noted that the arguments against "solicitation" in the second factor are identical to the arguments

[57] See fn 41 above. [58] See *Carter Hawley*, at 951–2.

[59] 511 F. Supp. 294 (D. Del. 1981) (hereinafter, "*Crane*" or the "*Crane* case").

[60] Ibid., at 303.

against "solicitation" in the first Wellman factor, and the argument that the offeror did not acquire a "substantial percentage of principal amount" for purposes of the second factor are identical to its arguments that it did not acquire a "large principal amount of the company's securities" for purposes of the eighth Wellman factor.

3.3 *Offer to purchase made at a premium to prevailing market price*

While the determination of whether a premium exists is generally uncontroversial, one court has been called upon to determine what market price the current offer is to be measured against for purposes of calculating the premium. In *Carter Hawley*,[61] the SEC contended that an issuer's offer to repurchase common stock, made in response to a competing third-party tender offer, should be measured against the pre-tender offer price of its stock, rather than the artificially inflated stock price due to the third party's competing tender offer. The court rejected the SEC's approach, stating that under such a definition "a premium will always exist when a target company makes open market purchases in response to a tender offer even though the increase in market price is attributable to the action of the third-party offeror and not the target company."[62] Instead, the court adopted the definition of "premium" urged by the SEC in its November 29, 1979 proposed amendments to the US Tender Offer Rules,[63] which stated that the existence or not of a premium should be determined by reference to the current market price of the securities being bought.[64] It is often argued that a purchase of debt securities is not purchase at a "premium" if the offer is made following the close of the market at the closing market price for that day.

As a general matter, the appropriate time against which the tender offer price should be measured is the time immediately before the first public announcement of the tender offer. In relation to purchases in the open market without any publicity, the appropriate measurement time shall be the time of purchase, which is when both parties are irrevocably committed to consummating the transaction.[65] The *market price* of the security is the price in the principal market on which the security trades. If the security trades among brokers or dealers over the counter, the market price should be the last sale price of the security that is generally

[61] See fn 41 above. [62] Ibid., at 951. [63] See SEC Release No. 16385. [64] Ibid., at 16.
[65] See *In re General Motors Class E Stock Buyout Securities Litigation*, 694 F. Supp. 1119, 1130 (D. Del. 1988).

available to the market. It must follow from this that there is no premium if purchases are made in the open market without any publicity or when a purchaser acquires the securities through a purchase program at prices that gradually increase due to prior purchases made in the program.

3.4 Terms of the offer are firm rather than negotiable

Although this factor appears very clear on its face, the courts have been confronted with challenges to the meaning of the term "firm" under the Wellman test. In *Hoover*,[66] the plaintiff claimed that the fourth Wellman factor had been satisfied because the offer letters sent by the defendant to the members of the Hoover family indicated that the offer was a "firm offer." However, the court made it clear that with respect to the fourth factor "firm" does not refer to the fact that acceptance of the offer will result in a binding contract (as was intended by the language in the defendant's letters), but rather to "the way in which the offering or sale price was determined."[67] To make this determination courts must look to whether the terms of the offer were determined unilaterally by the offeror, or whether they were subject to negotiation.[68]

Open market purchases do not result from a firm offer. Offers to negotiate a purchase of securities are, similarly, not "firm" offers for purposes of the Wellman test. An offeror can refute a claim that the terms of the offer were firm by demonstrating that different sellers managed to negotiate different terms in connection with a program of open market repurchases or similar transactions. The number of persons solicited in an offer to purchase securities is one of the principal factors in determining whether the offer is firm or open to negotiation: the more persons are solicited by the offeror, the more likely it will be that the terms of the offer will be "firm" and not "negotiable."

3.5 Offer subject to a minimum condition, and often subject to a fixed principal amount to be purchased

Despite the fact that the SEC included consideration of whether the offer is subject to a fixed maximum number of securities in this factor, the courts appear to universally ignore this consideration and focus solely on the presence of a minimum condition.[69] For example, in concluding that the

[66] See fn 42 above. [67] Ibid., at 17. [68] Ibid.
[69] See, e.g., *Wellman*, at 824; *Carter Hawley*, at 951; *Hoover*, at 17; *Brascan*, at 792.

defendant's offer had not satisfied the fifth factor of the Wellman test, the court in *Carter Hawley* disregarded the fact that the defendant's offer was subject to a fixed maximum condition, stating: "[w]hile [the defendant] indicated it would purchase up to 15 million shares, [its] purchases were not contingent on the tender of a fixed minimum number of shares."[70]

If a repurchase of debt securities is not subject to any minimum condition but, as is often the case, is subject to a fixed maximum principal amount to be purchased, it is likely that a court will focus on the lack of a minimum condition, while ignoring the fact that the offer is subject to a fixed maximum principal amount, and find that this factor has not been satisfied. Nevertheless, under certain circumstances, if a fixed maximum principal amount is used to exert pressure on solicitees either to sell debt securities quickly or miss the opportunity to do so, a court may reach a different conclusion.[71]

3.6 *Offer only open for a limited period of time*

Given that the act of placing time constraints on an investor's ability to consider an offer inevitably increases the very pressure on the investor that the Williams Act was designed to alleviate, the sixth and seventh Wellman factors (dealing with time limitations and selling pressure, respectively) are closely related. In *Carter Hawley*, an issuer publicly announced and subsequently executed a repurchase program in an attempt to defeat a third-party tender offer. The offer was to remain open for the entire period of the third-party tender offer, or until 15 million shares had been acquired. In the suit that followed, the SEC contended that since the issuer acquired the 15 million shares in a short period of time, the issuer's offer satisfied the sixth Wellman factor. Rejecting this argument, the court said that the time limitation in that case "was a product of ordinary market forces, not the terms of [the issuer's] repurchase program."[72]

Depending upon the overall circumstances, it is possible that the offer may be open for a limited period of time due to natural market pressures

[70] See *Carter Hawley*, at 952.

[71] Similarly, the court in *Wellman*, although in the context of determining that the defendants had applied pressure for purposes of the seventh factor, stated: "The [solicitees] were told that favorable responses were coming in fast, and it was implied that either they had better make a hurried acceptance of this attractive offer or their chance would be gone." *Wellman*, at 825.

[72] See *Carter Hawley*, at 952.

relating to the trading of securities among sophisticated investors and not as a coercive mechanism. Therefore, while the use of a fixed deadline clearly satisfies the sixth factor on its face, it is possible, depending on the facts and circumstances, that a court would give some credence to the "natural market pressures" argument and, at the least, give less weight to this factor in its balancing of the Wellman test as a whole.[73]

3.7 Offerees subject to selling pressure

One of the principal policy objectives and aims of Congress in enacting the Williams Act was to insulate investors from the pressures that forced them to make quick, uninformed decisions in response to tender offers.[74] The importance of the seventh Wellman factor was noted by the court in *Hoover*, when it stated that "[i]f an offer is otherwise far removed from a conventional tender offer, a court might still find a tender offer if the shareholders were pressured."[75] Similarly, the court in *Crane* stated: "Th[e *Wellman*] factors are not of equal significance; courts have emphasized that pressure on stockholders to decide whether to sell is the primary characteristic of a tender offer."[76]

The best explanation of the type of pressure the seventh factor focuses on was provided by the court in *Brascan*[77] in its assessment of the sixth Wellman factor. In *Brascan*, after its attempts at a friendly acquisition of the target failed, the bidder contacted a broker and indicated that if a certain number of shares of the target became available in the market, it might be willing to purchase them at a premium. Over the next couple of days, the bidder solicited between thirty and fifty institutional investors, and ten to fifteen individual shareholders holding large equity stakes in the target. As a result of these solicitations (and less substantial purchases from other brokers), the bidder was able to purchase approximately 24 percent of the outstanding shares of the target company. In its application of the Wellman test to these facts, the court in *Brascan* stated that the

[73] See *Wellman*, at 824 ("depending upon the circumstances involved in the particular case, one or more of the [eight Wellman factors] may be more compelling and determinative than the others").

[74] See *Hoover*, at 18. See also *Carter Hawley*, at 948 ("The [Williams] Act was also designed to provide shareholders an opportunity to examine all relevant facts in an effort to reach a decision without being subject to unwarranted pressure.").

[75] See *Hoover*, at 18. [76] See *Crane*, at 302. [77] See fn 51 above.

pressure the Williams Act was designed to alleviate was the potential pressure an investor faced when presented with an offer that combined a high premium with the threat that the offer may disappear.[78] Moreover, the court expressed doubt as to whether sophisticated investors can be subject to the type of pressure that the Williams Act was intended to curb.[79] Other courts have made it clear that, in their view, sophisticated investors are unlikely to be forced into uninformed, ill-considered decisions.[80] Although these courts did not explicitly address investor sophistication in their analyses of whether there was pressure for purposes of the seventh factor, the implication seems to be that, in the absence of specific facts supporting a different conclusion, sophisticated investors cannot be "pressured" for purposes of the Wellman test. On the other hand, where additional facts are present, at least one court has refused to give any consideration to the sophistication of the sellers. In *Wellman*, the court determined that since the sophisticated investors in its case were provided with minimal information about the offer or the bidder (other than the price being offered) and were given only hours to respond, they "were in no position to put their sophistication and experience to use."[81] Under such circumstances, said the court, "[S]ophistication and expertise cannot be relied on . . . to exempt [the] transaction from the reach of Section 14(d)."[82]

The extent of the pressure exerted in any transaction for the purchase of debt securities depends on a number of factors. First, one must look to the actual communications between the offeror's representatives (such

[78] See *Brascan*, at 792. See also *Carter Hawley*, at 952.

[79] The *Brascan* court stated: "The offerees were experienced professionals, in most cases institutional portfolio managers. Even assuming that such professional investors can be susceptible to 'pressure' in the sense in which the Williams Act is concerned, no such pressures were exerted." See *Brascan*, at 792.

[80] See *Kennecott Copper*, fn 52 above, at 1206 (affirming the district court's judgment based on the fact that the fifty shareholders solicited by the defendant off the exchange were sophisticated institutional shareholders unlikely to be forced into uninformed, ill-considered decisions); *D-Z Investment Co.*, fn 52 above, at 11 (stating, in dicta, that calls to sophisticated persons were not likely to pressure them into making uninformed, ill-considered decisions to sell); see also *Pin* v. *Texaco*, fn 52 above, at 1454 (in finding the Wellman test had not been satisfied, the court stated: "There is no assertion of pressure by Texaco on any member of the [sellers] to sell hastily. The complaint implies that the sellers were highly sophisticated."); *Hanson*, at 57 (concluding, under an alternative to the Wellman test, that there had been no tender offer, the court stated: "At least five of the sellers were highly sophisticated professionals, knowledgeable in the market and well aware of the essential facts needed to exercise their professional skills and to appraise [the] offer").

[81] See *Wellman*, at 823. [82] Ibid.

as brokers, dealers, or other similar sales forces) to determine whether any excessive measures were employed. Absent the use of any tactics comparable to those used by the solicitors in *Wellman*,[83] offerors should usually have a strong argument that sophisticated investors in debt securities are not the type of investors the Williams Act was intended to protect. As stated by the court in *Pin* v. *Texaco*:[84] "This is not a case in which poorly informed shareholders were induced to tender their shares to [the Company] through misleading or incomplete information, which is the evil that § 13(e) was enacted to remedy."[85] Rather, "the off-market purchases were made largely from sophisticated institutional shareholders who were unlikely to be forced into uninformed, ill-considered decisions."[86] Nevertheless, as the *Wellman* case demonstrated, the fact that the investors involved are sophisticated does not guarantee a favorable outcome.

Second, even if a court refused to consider the sophistication of the solicitees in its analysis, it would still need to conclude that the solicitees were subjected to the type of "pressure" that is the focus of the seventh factor. Under the *Brascan* court's formulation, such a conclusion is ultimately dependent upon the court's determination of whether a "premium" was offered under the third Wellman factor, and whether there were time constraints imposed by the offer under the sixth factor. Given the previous discussions regarding "premium" and time constraints, it is arguable that the only pressure placed on the investors was the limited time period.[87] Therefore, one could argue that absent a premium the "pressure" that the seventh factor focuses on is not present. The argument against the presence of "pressure" is further bolstered in certain circumstances by the fact that the time constraints, as stated in the discussion of the sixth factor, are a result of ordinary market pressures and, consequently, any pressure to sell in any transaction would be largely "the pressure of the marketplace and not the type of untoward pressure the tender offer regulations were designed to prohibit."[88] The plaintiffs may argue that

[83] Ibid., at 825 (in finding that the offerees were subject to pressure, the court stated: "The solicitors tried to exert a maximum amount of pressure on the solicitees they contacted. The latter were told that favorable responses were coming in fast, and it was implied that either they had better make a hurried acceptance of this attractive offer or their chance would be gone.").

[84] See fn 52 above. [85] Ibid., at 1453.

[86] See *Kennecott Copper*, fn 52 above, at 1206 (explaining the findings of the district court, and affirming its conclusion that there had been no tender offer).

[87] The court in *Wellman* noted time constraints as one (but not the only) element of selling pressure. See *Wellman*, at 874–5.

[88] See *Carter Hawley*, at 952.

the US Tender Offer Rules are intended to provide greater time periods, and thereby avoid pressure, in specified contexts.

The usual indications of an absence of selling pressure are the following: (i) the offer is subject to negotiations; (ii) the persons solicited by the offeror have access to all material information relating to a decision to tender or not the relevant securities; (iii) the persons solicited by the offeror are sophisticated and able to evaluate the merits of the offer; (iv) the offeror does not engage in high-pressure selling tactics; and (v) the persons solicited by the offeror can sell the securities to alternative sources of demand.

3.8 Public announcement of purchasing program precedes or accompanies rapid accumulations of large amounts of the company's securities

> When there has been no public announcement of a proposed offer . . . the purposes of the Williams Act would not be materially furthered by applying it to the offeror or the target company. When, however, a public announcement of a proposed offer has been made, the very dangers that the Act was intended to guard against came into play, and the application of sections 14(d) and 14(e) is thus appropriate. . . . Th[e] publicity create[s] a risk of pressure on sellers that the disclosure and remedial tender offer provisions of the Williams Act were designed to prevent.[89]

Courts have found that the "public announcement" may be satisfied by numerous activities including, but not limited to, the issuance of press releases outlining the details of the buying program,[90] letters from the company to its security holders concerning the repurchasing plan,[91] and filing disclosure documents with the SEC.[92] Nevertheless, certain courts have refused to find a "public announcement" under the Wellman test if the terms of the offer are publicized only to the extent required by law or stock exchange rules.[93] The court in *Crane* expressed the view that

[89] See *S-G Securities*, fn 41, at 1125. [90] Ibid., at 1126; *Carter Hawley*, at 952.

[91] See *Carter Hawley*, at 952. [92] Ibid.

[93] See *Crane*, at 303 (finding no public announcement where defendant "publicized its offer only to the extent required by law, and its press release . . . was required by the New York Stock Exchange"); see also *Carter Hawley*, at 950 (in finding there had been no active and widespread solicitation of the shareholders under the first Wellman factor, the court stated: "the only public announcements by CHH were those mandated by SEC or Exchange rules"; however, without analysis, the court subsequently determined that the eighth Wellman factor had been satisfied based on facts that included the issuance of a press release, sending a letter to the company shareholders, and filing documents with

excepting public announcements mandated by law from the meaning of the eighth factor is appropriate especially when the public announcement did not suggest that the company "wished to buy stock then in the hands of its stockholders."[94]

In addition to having a public announcement of a purchasing program, the eighth factor requires that this announcement be followed by a rapid accumulation of large amounts of stock. Neither the SEC nor the courts have adopted a definitive percentage threshold that would constitute "large amounts of the company's securities" for purposes of the Wellman test.[95] The court in *Crane*, when analyzing the second Wellman factor, took the position that accumulation of less than 5 percent of a company's outstanding shares was not "substantial" for purposes of the Wellman test. Since courts often interchange the second Wellman factor with the first and eighth Wellman factors, there is an argument that purchasing less than 5 percent of a company's stock would not constitute "a large amount of the company's securities" for purposes of the eighth Wellman factor.[96] On the other hand, in *Cattleman's Investment Company* v. *Fears*,[97] a case preceding *Wellman* and not applying the SEC's eight-factor test, the court held that the bidder's acquisition of approximately 7 percent of the target's outstanding shares over a two-month period as part of an attempt to gain control of the company constituted a tender offer.[98]

It seems entirely plausible that the court's reasoning in *Crane* was based on analogy to Section 14(d)(1) of the Securities Exchange Act and Rule 14d-3 adopted by the SEC thereunder, which exempt tender offers that result in the offeror beneficially owning less than 5 percent of the outstanding shares in a class from the purview of the US Tender Offer Rules. Similarly, Section 14(d)(8) of the Securities Exchange Act states that the terms of Section 14 of the Securities Exchange Act are inapplicable to offers by third-party bidders which, if consummated and aggregated with all other acquisitions of such stock by such bidder within the previous twelve months, do not exceed 2 percent of the class. Given that the exception in Section 14(d)(1) for tender offers of less than 5 percent of

the SEC). But see *S-G Securities*, at 1119–21 (finding there had been a tender offer where numerous press releases publicized the terms of the offer).

94 See *Crane*, at 303.

95 However, in SEC Release No. 16385, the SEC concluded that the fourth factor of the first tier of the SEC's proposed definition was "seeking acquisition of 5% or more of the class of securities."

96 See *Carter Hawley*, at 951–2.

97 See fn 47 above.

98 Ibid., at 1248.

the outstanding shares would seemingly make this provision unnecessary, Section 14(d)(8) may be an indication from the legislature that third-party acquisitions of less than 2 percent of a company's outstanding shares do not constitute tender offers.

On its face, the issuance of a press release by an issuer disclosing its intention to commence a debt repurchase program would likely be considered by a court to be a "public announcement of a purchasing program" for purposes of the Wellman test. However, given the case law holding that public announcements mandated by SEC or stock exchange rules do not constitute public announcements under the Wellman test, the issuer of the relevant securities or the offeror might be able to persuade a court that there was no "public announcement" for purposes of the Wellman test because the press release issued by the offeror was mandated pursuant to the applicable stock exchange rules to securities offered under Rule 144A under the Securities Act and listed on a US national securities exchange or a European securities market, and such announcement did not suggest the offeror would be purchasing securities then in the hands of its security holders. Even if its argument regarding public announcement failed, the issuer could still rely on *Crane* (and analogy to the exceptions in Section 14(d)(1) of the Securities Exchange Act and Rule 14d-3 thereunder), to the extent that it accumulates less than 5 percent of the outstanding principal amount of the relevant securities, and argue that its public announcement did not precede the rapid accumulation of large amounts of the issuer's securities.

3.9 Other considerations

In addition to the eight-factor Wellman test there are other factors that can be considered when attempting to determine whether a purchase of debt securities constitutes a tender offer. A review of the case law reveals no case where *Wellman* has been applied outside the corporate control context, for example in connection with purchases of debt securities. It is worth noting that although the case law addressing Williams Act violations has been limited to the corporate control context, the SEC itself has applied Section 14(d) of the Securities Exchange Act to circumstances not implicating corporate control, such as option repricing. Similarly, in a series of no-action letters during the mid-1980s and early 1990s, the SEC expressed its view that the obligation of a company to redeem preferred stock upon a shareholder's exercise of a *put right* attached to such preferred stock constitutes a tender offer within the meaning of the Securities

Exchange Act.[99] Moreover, it should be noted that a number of federal courts have applied Rule 14d-10 under the Securities Exchange Act broadly to cover employment and severance arrangements, and commercial arrangements with shareholders entered into substantially contemporaneously with tender offers. While this analysis has been rejected by many other federal courts, it does illustrate the willingness of at least some federal judges to stretch the US Tender Offer Rules when they perceive potential abuses.

An investigation of the case law reveals that there has been no reported case that has ever addressed the question of what constitutes a tender offer under circumstances remotely approximating a debt repurchase program. More interestingly, all the cases dealing with this issue have tended to focus on the concern for possible shifts in corporate control, a fact that is absent in debt repurchases. Determining the likelihood that a debt repurchase would be deemed to be a tender offer should such a case ever be commenced requires an analysis of the facts in light of the eight-factor Wellman test.

3.10 Final observations and link to Hanson test

The eight-factor Wellman test has generated general court approval. At the same time, the courts have cautioned against a formulaic application of the test or its elevation as the exclusive mandatory test. As the court observed in *Hanson*, many of the eight factors are relevant for purposes of determining whether a given solicitation of the purchase of securities amounts to a tender offer; the elevation of such a list to a mandatory "litmus test" appears to be both unwise and unnecessary. In any given case a solicitation may constitute a tender offer even though some of the eight factors are absent or, when many factors are present, the solicitation may nevertheless not amount to a tender offer because the missing factors outweigh those present.[100] The SEC has also observed that the eight factors are not entitled to equal weight and less than a majority of the factors need to be present to find a tender offer.[101] To our knowledge, no case weighs the factors in a way to facilitate the structuring of a transaction in a predictable fashion.

[99] See 1991 SEC No-Act. LEXIS 932; 1990 SEC No-Act. LEXIS 498; 1985 SEC No-Act. LEXIS 2155.

[100] See *Hanson*, at 824; *Carter Hawley*, at 950.

[101] See, e.g., Exchange Act Release 24976 (October 1, 1987).

Consequently, an alternative test based on the statutory purpose of the Williams Act, was proposed as the guiding principle in determining whether the Williams Act applies to private transactions for the purchase of securities. Since the purpose of Section 14(e) and (d) of the Securities Exchange Act is to protect the ill-informed solicitee in an offer to purchase securities, the question of whether a solicitation constitutes a "tender offer" within the meaning of the Securities Exchange Act must turn on whether the transaction is such that unless the protection of the US Tender Offer Rules apply there will be a substantial risk that solicitees will lack information needed to make a carefully considered appraisal of the proposal put before them.

4 The Hanson test

In *Hanson*, the Second Circuit emphasized the history of the Williams Act and the rationale for introducing tender offer regulation that applies to offers to purchase securities issued by public companies as well as securities issued by private companies. The court recognized that although the US Tender Offer Rules clearly apply to "classic" tender offers for publicly traded securities, in the case of privately negotiated transactions or solicitations for private purchases of securities many of the conditions leading to the enactment of the Williams Act for the most part do not exist. The number and percentage of security holders solicited are usually far fewer than those involved in public offers. The solicitation involves less publicity than a public tender offer, or none. The solicitees, who are frequently directors, officers, or substantial security holders of the issuer of the target securities, are more apt to be sophisticated, inquiring, or knowledgeable concerning the issuer's business, the offeror's objectives, and the impact of the solicitation on the issuer's business prospects. In short, the solicitee in the private transaction is less likely to be pressured, confused, or ill-informed regarding the businesses and decisions at stake than solicitees who are the subjects of a public tender offer.

The distinction between public solicitations and privately negotiated purchases of securities is fact-intensive and far from clear, and it is frequently difficult to determine whether transactions that have mixed elements of "public solicitation" and private trading are "tender offers" or private deals. The *Hanson* court accepted that the eight-factor Wellman test was useful in distinguishing tender offers subject to the US Tender Offer Rules from other types of transactions that were outside the federal regulatory framework. That said, the court in *Hanson* concluded that the elevation of such a list to a mandatory "litmus test" was unwise and unnecessary.[102] The court concluded that in any given case a solicitation may constitute a tender offer even though some of the eight factors are absent or, when many factors are present, the solicitation may nevertheless not amount to a tender offer because the missing factors outweigh those present.

On that basis, the *Hanson* court chose to be guided by the principle followed by the Supreme Court in deciding which transactions fall within the private offering exemption provided by Section 4(1) of the Securities Act, i.e., simply to look to the statutory purpose of the relevant legislation. In *SEC* v. *Ralston Purina Co.*,[103] the Supreme Court stated: "the applicability of Section 4(1) of the Securities Act should turn on whether the particular class of persons affected need the protection of the Securities Act. An offering to those who are shown to be able to fend for themselves is a transaction 'not involving any public offering'." Similarly, in the view of the *Hanson* court, since the purpose of the US Tender Offer Rules is to protect the ill-informed solicitee, the question of whether a solicitation constitutes a "tender offer" should turn on whether the transaction is such that, unless the procedural and substantive protections of the US Tender Offer Rules are followed, there will be a substantial risk that solicitees will lack information needed to make a carefully considered appraisal of the proposal put before them.

On application of this standard, the *Hanson* court was persuaded that the negotiation of five private purchases and one open market purchase of the relevant class of securities was not a "tender offer" within the meaning of the Williams Act for the following reasons: (i) out of a total 22,800 holders of the target securities, the number of holders solicited by the offeror (six in all) was miniscule compared with the numbers involved in public solicitations of the type against which the Williams Act was directed; (ii) at least five of the sellers of the target securities were highly sophisticated professionals, knowledgeable of the marketplace and well aware of the essential facts needed to exercise their professional skills and to appraise the offer, including the financial condition of the offeror as well as that of the issuer of the target securities, the likelihood that the purchases might block the competing bid, and the risk that if the offeror acquired more than 33.3 percent of the target securities certain

[102] See *Hanson*.

[103] See *SEC* v. *Ralston Purina Co.*, 346 U.S. 119, 73 S. Ct. 981, 97 L. Ed. 1494 (1953).

material commercial consequences would follow; (iii) the sellers were not "pressured" to sell their securities by any conduct that the Williams Act was designed to alleviate, but by the forces of the marketplace; (iv) there was no active or widespread advance publicity or public solicitation, which is one of the earmarks of a conventional tender offer; (v) the price received by the six sellers, $73.50 per share, unlike that appearing in most tender offers, can scarcely be dignified with the label "premium" because it was merely 1.4 percent higher than the benchmark market price; (vi) unlike most tender offers, the purchases were not made contingent upon the offeror acquiring a fixed minimum number or percentage of outstanding securities; and (vii) unlike most tender offers, there was no general time limit within which the offeror would make purchases of the relevant securities. In short, the totality of circumstances did not evidence any likelihood that there would be a substantial risk of ill-considered sales of the relevant securities by ill-informed security holders unless the offeror was required to comply with the US Tender Offer Rules.

Thus, it is apparent that the eight-factor Wellman test and the "totality of circumstances" Hanson test are similar since both consider the same factors. They differ because the totality of circumstances Hanson test ultimately determines the outcome of the analysis by reference to the purpose of the Williams Act and the response to one fundamental question: Is there a substantial likelihood that, unless the substantive and procedural protections of the Williams Act are afforded to holders of securities that are the subject of a solicitation to tender or sell such holders would be at a substantial risk of lacking the necessary information and consequently they would be likely to make ill-considered sales of the relevant securities? If the answer is, in light of the totality of the circumstances, yes, then a court is likely to determine that the relevant transaction is a tender offer within the meaning of the Williams Act and the US Tender Offer Rules.

5 Application of the tests in specific situations

Let us briefly examine the likely outcome of the analysis of the application of the two tests in different types of transactions for debt securities.

5.1 Open market purchases

Purchases of debt securities in the open market by the issuer (or an affiliate of the issuer) are not usually found to be "tender offers" within the meaning of the term under the provisions of the Williams Act. Courts and legal practitioners reach this conclusion under both the eight-factor test and the totality of circumstances test. A purchase of debt securities in the open market, directly by the purchaser or through a dealer, is probably not a solicitation of the relevant securities, certainly not an active and widespread solicitation, because there are no fixed terms, no premium involved, no conditionality on acquiring a certain amount of securities, no limited time period, no pressure to sell, and no publicity of the offer. For debt securities offered and sold in the institutional debt markets (to QIBs or other types of sophisticated investors), the sophistication of the likely sellers of those securities, especially for securities issued and traded in the high-yield market, precludes the finding that the holders of the relevant securities are likely to require the protections of the US Tender Offer Rules in making an informed selling decision.

5.2 *Privately negotiated purchases*

A typical privately negotiated purchase of debt securities is not a tender offer. When a potential purchaser of debt securities approaches one or more potential buyers of debt securities with a view to negotiating a purchase or series of related purchases, there is usually no active and widespread solicitation and no premium is offered; the terms are not fixed and firm, but negotiable; the purchases are not conditional on the acquisition of a set amount of securities; no time limit is imposed; no publicity surrounds the transaction; and the sellers are likely to be well informed and sophisticated.

As a result of both of the Wellman and Hanson tests, companies repurchase large amounts of equity and debt securities through open market and privately negotiated purchases conducted outside the scope of the Williams Act and the US Tender Offer Rules. Nonetheless, companies must be advised to keep both open market and privately negotiated purchases from falling into the trap of becoming subject to the US Tender Offer Rules. To achieve this objective, it is important to ensure that (i) each negotiation is independent of any other; (ii) each seller is sophisticated; (iii) no attempt is made to impose the same terms on all sellers or to set any fixed deadline for responding (a record of negotiation is helpful); and (iv) the offerees should not be coerced (e.g., telling the debt security holder that the security will subsequently become very illiquid).

It is fair to say that the determination is very fact-specific and does not lend itself easily to the safe application of bright-line tests. Ultimately, if a specific transaction structure undermines the overarching objectives of the Williams Act, as interpreted by federal and state courts and the rules and regulations of the SEC, then the offeror and its advisors should reconsider the structure. If the totality of circumstances and factors form a plausible framework for concluding that the transaction respects the regulatory aims of the Williams Act, then the US Tender Offer Rules may not be applicable. A series of privately negotiated purchases of securities held by sophisticated and suitably qualified investors, which securities had been distributed in a Rule 144A offering and remained in the hands of QIBs within the meaning of Rule 144A under the Securities Act, would not constitute a tender offer, in the absence of other factors, even if it resulted in the purchase of the entire amount of the relevant debt securities. Conversely, the acquisition of 25 percent of the principal amount of debt securities in a transaction or series of transactions offering a premium to the market price and creating pressure to sell through other means might be considered a tender offer within the meaning of the US Tender Offer Rules.

5.3 Other types of purchases

Redemption of debt securities in accordance with the terms of the relevant series is not a tender offer.[104] In connection with potential restructurings, a letter addressed to the holders of the debt securities to indicate whether they are interested in negotiating a debt restructuring is not a tender offer.[105] The settlement of litigation whereby investors were asked to choose, at their discretion, to maintain their investment in the relevant debt securities, convert the debt securities into equity, or maintain the investment but convert the debt securities at a later time was not a tender offer if the process was approved by the court. The US Tender Offer Rules do not apply to judicially approved settlement agreements where individual investors are more than adequately protected by procedures followed in settlement, and individual investors are given full notification of the terms of the offer, people, or groups involved, the purpose of offer, and the plans of the offeror.[106]

5.4 Differentiating between debt and equity tender offers

It should not escape our attention that the jurisprudence of the federal and state courts relating to the definition of a "tender offer" for purposes

[104] See *Howell* v. *Management Assistance, Inc.*, 519 F. Supp. 83, 86, 91 (S.D.N.Y. 1981).

[105] See *Rand* v. *Anaconda-Ericsson, Inc.*, 794 F.2d 843, 848 (2d Cir. 1986).

[106] See *Brucker* v. *Thyssen-Bornemisza Europe N.V.*, 424 F. Supp. 679 (D.C.N.Y. 1976).

of the regulatory framework established by the Williams Act has been formed over the years primarily, if not exclusively, in the context of disputes over the acquisition or exercise of corporate control through offers for the purchase of equity securities. Some of the factors applicable by the federal and state courts in the context of offers for equity securities are not particularly relevant or, at least, directly applicable to offers to purchase debt securities in the open market or otherwise (whether the purchases are made by the issuer or a third party). This distinction is not without practical consequences for those structuring liability management transactions. When considering various alternative structures for the offer to purchase debt securities, counsel or other transaction professionals are often tempted to apply by analogy arguments and concepts directly borrowed from offers to acquire equity securities. This approach may often lead to structures that are more conservative, for lack of a better word, than they should be. While the review of analogies to similar situations is always helpful and likely to inform sound transaction management, distinguishing the differences between equity and debt tender offers, and the differences between the underlying securities and the objectives of the relevant transactions, is a critical analytical tool. If the recharacterization of a bond repurchase program as a tender offer, in light of all the relevant factors, is not going to enhance investor protection in any discernible way, then it could be true that any analogy to a share buyback might have been misplaced.

3

Debt tender offers and Regulation 14E under the Securities Exchange Act

1 Introduction

Section 14(e) of the Securities Exchange Act empowered the SEC "in connection with any tender offer [...] by rules and regulations, [to] define, and prescribe means reasonably designed to prevent, such acts and practices as are fraudulent, deceptive, or manipulative." Pursuant to this rule-making power, and in connection with tender offers for all types of securities (equity securities, debt securities, and hybrid securities), the SEC adopted Regulation 14E under the Securities Exchange Act comprising several rules,[107] all reasonably designed to prevent fraudulent, deceptive, or manipulative acts or practices within the meaning of Section 14(e) of the Securities Exchange Act.[108] Section 14(e) was introduced as part of the Williams Act and its legislative purpose and motivation (i.e., the prevention of fraudulent or abusive practices in connection with tender offers) are extensively covered in Chapter 1.[109]

[107] The SEC has adopted the following rules under Section 14(e) of the Securities Exchange Act: (i) Rule 14e-1(a) (offer must remain open for twenty business days); (ii) Rule 14e-1(b) (offer must remain open for ten business days after certain changes in the terms of the offer); (iii) Rule 14e-1(c) (payment must be made promptly following the termination of the offer); (iv) Rule 14e-1(d) (extensions must be publicly announced); (v) Rule 14e-2 (position of the target company with respect to a tender offer); (vi) Rule 14e-3 (transactions in securities on the basis of material, non-public information in the context of tender offers); (vii) Rule 14e-4 (prohibited transactions in connection with partial tender offers); (viii) Rule 14e-5 (prohibiting purchases outside a tender offer); this rule applies only to tender offers for equity securities; (ix) Rule 14e-6 (repurchase offers by certain closed-end registered investment companies); (x) Rule 14e-7 (unlawful tender offer practices in connection with roll-ups); and (xi) Rule 14e-8 (prohibited conduct in connection with pre-commencement communications).

[108] See Rule 14e-1 under the Securities Exchange Act.

[109] Pursuant to the House Report, the proposed subsection (e) of Section 14 of the Securities Exchange Act was intended to affirm the fact that persons engaged in making or opposing tender offers or otherwise seeking to influence the decision of investors or the outcome of tender offer are under an obligation to make full disclosure of material information

The SEC rules comprising Regulation 14E were therefore adopted by the SEC pursuant to its regulatory authority under the Williams Act. In *US* v. *Chestman*,[110] the US Supreme Court clarified that in enacting Section 14(e) of the Securities Exchange Act, Congress had explicitly left a gap and therefore there was an express delegation of authority to the SEC to elucidate a specific provision of the statute by regulation. The views of the SEC when applying Regulation 14E (as well as the views of other regulatory agencies in relation to other similar regulations adopted by them) should be given controlling weight by the courts, unless they are "arbitrary, capricious, or manifestly contrary to the statute."[111] The Court clarified that when Congress delegates to an agency the power to promulgate rules and regulations, the subsequently adopted regulations encompass legislative effect. Therefore, a reviewing court was not free to circumvent those regulations, merely in view of a different interpretation of the statute. It was found that the plain language of Section 14(e) represented a broad delegation of rule-making authority. The statute explicitly directed the SEC to "define" fraudulent practices and to "prescribe means reasonably designed to prevent" such practices. Apart from the statute's language, the Court also examined the legislative history of Section 14(e) in order to bolster its interpretation, concluding that Congress intended to grant broad rule-making authority to the SEC. Notably, Senator Williams, the bill's sponsor, had asserted the "utmost necessity" of granting "full rulemaking powers" to the SEC in the area of tender offers in order to enable it to deal promptly and flexibly with problems in that area.

In summary, the SEC's views on the meaning and interpretation of Regulation 14E under the Securities Exchange Act are given considerable weight by the courts and, consequently, practicing lawyers structuring tender offers ought to be familiar with the SEC views (as expressed in interpretative guidance and SEC no-action letters)[112] on the rules comprising Regulation 14E.

to those with whom they deal. See H.R. Rep. No. 1711, 90th Cong., 2d Sess. 11 (1968); quoted in *U.S.* v. *Chestman*, 947 F.2d 551, 559.

110 Ibid. 111 Ibid.

112 See generally *Shearson Lehman Brothers, Inc.*, SEC No-Action Letter (December 2, 1986); *Merrill Lynch, Pierce, Fenner & Smith, Inc.*, SEC No-Action Letter (July 2, 1986); *Kidder, Peabody & Co., Inc.*, SEC No-Action Letter (May 5, 1986); *Salomon Brothers, Inc.*, SEC No-Action Letter (March 11, 1986); *Times Mirror Co.*, SEC No-Action Letter (November 15, 1994); *Goldman, Sachs & Co.*, SEC No-Action Letter (December 3, 1993); *Merrill Lynch, Pierce, Fenner & Smith, Inc.*, SEC No-Action Letter (July 19, 1993); *Salomon Brothers, Inc.*, SEC No-Action Letter (October 1, 1990); *Shearson Lehman Brothers, Inc.*, SEC No-Action Letter (December 3, 1986); *Kidder, Peabody & Co., Inc.*, SEC No-Action Letter (May 5,

2 Rule 14e-1 (unlawful tender offer practices)

Rule 14e-1 under the Securities Exchange Act, appearing first in the sequence of rules comprising Regulation 14E under the heading "Unlawful Tender Offer Practices," introduces four separate rules that are reasonably designed to prevent fraudulent, deceptive, or manipulative acts or practices within the meaning of Section 14(e) of the Securities Exchange Act and are applicable to any person who makes a tender offer (whether or not the tender offer is for equity, debt, or other securities):

- the "Length of the Offering Period" Rule or the "20 Business Days" Rule (Rule 14e-1(a));
- the "Extension of the Offering Period" Rule (Rule 14e-1(b));
- the "Prompt Payment" Rule (Rule 14e-1(c)); and
- the "Notice of Extensions" Rule (Rule 14e-1(d)).

Unless the context otherwise requires, all terms used in Regulation 14E have the same meaning as in the Securities Exchange Act and Rule 12b-2[113] under the Securities Exchange Act and, in addition, the definitions set forth in Rule 14d-1(g) under the Securities Exchange Act.

2.1 The "20 Business Days" Rule (Rule 14e-1(a))

Rule 14e-1(a) requires that a person making a tender offer (*tender offeror*) must hold such tender offer open for at least twenty business days[114] from the date such tender offer is first published or sent or given to *security holders*.[115]

1986); *First Boston Corp.*, SEC No-Action Letter (April 17, 1986); *Goldman, Sachs & Co.*, SEC No-Action Letter (March 26, 1986).

113 See Rule 12b-2 under the Securities Exchange Act for the following definitions, among others, that are commonly used in legal and regulatory analyses of the Williams Act and the federal US Tender Offer Rules: "affiliate," "amount," "common equity," "control," "fiscal year," "material," "registration statement," "registrant," "significant subsidiary," "subsidiary," "voting security," and "wholly-owned subsidiary."

114 The term "business days" means any days, other than Saturday, Sunday, or federal holidays in the United States, and consists of the time period from 12:01 a.m. through 12:00 midnight Eastern time. See Rule 14d-1(g)(3) under the Securities Exchange Act. As of the day of printing this book, the following days are federal holidays in the United States: New Year's Day, Birthday of Martin Luther King, Jr., Washington's Birthday, Memorial Day, Independence Day, Labor Day, Columbus Day, Veterans Day, Thanksgiving Day, and Christmas Day.

115 The term "security holders" means holders of record and beneficial owners of securities that are the subject of the relevant tender offer. See Rule 14d-1(g)(5) under the Securities Exchange Act. The term *beneficial owner* has the same meaning as that set forth in

In computing any time period under Regulation 14E, the date of the event which begins the running of such time period shall be included *except* that if such event occurs on a day other than a business day such period begins to run on and includes the first business day thereafter.[116] As a result, the day of the first publication of the tender offer documentation or the day such documentation is sent or given to security holders constitutes "Day One" of the tender offer period. The tender offeror must keep the depositary open during customary business hours on every business day of the tender offer period with the exception of the twentieth day, on which the depositary must be open until midnight unless the offer is held open for more than the minimum twenty business days, in which case the tender offeror must disclose this fact in the tender offer memorandum.[117] Consequently, an offer complying with the requirements of Rule 14e-1(a) cannot end before 12:00 midnight on the twentieth business day (including the day the tender offer documentation is first published or sent or given to security holders).[118]

Section 14(e) of the Securities Exchange Act and Regulation 14E do not state how the tender offer documentation should be "published or sent to security holders." It is the SEC staff's view that the tender offeror must make reasonable efforts to disseminate material information about the tender offer to security holders and that Rule 14d-4 can provide guidance in this area.

The dissemination methods set forth in Rule 14d-4 are:

- publishing the offering document in a newspaper;
- publishing a summary advertisement containing certain information in a newspaper and mailing to security holders a copy of the full offering document; or

Rule 13d-3 under the Securities Exchange Act. More specifically, a beneficial owner of a security is any person who, directly or indirectly, through any contract, arrangement, understanding, relationship, or otherwise has or shares: (i) voting power which includes the power to vote, or to direct the voting of, such security; and/or (ii) investment power, which includes the power to dispose, or to direct the disposition of, such security.

116 See Rule 14d-1(g)(3) under the Securities Exchange Act.

117 See Exchange Act Release No. 34–16623, March 5, 1980.

118 If time is of the essence and the issuer cannot afford to have the tender offer open for a period longer than the minimum statutory period of twenty business days, the tender offer documentation will normally specify that the offer will end at 11:59 p.m. on the twentieth business day from the commencement of the offer, which means that any tender received prior to midnight should be accepted. When the time of expiration of the offer period is not critical, it is often the case that the offer remains open until 17:00 p.m. (close of business), Eastern time, of the twenty-first day of the offer period.

• mailing the offering document to security holders using a security holder list.

Market conditions, however, often make it impractical to leave debt tender offers open for as long as twenty business days (or more in the event of federal holidays falling within the relevant tender offer period). The reason this requirement is problematic is that most debt tender offers are initiated by the tender offerors when interest rates are low (i.e., the issuer is retiring higher interest rate debt using proceeds from the issuance of lower interest rate debt). If interest rates decline during the twenty-day time period, then the issuer will not retire as much debt as it was planning to do; if interest rates increase, the new issuance will become more expensive and the entire liability management transaction may become uneconomical. Longer offer periods create uncertainty for the commercial success and viability of debt tender offers.

Paying attention to the legitimate concerns of issuers and their advisors, the SEC explicitly carved out an exception to the minimum tender offer period in no-action letters related to tender offers, for cash,[119] for investment-grade,[120] non-convertible debt securities, provided that the offer: (i) is made by the issuer for any and all securities of a particular class or series of non-convertible debt securities; (ii) is open to all record and beneficial holders of that class or series of debt securities; (iii) conforms to dissemination procedures designed to give all security holders a reasonable opportunity to participate in the tender offer; this includes dissemination of the offer on an expedited basis in situations where the tender offer is open for a period of less than ten calendar days; and (iv) is not made in response to or in anticipation of another tender offer for the issuer's securities.[121]

In many of the no-action letters in this area, the SEC has expressed the fundamental policy view that debt tender offers for cash, for any and all non-convertible debt securities of a particular class or series, pose far fewer regulatory concerns than the equity tender offers that prompted the

[119] The *Salomon Brothers, Inc.*, SEC No-Action Letter, fn 112 above, limits the availability of the shortened offer period to tender offers for cash. Consequently, exchange offers for investment-grade debt securities must still remain open for at least twenty business days.

[120] The SEC no-action letters that established these basic conditions did not initially clarify whether the debt should be rated investment grade or not. This additional requirement was clarified in 1990 in the *Salomon Brothers, Inc.*, SEC No-Action Letter, fn 112 above. An investment-grade rating from one rating agency should be sufficient in the event of split ratings.

[121] See fn 112 above.

enactment of the Williams Act.[122] Tender offers for debt securities meeting these requirements are typically held open for only ten calendar days and may be held open for as few as seven calendar days if the company uses expedited methods to deliver the tender offer materials to its holders. Such expedited methods generally include commencing the tender offer with a news release and a tombstone advertisement, delivering a letter to each registered holder on the day the tender offer is commenced, and contacting brokerage houses and depository institutions shortly after commencing the offer in order to expedite their dissemination concerning the offer.[123] Furthermore, these tender offers are also not subject to the provisions of Rule 14e-1 relating to the extension of the tender offer period. That said, experienced counsel often advise tender offerors to extend the tender offer if material changes to the terms of the tender offer occur so that security holders are given the opportunity to respond. This approach reflects a general caution against the risk of liability for fraudulent or manipulative practices under Section 14(e) of the Securities Exchange Act.

2.2 The Extension of the Offering Period Rule (Rule 14e-1(b))

Rule 14e-1(b) requires that the tender offeror must not increase or decrease (i) the percentage of the class of securities being sought, (ii) the consideration offered, or (iii) the dealer's soliciting fee to be given in a tender offer unless such tender offer remains open for at least ten business days from the date that notice of such increase or decrease is first published or sent or given to security holders; provided, however, that the acceptance of payment of an additional amount of securities not to exceed 2 percent of the class of securities that is the subject of the tender offer shall not be deemed to be an increase and, for the purposes of this provision, the percentage of a class of securities shall be calculated in accordance with Section 14(d)(3) of the Securities Exchange Act.

In addition, Rule 14d-4(d)(2) under the Securities Exchange Act requires, among other things, an extension of (i) five business days for material changes other than the price or number of shares sought; and (ii) ten business days for changes that are similar in significance to changes

[122] See, e.g., *Merrill Lynch, Pierce, Fenner & Smith, Inc.*, SEC No-Action Letter (July 2, 1986): "For example, because of the modest premiums typically offered in an issuer debt tender offer, it is not clear that participation in the tender offer by individual non-institutional debt holders would be materially increased by requiring that tender offer be held open for at least twenty business days."

[123] See *Shearson Lehman Brothers, Inc.*, SEC No-Action Letter (December 2, 1986).

in the price or percentage of securities being sought. It is the SEC staff's view that these time periods represent general guidelines that should be applied uniformly to all tender offers, including those that are subject only to Regulation 14E such as tender offers for debt securities.[124] The length of the required time extension is directly analogous to the materiality of the change and its likely impact on a holder's investment decision. The SEC staff applies a general rule of five business days for any material change in the terms of the tender offer (including waivers of conditions) that are not expressly subject to the longer extensions of ten or twenty business days. If the change relates to a term of the offer that is similar in significance to those changes requiring an extension of ten business days, practitioners generally tend to extend the offer for ten business days.[125]

The ten-day period runs concurrently with the twenty-day period.[126] Thus, if the relevant material change in the terms of the tender offer occurs and is announced on the ninth day of the tender offer period, the ten-day period will expire before the twenty-day period and, consequently, there will be no need to extend the twenty-day period. If a tender offeror makes a material change to the tender offer, the tender offeror must disseminate the changes in a manner reasonably likely to inform security holders of the change. The tender offeror generally should consider disseminating the change in the same manner as it disseminated the original offer.

2.3 Pricing mechanisms and the Extension of the Offering Period Rule

The cash consideration that the tender offeror promises to pay for the purchase of a certain principal amount of tender securities could be a fixed amount. For example, the tender offeror may offer to pay $450 for each

[124] See SEC Release No. 33–7760 (October 19, 1999): "As a result, exchange offers that commence early must remain open for at least: (i) five business days for a prospectus supplement containing a material change other than price or share levels; (ii) ten business days for a prospectus supplement containing a change in price, the number of shares sought, the dealer's soliciting fee, or other similarly significant change; (iii) ten business days for a prospectus supplement included as part of a post-effective amendment; and (iv) 20 business days for a revised prospectus when the initial prospectus was materially deficient; for example, failing to comply with the going-private rules or filing a "shell" document solely to trigger commencement and staff review. Of course, if a material change in the information previously disseminated to security holders occurred shortly before the expiration of the offer, a prospectus supplement would need to be disseminated to security holders and the offer extended for the appropriate length of time. *We also believe that these time periods represent general guidelines that should be applied uniformly to all tender offers, including those subject only to Regulation 14E.*" (Emphasis added.)

[125] Ibid. [126] See SEC Exchange Act Release 34–16384 (November 29, 1979).

$1,000 of principal amount of tender securities tendered and delivered for purchase.

More-sophisticated pricing mechanisms than fixed cash consideration have been developed and raise a number of legal issues under the applicable US Tender Offer Rules.

2.3.1 Dutch auctions

Debt tender offers are not subject to the "equal treatment" requirements of Rule 14d-10 under the Securities Exchange Act, which requires that tender offers for equity securities give each security holder the highest price paid to any other security holder. As a result, debt tender offers may be conducted as a Dutch auction. In a Dutch auction, instead of the tender offeror binding itself to a price, the holder of the tender securities submits the bid at a specified price, which the tender offeror is free to accept or reject. The offeror would accept securities for purchase, beginning with those for which the lowest price has been offered by the tendering holders and moving to higher prices until it has reached the desired number or principal amount of securities sought in the tender offer.

Pure Dutch auctions therefore can result in substantial savings for issuers because they enable them to avoid paying any single security holder more than the minimum price for which that particular security holder is willing to sell its securities. Variations of a less than pure Dutch auction, including modified Dutch auctions, are also permissible. In a modified Dutch auction, instead of the tender offeror binding itself to a price, the holder of the tender securities submits the bid at a specified price, which the tender offeror is free to accept or reject, but the tender offeror sets a minimum and maximum tender offer price at which the tender offeror is willing to purchase the tender securities tendered.

Under present SEC staff interpretations, modified Dutch auction tender offers are permitted subject to several conditions: (i) disclosure in the tender offer materials of the minimum and maximum consideration to be paid; (ii) pro rata acceptance throughout the offer with all securities purchased participating equally in prorationing; (iii) withdrawal rights throughout the offer; (iv) prompt announcement of the purchase price, if determined prior to the expiration of the offer; and (v) the purchase of all accepted securities at the highest price paid to any security holder under the offer. It is clear that conditions (ii), (iii), and (v), relating to proration, withdrawal rights, and "best price," apply only to equity tender offers.[127] Consequently, it follows that debt tender offers can be conducted as modified Dutch auctions on the condition that the tender offer materials set the minimum and maximum consideration to be paid and the purchase price is promptly announced after the expiration of the tender offer period. The offer may specify an overall monetary cap that it is prepared to pay, but may not set a range of the number or principal amount of securities to be purchased.[128]

2.3.2 Fixed-spread pricing

Rule 14e-1(b) requires that the tender offeror must not increase or decrease (i) the percentage of the class of securities being sought, (ii) the consideration offered, or (iii) the dealer's soliciting fee to be given in a tender offer unless such tender offer remains open for at least ten business days from the date that notice of such increase or decrease is first published or sent or given to security holders. In effect, Rule 14e-1(b) requires a ten-day notice period between changing the tender offer consideration and closing the tender offer.

This is very undesirable for debt tender offers, because the price of the security changes as interest rates change. As a result, issuers prefer to express the price as a formula based on a specified, US *Benchmark Treasury Security* (i.e., the dollar price changes as Treasury rates change).[129] Fixed-spread pricing allows a tender offeror to choose a specific yield spread between the debt being tendered for and a benchmark US Treasury security which matures at or near the earliest redemption date for such debt security. The purchase price is the present value of the tender security, discounted at an interest rate equal to the applicable spread (i.e., equal to the sum of the present value as of the payment date of all interest payments on the debt from the payment date until maturity or the earliest call date, any accrued interest and additional amounts, and any principal payments to and redemption premium at the earliest call date or maturity). While the actual price to be paid in the tender offer fluctuates during the tender offer (hence the potential violation of Rule 14e-1(b)), the formula for determining what the price will be is fixed. The SEC has provided no-action relief for debt tender offers for

[127] See SEC Release, *Amendments to Tender Offer Rules All-Holders and Best-Price* (July 11, 1986), fn 64.

[128] See *Alliance Semiconductor Corp.*, SEC No-Action Letter (September 22, 2006).

[129] See *Goldman, Sachs & Co.*, SEC No-Action Letter (March 26, 1986) (no-action position with respect to dealer-manager and issuer's noncompliance with Rules 14e-1(a) and (b) under the Securities Exchange Act).

investment-grade debt securities to be priced based on a *fixed spread* to a Treasury security rather than a fixed price.[130]

2.3.2.1 *Salomon Brothers* No-Action Letter (1990) The SEC initially granted a no-action letter in response to a request by Salomon Brothers, Inc.,[131] as dealer manager, to conduct tender offers for debt securities of issuers using a fixed-spread pricing methodology in conformity with the requirements of Rule 14e-1 under the Securities Exchange Act. Stating that issuer tender offers involving debt securities may "present considerations that differ from any and all or partial issuer tender offers for a class or series of equity securities or non-investment grade debt," the SEC granted Salomon Brothers's request to conduct issuer tender offers for debt securities at a price determined on each day during the tender offer period by reference to a stated fixed spread over the then current yield on a Benchmark Treasury Security, such *yield to be determined as of the date, or date preceding the date, of tender, subject to certain conditions.* Those conditions include that the issuer tender offer: (i) is an offer to purchase any and all debt securities of a particular class or series of the issuer for cash; (ii) is open to all record and beneficial holders of the debt securities; (iii) provides that information regarding the Benchmark Treasury Security is reported each day in a daily newspaper of national circulation; (iv) is conducted in a manner designed to afford all record and beneficial holders of the debt securities a reasonable opportunity to participate in the tender offer and, in the case of an offer for less than twenty days conducted in reliance on the earlier no-action letters, dissemination of the issuer tender offer is made on an expedited basis; (v) promptly pays all tendering holders of the debt securities after such securities are accepted for payment; and (vi) is not to be made in anticipation of or in response to other tender offers for the issuer's securities.

2.3.2.2 *Embassy Suites* No-Action Letter (1992) The SEC granted a similar no-action letter in response to a request by Embassy Suites, Inc.,[132] in

[130] See generally *Goldman, Sachs & Co.*, SEC No-Action Letter (December 3, 1993). "Enforcement action under Rule 14e-1 (a), (b), or (c) would not be recommended if a broker-dealer, acting as dealer-manager and an issuer conduct an issuer tender offer for non-convertible, *investment grade* debt securities at a price determined by a stated fixed-spread over the current yield on a specified Benchmark Treasury Security at the same time that the holder of the debt security tenders the security, subject to specified conditions."

[131] See *Salomon Brothers, Inc.*, SEC No-Action Letter (October 1, 1990) (hereinafter, the "*Salomon Brothers* Letter").

[132] See *Embassy Suites, Inc.*, SEC No-Action Letter (April 15, 1992) (hereinafter, the "*Embassy Suites* Letter").

which the staff stated it would not recommend that the SEC take enforcement action pursuant to Rule 14e–1(b) if Embassy Suites conducted a fixed-spread tender offer. The nominal purchase price in the offer was calculated with respect to the yield on a Benchmark Treasury Security as of the date preceding the date of tender, similar to the *Salomon Brothers* Letter, but not as of the date of tender as permitted in the *Salomon Brothers* Letter. The determination was based on the following conditions: (i) the subject security was investment-grade debt; it was not convertible into and did not otherwise have equity attributes; (ii) the offer would be for all cash for any and all of the outstanding notes; (iii) the offer would be made to all beneficial holders and all record-holders of the notes; (iv) the offer would be held open for at least twenty business days from the date the offer was first published or sent or given to noteholders; (v) because the nominal purchase price in the offer would be calculated with respect to the yield on the Benchmark Treasury Security determined as of the date preceding the date of tender, holders of the notes would have the entire business day to evaluate the nominal purchase price for that day; (vi) acceptance for payment would occur on a daily basis; (vii) all tendering noteholders would be paid promptly for their tendered notes after such securities are accepted for payment; (viii) the offer would not be made in anticipation of or in response to other tender offers for any other securities; (ix) since the pre-offer agreements between the issuer and the tender offeror eliminated any risk that the tender offeror could use the notes acquired in the offer to attempt to influence the issuer, there were no control implications to the offer; (x) the tender offeror had the same economic interests in the pricing and completion of the offer and the retirement of the notes as an issuer of debt securities would have in an issuer debt tender offer; (xi) it would be a condition of the offer that information regarding the Benchmark Treasury Security would be reported each day in a specified daily newspaper of national circulation; and (xii) in connection with the offer, the tender offer material would be distributed to noteholders on an expedited basis and would contain, in the manner stated in the letter, all pertinent information.

2.3.2.3 *Merrill Lynch, Pierce, Fenner & Smith Incorporated* (SEC No-Action Letter, July 19, 1993, hereinafter, the "Merrill Lynch Letter")
Merrill Lynch proposed to use a fixed-spread pricing methodology in connection with issuer tender offers that would be conducted in general conformity with the *Salomon Brothers* and the *Embassy Suites* Letters. However, the nominal purchase price in the offer would be calculated

by reference to a stated fixed spread over the most current yield on a Benchmark Treasury Security determined at the time that the holder of the debt security tenders the security (that is, in "real time") rather than by reference to the yield on a Benchmark Treasury Security as of the date, or the date preceding the date, of tender. The offer would be conducted in compliance with all relevant procedural requirements of the *Salomon Brothers* and *Embassy Suites* Letters, except as provided in the above sentence, and would be conducted in compliance with certain additional procedures described below.

An offer made under the Merrill Lynch proposal would include the following terms: (i) each offer would be an offer to purchase any and all securities of the class or series of the issuer's debt securities for cash; (ii) each offer would be open to all record and beneficial holders of the debt securities; (iii) each offer would indicate (a) in which daily newspaper of national circulation information regarding the closing yield of the Benchmark Treasury Security may be found each day, (b) which reference source Merrill Lynch intended to use as the definitive reference source for current yield information on the Benchmark Treasury Security, and (c) that the current yield on the Benchmark Treasury Security and the resulting nominal purchase price of the debt securities would be accessible on a real-time basis by either calling Merrill Lynch collect or through an 800 (toll-free) telephone number established by Merrill Lynch for each offer; (iv) each offer would be conducted in a manner designed to afford all record and beneficial holders of the debt securities a reasonable opportunity to participate in the issuer debt tender offer, and in the case of an offer conducted in reliance on the earlier 1986 no-action letters, dissemination of the offer would be made in accordance with those letters; (v) all tendering holders would be paid promptly for their tendered debt securities after such debt securities are accepted for payment; and (vi) no offer would be made in anticipation of or in response to other tender offers for any other securities of the issuer.

In addition, the tender offer material distributed to holders of the debt securities in connection with an offer shall: (i) identify the specific Benchmark Treasury Security; (ii) designate the fixed spread to be added to the yield on the Benchmark Treasury Security; (iii) identify the reference source to be used to establish the yield on the Benchmark Treasury Security; (iv) describe the methodology to be used to calculate the nominal purchase price to be paid with respect to the debt securities; (v) state the nominal purchase price that would have been payable under the offer based on the applicable reference yield prevailing immediately preceding the commencement of the offer; (vi) disclose that the issuer understands that current yield information for the debt securities and the Benchmark Treasury Security is available through other reference sources, disclosing such sources; and (vii) state that holders may contact the dealer manager collect or through an 800 (toll-free) telephone number for current information regarding the yield on the Benchmark Treasury Security and the resulting nominal purchase price.

Consequently, the applicable fixed spread and the manner in which the nominal purchase price shall be determined are known by the holders of the debt securities upon commencement of the offer, and any change in such spread or method of calculating the nominal purchase price is to be treated as a change in the consideration offered for purposes of Rule 14e–1(b). Current yields on US Treasury securities are widely published on a daily basis, including, for example, in *The Wall Street Journal*, *The New York Times*, and other electronic and printed resources. As noted above, the dealer manager shall also establish an 800 (toll-free) telephone number and a collect telephone number whereby holders of the debt securities are able to access on a real-time basis information regarding the current yield on the Benchmark Treasury Security and the resulting nominal purchase price.

The no-action letter noted that the use of real-time fixed-spread pricing has distinct advantages, both for the holders of the debt securities and for the issuer, over both fixed nominal purchase price offerings and mixed pricing, whereby the nominal purchase price is adjusted at arbitrary intervals through the application of fixed spreads. Without this technique, normal tender offer pricing methods freeze nominal purchase prices for arbitrary periods of time, however volatile market conditions actually are, and expose the offeror and holder of the debt securities to market risks. Fixed-income securities are not traded on the basis of a fixed price, but rather are traded on the basis of yield. If a dollar price is quoted for a fixed-income security, that price is converted by participants in the fixed-income markets into a yield, and is compared to a benchmark yield (generally the current yield on a US Treasury security of comparable maturity), in order to evaluate the effective cost of the security. The use of real-time fixed-spread pricing, therefore, permits an issuer to conduct a tender offer for its debt securities, and permits the holders of debt securities to evaluate the terms of an offer, in a manner that is consistent with the prevailing market practice for tendering certain debt securities and the purchase of debt securities. Real-time fixed-spread pricing produces a potential benefit to fixed-income investors who, in connection with a tender offer, generally elect to purchase a new debt security in connection with their decision to tender the debt security that is the subject of the tender offer. The decision on whether or not to sell into a tender offer is made in connection with a decision to buy another security, and the *buy-side* and *sell-side* are viewed as part of a single transaction.

2.3.2.4 *Goldman Sachs* (1993) Goldman Sachs[133] proposed to act as dealer manager in a tender offer where: (i) the price for the tender securities tendered at any time during ordinary trading hours on any business day during the tender period would be calculated, in accordance with the standard market convention for pricing fixed-income securities, as the present value of future payments on the tender securities (excluding accrued interest to the date of settlement) discounted at an interest rate equal to a stated fixed spread over the yield on a Benchmark Treasury Security as reported at the time of the tender by an electronic quotation service, plus accrued interest on the tender securities to the date of settlement; (ii) tender securities would be tendered in the conventional manner in which securities are bought and sold in the open market (i.e., orally in a telephone call between the dealer (as representative of the issuer) and the broker, dealer, commercial bank, trust company, or similar institution beneficially owning, or representing the beneficial owner of, the tender securities); (iii) tender securities tendered during the tender offer period would be deemed to be irrevocably accepted by the issuer upon valid tender; (iv) if the issuer determines not to make a simultaneous settlement procedure available to holders of target securities, then validly tendered tender securities would be paid for within a period of days after the date of tender not longer than the standard settlement time frame for ordinary securities trades; and (v) if the issuer determines to make a simultaneous settlement procedure available to holders of tender securities, then (a) tender securities validly tendered by a holder electing to receive payment on the single simultaneous settlement date specified in the offer (the "Simultaneous Settlement Date"), and tender securities validly tendered a number of days prior to such Simultaneous Settlement Date that falls within the standard settlement time frame, would be paid for on such Simultaneous Settlement Date; and (b) all other validly tendered tender securities (i.e., tender securities tendered a number of days prior to such Simultaneous Settlement Date that falls outside the standard settlement time frame by a holder not electing to receive payment on such Simultaneous Settlement Date) would be paid for within the standard settlement time frame.

[133] See *Goldman, Sachs & Co.*, SEC No-Action Letter (December 3, 1993).

The type of offer described above using the Simultaneous Settlement Procedure differs from the fixed-spread tender offers described in the *Salomon Brothers* and *Merrill Lynch* Letters in two respects. First, under a continuously priced fixed-spread tender offer described above, the yield of the Benchmark Treasury Security is determined not daily but on a continuous basis; as a result, the price to be paid for tender securities by the issuer is not artificially "frozen" over the course of an entire day but instead varies throughout each day depending on the yield of the Benchmark Treasury Security at the specific time at which the tender securities are tendered. Second, although tender securities will be irrevocably accepted for payment on a continuous basis throughout the tender offer period, the issuer will pay for validly tendered tender securities on a single Simultaneous Settlement Date promptly after the termination of the tender offer if the holders of such tender securities elect to receive payment on such Simultaneous Settlement Date or such Simultaneous Settlement Date is a number of days after the date of tender that falls within the standard settlement time frame. Since the cash paid in the tender offer will include accrued interest on the tender securities to the date of settlement (in accordance with market practice for the settlement of trades in fixed-income securities), holders tendering early in the tender offer period will normally benefit from delayed settlement.

The no-action relief was granted under the condition that each tender offer would: (i) be an offer to purchase for cash any and all of the tender securities; (ii) be conducted in a manner designed to afford all record and beneficial holders of the tender securities a reasonable opportunity to participate in the offer; (iii) identify the specific Benchmark Treasury Security to be used in calculating the price; (iv) specify the fixed spread to be added to the quoted yield on such Benchmark Treasury Security in calculating the price; (v) identify a daily newspaper of national circulation that is expected to report daily yield data regarding such Benchmark Treasury Security; (vi) identify the specific quotation service to be used as the definitive reference source for current-yield data regarding such Benchmark Treasury Security in calculating the price; (vii) provide a mechanism for holders of tender securities to obtain quotes of the current yield on the Benchmark Treasury Security and the resulting nominal purchase price of the tender securities on a continuous basis by calling a specified telephone number (collect or toll-free); (viii) disclose the assumptions and methodologies to be used in calculating the price to be paid with respect to tender securities tendered at a particular time; (ix) be conducted in a manner designed to afford all record and beneficial holders of tender securities a reasonable opportunity to participate in the manner described herein; (x) in the case of an offer that would remain open for fewer than twenty business days, be disseminated on an expedited basis; (xi) disclose the price that would have been payable under the offer based on the yield of such Benchmark Treasury Security as reported by the relevant quotation service at a specified time as close to commencement of the offer as practicable; and (xii) in the case of an offer using the simultaneous settlement procedure, specify the Simultaneous Settlement Date (which date will occur promptly after termination of the offer and in no event longer than the standard settlement time frame).

Furthermore, in connection with each offer, the relevant dealer would be obligated to: (i) make and maintain records showing (a) the date and time of each tender thereunder, (b) the current yield on the Benchmark Treasury Security at the time of such tender, (c) the purchase price of tendered tender securities based on that yield, and (d) in the case of an offer using the simultaneous settlement procedure, whether or not a holder tendering tender securities elected to receive payment on the Simultaneous Settlement Date specified in the offer rather than within the standard settlement time frame; and (ii) send a confirmation to each holder tendering tender securities, not later than one business day after the date of tender, specifying the date and, if requested, the time of tender, the price to be paid for such tender securities, and the settlement date. Also, the dealer should insure that, during any tender offer, neither the dealer nor the tender offeror, nor any affiliated purchasers thereof, would engage in any transactions in the tender securities or Benchmark Treasury Security for the purpose of creating actual, or apparent, active trading in, or raising or depressing the price of, the tender securities or Benchmark Treasury Security, and no tender offer would be made in anticipation of or in response to other tender offers for the issuer's securities.

In a tender offer conducted as contemplated by the *Salomon Brothers* Letter, the relative value may vary over the course of the day since the price is artificially frozen on a daily basis. In contrast, in a continuously priced fixed-spread tender offer, the yield over the yield of the specified Benchmark Treasury Security, and therefore the relative value, remains constant throughout the tender period. Continuous fixed-spread pricing has distinct advantages, both for issuers and holders, over the daily fixed-spread pricing mechanism contemplated by earlier no-action letters. Interest rates can fluctuate significantly during the course of a day; continuous fixed-spread pricing further reduces the interest rate risk to which daily fixed-spread pricing subjects the issuer and the holders.

2.3.2.5 18-day and 20-day fixed-spread pricing Unlike "real-time" fixed-spread pricing, where the price paid to each tendering holder varies depending on the yield of the Benchmark Treasury Security at the time of tender, an alternative structure has also been allowed, in which the fixed spread is announced at the commencement of the tender offer and remains unchanged during the offer period but the nominal price is fixed by the tender offeror only on the eighteenth day of the offer.[134]

In granting the requested no-action relief, the SEC staff set the following conditions:

- the relevant securities should be represented as being valued by investors on the basis of their yield, taking into account the issuer's credit spread, compared to a benchmark yield, and the yield of the securities should fluctuate in response to changes in prevailing interest rates;
- the offer to purchase should identify the electronic quotation service to be used as the definitive reference source for yield data regarding the Benchmark Treasury Security in calculating the nominal purchase price and where yield data regarding such US Treasury security will be available during the tender offer;
- the fixed-spread pricing formula for determining the offer price should be disclosed in the tender offer materials disseminated to security holders; the formula will remain fixed throughout the duration of the tender offer unless the offer is revised to provide a fixed price or there is a change in the formula, in which case the offer period will be extended; and the formula will be based on a specific Benchmark Treasury Security to be used in calculating the nominal purchase price and specify the fixed spread to be added to the yield on such Benchmark Treasury Security;
- the formula to be used to determine the nominal purchase price per subject security, as well as a hypothetical nominal purchase price based on the applicable reference yield immediately preceding the commencement of the tender offer, should also be disclosed in such offer to purchase. The offer to purchase will include as annexes a detailed schedule setting forth the formula for determining the nominal purchase that will be paid for the securities, as well as a schedule illustrating how the hypothetical nominal purchase price has been calculated;
- the offeror should provide a toll-free telephone number that will enable security holders to determine a hypothetical nominal purchase price as

[134] See *BBVA Privanza International*, SEC No-Action Letter (December 23, 2005).

of the date of a holder's inquiry as well as to answer questions holders of the securities may have regarding the tender offer;

- the final offer price should be set at least two trading days prior to the scheduled expiration of the offer; and
- the offeror should issue a press release to publicly announce the final offer price prior to the close of business on the pricing date.

More recent no-action letters, keeping with the spirit of the provisions discussed above, allowed "20-day" pricing in exchange and tender offers where the final exchange ratio or nominal tender price is determined on the basis of an averaging period ended on the expiration date of the offer. The same procedural and substantive requirements discussed above are also essential features of this structure.[135]

2.3.2.6 High-yield debt securities Using fixed spreads over Benchmark Treasury Securities as the pricing mechanism for *high-yield* (non-investment-grade) tender offers has evolved into standard industry practice. Although the SEC has not yet, to our knowledge, issued a release or no-action letter explicitly permitting this evolution (which it had hitherto expressly forbidden), the SEC has apparently given telephonic comfort to high-yield debt issuers that it would not pursue enforcement actions pursuant to such transactions.

After it initially became known that the SEC gave telephonic comfort, high-yield debt issuers would seek such assurances as a matter of course. The practice has since developed further, where high-yield debt issuers now proceed in launching debt tender offers outside the confines of Rules 14e-1(a) and (b), *without* consulting the SEC. The SEC staff has required offerors wishing to use the pricing formula for high-yield debt securities to submit a letter to the SEC outlining the terms of the proposed tender offer and stating, among other things, that the debt is held predominantly by institutional investors, trading volume is reasonably active, the market for the debt is relatively liquid in comparison to debt issues of comparable rating, size and age, and one or more institutions currently make a market in the debt.[136] In addition, the reference security benchmark has in practice been fixed-spread over other government securities. In general, in granting informal telephonic relief, the SEC staff

[135] See generally *Thermo Fisher Scientific, Inc.*, SEC No-Action Letter (November 13, 2009) (hereinafter, the "*Thermo Fisher* Letter"); *Kraft Foods, Inc.*, SEC No-Action Letter (July 1, 2008).

[136] See generally David Brittenham and Peter Loughram, "Doing a Debt Tender Offer and Consent Solicitation," 21 *Insights: The Corporate and Securities Law* 9 (2007).

have asked for assurances in the following areas: (i) the date for fixing the actual tender offer price must be no later than the second business day prior to the expiration of the tender offer; (ii) at least two firms make a market in the high-yield securities; (iii) there is some minimum level of trading activity in the debt securities and the securities trade generally on a spread-to-treasuries basis; (iv) the period for consenting to exit amendments and receiving the consent fee ends at least five business days prior to the expiration of the tender offer period; and (v) in the event of debt tender offers with exit consent solicitations, assurances that there would not be a material adverse change in the trading price of bonds that were not tendered and accepted in the tender offer. In practice, offers conducting tender offers combined with consent solicitations using the *10 plus 10* business days structure will find it impossible to make representation (v) because it is difficult to provide assurances that the results of the consent solicitation would not have any material adverse impact on the trading price of the bonds. Thus, fixed-spread offers for high-yield debt securities typically determine the nominal price paid in the tender offer during the first ten business days.

2.3.2.7 Other types of transactions Similar mechanisms have been used in a variety of different transactions, always following the same logic in the determination of the tender offer price.[137] For example, in a no-action letter for Citizens Republic Bancorp, Inc.,[138] the SEC granted no-action relief relating to Rule 14e-1(b) permitting the tender offeror to issue a fixed dollar value of its common stock in exchange for its outstanding non-convertible subordinated notes and trust-preferred securities, with the final number of shares of common stock to be issued being determined on the expiration date of the exchange offer. Subsequent to the *Citizens Republic* Letter, in the *Thermo Fisher* Scientific Letter, the SEC granted no-action relief relating, among others, to Rule 14e-1(b) with respect to an offer with a fixed-spread pricing mechanism and with structural protections, such as the daily publishing of indicative calculated purchase prices on a web page. The pricing mechanism in the *Thermo Fisher* Letter included: (i) the formula component and the fact that the *fixed cash payment would be fixed* and would remain constant during the tender

[137] For a comprehensive review of the various fixed-spread pricing mechanisms used in tender offers under the provisions of Rule 14e-1(b) under the Securities Exchange Act with special dispensation from the SEC, see *Textron, Inc.*, SEC No-Action Letter (October 7, 2011).

[138] August 21, 2009 (hereinafter, the "*Citizens Republic* Letter").

offer (subject to the minimum and maximum purchase prices described in the tender offer); (ii) the final purchase price would be based on readily observable trading prices for securities listed on a national securities exchange; (iii) the tender offeror would issue a press release announcing the final purchase price and post the final purchase price to the web page described above promptly following the close of trading on the expiration date of the tender offer, thus allowing investors time for tenders and withdrawals following the determination of the final purchase price; and (iv) the tender offer would include a toll-free telephone number and a link to a web page through which holders of the tender securities can access indicative purchase prices, enabling holders to predict whether the final purchase price would make participation in the tender offer economically beneficial to them.

In the *Citizens Republic* Letter, the consideration for the purchase of the tender securities was not cash but the issuance of common shares. The SEC provided no-action relief for an exchange offer of non-convertible subordinated notes and trust-preferred securities for common shares. The issuer would issue common shares having a value (based on their average volume-weighted average price) equal to a fixed dollar amount specified in the offering documentation. The no-action relief was provided on the basis that: (i) the tender offeror should disclose a specified dollar value of its common shares to be issued for each tender security accepted for exchange; (ii) the formula for determining the number of common shares to be issued in exchange for target securities, the cap on the consideration, and the method for determining the prioritization of acceptances have been disclosed in the offering materials disseminated to security holders; (iii) the formula, the cap, and the prioritization of acceptances would remain fixed throughout the duration of the tender and exchange offer; and, if there is a change in the formula, the cap, or the prioritization of acceptances, the tender and exchange offer would remain open for at least ten business days; (iv) the common shares offered as consideration in the tender and exchange offer and used as the reference security in the pricing mechanism should be listed on the Nasdaq Global Select Market; (v) the tender offeror should publish on a website maintained for the tender and exchange offer the daily indicative calculated per share values and exchange ratios, and provide a toll-free telephone number that its security holders can use to obtain tender and exchange offer pricing-related information; (vi) the tender offeror should publish the final exchange ratio on the exchange offer website and in a press release no later than 4:30 p.m., Eastern time, on the expiration date of the tender and exchange, and electronically file that information pursuant to Rule 165 under the Securities Act with the SEC; (vii) the tender offeror should use a proration mechanism to determine the exact amount of tendered tender securities to be accepted for exchange, in the event that accepting the total number of tender securities tendered would necessitate the issuance of shares in excess of the maximum amount available for payment; and (viii) the tender and exchange offer should disclose that the tender offeror would be seeking to buy up to all the tender securities, subject to certain terms and conditions being satisfied.

In the *Lloyds Banking Group plc* No-Action Letter,[139] the staff provided no-action letter relief under Rule 14e-1(b) for an exchange offer of non-convertible notes for ordinary shares, where the pricing formula included as a data input the US dollar/UK pound exchange rate. The exchange ratio was reported on Bloomberg on each trading day in the trading period prior to the expiration date.

2.4 *The Prompt Payment Rule (Rule 14e-1(c))*

Rule 14e-1(c) mandates prompt payment. The tender offerer must pay the consideration offered or return the tender securities deposited by or on behalf of security holders promptly after the termination or withdrawal of the tender offer. To protect tendering security holders, the tender offeror must pay the consideration promptly after termination of the offer. Similarly, returning securities that were not purchased ensures that the deposited securities are not tied up for a long period of time.

The term "promptly" is not defined. The SEC staff has stated that "promptly" may be determined by reference to the practices of the financial community, including current settlement practices. In most cases, the current settlement practice is for the payment of funds and the delivery of securities no later than the third business day after the date of the transaction. The SEC staff views payment within these time periods as "prompt" under Rule 14e-1(c).[140] There is one caveat to this rule: the payment may be delayed until certain regulatory approvals are obtained.[141] Furthermore, the rule does not obligate the tender offeror to have

[139] May 28, 2010. [140] See Exchange Act Release, No. 34–30967 (July 28, 1992).

[141] Rule 14e-1(c) under the Securities Exchange Act requires that a bidder in a tender offer either pay the consideration offered or return the securities tendered "promptly" after the withdrawal or termination of the tender offer. If payment is delayed because the bidder must obtain approvals from regulatory agencies before completing the purchase, the SEC staff ordinarily (depending on the length of the delay) will not deem a violation of Rule 14e-1(c) to have occurred, provided the tender offer materials fully disclosed the

financing in place to pay for the tender securities before launching the tender offer.

Early payment is also possible. The SEC staff has informally stated that the payment of full consideration to consenting holders prior to the expiration of a tender offer and consent solicitation is permissible. This structure permits the tender offeror to complete an acquisition or other transaction involving a debt tender offer with indenture amendments as soon as the required majority of holders of tender securities have tendered their bonds and consented to the indenture amendments, because the amendments become operative when the tender offeror begins accepting tendered securities for payment.[142] The tender offer is then held open for the remaining period of the twenty business days following the completion of the transaction. By settling the purchase of the securities and the delivery of the cash payment early, the issuer saves the additional interest that would accrue until the expiration of the tender offer and, arguably, the holder is also protected against future adverse movements in interest rates by realizing the cash value of the securities early and, on that basis, being able to reinvest the proceeds in a timely fashion. Early settlement is also possible in tender offers for less than the entire principal amount of securities outstanding. While early settlement in full of tendered securities in partial tender offers may create undue pressure to settle early, it is intellectually and from an investor protection standpoint more consistent with the objectives of the Williams Act to settle early only the relevant pro rata portion of tendered securities in partial tender offers (for example, in a tender offer for up to 80 percent of the outstanding principal amount, the offeror should be able to settle early up to 80 percent of the tendered securities (but no more than that) to ensure that all tendering holders are treated fairly on a pro rata basis).

Early settlement while withdrawal rights are available is not possible.

2.5 The Notice of Extensions Rule (Rule 14e-1(d))

If the tender offeror extends the length of the tender offer, the tender offeror must issue a notice of such extension by a press release or other public announcement, which notice shall include disclosure of the approximate number of securities deposited to date and shall be issued no later than the earlier of (i) 9:00 a.m. Eastern time, on the next business

possibility of such delay. See SEC Division of Corporation Finance, *Manual of Publicly Available Telephone Interpretations*, para 29, July 1997.

142 See Brittenham and Loughram, fn 136 above.

day after the scheduled expiration date of the tender offer, or (ii) if the class of securities which is the subject of the tender offer is registered on one or more national securities exchanges, the first opening of any one of such exchanges on the next business day after the scheduled expiration date of the tender offer. In practice, an extension of the length of a tender offer is commonly notified through the issuance of a press release or other public announcement to the Dow Jones News Service, Bloomberg, and similar services.

2.6 Withdrawal rights

The tender offeror is not required to offer withdrawal rights to security holders tendering their securities in a debt tender offer that is subject to Regulation 14E but not subject to Regulation 14D under the Securities Exchange Act. Nevertheless, if the tender offeror makes a material change to the terms of the tender offer or waives a material condition of the tender offer, the tender offeror is well advised to allow any security holders that tendered and deposited their securities to withdraw.[143] The ability to withdraw a tender while the tender offer is still open can influence an investor's decision on whether to tender or not. The offeror should disclose clearly whether security holders have the right to withdraw the securities they tendered during the offer. If no withdrawal rights are offered, the disclosure should warn the holders that any tenders cannot be withdrawn. The disclosure should also clearly state, if applicable, that if the offeror extends the offer, the securities tendered before the extension can still not be withdrawn. If withdrawal rights are offered, the disclosure should explain fully the procedures for withdrawing tendered securities.[144]

In combined tender offers and consent solicitations, the tender of the securities and the consent are typically linked. The tendering security holder is not allowed to withdraw consent without withdrawing the tendering of the tender securities. Bond indentures, however, typically provide that consents to amendments may be revoked before they become effective. Thus, to insure the enforceability of consents, it is customary to allow withdrawal rights until the requisite consents have been obtained

[143] The right to withdraw is the natural and logical extension of the obligation of the offer to extend the offer period in the event of a material change in the terms of the tender offer.

[144] See SEC, *Commission Guidance on Mini-Tender Offers and Limited Partnership Tender Offers*, Release No. 34–43069, July 31, 2000 (the "Mini-Tender Offer Release").

and a supplemental indenture executed. The holder is permitted to withdraw the consent, but must also withdraw the tender in doing so. Giving withdrawal rights until the consents have been effective and the supplemental indenture has been signed is intended to avoid a dispute that the securities that were tendered prior to that time had become beneficially owned by the offeror and, as a result, could not be taken into account for purposes of the consent. Allowing holders to withdraw their consents defends against the argument that beneficial ownership passes to the offeror at the time of the tender.

2.7 The "10 plus 10" tender offer and consent solicitation structure

One of the transaction structures that is often employed by issuers and their counsel in connection with liability management transactions is a fixed-price tender offer for any and all of the issuer's outstanding debt securities, combined with a concurrent consent solicitation to certain amendments of the terms of the securities. The tender offer is open for at least twenty business days but holders are incentivized to tender their securities early through the payment of an *early tender* premium for those tenders received any time from the commencement of the tender offer to (and including) the close of business on the tenth business day of the offer (the *early tender period*). Holders delivering their tenders during the early tender period receive a payment (usual $10–$50 for every $1,000 of principal amount of securities tendered) that is additional to the tender offer consideration payable to those holders delivering their tenders after the expiration of the early tender period but before the expiration of the tender offer period. Holders tendering after the expiration of the early tender period only receive the tender offer consideration (without any additional early tender premium). To further ensure that the structure creates the right incentives for holders to consent to the amendments of the terms of the securities being sought in the concurrent consent solicitation, the terms of the offer typically provide that (i) any tender of the relevant securities is deemed automatically to be a consent for the relevant amendments, so that securities cannot be tendered without the relevant consents relating to those securities being delivered, and (ii) consents delivered to the issuer without tenders of the relevant security can benefit from the payment of a consent solicitation fee only if delivered during the early tender period. Thus, tenders and consents can be delivered after the early tender period but without the relevant holders being entitled to receive the early tender payment or the consent solicitation fee; tenders and consents can be delivered during the early tender period subject to payment of the early tender fee and the consent solicitation fee; consents can be delivered without tendering the relevant securities; and tenders are automatically deemed to be consents for the relevant amendments regardless of the time of delivery of the relevant tenders. This structure insures that holders are encouraged to tender and consent early and not tender only shortly before the expiration of the relevant tender offer period of twenty business days. Absent any incentives to tender and consent early, holders typically tender shortly before the expiration of the relevant period because they normally prefer to monitor the interest rate environment before they decide if the tender consideration offered is attractive or not.

The staff of the SEC has considered this structure and concluded that the expiration of the early tender period leads to a decrease of the consideration offered to tendering and consenting holders. Since Rule 14e-1(b) under the Securities Exchange Act requires every tender offer to remain open for a period of at least ten business days following a decrease in the consideration offered to security holders, a tender offer must remain open for at least ten business days from the date of notice to the security holders that the early tender and consent period has expired (including any extensions thereof).[145] The staff view the termination of the early consent payment as a decrease of the total consideration offered in the tender offer and, consequently, the requirements of Rule 14e-1(a) and (b) are complied with only when the tender offer period is at least twenty business days and the offer remains open for at least ten business days after the expiration of the early tender and consent period.

2.8 *"Waterfall" structures*

Another structure for tender or exchange offers in debt securities, especially when the issuer would like to retire several series of outstanding

[145] See *Playtex, Inc.*, SEC No-Action Letter (November 22, 1987). In the end, the staff accepted in *Playtex* that the offer will remain open for at least twenty business days from the date of its commencement. The consent solicitations may expire on the fifteenth (not the tenth) business day after commencement. Holders who desire to accept the tender offer must consent and holders who desire only to consent need not accept the tender offer but only give their consents. The staff granted the no-action relief on the basis of a period of only five business days from the expiration of the consent solicitation deadline on the basis of the specific representations made by the issuer regarding other features of the tender offer, including the giving of withdrawal rights to tendering and consenting holders until the end of the offer period and the commitment to offer to all holders the best price offered to any holder.

securities, is the *waterfall* structure. In this structure, the offeror typically offers to acquire up to all the securities of each class subject to the tender offer but goes on to disclose that the offeror will not pay more than a specified amount of consideration or, in an exchange offer, will not issue more than a certain number or principal amount of exchange securities. The offering documentation states that if accepting for exchange or tender all the relevant securities tendered in the transaction would cause the offeror to exceed the specified limit, the offeror will first accept subordinated securities before accepting any senior securities and, if there are several classes of subordinated and senior securities included in the offer, the offeror will specify the classes that will be accepted in the order that they will be accepted. Finally, if the acceptance of all the securities of the last class to be accepted would cause the offeror to exceed the specified limit, the offeror announces that it would accept tenders of the relevant securities of that last class on a pro rata basis. This approach, in which an offeror prioritizes acceptances of different classes of securities in an exchange offer or tender offer and prorates acceptances for the lowest-priority class accepted, is sometimes referred to as a "waterfall" structure, because the consideration flows first to the first priority securities and only the remaining consideration flows to lower-priority securities.

A waterfall structure raises the question of compliance with Rule 14e-1(b), which requires that following the announcement of any increase or decrease in the percentage of the class of securities being sought, the offer must remain open for at least ten business days. In a 2009 no-action letter,[146] the staff of the SEC clarified the position and granted the no-action relief on the following conditions:

- the specified dollar value of the securities issuable for each subject security accepted for exchange shall be disclosed;
- the formula for determining the number of securities to be issued in exchange for the subject securities, the cap on the consideration, and the method for determining the prioritization of acceptances should be disclosed in the offering materials disseminated to security holders; the formula, the cap, and the prioritization of acceptances will remain fixed throughout the duration of the exchange offer; and, if there is a change in the formula, the cap, or the prioritization of acceptances, the exchange offer must remain open for at least ten business days;

[146] See the *Citizens Republic* Letter.

- the securities offered as consideration in the exchange offer and used as the reference security in the pricing mechanism are listed on a national securities exchange;
- the offeror shall publish on a website maintained for the exchange offer the daily indicative calculated per share values and exchange ratios and has provided a toll-free telephone number that its security holders can use to obtain exchange offer pricing-related information;
- the offeror shall publish the final exchange ratio on the exchange offer website and in a press release no later than 4:30 p.m., Eastern time, on the expiration date of the exchange offer, and electronically file that information pursuant to Rule 165 under the Securities Act on Form 425;
- the offeror shall make available all the necessary forms and notices of withdrawal in its printed materials and on the exchange offer website, shall permit tenders and withdrawals to be made until 11:59 p.m. on the expiration date, and shall have disclosed the procedures for making tenders and withdrawals in the offering materials disseminated to security holders;
- the offeror shall use a proration mechanism to determine the exact amount of tendered securities to be accepted for exchange in the event that accepting the total number of securities tendered would necessitate the issuance of shares in excess of the maximum amount available for payment; and
- the exchange offer shall disclose that the offeror is seeking to buy up to all of the subject securities, subject to certain terms and conditions being satisfied.

Regulation 14E does not require pro rata acceptances of securities tendered in debt tender offers.[147] In partial tender offers for less than the entire outstanding principal amount of the subject securities, the offeror may specify that tendered securities would be accepted for purchase on a pro rata basis or, alternatively, that securities tendered up to a certain point in time would be accepted in full and any securities tendered after the relevant cut-off time would not be accepted at all. The SEC has recognized that a pro rata provision has a direct bearing on the amount of time available for an investment decision. If no pro rata provision exists, the offer can, in effect, be open for less than twenty business days for those tendering early because tendered securities are purchased on a first

[147] Pro rata acceptance of partial tender offers is expressly mandated in equity tender offers. See Rule 14d-8 under the Securities Exchange Act.

come, first served basis. The SEC does, however, accept the practice of not giving pro rata rights in debt tender offers that are subject to Regulation 14E.[148]

3 Rule 14e-2 (Position of subject company with respect to a tender offer)

As a means reasonably designed to prevent fraudulent, deceptive, or manipulative acts or practices within the meaning of Section 14(e) of the Securities Exchange Act, the *subject company*,[149] no later than ten business days from the date the tender offer is first published or sent or given, shall publish, send, or give to security holders a statement disclosing that the subject company: (i) recommends an acceptance or rejection of the tender offer; (ii) expresses no opinion and remains neutral regarding the tender offer; or (iii) states that it is unable to take a position regarding the tender offer. The subject company must provide the reasons for the position taken. Material changes in the target's response to the tender offer must be promptly published or sent to its security holders. Generally, in practice, this requirement can be satisfied either through an appropriate press release or by including the target's recommendation in the relevant offer documents.

The regulatory aim of the rule is not difficult to discern: The subject company's position with respect to a tender offer can have a determinative effect on the outcome of a tender offer and thus is material to security holders. The subject company therefore should not be permitted to state its position when it maximizes its tactical advantage and to remain silent when it does not. Such complete discretion increases the likelihood for ill-considered decision-making by security holders and the possibility for fraudulent, deceptive, or manipulative acts or practices by the subject company and others. It is also inconsistent with the neutrality between tender offerors and subject companies sought to be achieved by the Williams Act. Stated differently, Rule 14e-2(a) insures that public security holders confronted with a tender offer will not be required to respond without adequate information. In debt tender offers by the issuer

[148] See the Mini-Tender Offer Release, fn 145 above: "The bidder should disclose clearly whether tendered securities will be accepted on a pro rata basis if the offer is oversubscribed. If shares will not be accepted on a pro rata basis, the disclosure should describe the effect on security holders."

[149] The *subject company* is the issuer of the securities that are sought by a tender offeror pursuant to a tender offer. See Rule 14d-1(g)(7) under the Securities Exchange Act.

of the tender securities, the offering materials usually contain a statement of position.

4 Rule 14e-3 (Transactions in securities on the basis of material, non-public information in the context of tender offers)

Rule 14e-3 under the Securities Exchange Act[150] prohibits insider trading and tipping based on information relating to a tender offer. It contains four basic parts: (i) the basic prohibition on insider trading unless disclosure is made (Rule 14e-3(a)); (ii) the Chinese Wall defense (Rule 14e-3(b)); (iii) two additional exemptions (Rule 14e-3(c)); and (iv) the tipping prohibition (Rule 14e-3(d)).

The basic prohibition is set forth in Rule 14e-3(a) (emphasis added):

> [I]f any person has taken a substantial step or steps to commence, or has commenced, a tender offer (the "offering person"), *it shall constitute a fraudulent, deceptive or manipulative act or practice* within the meaning of Section 14(e) [of the Securities Exchange Act] for any other person who is in possession of material information relating to such tender offer which information he knows or has reason to know is nonpublic and which he knows or has reason to know has been acquired directly or indirectly from: (1) the offering person, (2) the issuer of the securities sought or to be sought by such tender offer, or (3) any officer, director, partner or employee or any other person acting on behalf of the offering person or such issuer, *to purchase or sell or cause to be purchased or sold* any of such securities or any securities convertible into or exchangeable for any such securities or any option or right to obtain or to dispose of any of the foregoing securities, unless within a reasonable time prior to any purchase or sale such information and its source are publicly disclosed by press release or otherwise.

This is a very broad insider trading prohibition. It provides that, if a tender offeror has taken a "substantial step"[151] to commence a tender offer, no

[150] In its long history, the constitutionality and validity of Rule 14e-3 has been challenged several times without success. See, e.g., *U.S.* v. *Chestman*, fn 109 above.

[151] What is a "substantial step" towards the commencement of a tender offer is a question of fact. It is clear that no tender offer has to exist for a cause of action under Rule 14e-3 under the Securities Exchange Act to arise. Based on existing case law and SEC practice, any of the following actions would be considered a substantial step towards the commencement of a tender offer: hiring a financial advisor or law firm; executing a confidentiality agreement; discussing a range of values; meeting with investment bankers and other advisors; adopting a resolution to proceed with a tender offer; the commencement of the drafting of a tender offer memorandum; formulating a plan or proposal to make a tender offer; arranging financing for the tender offer; and/or preparing or authorizing the preparation of tender offer documentation.

other person[152] who possesses[153] material[154] information relating to such tender offer,[155] which he or she knows or has reason to know[156] has been acquired directly or indirectly from the tender offeror, the issuer of the tender securities, or any of their officers, directors, partners, or employees, or persons acting on their behalf,[157] can buy or sell the tender securities,[158] or any securities convertible into or exchangeable for any such securities, unless, within a reasonable period of time[159] prior to any purchase or sale, such information and its source[160] are publicly disclosed.[161]

Rule 14e-3(b) creates a defense against the risk of violation of paragraph (a) of Rule 14e-3 through the establishment of a *Chinese Wall.* A legal person (i.e., any person other than a natural person) such as a financial institution, a company, an investment management firm, and others

[152] The tender offeror, including the issuer preparing for a tender offer of its own securities, is not subject to the prohibition. The tender offeror would, of course, be subject to the general prohibition against insider trading of Rule 10b-5 under the Securities Exchange Act and Section 14(e) of the Securities Exchange Act.

[153] "Possession" means actual knowledge of the relevant information regardless of source and legality or not of the acquisition of such knowledge.

[154] The person need not know or have reason to know that the information is material. A fact about a tender offer can be material even though the relevant person does not know the type of transaction that would occur, the price, or when it might take place.

[155] The information must relate to the tender offer. Having material non-public information about the issuer of the tender offer securities (other than the tender offer) or information relating to the tender offeror is not an essential element of a cause of action under Rule 14e-3 under the Securities Exchange Act. "Information relating to a tender offer" is broad enough to cover: the fact that a tender offer is being considered or prepared; the details of the tender offer; its objectives, purposes and timing; valuation and expected price ranges; and/or plans to increase or decrease the offered consideration and other elements of the tender offer.

[156] The person must "know" or must "have reason to know." "Reason to know" is a negligence-based standard. The person may not know but, if she or he has reason to know, her or his actions are actionable.

[157] E.g., legal counsel or financial printer.

[158] Both purchases and sales are actionable. Offers of securities that do not result in purchases or sales are not actionable. Thus, the rule is not violated by a person who aborts a prospective sale or purchase after learning material non-public information regarding a tender offer.

[159] What a "reasonable period of time" is will depend on the circumstances.

[160] The rules require full and complete disclosure of both the information relating to the tender offer and the person highest up the chain of information flow of which the person making disclosure has actual knowledge. The disclosure must cover the identity of the tender offeror, the identity of the issuer of the target securities, a statement that the offeror has determined to make a tender offer for a class of securities of the issuer of the target securities, the amount of consideration to be offered, and the amount of securities to be sought in the tender offer.

[161] Any method that constitutes public disclosure is sufficient.

will not violate Rule 14e-3(a) if such person can demonstrate that: (i) the individual(s) making the investment decision on behalf of such person to purchase or sell any security described in paragraph (a) of the rule or to cause any such security to be purchased or sold by or on behalf of others did not know the material, non-public information; and (ii) such person had implemented one or a combination of policies and procedures, reasonable under the circumstances, taking into consideration the nature of the person's business, to insure that individual(s) making investment decision(s) would not violate the prohibition of paragraph (a), which policies and procedures may include, but are not limited to, those which restrict any purchase or sale, and causing any purchase and sale of any such security or those which prevent such individual(s) from knowing such information.

Rule 14e-3(c) exempts two types of transactions from the general prohibition of Rule 14e-3(a): (i) purchase(s) of any security described in paragraph (a) by a broker or by another agent on behalf of an offering person; or (ii) sale(s) by any person of any security described in paragraph (a) to the offering person.

The first exemption seeks to protect brokers or dealers purchasing securities subject to a tender offer on behalf of the tender offeror when, for example, the tender offeror has disclosed material non-public information relating to the tender offer to such broker or dealer. The second exemption allows any person to sell any security subject to a tender offer to the tender offeror if the tender offeror is the ultimate source of the material non-public information.

Finally, Rule 14e-3(d) prohibits certain types of persons from communicating material non-public information to any other person under circumstances in which it is reasonably foreseeable that such communications are likely to result in a violation of Rule 14e-3.

It shall therefore be unlawful for any person described below to communicate material, non-public information relating to a tender offer to any other person under circumstances in which it is reasonably foreseeable that such communication is likely to result in a violation of Rule 14e-3 *except* communications made in good faith: to the officers, directors, partners, or employees of the offering person, to its advisors or to other persons involved in the planning, financing, preparation, or execution of such tender offer; to the issuer whose securities are sought or to be sought by such tender offer; or to its officers, directors, partners, employees, or advisors or to other persons involved in the planning, financing, preparation, or execution of the activities of the issuer with respect to such tender offer; or to any person pursuant to a requirement of any statute, rule, or regulation promulgated thereunder.[162] The persons covered by the prohibition are the tender offeror or its officers, directors, partners, employees, or advisors; the issuer of the securities sought or to be sought by such tender offer or its officers, directors, partners, employees, or advisors; anyone acting on behalf of the persons set forth in the preceding sentence or the issuer; and any person in possession of material information relating to a tender offer which information he or she knows or has reason to know is non-public and which he or she knows or has reason to know has been acquired directly or indirectly from any of the above.[163]

5 Rule 14e-4 (Prohibited transactions in connection with partial tender offers)

Rule 14e-4 prohibits certain transactions in connection with short tendering for less than the outstanding principal amount of the relevant class of tender securities (*partial tender offers*).

Under the rule, it shall be unlawful for any person acting alone or in concert with others, directly or indirectly, to tender[164] any *subject security*[165] in a partial tender offer[166] (i) for his or her own account unless at the time of tender, and at the end of the proration period or period during which securities are accepted by lot (including any extensions thereof), he or she has a *net long position*[167] equal to or greater than the

[162] See, for example, *SEC* v. *Gallahair*, Not Reported in F. Supp. 2d, 2009 WL 1084742, N.D. Cal., April 14, 2009 (NO. 08 CV 05134 SBA).

[163] Ibid.

[164] For purposes of this rule, a person shall be deemed to "tender" a security if he or she (i) delivers a subject security pursuant to an offer, (ii) causes such delivery to be made, (iii) guarantees delivery of a subject security pursuant to a tender offer, (iv) causes a guarantee of such delivery to be given by another person, or (v) uses any other method by which acceptance of a tender offer may be made. See Rule 14e-3(a)(4) under the Securities Exchange Act.

[165] The term "subject security" means a security that is the subject of any tender offer or request or invitation for tenders. See Rule 14e-4(a)(3) under the Securities Exchange Act.

[166] The term "partial tender offer" means a tender offer or request or invitation for tenders for less than all of the outstanding securities subject to the offer in which tenders are accepted either by lot or on a pro rata basis for a specified period, or a tender offer for all the outstanding shares that offers a choice of consideration in which tenders for different forms of consideration may be accepted either by lot or on a pro rata basis for a specified period. See Rule 14e-3(a)(5) under the Securities Exchange Act.

[167] The amount of a person's "net long position" in a subject security shall equal the excess, if any, of such person's "long position" over such person's "short position." For the purposes of determining the net long position as of the end of the proration period and

amount tendered in the subject security and will deliver or cause to be delivered such security for the purpose of tender to the person making the offer within the period specified in the offer; or an *equivalent security*[168] and, upon the acceptance of his or her tender will acquire the subject security by conversion, exchange, or exercise of such equivalent security to the extent required by the terms of the offer, and will deliver or cause to be delivered the subject security so acquired for the purpose of tender to the person making the offer within the period specified in the offer; or (ii) for the account of another person unless the person making the tender possesses the subject security or an equivalent security, or has a reasonable belief that, upon information furnished by the person on whose behalf the tender is made, such person owns the subject security or an equivalent security and will promptly deliver the subject security or such equivalent security for the purpose of tender to the person making the tender.

for tendering concurrently to two or more partial tender offers, securities that have been tendered in accordance with the rule and not withdrawn are deemed to be part of the person's long position. Such person's long position is the amount of subject securities that such person: (i) or his or her agent has title to or would have title to but for having lent such securities; (ii) has purchased, or has entered into an unconditional contract, binding on both parties thereto, to purchase but has not yet received the subject security; (iii) has exercised a standardized call option for; (iv) has converted, exchanged, or exercised an equivalent security for; or (v) is entitled to receive upon conversion, exchange, or exercise of an equivalent security. Such person's short position is the amount of subject securities or subject securities underlying equivalent securities that such person: (i) has sold, or has entered into an unconditional contract, binding on both parties thereto, to sell; (ii) has borrowed; (iii) has written a non-standardized call option, or granted any other right pursuant to which his or her shares may be tendered by another person; or (iv) is obligated to deliver upon exercise of a standardized call option sold on or after the date that a tender offer is first publicly announced or otherwise made known by the bidder to holders of the security to be acquired, if the exercise price of such option is lower than the highest tender offer price or stated amount of the consideration offered for the subject security. For the purpose of this paragraph, if one or more tender offers for the same security are ongoing on such date, the announcement date shall be that of the first announced offer. See Rule 14e-4(a)(1) under the Securities Exchange Act. The term "standardized call option" means any call option that is traded on an exchange, or for which quotation information is disseminated in an electronic inter-dealer quotation system of a registered national securities association. See Rule 14e-4(a)(6) under the Securities Exchange Act.

168 The term "equivalent security" means (i) any security (including any option, warrant, or other right to purchase the subject security), issued by the person whose securities are the subject of the offer, that is immediately convertible into, or exchangeable or exercisable for, a subject security; or (ii) any other right or option (other than a standardized call option) that entitles the holder thereof to acquire a subject security, but only if the holder thereof reasonably believes that the maker or writer of the right or option has title to and possession of the subject security and upon exercise will promptly deliver the subject security. See Rule 14e-4(a)(2) under the Securities Exchange Act.

6 Rule 14e-8 (Prohibiting conduct in connection with pre-commencement communications)

Rule 14e-8 under the Securities Exchange Act is another anti-fraud rule in connection with tender offers. More specifically, under the provisions of Rule 14e-8, it is a fraudulent, deceptive, or manipulative act or practice within the meaning of Section 14(e) of the Securities Exchange Act for any person to publicly announce that the person (or a party on whose behalf the person is acting) plans to make a tender offer that has not yet been commenced, if the person: (i) is making the announcement of a potential tender offer without the intention of commencing the offer within a reasonable time and completing the offer; (ii) intends, directly or indirectly, for the announcement to manipulate the market price of the securities of the tender offeror or the issuer of the tender securities; or (iii) does not have the reasonable belief that the person will have the means to purchase securities to complete the offer.[169]

7 Disclosure requirements in debt tender offers

As has become apparent from the discussion of the various anti-fraud rules adopted by the SEC under the rule-making power of Section 14(e) of the Securities Exchange Act, the SEC has not yet promulgated specific disclosure requirements applicable to tender offers for debt securities outside the scope of Section 14(d) of the Securities Exchange Act and Regulation 14D thereunder.

In July 2000, the SEC issued an interpretative release providing guidance in relation to the disclosure and dissemination of tender offers that result in the bidder holding 5 percent or less of a class of outstanding securities of an issuer.[170] These mini-tender offers are generally structured to result in ownership of not more than 5 percent of a class of securities to avoid the filing, disclosure, and procedural requirements of the equity tender offer rules adopted under Section 14(d) of the Securities Exchange Act and

[169] Another significant prohibition created by the SEC in Regulation 14E is the prohibition on purchases of subject securities outside a tender offer. See Rule 14e-5 under the Securities Exchange Act. Under Rule 14e-5, no "covered person" may directly or indirectly purchase or arrange to purchase any "subject securities" or any related securities except as part of the tender offer. The prohibition applies only to equity securities and will not be considered further in this book.

[170] See the Mini-Tender Offer Release, fn 145 above.

Regulation 14D thereunder. The SEC pointed out that, while Congress limited the application of Section 14(d) of the Securities Exchange Act to tender offers that would result in ownership of more than 5 percent of a class of securities, the general anti-fraud provisions of Section 14(e) of the Securities Exchange Act have no similar limitation. Consequently, security holders faced with a tender offer outside the scope of Section 14(d) of the Securities Exchange Act (including a mini-tender offer) are entitled to the protection of Section 14(e) and Regulation 14E thereunder.[171] In the interpretative guidance, the SEC expressly commented that Section 14(e) and Regulation 14E applied to all tender offers, even where the offer is for less than 5 percent of the outstanding securities and offers for any type of security, *including debt.*[172] Thus, the views of the SEC in relation to the disclosure and dissemination requirements applicable to mini-tender offers subject to Regulation 14E under the Securities Exchange Act reflect the views of the staff on the general disclosure and dissemination requirements in tender offers that are subject to Regulation 14E but not Section 14(d) and Regulation 14D under the Securities Exchange Act such as tender offers for debt securities.

7.1 Disclosure guidelines

The SEC believes that security holders need better and clearer disclosure in tender offers subject to Regulation 14E under the Securities Exchange Act. To avoid liability under the anti-fraud provisions of Section 14(e) of the Securities Exchange Act, the SEC has recommended that tender offerors consider the following issues in crafting disclosures in the tender offer documents that are provided to security holders.[173]

Offer price. Price information is material to security holders. Because tender offers typically are made at prices that are at a premium to the market, investors could reasonably assume that every offer includes a premium. Bidders should disclose clearly if the offer price is below the market price. If the price offered is below the market price when the offer commences, the disclosure should clearly explain this prominently in the document. Also, the explanation should include the market price (or the bid and ask prices) on the day of commencement, or the most recent practicable date. If there is no liquid market for the securities, the bidder should disclose, if known, the latest price at which the security sold,

[171] Ibid. [172] Ibid.

[173] Ibid. The disclosure guidance that follows summarizes the Mini-Tender Offer Release.

including the date of sale, or the latest bid and ask prices. Some offers have been made at, or slightly above, the market price of the security. The offer is then repeatedly extended until the market price rises above the offer price. These offers generally do not have withdrawal rights. The tender offeror then purchases the securities below the market price. If the tender offeror intended never to purchase the securities unless the market price rose above the offer price, and did not disclose this intention, the SEC is of the view that this would be a "fraudulent, deceptive or manipulative practice" within the meaning of Section 14(e) of the Securities Exchange Act.

Price changes. A tender offeror's intention to reduce the offering price based on distributions made to security holders by the issuer of the tender securities and fees imposed by the tender offeror is material information in the view of the SEC. In describing the offer price, the tender offeror should disclose, if applicable, that the price may be reduced by any distributions or fees and the amount, if known. If the tender offeror changes the price, the tender offer would obviously need to be extended for ten business days as provided by Rule 14e-1(b) under the Securities Exchange Act.

Withdrawal rights. The ability to withdraw a tender while the offer is open can influence an investor's decision on whether to tender. The tender offeror should disclose clearly whether security holders have the right to withdraw the securities they tendered during the offer. If no withdrawal rights exist, the disclosure should indicate that security holders who tender their securities cannot withdraw their securities from the tender offeror. The disclosure should also clearly state, if applicable, that if the tender offeror extends the offer, the securities tendered before the extension still cannot be withdrawn and may be held through the end of the offer until payment. If withdrawal rights do exist, the disclosure should explain fully the procedures for withdrawing tendered securities.

Pro rata acceptance. A pro rata provision has a direct bearing on the amount of time available for an investment decision. If no pro rata provision exists, the offer can, in effect, be open for fewer than twenty business days because securities will be purchased on a first come, first served basis. The tender offeror should disclose clearly whether tendered securities will be accepted on a pro rata basis if the offer is oversubscribed. If securities will not be accepted on a pro rata basis, the disclosure should describe the effect on security holders.

Target recommendation. Security holders should be advised, before an investment decision is made, that additional, material information will come from the management of the issuer of the tender securities. This disclosure is especially important in instances where withdrawal rights do not exist. The tender offeror should disclose that if the issuer is aware of the offer, the issuer is required to make a recommendation to security holders regarding the offer within ten business days of commencement. The SEC encourages tender offerors to send the offering document to the issuer of the tender securities at the commencement of the tender offer so the issuer can comply with its obligation under Rule 14e-2 under the Securities Exchange Act to make a recommendation regarding the tender offer.

Identity of tender offeror. Identification of the tender offeror provides security holders with insight regarding financial resources, its capacity to pay for tendered securities, and historical business practices. The tender offeror should completely and accurately disclose its identity, including the controlling persons of the tender offeror and promoters. For example, it may be meaningful to disclose the controlling security holders, executive officers, and directors of a corporate tender offeror, or the general partner (and its controlling persons) of a partnership tender offeror. The tender offeror also should disclose any affiliation between the issuer of the tender securities and the tender offeror.

Plans or proposals. In deciding whether to tender, it may be material to know whether the tender offeror intends to continue the acquisition program at some future point. The tender offeror should disclose its plans or proposals regarding future tender offers of the securities of the same issuer.

Ability to finance offer. Security holders need to know whether the tender offeror has the ability to buy the securities. The tender offeror should disclose whether it has the funds necessary to consummate the offer. If the tender offeror does not have the financing for the offer (e.g., cash or a commitment letter from a bank) at the commencement of the offer, the tender offeror should clearly state that it cannot buy the securities until it obtains financing. Tender offerors in some types of tender offers often do not have the financing necessary to purchase the securities in the offer. In many cases they merely accept the securities in the offer and then attempt to sell those securities in the market and use the proceeds to pay the security holders who tendered. When the offer is made at a premium, tender offerors sometimes improperly hold the securities and wait for the market price to rise above the offer price before they attempt to sell the securities in the market. This plan is not disclosed to security holders. The SEC believes that this method of financing tender offers is inappropriate and may be a "fraudulent, deceptive or manipulative practice" within the meaning of Section 14(e) of the Securities Exchange Act. The SEC further recalls that Rule 14e-8(c) under the Securities Exchange Act expressly prohibits a person from publicly announcing a tender offer if that person "does not have the reasonable belief that the person will have the means to purchase the securities to complete the offer." Furthermore, this method of financing does not comply with the prompt payment the requirement of Rule 14e-1(c) under the Securities Exchange Act.

Conditions to the offer. The SEC considers it important for security holders to be able to evaluate the genuineness of the offer. It therefore believes that a tender offer can be subject to conditions only where the conditions are based on objective criteria, and the conditions are not within the tender offeror's control. If the conditions are not objective and are within the tender offeror's control (e.g., the offer may be terminated for any reason or may be extended indefinitely), the SEC is concerned that the offer would be illusory and may constitute a "fraudulent, deceptive or manipulative" practice within the meaning of Section 14(e). It therefore advises that the tender offeror should disclose all material conditions to the offer.

Extensions of the offer. The SEC believes that a tender offeror's ability and intention to extend the offer period is material information. This information is particularly important when there are no withdrawal rights. Security holders will be unable to withdraw securities tendered even if the offer is extended and securities are locked up for an unexpectedly long time. The initial disclosure materials should state whether the offer could be extended, whether the tender offeror intends to extend the offer, under what circumstances the tender offeror would extend and, if the tender offeror intends to extend, the anticipated length of any extension. If the offer is extended after the initial disclosure materials are provided to security holders, the tender offeror should publicly announce this fact.

7.2 Dissemination guidelines

In recommending appropriate dissemination practices, the SEC reflects on the Congressional intention in enacting the Williams Act as a mechanism for protecting investors in tender offers. The SEC points out that in enacting the Williams Act, Congress stressed the importance of not merely specifying disclosure requirements but also ensuring that information is communicated to security holders. The tender offeror in a tender offer must make reasonable efforts to disseminate material information about the tender offer to security holders. The failure to disseminate the disclosure frustrates the purpose of the US Tender Offer Rules.

Rule 14e-1(a) states that a tender offer must be held open for twenty business days from the date the offer is first "published or sent to security holders." Section 14(e) and Regulation 14E do not state how tender offers should be "published or sent to security holders." However, Rule 14d-4, which applies only to tender offers subject to Section 14(d) and Regulation 14D, provides guidance in this area. Rule 14d-4 sets forth three alternative methods of dissemination for cash tender offers. The purpose of Rule 14d-4 is to add content and clarity to the term "published or sent or given" in Section 14(d)(1). Dissemination under Rule 14d-4 is deemed "published or sent or given to security holders" for purposes of Section 14(d)(1). These dissemination methods are as follows:

- publishing the offering document in a newspaper;
- publishing a summary advertisement containing certain information in a newspaper and mailing to security holders a copy of the full offering document upon request; or
- mailing the offering document to security holders using a security holder list.

Rule 14d-4 also provides that these methods of dissemination are not exclusive or mandatory.

Depending on the facts and circumstances, adequate publication of a tender offer under Rule 14d-4 may require publication of the offering document in a newspaper with a national circulation or may only require publication in a newspaper with a metropolitan or regional circulation. Publication in all editions of a daily newspaper with a national circulation will always constitute adequate publication for purposes of Rule 14d-4.

The SEC believes that dissemination of material information using mechanisms the tender offeror knows or is reckless in not knowing are inadequate would be a "fraudulent, deceptive or manipulative" practice within the meaning of Section 14(e) and Rule 14e-1. For example, the SEC believes that merely sending the offering documents to the Depositary Trust Corporation ("DTC") is not an adequate means of communicating the information to security holders. DTC is not in business to, and in fact does not, disseminate the tender offer materials to security holders. DTC sends only limited notice information to its participants about tender offers. As a result, the tender offeror has no reasonable assurance that dissemination to DTC and then through broker-dealers or banks will satisfy the requirements of Section 14(e). Furthermore, many tender offerors have refused to pay broker-dealers and banks the costs of forwarding information to security holders. Consequently, the tender offer document does not consistently reach security holders to whom the offer is made. It is the tender offeror's obligation to assure that security holders get material information about the tender offer. If a tender offeror adequately disseminates the information to security holders through another method, such as one of the methods provided in Rule 14d-4, the bidder also may send the information to DTC for forwarding to its participants.

Also, the SEC believes that only posting the information on a website would not be adequate dissemination. By merely posting a tender offer on a website, the bidder does not adequately publish the offer, nor is the offer deemed sent to security holders. If a tender offeror makes a material change to the tender offer, the tender offeror must disseminate the changes in a manner reasonably likely to inform security holders of the change. The tender offeror generally should disseminate the change in the same manner as it disseminated the original offer.

4

Debt tender offers and capital markets regulation in the European Union and the United Kingdom

1 Introduction

The regulation of securities markets (including the regulation and supervision of the issuance of securities, the sale and purchase of securities, and the conduct of tender offers for securities) across the member states of the European Union, including the United Kingdom, is an evolving regulatory system. The underlying objective of the securities laws adopted by the European Union[174] in the form of various directives, regulations, and other implementing measures is the construction of a single pan-European securities and investment services market across the member states of the European Union through the harmonization of the national laws and regulations of the individual member states. This regulatory system has for certain member states and in respect of specific regulatory areas resulted not simply in the application of common European standards but also in the establishment of entirely new systems of regulation of national markets which were previously lightly regulated or unregulated.

The first signs of an independent pan-European system of regulation of securities transactions can be traced to a recommendation in 1977 by the European Commission, the guardian of the institutional and legal integration of the member states of the European Union under a common system of law, for the introduction or creation of a European Code of Conduct Relating to Transactions in Transferable Securities.[175]

Several other legislative measures (in the form of directives) followed in the 1970s, 1980s, and 1990s on matters relating to conditions for the

[174] The Treaty on the Functioning of the European Union amended and replaced, with effect from December 1, 2009 upon the entry into force of the Treaty of Lisbon, the Treaty Establishing the European Community. See fn 192 below.

[175] Commission Recommendation 77/534/EEC of July 25, 1977 concerning a European code of conduct relating to transactions in transferable securities, OJ L 212, 20.8.1977, pp. 37–43.

admission of securities to official stock exchange listings,[176] the requirements for the preparation of listing particulars,[177] information requirements imposed on companies the shares of which have been admitted to official stock exchange listing,[178] information requirements when a major holding in a listed company is acquired or disposed of,[179] the conduct and pursuit of investment services,[180] and regulations on insider dealing and the mutual recognition of public-offer prospectuses as stock exchange listing particulars.[181]

The adoption of the Financial Services Action Plan (the "FSAP")[182] in 1999 and the political endorsement of that policy plan by the heads of state and government of the EU member states during the Stockholm European Council in 2001 accelerated the process of harmonization of the regulation of EU securities markets.[183]

The FSAP, an ambitious collection of various policy measures in the areas of securities regulation and financial services, was implemented during the following five years through a number of legislative initiatives in the form of directives, regulations, and several level-2 measures.[184]

[176] Council Directive 79/279/EEC of March 5, 1979 coordinating the conditions for the admission of securities to official stock exchange listing, OJ L 66, 16.3.1979, pp. 21–32.

[177] Council Directive 80/390/EEC of March 17, 1980 coordinating the requirements for the drawing-up, scrutiny, and distribution of the listing particulars to be published for the admission of securities to official stock exchange listing, OJ L 100, 17.4.1980, pp. 1–26.

[178] Council Directive 82/121/EEC of February 15, 1982 on information to be published on a regular basis by companies the shares of which have been admitted to official stock-exchange listing, OJ L 48, 20.2.1982, pp. 26–9.

[179] Council Directive 88/627/EEC of December 12, 1988 on the information to be published when a major holding in a listed company is acquired or disposed of, OJ L 348, 17.12.1988, pp. 62–5.

[180] Council Directive 93/22/EEC of May 10, 1993 on investment services in the securities field, OJ L 197, 6.8.1993, p. 58.

[181] Council Directive 90/211/EEC of April 23, 1990 amending Directive 80/390/EEC in respect of the mutual recognition of public-offer prospectuses as stock exchange listing particulars, OJ L 112, 3.5.1990, pp. 24–5.

[182] Commission Communication of May 11, 1999, "Implementing the Framework for Financial Markets: Action Plan," COM (1999) 232 final.

[183] See generally Luca Enriques and Matteo Gatti, "Is There a Uniform EU Securities Law After the Financial Services Action Plan?" 14 *Stanford Journal of Law, Business and Finance* 43 (2008–2009).

[184] In connection with financial and securities regulation, legislative measures adopted at the EU level are either "level-1" directives and regulations (containing the main principles and rules) or "level-2" directives and regulations (containing more detailed provisions and, due to a more flexible law-making process, being subject to amendment and modification as often as necessary to adapt to changing financial market conditions). In addition to the two levels (1 and 2), the European Securities and Markets Authority issues guidelines

In the field of securities markets regulation, several level-1 directives and regulations, complemented by level-2 measures, have been adopted and are presently in force, including in matters such as the markets in financial instruments,[185] the harmonization of international accounting standards,[186] regulatory standards applicable to securities offerings and prospectuses,[187] insider trading and market manipulation,[188] takeover bids,[189] and mandatory disclosure by issuers of listed securities.[190]

With the exception of the European Directive on Takeover Bids (the "Takeover Directive"), which applies only to equity securities (or, to be precise, securities with voting rights) and not to debt securities, there is no distinct system of tender offer regulation in the European Union that would be analogous to Section 14(e) of the Securities Exchange Act, and Regulation 14D and Regulation 14E thereunder. This does not mean that debt tender offers or purchases of debt securities in the open market or in privately negotiated transactions are outside the scope of the European securities laws. The purpose of this chapter is to identify and discuss those regulations, directives, and other provisions of EU law that apply in connection with tender offers and similar transactions in debt securities.

2 The legal basis of EU securities regulation

The various EU legislative measures adopted towards the establishment of a common integrated European securities markets are based on the

for the implementation and uniform application of level-1 and level-2 legislative and regulatory measures. For a detailed description of this multi-layered standard-setting process, see Eilis Ferran, *Building an EU Securities Market* (Cambridge University Press, 2004), pp. 61–84.

185 Directive 2004/39/EC of the European Parliament and of the Council of April 21, 2004 on markets in financial instruments amending Council Directives 85/611/EEC and 93/6/EEC and Directive 2000/12/EC of the European Parliament and of the Council and repealing Directive 93/22/EEC, 2004 OJ L 145 1 (also known as the "MIFID").

186 Regulation 1606/2002/EC of the European Parliament and of the Council of July 19, 2002 on the application of international accounting standards, 2002 OJ L 243 1.

187 Prospectus Directive, fn 6 above.

188 Directive 2003/6/EC of the European Parliament and of the Council of January 28, 2003 on insider dealing and market manipulation (market abuse), OJ L 96, 12.4.2003, pp. 16–25.

189 Directive 2004/25/EC of the European Parliament and of the Council of April 21, 2004 on takeover bids, OJ L 142, 30.4.2004, pp. 12–23 (the "Directive on Takeover Bids").

190 Directive 2004/109/EC of the European Parliament and of the Council of December 15, 2004 on the harmonization of transparency requirements in relation to information about issuers whose securities are admitted to trading on a regulated market and amending Directive 2001/34/EC, 2004 OJ L 390, 38.

recognition that the economic objectives of the European Union can only be achieved if sufficient capital is available, and the sources of capital are sufficiently diversified to enable investments in the common market to be financed as rationally as possible without national borders and national laws being impediments to the integration of financial markets. The role of the securities markets is to permit the free and rational allocation of capital and, consequently, the proper working and interpenetration of the securities markets must be regarded as an essential aspect of the establishment of a common European securities market.

The philosophy underpinning the European system of securities and financial markets regulation is the cooperation of national authorities (legislative, executive, and judicial) towards the harmonization of national laws as a means to solving the problems associated with multiple legal systems adopting different laws and regulations, and applying those laws and regulations to cross-border transactions within the European economic area, which is supposed to be an integrated financial market akin to one single national market.

2.1 The Treaty on the Functioning of the European Union

The EU regulatory framework relating to transactions in securities and the functioning of securities markets is based on the Treaty objective of constructing a common integrated European market (Article 26 of the Treaty).[191] The European Union has the legal right, enshrined in the Treaty, to adopt measures with the aim of establishing or ensuring the functioning of the internal market, which shall comprise an area without internal frontiers in which the free movement of goods, persons, services, and capital is ensured in accordance with the provisions of the Treaty.[192] A single integrated securities market across the European countries, within which investment services providers, investors, and issuers of securities can access national markets, should generate a more efficient, liquid, and deeper capital market in Europe for the benefit of investors and issuers. In

[191] References to the "Treaty" are to the Consolidated Version of the Treaty on the Functioning of the European Union, Official Journal C 83 of 30.3.2010. The Treaty on the Functioning of the European Union amended and replaced, with effect from December 1, 2009 upon the entry into force of the Treaty of Lisbon, the Treaty Establishing the European Community. Articles, sections, chapters, titles, and parts of the Treaty Establishing the European Community were renumbered into the relevant provisions of the Treaty on the Functioning of the European Union (Treaty of Lisbon, Article 5 and Annex).

[192] Article 26 of the Treaty.

the absence of legislative coordination among the member states, several cumulatively applicable systems of securities regulation apply to cross-border transactions and, consequently, market participants are required to comply with multiple regulatory regimes.

To achieve the objective of establishing an integrated common European securities market, the Treaty makes available to policy-makers two principal legal instruments that can be (and have been) used cumulatively in pursuit of the common goal: first, the removal of direct regulatory obstacles to the free movement of capital and services through the prohibition of all restrictions on the provision of services and the movement of capital across borders; and second, the adoption of harmonized common regulatory standards regulating European securities markets with the aim of abolishing the different national laws governing securities transactions and replacing them with a common European regulatory system of securities regulations. All of the EU directives[193] or regulations[194] relating to securities markets currently in force are measures that either abolish direct restrictions on the free movement of capital or services across borders, or introduce common European regulatory standards, in all cases as part of the effort to create a single European securities market.

2.2 The freedom of services and the free movement of capital

The basic economic freedoms that are directly relevant to the establishment of a well-functioning European securities market, i.e., the free movement of services and the free movement of capital, were established by the original Treaty of Rome in 1957 and have remained the fundamental economic constitution of the European integration project ever since. Regarding the free movement or provision of services, Article 56 of the Treaty simply provides that "restrictions on the freedom to provide services within the Union shall be prohibited in respect of nationals of member states who are established in a member state other than that of the person to whom the services are intended." Even more laconically, in relation to the free movement of capital, Article 63 of the Treaty provides

[193] A *Directive* is one of the types of legal acts that can be adopted by the institutions of the European Union in accordance with a specific procedure prescribed in the Treaty. It is a binding legal measure, as to the result to be achieved, upon each member state to which it is addressed, but leaves to the national authorities the choice of form and methods.

[194] A *Regulation* is also a type of legal act that can be adopted by the institutions of the European Union in accordance with the Treaty. A Regulation has general application. It is binding in its entirety and directly applicable in all member states.

that "all restrictions on the movement of capital between member states and between member states and third countries shall be prohibited."

It is now settled law that the free movement of services requires not only the elimination of all discrimination against a person providing services on the ground of his or her nationality but also the abolition of any restriction, even if it applies without distinction to national providers of services and to those of other member states, when it is liable to prohibit or otherwise impede the activities of a provider of services established in another member state where he or she lawfully provides similar services.[195] The country of destination must recognize the equivalence of the law of the country of origin and should not impose national measures the effect of which is equivalent to the effect of the legislative and administrative action in the country of origin. Compliance with the rules in the "home country" suffices to secure market access in the country of destination without being subject to "prohibiting" or "impeding" measures applicable therein. This mandatory "mutual recognition" of national laws retreats only in cases where the measures of the regulating country of destination are "justified by imperative reasons relating to the public interest"[196] and only if that interest "is not protected by the rules to which the person providing the services is subject in the member state in which he is established"[197] in which case mutual recognition is restored.

The abolition of all capital controls and the establishment of free movement of capital or, more specifically, the removal of all restrictions on cross-border financial transactions has been a critical requirement for the establishment of a common European securities market. Certainly, capital account liberalization has also been an essential element of the European Monetary Union, which in turn is also based on the completion of the single European market for capital and securities transactions. Following a history of gradual and incomplete capital movement liberalization in the 1970s and 1980s, the Directive on Capital Movements[198] finally in 1988 established the free movement of capital among member states, repealing all earlier directives on the topic and liberalizing certain capital movements which had previously been restricted. Another significant effect of the Directive on Capital Movements was that it created the essential legal environment which made the adoption of a series of EU measures on securities markets and investment services possible.

[195] See Case C-76/90 *Säger* [1991] ECR I-4221. [196] Ibid., para 15. [197] Ibid.

[198] Council Directive 88/361/EEC of June 24, 1988 for the implementation of Article 67 of the Treaty, OJ L 178, 8.7.1988, pp. 5–18.

The present version of Article 63 of the Treaty is now the controlling provision on capital movements across the member states of the European Union. It provides that, within the framework set forth in the Treaty, all restrictions on the movement of capital are prohibited. The Treaty introduces certain derogations from the fundamental principle. For example, the institutions of the European Union may adopt, in accordance with the relevant procedure, measures on the movement of capital to or from third countries involving direct investment, the establishment of branches or subsidiaries, the provision of financial services, or the admission of securities of third-country issuers to capital markets.[199] In addition, member states may take all requisite measures to prevent violations of national law and regulations, particularly in the field of taxation and the prudential supervision of financial institutions, or to lay down procedures for the declaration of capital movements for purposes of administrative or statistical information, or to take measures that are justified on grounds of public policy or public security.[200]

2.3 Liability management transactions and the treaty freedoms

The sale or purchase of debt securities (in tender offers, in the open market, or in privately negotiated transactions) or the exchange of securities for other securities in exchange offers are subject to laws and regulations in all EU member states, which laws and regulations may restrict, directly or indirectly, the relevant transactions. Laws and regulations in EU member states that may raise obstacles in the ability of issuers and/or investors to execute liability management transactions across borders can be scrutinized for compliance with the economic freedoms established under the provisions of the Treaty.

According to consistent case law of the European Court of Justice (the "ECJ"), the Treaty generally prohibits restrictions on movements of capital between member states.[201] In the absence of a definition in the Treaty of "movements of capital" for the purposes of the Treaty prohibition of restrictions, the ECJ has recognized the list annexed to the Directive on Capital Movements as having indicative value.[202] Movements of capital

[199] Treaty, Article 64(2). [200] Treaty, Article 65(1)(b).

[201] See, to that effect, Case C-483/99 *Commission* v. *France* [2002] ECR I-4781, paras. 35 and 40, and Case C-98/01 *Commission* v. *United Kingdom* [2003] ECR I-4641, paras. 38 and 43.

[202] The movements of capital between member states of the European Union fully liberalized by the Treaty cover all capital transactions in the broadest possible sense, including all the operations necessary for the purposes of capital movements (the conclusion and performance of the transaction and related transfers) between residents of different member

for the purposes of the Treaty therefore include, among other things, the acquisition of shares, debt securities, or other capital markets instruments on the capital markets solely with the intention of making a financial investment without any intention of influencing the management and control of the undertaking.[203] The ECJ has stated that national measures must be regarded as "restrictions" within the meaning of the Treaty and the relevant rules prohibiting restrictions on the movement of capital if they are likely to prevent or limit the acquisition of securities issued by issuers in another EU country or to deter investors of other member states from investing in their capital.[204]

Thus, any law or regulation that would be likely to prevent, directly or indirectly, investors or issuers in one member state from engaging in liability management transactions with issuers and investors, respectively, in another member state would be contrary to the fundamental economic freedom of movement of capital across the European Union.

2.4 The Treaty basis of the harmonization of national securities laws

Where the single European market in securities activities and investment services cannot be achieved solely by the elimination of discriminatory or

states, operations carried out by any natural or legal person (including operations in respect of the assets or liabilities of member states or of other public administrations and agencies), access for the economic operator to all the financial techniques available in the market approached for the purpose of carrying out the operation in question, operations to liquidate or assign assets built up, repatriation of the proceeds of the liquidation thereof or the immediate use of such proceeds, and operations to repay credits or loans. The freedom to move capital applies to: (i) direct investments; (ii) investments in real estate; (iii) operations in securities normally dealt in on the capital markets, including the acquisition by nonresidents of domestic securities dealt in on a stock exchange, the acquisition by residents of foreign securities dealt in on a stock exchange, the acquisition by nonresidents of domestic securities not dealt in on a stock exchange, the acquisition by residents of foreign securities not dealt in on a stock exchange, the admission of securities to a capital market, introduction on a stock exchange, issuance and placement on a capital market, and the administration of foreign securities to the domestic capital market; (iv) transactions in securities and other instruments in the money market; (v) operations in current and deposit accounts with financial institutions; (vi) the provision of credit related to commercial transactions; (vii) financial loans and credits; (viii) sureties, other guarantees, and rights of pledge; (ix) transfers in performance of insurance contracts; (x) personal capital movements such as loans, gifts, endowments, dowries, and inheritances; (xi) the physical import and export of financial assets such as securities and currencies; and (xii) other capital movements not falling in any of the above categories. See Council Directive 88/361/EEC of June 24, 1988 for the implementation of Article 67 of the Treaty.

[203] Ibid.

[204] See, for example, to that effect, in particular, *Commission* v. *France*, para 41; Case C-174/04 *Commission* v. *Italy* [2005] ECR I-4933, paras 30 and 31; and Case C-265/04 *Bouanich* [2006] ECR I-923, paras. 34 and 35.

other direct barriers alone, the Treaty establishes the legal basis for the harmonization of national laws through the adoption of common European laws and regulations. All EU laws and regulations relating to prospectuses, investment services, listings of securities, market abuse, reporting and transparency obligations, accounting standards, and other areas relating to securities and capital markets are based on a Treaty provision that empowers the European Union to act.

For the most part, the legislative measures adopted by the European Union in the field of securities regulation are based on those Treaty provisions that allow the institutions of the European Union to adopt such measures as would be necessary to achieve the liberalization of a specific service or sector[205] or those Treaty provisions that allow the European Union to adopt directives or regulations for the approximation of laws, regulations, or administrative actions in the member states which have as their objective the establishment and the functioning of the internal market.[206]

3 The EU Directive on Takeover Bids

The closest equivalent to the Williams Act in the European Union is the Directive on Takeover Bids.[207] Adopted in 2004, this Directive required EU countries to adopt such national laws, regulations, and other measures as would be necessary to give effect, implement, or comply with the provisions of the Directive no later than May 20, 2006.

The Directive on Takeover Bids was a significant legislative initiative towards the creation of a single European capital market and the protection of investors. It was based on the belief that it was necessary to coordinate and harmonize certain regulatory safeguards which individual member states required of companies with securities listed on securities exchanges in connection with takeover bids or changes of control with a view to making such regulatory safeguards equivalent throughout the European Union and protecting the interests of the holders of the relevant securities.[208] It was also considered necessary to create clarity and

[205] See Treaty, Article 50 (*ex* Article 44 TEC): "In order to attain freedom of establishment as regards a particular activity, the European Parliament and the Council, acting in accordance with the ordinary legislative procedure and after consulting the Economic and Social Committee, shall act by means of directives." See also Treaty, Article 59: "In order to achieve the liberalisation of a specific service, the European Parliament and the Council, acting in accordance with the ordinary legislative procedure and after consulting the Economic and Social Committee, shall issue directives."

[206] See Treaty, Articles 114 and 115.

[207] See fn 190 above.

[208] See Directive on Takeover Bids, Recitals 1 and 2.

transparency throughout the European Union in respect of legal issues to be settled in the event of takeover bids and to prevent patterns of corporate restructuring within the European Union from being distorted by arbitrary differences in governance and management cultures.[209]

The degree to which the national implementation of the Directive on Takeover Bids has changed the law and market practice in each of the member states of the European Union varies considerably. For example, in the United Kingdom, the overall impact on the law and practice has not been particularly significant. Other countries that had previously lacked a comprehensive system of regulation of takeover bids and changes of corporate control have seen more significant legal and practical changes.

3.1 Scope of application and main provisions

The Directive on Takeover Bids establishes regulatory standards relating to takeover bids for the securities of companies governed by the laws of member states, where all or some of those securities are admitted to trading on a regulated securities market in one or more member states. *Takeover bid* means a public offer (other than by the offeree company itself) made to the holders of the securities of a company to acquire all or some of those securities, whether mandatory or voluntary, which follows or has as its objective the acquisition of control of the offeree in accordance with the relevant national laws. The *offeree company* is the company, the securities of which are the subject of a takeover bid and the *offeror* is any natural or legal person making a takeover bid. The term "securities" means transferable securities carrying voting rights in a company.

It is therefore clear that the Directive on Takeover Bids does not apply to offers to purchase debt securities or any other securities that do not carry voting rights. The Directive on Takeover Bids is also not applicable to offers to purchase debt or equity securities made by the issuer of those securities.

One of the principles underlying the regulatory standards introduced by the Directive on Takeover Bids is the protection of holders of securities, particularly those with minority holdings, when control of their companies has been acquired. The member states should ensure such protection by obligating the person who has acquired control of a company to make an offer to all the holders of that company's securities for all their holdings at an equitable price in accordance with a common definition. To reduce the scope for insider dealing, an offeror should be required to

[209] Ibid, Recital 3.

announce his or her decision to launch a bid as soon as possible and to inform the supervisory authority promptly.[210] The holders of securities should be properly informed of the terms of the bid by means of an offer document, and appropriate information should also be given to the representatives of the company's employees or to the employees directly.[211]

To promote these regulatory and investor protection objectives, the Directive on Takeover Bids establishes certain general principles[212] that must be implemented by all member states of the European Union through appropriate legislative, regulatory, and other measures:

- all holders of the securities of an offeree company of the same class must be afforded equivalent treatment; moreover, if a person acquires control of a company, the other holders of securities must be protected;
- target security holders should be given sufficient time and information to enable them to reach a properly informed decision on a bid and the target board of directors should give its opinion on the effects of the bid on employment and the locations of business;
- the target board of directors must act in the interests of the company as a whole and must not deny the holders of securities the opportunity to decide on the merits of the bid;
- false markets must not be created in the securities of the offeree company, of the offeror company, or of any other company concerned in the bid in such a way that the rise or fall of the prices of the securities becomes artificial and the normal functioning of the markets is distorted;
- an offeror must announce a bid only after ensuring that he or she can fulfill in full any cash consideration, if such is offered, and after taking all reasonable measures to secure the implementation of any other type of consideration; and
- an offeree company must not be hindered in the conduct of its affairs for longer than is reasonable by a bid for its securities.

Under the Directive on Takeover Bids, member states of the European Union are required to designate an authority to supervise bids which can be a public or private body. The Directive on Takeover Bids requires member states to implement a mandatory bid requirement for the acquisition of shares above a certain threshold, at an equitable price. The threshold at which a bid must be made is left for member states to determine.

[210] Ibid., Recitals 12–13. [211] Ibid. [212] Ibid., Article 3.

The Directive further requires member states to enact provisions enabling a bidder to squeeze out minority shareholders at a fair price once it has obtained a percentage threshold (between 90 and 95 percent, at the discretion of the member states) of the target's voting share capital and to provide minority shareholders with a reciprocal right upon a bidder's shareholding reaching such threshold. The Directive on Takeover Bids also contains a number of other provisions, common in regulatory frameworks regulating the change of corporate control, including provisions relating to frustrating actions and "breakthrough" provisions, publication of offer document, fair price considerations, the time allowed for acceptance, the legal obligations of the board of directors, the lapsing and revision of bids, irrevocability, and the disclosure of results.

3.2 Impact of Directive on Takeover Bids

The Directive on Takeover Bids has led to a significant degree of legal harmonization of the law, corporate practice of takeover bids, and changes of corporate control across the member states of the European Union. Nevertheless, its impact varies considerably between member states. For example, its implementation has triggered few changes of law and practice in the United Kingdom but led to a substantial revision of the relevant law in other countries (e.g., Greece, Spain, and Portugal) without a historical tradition of regulating tender offers.

In relation to the law of liability management transactions (debt tender offers, exchange offers, debt repurchases, or debt buybacks), the Directive on Takeover Bids has not followed the example of the Williams Act or introduced any general anti-fraud provision that would be applicable to offers of all types of securities. The Directive on Takeover Bids applies only to equity securities with voting rights and, consequently, it has not had any direct impact on the law of tender offers and liability management transactions. Indirectly, the Directive on Takeover Bids established certain general principles relating to public offers for the purchase of securities that are rules against market abuse of universal application and applicable, through the rules governing market abuse, to all types of offers for the purchase or exchange of securities (including debt securities). Finally, the Directive does not provide any regulatory framework for the procedural and substantive aspects of tender offers, such as a mandatory length for an offer period, conditions attached to a tender offer, a best-price rule, a pro rata rule, competing bids, and other important areas that remain with the legislative competence of member states. As a result, the procedural and substantive requirements for tender offers continue to be diverse throughout the European Union.

4 The EU Directive on Insider Dealing and Market Manipulation

The EU Directive on Insider Dealing and Market Manipulation[213] was considered a necessary measure towards the establishment of an integrated European securities regulatory framework. The then existing European legal framework to protect investors and the markets against insider dealing and market manipulation was considered to be incomplete. Legal requirements varied from one member state to another, leaving market participants often uncertain over concepts, definitions, and enforcement. In some member states there was no legislation addressing the issues of price manipulation and the dissemination of misleading information to investors. In addition, new financial and technical developments had enhanced the incentives, means, and opportunities for market abuse through new products, new technologies, increasing cross-border activities, and the Internet.

The Market Abuse Directive was formally introduced in December 2002. It aims to ensure the integrity of community financial markets and to enhance investor confidence in those markets. It provides an EU-wide prohibition on insider dealing and market manipulation, and prohibits selective disclosure. Furthermore, it upgrades the legal framework for the disclosure of inside information by insiders of financial instruments and establishes certain other regulatory requirements in relation to conflicts of interest, the execution of share buyback programs, and the carrying out of stabilization activities.

The Market Abuse Directive aims to prevent and punish a range of different types of conduct, such as entering into, recommending, or inducing transactions involving financial instruments on the basis of inside information, unduly disclosing inside information to third parties (tipping), or manipulating the market through the dissemination of false information or various types of fraudulent, manipulative, or abusive transactions. The Directive uses two main regulatory tools: sanctions for those engaging in insider trading and other prohibited activities; and preventive or prophylactic rules limiting the risk that prohibited activities are likely to

[213] Directive 2003/6/EC of the European Parliament and of the Council of January 28, 2003 on insider dealing and market manipulation (market abuse), OJ L 96, 12.4.2003 (the "Market Abuse Directive"), pp. 16–25.

occur (such as the duty of issuers of listed financial instruments to publicly disclose any inside information promptly through adequate means of dissemination to the market).

4.1 *Insider dealing*

The combined effect of Articles 2, 3, and 4 of the Market Abuse Directive is to prohibit three types of activities:

- any *primary insider*[214] or any *secondary insider*[215] acquiring or disposing or attempting to acquire or dispose of *financial instruments*[216] on the basis of *inside information*;[217]

[214] A *primary insider* is any person who possesses the relevant information: (i) by virtue of his or her membership of the administrative, management, or supervisory bodies of the issuer; (ii) by virtue of his or her holding in the capital of the issuer; (iii) by virtue of his or her having access to the information through the exercise of his or her employment, profession, or duties; (iv) by virtue of his or her criminal activities. Where the relevant person is a legal person, the prohibition laid down in that paragraph shall also apply to the natural persons who take part in the decision to carry out the transaction for the account of the legal person concerned.

[215] A *secondary insider* (or *tipee*) is any person, other than a primary insider, who possesses inside information while that person knows, or ought to have known, that it is inside information. According to Recital 18 of the Market Abuse Directive, competent authorities should consider what a normal and reasonable person would know or should have known in the circumstances. Moreover, the mere fact that market-makers, bodies authorized to act as counterparties, or persons authorized to execute orders on behalf of third parties with inside information confine themselves, in the first two cases, to pursuing their legitimate business of buying or selling financial instruments or, in the last case, to carrying out an order dutifully, should not in itself be deemed to constitute the use of such inside information.

[216] For purposes of the Market Abuse Directive, "financial instrument" shall mean: (i) *transferable securities* as defined in Council Directive 93/22/EEC of May 10, 1993 on investment services in the securities field; (ii) units in collective investment undertakings; (iii) money-market instruments; (iv) financial-futures contracts, including equivalent cash-settled instruments; (v) forward interest rate agreements; (vi) interest rate, currency, and equity swaps; (vii) options to acquire or dispose of any instrument falling into these categories, including equivalent cash-settled instruments; this category includes, in particular, options on currency and on interest rates; (viii) derivatives on commodities; and (ix) any other instrument admitted to trading on a regulated market in a member state or for which a request for admission to trading on such a market has been made.

[217] For purposes of the Market Abuse Directive, "inside information" shall mean information of a precise nature which has not been made public, relating, directly or indirectly, to one or more issuers of financial instruments or to one or more financial instruments and which, if it were made public, would be likely to have a significant effect on the price of those financial instruments or on the price of related derivative financial instruments. In relation to derivatives on commodities, "inside information" shall mean information of

- any primary insider or secondary insider disclosing inside information to any other person unless such disclosure is made in the normal course of the exercise of his or her employment, profession, or duties; and
- any primary insider or secondary insider recommending or inducing another person, on the basis of inside information, to acquire or dispose of financial instruments to which that information relates.

For purposes of the prohibitions introduced by the Market Abuse Directive, "inside information" means (i) information of a precise nature, (ii) which has not been made public, (iii) relating, directly or indirectly, to one or more issuers of financial instruments or to one or more financial instruments, and (iv) which, if it were made public, would be likely to have a significant effect on the price of those financial instruments or on the price of related derivative financial instruments. We will examine each element of the definition below.

Non-public information. The Market Abuse Directive does not contain a precise definition of what is non-public information. It is generally accepted that information that has been disclosed to the public is no longer non-public information.[218] Other information based on publicly available information, including research, projections, and analysis, should also not be regarded as non-public information.

Information relating, directly or indirectly, to the issuer or one or more financial instruments. Information relating to the issuer of a security or to one or more series of securities includes information on the operations and financial results of the issuer, recent developments, the composition of the board of directors or of the shareholders, corporate policy, dividend policy, litigation, potential mergers or acquisitions, the development of new technologies, and other facts and developments relating to operations, financial profiles, corporate structure, or personnel.[219] Information

a precise nature which has not been made public, relating, directly or indirectly, to one or more such derivatives and which users of markets on which such derivatives are traded would expect to receive in accordance with accepted market practices on those markets. For persons charged with the execution of orders concerning financial instruments, "inside information" shall also mean information conveyed by a client and related to the client's pending orders, which is of a precise nature, which relates directly or indirectly to one or more issuers of financial instruments or to one or more financial instruments, and which, if it were made public, would be likely to have a significant effect on the price of those financial instruments or on the price of related derivative financial instruments.

[218] See Emilios Avgouleas, *The Mechanics and Regulation of Market Abuse, A Legal and Economic Analysis* (Oxford University Press, 2005), pp. 255–6.

[219] For these purposes, examples of information that directly concerns the issuer include: changes in control and control agreements; changes in management and supervisory

that directly relates to one or more series of securities includes decisions regarding the status and marketability of the financial instruments of an issuer, decisions and information relating to purchases, offers to purchase, repurchases, redemptions, or repayments of securities, which directly affect relevant financial instruments.

Information which indirectly relates to the issuer or the issuer's securities is very difficult to identify. The Market Abuse Directive states that information that could have a significant effect on the evolution and formation of the prices of a regulated market as such could be considered as information that indirectly relates to one or more issuers of financial instruments or to one or more related derivative financial instruments.[220] CESR (now defunct and replaced by the European Securities and Markets Authority) offered an indicative and non-binding list of information items that would usually only concern the issuer indirectly, including data and statistics, rating agencies' reports, research, recommendations or suggestions concerning the value of listed financial instruments, central bank decisions concerning interest rates, a government's decision concerning taxation, industry regulation, debt management and similar matters, decisions concerning changes in the governance rules of market indices, and especially regarding their composition, regulated and unregulated

boards; changes in auditors or any other information related to the auditors' activity; operations involving the capital or the issuance of debt securities or warrants to buy or subscribe for securities; decisions to increase or decrease the share capital; mergers, splits, and spin-offs; purchase or disposal of equity interests or other major assets or branches of corporate activity; restructurings or reorganizations that have an effect on the issuer's assets and liabilities, financial position, or profits and losses; decisions concerning buyback programs or transactions in other listed financial instruments; changes in the class rights of the issuer's own listed shares; filing of petitions in bankruptcy or the issuing of orders for bankruptcy proceedings; significant legal disputes; the revocation or cancellation of credit lines by one or more banks; the dissolution or verification of a cause of dissolution; relevant changes in the assets' value; insolvency of relevant debtors; reduction of real properties' values; the physical destruction of uninsured goods; new licenses, patents, registered trademarks; decrease or increase in the value of financial instruments in a portfolio; decrease in value of patents rights, or intangible assets due to market innovation; receiving an acquisition's bids for relevant assets; innovative products or processes; serious product liability or environmental damages cases; changes in expected earnings or losses; relevant orders received from customers, their cancellation, or important changes; withdrawal from or entering into new core business areas; relevant changes in the investment policy of the issuer; the ex-dividend date, the dividend payment date, and the amount of the dividend; and changes in dividend policy payments. See generally Committee of European Securities Regulators ("CESR"), *Advice on Level 2 Implementing Measures for the Proposed Market Abuse Directive*, December 2002, p. 15, available at www.esma.europa.eu/system/files/02_089d.pdf. Accessed June 11, 2013.

[220] See the Market Abuse Directive, Recital 16.

markets' decisions concerning rules governing the markets, competition and market authorities' decisions concerning listed companies, relevant orders by government bodies, regional or local authorities, or other public organizations, relevant orders to trade financial instruments, a change in trading mode (e.g., information relating to knowledge that an issuer's financial instruments will be traded in another market segment, such as changing from continuous trading to auction trading), or a change of market-maker or dealing conditions.[221]

Information of a precise nature. Information shall be deemed to be of a precise nature if the following conditions are met: (i) it indicates a set of circumstances which exists or may reasonably be expected to come into existence, or an event which has occurred or may reasonably be expected to occur; and (ii) it is specific enough to enable a conclusion to be drawn as to the possible effect of that set of circumstances or event on the prices of financial instruments or related derivative financial instruments.[222] In deciding whether a piece of information is precise, the following factors are to be taken into consideration: first, the underlying matter or event to which the information refers is true or could reasonably be expected to become true in the future; and, second, the information is specific enough to allow a conclusion to be drawn about its impact on the prices of securities.[223] A "set of circumstances which exists or may reasonably be expected to come into existence or an event which has occurred or may reasonably be expected to do so" refers to future circumstances or events from which it appears, on the basis of an overall assessment of the factors existing at the relevant time, that there is a realistic prospect that they will come into existence or occur. However, that notion should not be interpreted as meaning that the magnitude of the effect of that set of circumstances or that event on the prices of the financial instruments concerned must be taken into consideration.[224]

A matter or an event is true when it is based on firm and objective evidence, which can be communicated accurately (as opposed to rumors),

[221] See *Advice on Level 2 Implementing Measures for the Proposed Market Abuse Directive*, p. 17, fn 220 above.

[222] See Commission Directive 2003/124/EC of December 22, 2003 implementing Directive 2003/6/EC of the European Parliament and of the Council regarding the definition and public disclosure of inside information and the definition of "market manipulation," Article 1(1), OJ L 339, 24.12.2003, pp. 70–2 (the "Directive on Public Disclosure").

[223] See *Advice on Level 2 Implementing Measures for the Proposed Market Abuse Directive*, p. 10, fn 220 above.

[224] See European Court of Justice, *Geltl* v. *Daimler AG* (C-19/11) [2012] C.M.L.R. 32, para. 56.

i.e., if it can be proven to have happened or to exist. If the information derives from a stage process, every fact to do with the process, as well as the totality of the process itself, is precise information and therefore could be inside information, unless it consists only of rumors. The matter or event referred to could become true in the future: contingencies relating to the actual occurrence of the referred-to matter or event do not mitigate the precise nature of the information. For instance, the fact that an expected merger does not occur at the end of a negotiation process, does not preclude the classification of such negotiations as precise information.

A piece of information allows a conclusion to be drawn about its impact on prices, either when it would enable a reasonable investor to make an investment decision without (or at very low) risk or when it is likely to be exploited immediately in the market. Moreover, a piece of information that comprehends more than one matter or event and some of them are not precise, could be considered precise as far as it concerns precise matters or events. For instance, a takeover bid can be considered to be precise information and constitute inside information even though the bidder has not yet decided the price of the bid. A piece of information could be considered precise even if it refers to matters or events that could be alternatives. For instance, the matter or event that concerns a takeover bid on one of two companies can be considered precise information and therefore could be inside information. An investor could abuse this information by trading in shares of the two companies.[225]

In the case of a process that is intended, over the course of a number of intermediate steps, to bring about a particular set of circumstances or to give rise to a particular event (a "protracted process"), even information concerning facts – current or past – which relate to the intermediate steps and which are connected to bringing about the future set of circumstances or future event may be regarded as precise information and, accordingly, as inside information, provided that all the other preconditions laid down in those directives are also satisfied.[226]

Price-sensitive information. Inside information is price sensitive information. Price-sensitive information is information which, if it were made public, would be likely to have a significant effect on the prices of those financial instruments or on the price of related derivative financial instruments. In other words, information is price sensitive if a reasonable

[225] Directive on Public Disclosure, fn 223 above.

[226] See European Court of Justice, *Geltl* v. *Daimler AG* (C-19/11) [2012] C.M.L.R. 32, paras. 38–40.

investor would be likely to use it as part of the basis of his or her investment decisions.[227]

In its guidance to the markets, CESR pointed out that market participants have to be able to assess beforehand whether the information is price sensitive, in order to be able to act accordingly, regarding the duties of confidentiality, prompt disclosure, and the prohibition on entering into transactions.[228] In practice, this means that the assessment of whether or not the information is price sensitive has to consider the foreseeable market impact of the relevant information at the moment when the information has not yet been disclosed and the market impact is not yet measurable. This is obviously a difficult *ex-ante* analysis, i.e., an analysis of the likely impact of a set of facts before the relevant facts become publicly available and capable of affecting market decisions.[229] In order to perform this *ex-ante* analysis, any (relevant) information available at the time has to be taken into account. A piece of information could be considered as likely to have a significant effect on prices of financial instruments even though, when the piece of information is published, it would not actually produce any effect.[230] Mere possibility is not enough; the assessment requires a reasonable expectation that the effect on the price caused by the relevant information would be probable. On the other hand, a degree of probability close to certainty is not required either.[231]

Regarding the various factors to be taken into account, fixed thresholds of price movements or quantitative criteria alone are not a suitable means of determining the significance of a price movement.[232] It is also difficult to differentiate according to markets, market segments, or different types of securities (bonds, securities, or derivatives). In considering whether the effect on the price of financial instruments, or on the price of related derivative financial instruments, is likely to occur, all market variables that affect the financial instrument in question should be taken into account. These variables would include prices, returns, volatilities, liquidity, price relationships among financial instruments, volume, supply, demand, order books, the timing of pricing and news' disclosures, rules governing the exchange and market microstructure, and others.[233] Given that this is an *ex-ante* test, it is unsurprisingly irrelevant whether or

[227] See the Directive on Public Disclosure, Article 1(2).

[228] See *Advice on Level 2 Implementing Measures for the Proposed Market Abuse Directive*, p. 9, fn 220 above.

[229] Ibid. [230] Ibid. [231] Ibid. [232] Ibid. [233] Ibid.

to what extent the price actually changes when the information eventually becomes publicly known. This does not preclude the fact that the actual impact on prices might be relevant as an indicator for the investigation of a possible infraction.[234]

Regarding the information's likelihood of having a significant influence on prices, CESR suggested that a piece of information would be likely to have a significant effect on the price of a financial instrument when it is information that a reasonable investor in the given circumstances would be likely to take into account for his or her investment decision.[235] This assessment should take into consideration the following factors:

- the anticipated magnitude of the referred matter or event in light of the totality of the *company's activity*;
- the relevance of the information regarding the main determinants of the *financial instrument's price*;
- the reliability of the source; and
- all market variables that affect the financial instrument in question.[236]

Subsequent information may be used to check the presumption that the *ex-ante* information was price sensitive, but should not be used to take action against someone who drew reasonable conclusions from *ex-ante* information available to him or her.[237] In determining whether the information is likely to have a significant effect on prices in light of the factors stated above, there are some useful indicators that should be taken into consideration: (i) the type of information is the same as information which has, in the past, had a significant effect on prices; (ii) preexisting analyst's research reports and opinions indicate that the type of information in question is price sensitive; and (iii) the issuer itself has already treated similar events as inside information.

Exemptions and defenses. The stabilization of financial instruments or trading by an issuer in its own shares in connection with a buyback program can be legitimate activities in certain circumstances and are not, *ipso facto*, regarded as market manipulation or insider dealing if conducted in accordance with the legal requirements set forth in the Market Abuse Directive.[238] In addition, the general prohibitions on insider dealing do not apply to any transactions conducted in the discharge when due of an obligation to acquire or dispose of financial instruments where that obligation results from an agreement concluded before the person concerned

[234] Ibid. [235] Ibid. [236] Ibid. [237] Ibid., Recital 2.
[238] Ibid., Article 8 and Recital 33.

possessed inside information.[239] Moreover, the mere fact that market-makers, bodies authorized to act as counterparties, or persons authorized to execute orders on behalf of third parties with inside information confine themselves, in the first two cases, to pursuing their legitimate business, or buying or selling financial instruments or, in the last case, to carrying out an order dutifully, should not in itself be deemed to constitute use of such inside information.[240] In addition, having access to inside information relating to another company and using it in the context of a public takeover bid for the purpose of gaining control of that company or proposing a merger with that company should not in itself be deemed to constitute insider dealing.[241]

4.2 Market manipulation

Like insider dealing, *market manipulation* is a species of market abuse that the Market Abuse Directive and the implementing national legislation are seeking to eradicate. Laconically, the Market Abuse Directive provides that "member states shall prohibit any person from engaging in market manipulation."[242]

The Market Abuse Directive defines three types of market manipulation, each being sufficient to create a prohibited offense: (i) transactions or orders to trade: (a) which give, or are likely to give, false or misleading signals as to the supply of, demand for, or the price of financial instruments, or (b) which secure, by a person, or persons acting in collaboration, the price of one or several financial instruments at an abnormal or artificial level, unless in each case (a) and (b) the person who entered into the transactions or issued the orders to trade establishes that his or her reasons for so doing are legitimate and that these transactions or orders to trade conform to accepted market practices in the regulated market concerned; (ii) transactions or orders to trade that employ fictitious devices or any other form of deception or contrivance; and (iii) the dissemination of information through the media (including the Internet), or by any other means, which gives or is likely to give, false or misleading signals as to financial instruments, including the dissemination of rumors and false or misleading news, where the person who made the dissemination knew, or ought to have known, that the information was false or misleading.[243]

The Market Abuse Directive expressly provides that the definitions of "market manipulation" shall be adapted so as to insure that new patterns

[239] Ibid., Article 2(3). [240] Ibid., Recital 18. [241] Ibid.

[242] See the Market Abuse Directive, Article 5.

[243] See the Market Abuse Directive, Article 1(2).

of activity that in practice constitute market manipulations can be included. An indicative, non-exhaustive, list of manipulative practices, all derived from the core definition set forth above, is also offered in Article 1(2) of the Market Abuse Directive: (i) conduct by a person, or persons acting in collaboration, to secure a dominant position over the supply of or demand for a financial instrument which has the effect of fixing, directly or indirectly, purchase or sale prices or creating other unfair trading conditions; (ii) the buying or selling of financial instruments at the close of the market with the effect of misleading investors acting on the basis of closing prices; and (iii) taking advantage of occasional or regular access to the traditional or electronic media by voicing an opinion about a financial instrument (or indirectly about its issuer) while having previously taken positions on that financial instrument and profiting subsequently from the impact of the opinions voiced on the price of that instrument, without having simultaneously disclosed that conflict of interest to the public in a proper and effective way.[244] Therefore, the Market Abuse Directive prohibits price manipulations or misleading trades; artificial transactions and "wash sales"; and information-based manipulations effected through the dissemination of false and misleading information.

The Directive on the Public Disclosure of Inside Information[245] describes a number of facts and circumstances that should be treated by public authorities and enforcement agencies as potential signs of market manipulation. The non-exhaustive signals, which should not necessarily be deemed in and of themselves to constitute market manipulation, are as follows:

- the extent to which orders to trade given or transactions undertaken represent a significant proportion of the daily volume of transactions in the relevant financial instrument on the regulated market concerned, particularly when these activities lead to a significant change in the price of the financial instrument;
- the extent to which orders to trade given or transactions undertaken by persons with a significant buying or selling position in a financial instrument lead to significant changes in the price of the financial instrument or related derivative or underlying asset admitted to trading on a regulated market;

[244] See generally Emilios Avgouleas, "A Critical Evaluation of the New EC Financial-Market Regulations: Peaks, Troughs, and the Road Ahead," 18 *Transnational Lawyer* 179 (2004–2005), at 206–7.

[245] See the Directive on Public Disclosure, fn 223 above.

- whether transactions undertaken lead to no change in beneficial ownership of a financial instrument admitted to trading on a regulated market;
- the extent to which orders to trade given or transactions undertaken include position reversals in a short period of time and represent a significant proportion of the daily volume of transactions in the relevant financial instrument on the regulated market concerned, and might be associated with significant changes in the price of a financial instrument admitted to trading on a regulated market;
- the extent to which orders to trade given or transactions undertaken are concentrated within a short time span in the trading session and lead to a price change which is subsequently reversed;
- the extent to which orders to trade given change the representation of the best bid offer prices in a financial instrument admitted to trading on a regulated market, or more generally the representation of the order book available to market participants, and are removed before they are executed; and
- the extent to which orders to trade are given or transactions are undertaken at or around a specific time when reference prices, settlement prices, and valuations are calculated and lead to price changes which have an effect on such prices and valuations.[246]

In the same vein, the Directive on the Public Disclosure sets forth a non-exhaustive list of manipulative practices that should be considered, not necessarily in themselves but together with other transactions or orders to trade, as potential signals of the employment of fictitious devices or any other form of deception or contrivance: (i) whether orders to trade given or transactions undertaken by persons are preceded or followed by the dissemination of false or misleading information by the same persons or persons linked to them; and (ii) whether orders to trade are given or transactions are undertaken by persons before or after the same persons or persons linked to them produce or disseminate research or investment recommendations that are erroneous, biased, or demonstrably influenced by material interest.[247]

4.3 Forms and techniques of market manipulation in liability management transactions

In regulating market manipulation, the law aims to prohibit, to the fullest extent possible, the full range of activities, actions, devices, or schemes

[246] Ibid. [247] Ibid.

that might be used to manipulate securities prices in the sale and purchase of securities. The legislative intent of a broadly defined regulatory offense can be observed in the available definitions of "market manipulation" under the securities laws in the United States and the European Union.

In *Santa Fe Industries*,[248] for example, the US Supreme Court held that the boundaries of market manipulation remained intentionally undefined, reflecting Congress's intention to prohibit the full range of ingenious devices that might be used to manipulate securities prices. Similarly, in the antitrust context, the US Supreme Court held that market manipulation in its various manifestations is implicitly an artificial stimulus applied to (or at times a brake on) market prices, a force which distorts those prices, a factor that prevents the determination of those prices by free competition alone.[249] In *Cargill, Inc.* v. *Hardin*,[250] a seminal manipulation case, the US Court of Appeals (eighth) accepted that manipulative conduct and the methods and techniques of manipulation were limited "only by the ingenuity of man" and defined "manipulation" as any intentional conduct resulting in a price that does not reflect basic forces of supply and demand.[251] As a result, the US regulatory regime prohibits manipulative activities in the sale or purchase of securities through *general clauses* prohibiting any *manipulative* or *deceptive* actions, directly or indirectly, in connection with the sale or purchase of any security, without prescribing in any indicative or exhaustive manner a list of specific activities or actions that would be considered manipulative or deceptive.[252] In the European Union, the Market Abuse Directive similarly defines "market manipulation" in very broad terms,[253] and the same approach is followed in the United Kingdom by the regulatory framework against market abuse established under the Financial Services and Markets Act 2000 (the "FSMA").[254] While the applicable regulatory framework has not provided a rigid definition of "market manipulation" for the reasons stated above, it is equally true that market manipulation as a criminal or regulatory offense requires two essential elements: price artificiality and intentional conduct. The result of any successful manipulation, regardless

248 430 U.S. 462 (97 S. Ct. 1292, 51 L. Ed. 2d 480).

249 *United States* v. *Socony-Vacuum Oil Co.*, 310 U.S. 150, 223, 60 S. Ct. 811, 844 (1940).

250 *Cargill, Inc.* v. *Hardin*, 452 F.2d 1154 (C.A. 8, 1971).

251 Ibid., at 1163.

252 Section 10(b) of the Securities Exchange Act; Section 15(c)(1) of the Securities Exchange Act; Rule 10b-5 under the Securities Exchange Act.

253 See above section 4.2.

254 See section 5.2 below for a full description of the definition of "market abuse" and fact patterns under the FSMA and the Financial Services Authority Handbook of Rules and Guidance (the "FSA Handbook").

of the method or technique used, is the *intentional* creation of an artificial price.

In relation to the methods and techniques of market manipulation in securities transactions, the view of the US Court of Appeals in *Cargill, Inc.* v. *Hardin*[255] that the manipulative techniques and devices are limited only by the "ingenuity of man" is not very far from the truth. The judicial, regulatory, and enforcement history of violations of the securities laws reveal an extraordinary range of actions, devices, schemes, omissions, deceptions, and fraudulent activities, all of which were intentionally designed by manipulators to cause artificial effects in connection with the purchase or sale of securities or induce the purchase or sale of securities. The techniques or methods of market manipulation can be broadly classified into the following broad categories: (i) misrepresentations and/or false rumors; (ii) artificial transactions; (iii) purchases or sales of securities with manipulative intent; (iv) contract-based manipulations; and (v) abuses of market power.

Misrepresentations and/or false rumors. The most basic form of market manipulation is the distribution, dissemination, or publication of false information or false statements in connection with a security (or the issuer of a security) or generally false information or rumors in relation to economic or political affairs in general. Manipulators often publish, disseminate, or distribute false information or rumors in order to increase or decrease the price of a security and, as a result, profit from a transaction in that security. In relation to liability management transactions, for example, any false statement or rumor that would likely have the effect of decreasing the market price of a tender security or a security that may be the subject of a purchase program in the open market could be considered manipulative conduct. Even more deceptive are false statements and/or false rumors disseminated by insiders who are perceived by the market as holding superior information. There is little doubt, if any, that manipulative behavior through the dissemination of false statements and/or false rumors such as deliberate misreporting by insiders or the deliberate inclusion of misleading statements in an offering document constitute obvious instances of fraud, and in that respect manipulation is a type of securities fraud.

Artificial transactions. Artificial transactions are fictitious transactions. The most common form of an artificial or fictitious transaction is the so-called "wash sale," in which the same person initiates both a "buy"

[255] See fn 251 above.

and a "sell" order for the same security at the same price, producing a recorded transaction in the market when in fact there is no change in the beneficial ownership of the relevant security. Another form of an artificial or fictitious transaction is the *matched order*, in which an order for the purchase or sale of a security is made with the knowledge that an order or orders for the sale or purchase of securities, respectively, substantially of the same size, at substantially the same time, and at substantially the same price is made by or for the same or different parties.[256] Artificial transactions convey false information to the market about the state of supply and demand for a particular security by creating an impression that there is market interest or market activity in a specific security when, actually, there is nothing of the sort. In the case of artificial transactions, the dissemination of misleading information is the product of the sales and/or purchases of the securities themselves, not the product of false statements or rumors. Market manipulation through artificial transactions is prohibited by the Market Abuse Directive and the Securities Exchange Act[257] and treated as fraud at common law.[258] In connection with tender offers, this particular form of market manipulation can be observed in the event of an announcement of the commencement of an *illusory* tender offer, i.e., a tender offer that the offeror does not intend to complete, which may be followed by sales of tender securities by the offeror. Since the announcement of the commencement of the tender offer usually increases the market price of the tender securities, there is potential for abusive behavior if the offeror takes advantage of the increased market prices to effect sales in the relevant securities following the announcement of the commencement of the tender offer.

Purchases or sales of securities with manipulative intent. The purchase or sale of securities by any person, creating actual or apparent active trading in such security, or raising or depressing the price of such security, for the purpose of inducing the purchase or sale of such security by others is one of the most aggressive forms of market manipulation in the securities markets. The technique is simple: by buying and selling securities, manipulators purport to increase or decrease securities prices through purchases or sales. Sales and purchases of securities can affect such securities' market price, either because the transactions themselves are seen as carriers of new information or because markets present asymmetries between supply and demand for a particular security. Investors are affected by

[256] See, for example, Section 9 of the Securities Exchange Act. [257] Ibid.

[258] See, for example, *Scott* v. *Brown, Doering, McNab & Co* [1892] 2 QB 724.

the content of such information conveyed through the announcement of transactions in a number of ways that have been the topic of intense research and academic dialog over the years.[259] The most successful trade-based manipulations involve *pumping and dumping* techniques in which the securities are initially purchased to create the appearance of market demand, thus increasing prices, and then sold at inflated prices.

In relation to debt securities, any repurchases of debt securities by the issuer of such securities or an affiliate of the issuer in the open market or in privately negotiated transactions (*bond buybacks*) may provide a positive signal to the market that the debt securities in question are undervalued. They may also lead to pricing inefficiencies, especially if they precede other corporate actions (including a liability management transaction). In addition, the knowledge of a pending bond buyback program, which has not yet been publicly announced, is highly valuable inside information that may be used for financial gain.[260]

[259] See, for example, Steve Thel, "The Mechanics of Market Manipulation," 79 *Cornell Law Review* 219 (1994), pp. 237–9.

[260] The repurchase of equity securities by the issuer of such securities is subject to strict disclosure obligations and trading restrictions due to its potential for manipulative effects. See Commission Regulation (EC) No 2273/2003 of December 22, 2003 implementing Directive 2003/6/EC of the European Parliament and of the Council regarding exemptions for buyback programs and the stabilization of financial instruments. Although the conditions are not applicable to debt securities, consideration should be given to applying the provisions by analogy in connection with repurchases of debt securities. In relation to debt securities, issuers should also take into account the recommendations of good market practice issued in 2001 by the International Capital Market Association (the "ICMA"). The ICMA recognizes that although issuers' buyback policies necessarily differ, it would help to create a more efficient market, and increase transparency for investors, if issuers that intend to buy back their own debt securities were to disclose their respective buyback policies clearly in public (e.g., on their websites, or by press release). In setting forth their buyback policies, it is recommended that issuers should: disclose their overall policy on buying back their own debt (e.g., whether this is on a case-by-case basis or they follow predefined patterns or objectives such as the provision of a particular liquidity to investors); disclose their specific policy on buying back private placements (e.g., whether they are willing to buy back up to 100 percent of the issue outstanding); disclose their specific policy on buying back public issues; disclose, as a result of buybacks, holdings that are material in an appropriate manner that is consistent with relevant regulations for preventing market abuse; disclose, through appropriate channels, whether public debt that has been bought back has been redeemed or cancelled; and/or whether it may be held so as to be made available for resale in the market. When issuers implement the buyback policies they have disclosed by undertaking buybacks, it is recognized that they may choose not to announce the buybacks they have undertaken until after a date set by each issuer to the extent permitted by the relevant regulations for preventing market abuse. In relation to the threshold of materiality, the ICMA points out that while there is no universal definition of "materiality" in terms of an exact percentage threshold, for the

Contract-based manipulations. Contract-based manipulations are transactions in which the trader's profit results from his or her ability to trigger a contractual right or benefit by trading in circumstances in which the gains from triggering the contractual right could outweigh the losses incurred by the alleged manipulator at the time of the contract. These transactions aim to influence the value of financial contracts or commercial deals, the outcome or profitability of which depends on reported market prices on some underlying security, by affecting the market prices of the relevant security.

Market power manipulations. This form of market manipulation involves conduct by a person to secure a dominant position over the supply of or demand for a security which has the effect of fixing, directly or indirectly, purchase or sale prices or creating other unfair trading conditions. The possession of market power is not manipulative per se. The determining factor is whether the manipulator exercises his or her control to dictate the price of a security. If a person has control or dominant position in the relevant security, then manipulative conduct is observed when two conditions are met: first, the positions have been built up with manipulative intent; and, second, they result in distorted prices.

5 The regulation of market abuse in the United Kingdom and liability management transactions

5.1 Introduction

Historically, the regulatory and legal framework in the United Kingdom addressing improper or abusive market behavior consisted, first, of criminal sanctions for insider dealing and misleading statements and practices,[261] and, second, of supervisory and disciplinary powers over regulated firms and individuals. In the regulatory debate leading to the FSMA, the then existing framework was generally considered incomplete and, consequently, the gap was filled by the market abuse prohibitions

purpose of this recommendation the repurchase of less than 10 percent of the outstanding aggregate principal amount would not be deemed material. See ICMA, *Guidance on Buy-backs by Government, Government Agency and Supranational Issuers*, April 2011, available at www.icmagroup.org/assets/documents. Accessed June 11, 2013.

[261] See, for example, Section 12 of the Prevention of Fraud (Investments) Act 1939 and Section 13 of the Prevention of Fraud (Investments) Act 1958; see also Section 47 of the Financial Services Act 1986.

now found in Sections 118–132 of the FSMA and the explanatory regulations of the FSA Handbook. Another important milestone in the development of the structure of the market abuse regime in the United Kingdom was the implementation of the provisions of the Market Abuse Directive in July 2005.

Due to the implementation of the Market Abuse Directive in the United Kingdom, both the official definition and the general understanding of market abuse violations had to be amended. In the Joint Consultation Paper, the FSA and the Treasury described market abuse as "insider dealing and market manipulation, arising in circumstances where investors have been unreasonably disadvantaged by others. It prevents full and proper market transparency and undermines market integrity and investor confidence."[262]

5.2 The description of market abuse

The description of market abuse for purposes of the regulatory framework in the United Kingdom is found in Section 118 of the FSMA, which defines "market abuse" as the behavior (whether by one person alone or by two or more persons jointly or in concert) in relation to qualifying investments (i.e., securities and other financial instruments) admitted to trading on a securities market falling within any one or more of the following types of conduct:[263]

- where an insider deals, or attempts to deal, in a qualifying investment or related investment on the basis of inside information relating to the investment in question;
- where an insider discloses inside information to another person otherwise than in the proper course of the exercise of his or her employment, profession, or duties;
- where behavior is based on information that is not generally available to those using the market but which, if available to a regular user of the market, would be, or would be likely to be, regarded by him or her as relevant when deciding the terms on which transactions in qualifying investments should be effected, and is likely to be regarded by a regular user of the market as a failure on the part of the person concerned to

[262] See FSA and HM Treasury, *UK Implementation of the EU Market Abuse Directive, A consultation document*, June 2004, available at www.fsa.gov.uk/pubs/other/eu_mad.pdf. Accessed June 11, 2013.

[263] Section 118 of the FSMA.

observe the standard of behavior reasonably expected of a person in his or her position in relation to the market;

- where the behavior consists of effecting transactions or orders to trade (otherwise than for legitimate reasons and in conformity with accepted market practices in the relevant market) which (i) give, or are likely to give, a false or misleading impression as to the supply of, or demand for, or as to the price of, one or more qualifying investments; or (ii) secure the price of one or more such investments at an abnormal or artificial level;
- where the behavior consists of effecting transactions or orders to trade that employ fictitious devices or any other form of deception or contrivance;
- where the behavior consists of the dissemination of information by any means that gives, or is likely to give, a false or misleading impression as to a qualifying investment by a person who knew or could reasonably be expected to have known that the information was false or misleading; and
- where the behavior (i) is likely to give a regular user of the market a false or misleading impression as to the supply of, demand for, or the price or value of, qualifying investments; or (ii) would be, or would be likely to be, regarded by a regular user of the market as behavior that would distort, or would be likely to distort, the market in such an investment, and the behavior is likely to be regarded by a regular user of the market as a failure on the part of the person concerned to observe the standard of behavior reasonably expected of a person in his or her position in relation to the market.

The FSA has issued guidance in the FSA Handbook in determining whether or not behavior amounts to market abuse. Based on the seven types of behavior listed above, the FSA has provided non-exhaustive details of certain types of conduct that will amount to market abuse, along with published particulars of factors that the FSA will take into account in deciding whether certain behavior will amount to market abuse or not. The FSA guidance reflects the Market Abuse Directive's list of proscribed conduct that could constitute or contribute to market abuse. The following behaviors are market abuse according to the FSA:

Insider trading.[264] (i) Dealing on the basis of inside information that is not trading information; (ii) front running/pre-positioning – that is, a transaction for a person's own benefit, on the basis of and ahead of an

[264] See generally the FSA Handbook, MAR 1.3.2.

order (including an order relating to a bid) which he or she is to carry out with or for another (in respect of which information concerning the order is inside information), which takes advantage of the anticipated impact of the order on the market or auction clearing price; (iii) in the context of a tender offer for equity securities, an offeror or potential offeror entering into a transaction in a qualifying investment, on the basis of inside information concerning the proposed bid, which provides merely an economic exposure to movements in the price of the target company's shares (e.g., a spread bet on the target company's share price); and (iv) in the context of a tender offer for equity securities, a person who acts for the offeror or potential offeror dealing for his or her own benefit in a qualifying investment or related investments on the basis of information concerning the proposed bid which is inside information. The FSA has identified a number of factors that it will take into account in deciding whether information is generally available for purposes of the insider trading regulations, including whether the information has been disclosed to a prescribed market through a press release or other regulatory information service, whether the information has been disclosed in accordance with the rules of the relevant prescribed market, and whether the information is contained in records open to public inspection or can be accessed publicly.

Improper disclosure.[265] (i) Disclosure of inside information by the director of an issuer to another in a social context; and (ii) selective briefing of analysts by directors of issuers or others who are persons discharging managerial responsibilities.

Misuse of information.[266] (i) Dealing or *arranging deals* in qualifying investments based on relevant information that is not generally available and relates to matters that a regular user would reasonably expect to be disclosed to users of the particular prescribed market or prescribed auction platform but which does not amount to market abuse (insider dealing) (whether because the dealing relates to a qualifying investment to which Section 118(2) of the FSMA does not apply or because the relevant information is not inside information); and (ii) a director giving relevant information that is not generally available and relates to matters that a regular user would reasonably expect to be disclosed to users of the particular prescribed market, to another otherwise than in the proper course of the exercise of his or her employment or duties, in a way that does not amount

[265] See generally the FSA Handbook, MAR 1.4.2.
[266] See generally the FSA Handbook, MAR 1.5.2.

to market abuse (improper disclosure) (whether because the relevant information is not inside information or for some other reason).

Manipulating transactions.[267] (i) Buying or selling qualifying investments at the close of the market with the effect of misleading investors who act on the basis of closing prices, other than for legitimate reasons; (ii) *wash trades* – that is, a sale or purchase of a qualifying investment where there is no change in beneficial interest or market risk, or where the transfer of beneficial interest or market risk is only between parties acting in concert or collusion, other than for legitimate reasons; (iii) *painting the tape* – that is, entering into a series of transactions that are shown on a public display for the purpose of giving the impression of activity or price movement in a qualifying investment; (iv) entering orders into an electronic trading system, at prices that are higher than the previous bid or lower than the previous offer, and withdrawing them before they are executed, in order to give a misleading impression that there is a demand for or a supply of the qualifying investment at that price; (v) the buying or selling in the secondary market of qualifying investments or related derivatives prior to the auction with the effect of fixing the auction clearing price for the auctioned products at an abnormal or artificial level or misleading bidders in the auction, other than for legitimate reasons; (vi) transactions or orders to trade by a person, or persons acting in collusion, that secure a dominant position over the supply of or demand for a qualifying investment and which have the effect of fixing, directly or indirectly, purchase or sale prices or creating other unfair trading conditions, other than for legitimate reasons; (vii) transactions where both buy and sell orders are entered at, or nearly at, the same time, with the same price and quantity by the same party, or different but colluding parties, other than for legitimate reasons, unless the transactions are legitimate trades carried out in accordance with the rules of the relevant trading platform (such as *crossing trades*); (viii) entering small orders into an electronic trading system at prices that are higher than the previous bid or lower than the previous offer, in order to move the price of the qualifying investment, other than for legitimate reasons; (ix) an *abusive squeeze* – that is, a situation in which a person: (a) has significant influence over the supply of, or demand for, or delivery mechanisms for a qualifying investment or related investment or the underlying product of a derivative contract; (b) has a position (directly or indirectly) in an investment under which quantities of the qualifying investment, related investment, or product in

[267] See generally the FSA Handbook, MAR 1.6.2 and 1.6.4.

question are deliverable; and (c) engages in behavior for the purpose of positioning at a distorted level the price at which others have to deliver, take delivery, or defer delivery to satisfy their obligations in relation to a qualifying investment (the purpose need not be the sole purpose for entering into the transaction or transactions, but must be an actuating purpose); (x) parties who have been allocated qualifying investments in a primary offering colluding to purchase further tranches of those qualifying investments when trading begins, in order to force the price of the qualifying investments to an artificial level and generate interest from other investors, and then sell the qualifying investments; (xi) transactions or orders to trade employed so as to create obstacles to the price falling below a certain level, in order to avoid negative consequences for the issuer (for example, a downgrading of its credit rating); (xii) trading on one market or trading platform with a view to improperly influencing the price of the same or a related qualifying investment that is traded on another prescribed market; and (xiii) conduct by a person, or persons acting in collusion, that secures a dominant position over the demand for a qualifying investment which has the effect of fixing, directly or indirectly, auction clearing prices or creating other unfair trading conditions, other than for legitimate reasons.

According to the FSA, the following factors are to be taken into account when considering whether behavior is for "legitimate reasons," and are indications that it is not:[268] (i) if the person has an actuating purpose behind the transaction to induce others to trade in, bid for, or to position or move the price of, a qualifying investment; (ii) if the person has another, illegitimate, reason behind the transactions, bid, or order to trade; and (iii) if the transaction was executed in a particular way for the purpose of creating a false or misleading impression. The following factors are to be taken into account when considering whether behavior is for "legitimate reasons," and are indications that it is: (i) if the transaction is pursuant to a prior legal or regulatory obligation owed to a third party; (ii) if the transaction is executed in a way that takes into account the need for the market or auction platform as a whole to operate fairly and efficiently; (iii) the extent to which the transaction generally opens a new position, so creating an exposure to market risk, rather than closes out a position and so removes market risk; and (iv) if the transaction complied with the rules of the relevant prescribed markets or prescribed auction

[268] Ibid.

platform about how transactions are to be executed in a proper way (e.g., rules on reporting and executing cross-transactions).

Moreover, according to the FSA, the following factors are to be taken into account in determining whether or not a *person's behavior* amounts to market abuse (manipulating transactions):[269] (i) the extent to which orders to trade given, bids submitted, or transactions undertaken represent a significant proportion of the daily volume of transactions in the relevant qualifying investment in the regulated market or prescribed auction platform concerned, particularly when these activities lead to a significant change in the price of the qualifying investment; (ii) the extent to which orders to trade given, bids submitted, or transactions undertaken by persons with a significant buying or selling position in a qualifying investment lead to significant changes in the price of the qualifying investment-related derivative, or underlying asset, admitted to trading on a regulated market; (iii) whether transactions undertaken lead to no change in beneficial ownership of a qualifying investment admitted to trading on a regulated market; (iv) the extent to which orders to trade given or transactions undertaken include position reversals in a short period and represent a significant proportion of the daily volume of transactions in the relevant qualifying investment on the regulated market concerned, and might be associated with significant changes in the price of a qualifying investment admitted to trading on a regulated market; (v) the extent to which orders to trade given or transactions undertaken are concentrated within a short time span in the trading session and lead to a price change which is subsequently reversed; (vi) the extent to which orders to trade given change the representation of the best bid or offer prices in a financial instrument admitted to trading on a regulated market, or more generally the representation of the order book available to market participants, and are removed before they are executed; and (vii) the extent to which orders to trade are given or transactions are undertaken at or around a specific time when reference prices, settlement prices, and valuations are calculated and lead to price changes that have an effect on such prices and valuations.

According to the FSA, the following factors are to be taken into account in determining whether or not a person's behavior amounts to market abuse (manipulating transactions): (i) the extent to which the person had a direct or indirect interest in the price or value of the qualifying investment or related investment; (ii) the extent to which price, rate,

[269] Ibid.

or option volatility movements, and the volatility of these factors for the investment in question, are outside their normal intra-day, daily, weekly, or monthly range; and (iii) whether a person has successively and consistently increased or decreased his or her bid, offer, or the price he or she has paid for a qualifying investment or related investment.

Manipulating devices.[270] (i) Taking advantage of occasional or regular access to the traditional or electronic media by voicing an opinion about a qualifying investment (or indirectly about its issuer, if applicable) while having previously taken positions on, or submitted bids in relation to, that qualifying investment and profiting subsequently from the impact of the opinions voiced on the price of that instrument, without having simultaneously disclosed that conflict of interest to the public in a proper and effective way; (ii) a transaction or series of transactions that is or are designed to conceal the ownership of a qualifying investment, so that disclosure requirements are circumvented by the holding of the qualifying investment in the name of a colluding party, such that disclosures are misleading in respect of the true underlying holding. These transactions are often structured so that market risk remains with the seller. This does not include nominee holdings; (iii) *pump and dump* – i.e., taking a long position in a qualifying investment and then disseminating misleading positive information about the qualifying investment with a view to increasing its price; and (iv) *trash and cash* – i.e., taking a short position in a qualifying investment and then disseminating misleading negative information about the qualifying investment, with a view to driving down its price.[271]

Dissemination.[272] (i) Knowingly or recklessly spreading false or misleading information about a qualifying investment through the media, including in particular through a press release or similar information channel; and (ii) undertaking a course of conduct in order to give a false or misleading impression about a qualifying investment.

Distortion.[273] (i) The movement of physical commodity stocks, which might create a misleading impression as to the supply of, or demand for, or the price or value of, a commodity or the deliverable into a commodity futures contract; and (ii) the movement of an empty cargo ship, which might create a false or misleading impression as to the supply of, or the

[270] See generally the FSA Handbook, MAR 1.7.2. [271] Ibid.
[272] See generally the FSA Handbook, MAR 1.8.3.
[273] See generally the FSA Handbook, MAR 1.9.2.

demand for, or the price or value of, a commodity or the deliverable into a commodity futures contract.

6 Equal treatment of holders of debt securities in the United Kingdom

Issuers with debt securities listed on the London Stock Exchange are subject to Rule 6.1.3 of the Disclosure Rules and Transparency Rules of the FSA Handbook. Rule 6.1.3 provides that an issuer of debt securities must insure that all holders of debt securities ranking pari passu are given equal treatment in respect of all the rights attaching to those debt securities. Consequently, an issuer of debt securities listed on the London Stock Exchange may not, for example, exclude certain holders from a tender offer or offer tender offer consideration to certain holders that is not available to all holders of the same securities. This *equal treatment* requirement is part of the common transparency obligations for listed securities introduced in all of the EU member states as part of the implementation into national law of the EU Transparency Directive.[274]

[274] Directive 2004/109/EC of the European Parliament and of the Council of December 15, 2004 on the harmonization of transparency requirements in relation to information about issuers whose securities are admitted to trading on a regulated market and amending Directive 2001/34/EC, OJ L 390, 31.12.2004, pp. 38–57.

5

Exchange offers for debt securities

1 Introduction

The objective of most corporate debt restructurings or liability management transactions is the restoration of the financial health of the issuer or borrower and the preservation of the business enterprise as a going concern or, failing that, the orderly liquidation or reorganization of the business. If cash is available to the issuer, the issuer may be able to purchase the debt securities at a discount or finance a tender offer. If cash is not available, the liability management or debt restructuring transaction must be structured as an exchange offer.

In a debt exchange offer, the issuer of the debt securities (or an affiliate of the issuer, which can be the parent company, a subsidiary company, or a company under common control with the issuer) offers to issue new debt securities or a combination of debt securities, cash, equity securities, warrants, and any other non-cash consideration in exchange for its outstanding debt securities that the issuer would like to retire or restructure. The holders of the existing securities tender the securities and, following the acceptance of the tender by the tender offeror, the tender offeror issues new debt or equity securities and other types of cash and non-cash consideration in exchange for the tender securities accepted for purchase. Therefore, a debt exchange offer is the purchase of the issuer's debt securities by the issuer for non-cash consideration in the form of newly issued debt securities (in a debt-for-debt exchange offer), equity securities (in a debt-for-equity exchange offer), or a combination of non-cash consideration and cash consideration.

The objective of the transaction is the exchange, replacement, and/or modification of outstanding financial obligations issued in the past (often years earlier) in connection with capital-raising transactions, mergers or acquisitions, strategic investments, and other forms of business combinations.

1.1 *Objectives of debt exchange offers*

Exchange offers enable issuers to reduce the principal amount outstanding of their issued debt securities (by exchanging debt securities for newly issued debt securities having a lower principal amount or equity securities), maximize cash flows, and reduce interest payments on the outstanding debt securities (by exchanging the outstanding debt securities for newly issued debt securities having lower interest payments), and extend the maturity dates of outstanding debt securities, make changes to the non-financial terms of the existing debt securities, or effect any combination of the foregoing. These results are achieved through the issuance of new securities in consideration for the purchase of the outstanding debt securities by the issuer itself (or an affiliate of the issuer).

A broad range of financial remedies is pursued through the exchange of one or more series of outstanding securities for newly issued securities having different terms, including the suspension or reduction of interest and/or dividend payments, the extension of maturities, the elimination of amortization requirements, the refinancing of existing obligations, the forgiveness of the outstanding principal amount or interest payments due, and others.

1.2 *Legal framework of debt exchange offers*

An exchange offer is therefore a combination of two separate transactions:

- a *tender offer* by the issuer for the tender of the outstanding securities; and
- the *offer and sale of new securities* in exchange for the purchase of the tendered securities in the tender offer.

Consequently, an exchange offer is subject to all the regulatory and legal requirements applicable to tender offers for the relevant securities, and the securities laws applicable to the offer and sale of the newly issued securities. For this reason, the documentation for an exchange offer will be more detailed than that for a cash tender offer to the extent that the offering memorandum must describe the business and financial condition of the issuer and the terms and conditions of the new securities (in addition to the terms and conditions of the tender offer). An exchange offer is also subject to the full application of the securities laws relating to the offer and sale of securities. Although each corporate debt restructuring or liability management exercise in the form of an exchange offer is unique and subject to its own individual facts and circumstances, it generally involves a number of related transactions that raise securities laws ramifications, tax and accounting ramifications, insolvency and bankruptcy laws, contract laws, listing rules and regulations, disclosure regulations, and other complex legal issues.

For purposes of the US federal securities laws, the new securities must be registered under the Securities Act or be exempt from registration thereunder. Thus, one can make a distinction between a *registered exchange offer*, in which the newly issued securities are registered under Section 5 of the Securities Act and subject to SEC review, and a *private* or *exempt exchange offer*, in which the newly issued securities are exempt from the registration and prospectus delivery requirements of the Securities Act. The issuer and other offering participants will also be subject to securities laws liabilities, whereas the underwriters and other offering participants (other than the issuer) will need to conduct customary legal due diligence in connection with the offer and sale of the new securities.

In planning an exchange offer, the main issues considered by the issuer and its advisors are (i) the terms of the newly issued securities offered to existing holders, including the principal amount and coupon, (ii) registration and disclosure requirements under the Securities Act and the availability of exemptions, (iii) tax and accounting considerations, (iv) the likely impact of the exchange offer on the issuer's credit rating, and (v) the mechanics and documentation of the exchange offer, including timing and process, any exclusions of certain categories of holders from the scope of the exchange offer, required participation levels and withdrawal rights, the expiration time, and other pertinent procedural requirements.

1.3 Debt exchange offers by multinational companies across multiple jurisdictions

For complex corporate groups with cross-border operations, the conduct of an exchange offer for outstanding debt securities, benefiting from credit support in the form of guarantees or security in many different jurisdictions, is subject to additional complexities. Many issuers of distressed debt securities, especially in Europe, have subsidiaries, operations, assets, and creditors in multiple jurisdictions. The insolvency laws of those jurisdictions may vary greatly, adding to the complexity, some favoring secured creditors and others favoring non-creditor stakeholders such as employees. In negotiating the terms of a corporate debt restructuring in the form of an exchange offer, the issuer and the different creditor groups negotiate the terms of the restructuring on the basis of the treatment their claims are likely to receive in formal bankruptcy or insolvency proceedings. The likely outcome in such formal bankruptcy or insolvency proceedings casts a dark shadow over the efforts of the various parties to complete a sensible restructuring of the issuer's financial and other obligations, which can take the form of an exchange offer of the issuer's outstanding debt securities.

The high degree of uncertainty over the likely outcome of the formal insolvency process makes it difficult for the creditor groups and the issuer to understand the parameters and limits of their negotiating position and, on that basis, negotiate the terms of the debt exchange offer using the appropriate mix of debt and maturity relief, additional credit support, and/or additional equity incentives.

Furthermore, consensual corporate restructurings that involve the restructuring of debt securities in the form of debt exchange offers present additional complications because the debt securities are held anonymously in book-entry form through a global network of custodians, sub-custodians, and other types of institutional investors. Since it is difficult to identify and negotiate with several different holders of the relevant debt securities, it is extremely difficult to reach agreement among such creditors to avoid enforcement or liquidation when the financial situation of the issuer is desperate or after an event of default (particularly a payment default) has occurred. The objective must always be to effect the liability management or restructuring transaction as soon as possible and, in any event, before any event of default has occurred. In that respect, a debt exchange offer presents an efficient technique of restructuring marketable debt securities.

2 Types of exchange offers

Exchange offers involve two separate securities transactions, namely a tender offer for the relevant debt securities and an issuance of new securities, each of those transactions being the legal consideration offered to the counterparty for the performance of the counterparty's obligations. In the tender offer, the holders of the relevant debt securities to be restructured are offered the opportunity to tender such debt securities to the issuer thereof and the issuer promises, subject to certain conditions, to accept the tendered securities for purchase. The purchase price or the consideration offered to tendering holders is the issuance by the issuer (or an affiliate of the issuer), and the delivery to tender holders on the completion of the transaction, of new securities (either debt or equity securities) and, in certain cases, additional value in the form of other types of cash and/or non-cash consideration in accordance with the commercial agreement underlying the debt exchange.

Since the exchange offer involves the offer and sale of new securities by the issuer to the holders of existing securities *for value* (such value being the delivery by the holders to the issuer of the existing debt securities tendered), the offer and sale of the new securities by the issuer must be registered under Section 5 of the Securities Act or be exempt from registration under one of the available exemptions under the Securities Act.

The available exemptions from registration under the Securities Act relating to corporate debt restructurings in the form of debt exchange offers are the following:

(i) exchange offers that comply with the requirements of Section 3(a)(9) of the Securities Act (exempting exchanges of securities exclusively with existing security holders);
(ii) exchange offers that comply with the requirements of Section 4(2) of the Securities Act (exempting debt exchanges in which the new securities offered are placed in transactions not involving any public offering);
(iii) exchange offers that comply with the requirements of Section 3(a)(10) of the Securities Act (exempting exchanges of securities effected through a fair judicial or administrative process); and
(iv) exchange offers conducted as offshore transactions outside the territorial scope of application of the US federal securities laws pursuant to Regulation S under the Securities Act.

An exchange offer is also, in part, a tender offer to the holders of the existing securities. Consequently, the exchange offer must comply with the requirements of the US Tender Offer Rules or be structured as an exclusionary tender offer outside the United States and the scope of application of the US Tender Offer Rules.

Exchange offers registered under Section 5 of the Securities Act and exchange offers benefiting from one of the exemptions from registration have a number of advantages and disadvantages relating to applicable legal framework and transaction costs.

The general advantages of *exempt* or *unregistered* debt exchange offers are related to the avoidance of the registration and prospectus delivery requirements of the Securities Act and the rules and regulations thereunder. Unregistered exchange offers for debt securities can be conducted without the filing of a registration statement with the SEC and the procedural and liability rules emanating from registration under the Securities

Act. They are also outside the scope of the cumbersome US Tender Offer Rules applicable to equity securities. On the other hand, unregistered debt exchange offers must comply with the relevant exemptions from registration under the Securities Act, which may restrict the flexibility of the parties in certain aspects of the structuring and execution of the transaction. For example, one of the conditions for the availability of the Section 3(a)(9) exemption is that the issuer may not pay anyone, including a financial or other advisor, to solicit participation in the debt exchange, which may adversely affect the prospects of success of the transaction. Furthermore, in a Section 4(2) debt exchange structured as a private placement of securities not involving a public offering under the Securities Act, the issuer may not offer the new securities to investors who are not QIBs within the meaning of Rule 144A under the Securities Act. This limitation could mean that only a registered exchange offer may be possible in the case of the restructuring of debt securities held by a large number of retail investors. Finally, securities offered in unregistered exchange offers may be subject to resale limitations, which could also diminish the commercial desirability of an unregistered exchange offer.

3 Registered exchange offers

If the debt securities are widely held, especially if they are held by retail investors, an exchange offer registered under Section 5 of the Securities Act may be the appropriate technique for effecting the corporate debt restructuring that the issuer is seeking to achieve. A registered exchange offer is subject to the full requirements of SEC registration, requires the filing and SEC review of a prospectus for the offer and sale of the new securities, and exposes the issuer of the securities and the other offering participants to the full scope of securities laws liabilities under Sections 11 and 12 of the Securities Act.

On the other hand, the issuer and its advisors are free to hire professional assistance to solicit participations in the debt exchange and may approach retail investors subject to the requirements of Section 5 of the Securities Act and the rules and regulations thereunder relating to publicity in connection with a registered offering of securities. Finally, the securities issued in a registered exchange offer are freely transferable by non-affiliates of the issuer and not subject to any resale limitations or compliance of such resales with the registration requirements of the Securities Act. A registered exchange offer will often be used where a refinancing or restructuring proposal is particularly complex, i.e., involving debt securities held by a broad range of investors, and the holders of the relevant securities are well organized and may seek to litigate the proposed restructuring.

3.1 Filing a registration statement with the SEC

Securities offered in a registered exchange offer by a foreign private issuer must be registered with the SEC on Form F-4 under the Securities Act. The key information that must be provided in the registration statement filed on Form F-4 includes the information relating to the terms of the tender offer, a business description of the company issuing the securities to be registered, a description of the securities offered by the offeror and audited financial statements of the offeror, the risks associated with the exchange offer and the business of the issuer of the new securities, and pro forma financial information showing the effect of the exchange offer, often showing the pro forma impact of the exchange offer on the basis of different acceptance levels of the debt exchange. If the registrant qualifies to use the short-form registration statement on Form F-3, which permits incorporation of information by reference to previously filed documents, Form F-4 may likewise incorporate by reference with respect to the qualifying company.

3.2 Early commencement (Rule 162 under the Securities Act)

Section 5(a) of the Securities Act prohibits the issuer from selling, directly or indirectly, securities or carrying securities for the purpose of sale or for delivery after sale unless a registration statement is in effect as to such securities. This statutory prohibition of Section 5 is modified by Rule 162 under the Securities Act in relation to registered exchange offers, which allows issuers of debt securities to commence an exchange offer on the filing of the Securities Act registration statement, rather than on its effectiveness. Without the exemption from Section 5(a) offered by Rule 162, the offer by the issuer of debt securities to holders thereof to tender the securities into the exchange offer would constitute a prohibited and illegal "sale" if the securities would be tendered without an effective registration statement. Rule 162 provides relief against the consequences of violation of Section 5 of the Securities Act by establishing what is known as the *early commencement* rule.[275]

[275] Early commencement is not available for going-private transactions under Rule 13e-3 under the Securities Exchange Act or roll-up transactions under Item 901 of Regulation

More specifically, Rule 162(a) under the Securities Act provides that, notwithstanding Section 5(a) of the Securities Act, an offeror may solicit tenders of securities in an exchange offer before a registration statement is effective for the security offered, so long as no securities are purchased until the registration statement is effective and the tender offer has expired in accordance with the applicable US Tender Offer Rules. The exchange offer may not expire until after the mandatory 20-business-day tender offer period has expired. Under early commencement pursuant to Rule 162 under the Securities Act, the holders of the debt securities may tender securities into the exchange offer before the registration statement is effective, may withdraw tendered securities at any time until they are purchased by the offeror, and must receive a disclosure document before having to make an investment decision.

For exchange offers for debt securities, the early commencement relief of Rule 162 under the Securities Act is only available subject to the following conditions: (i) the offeror provides withdrawal rights to the same extent as would be required if the exchange offer were subject to the requirements of the equity tender offer rules of Rules 13e-4 or 14d-1 under the Securities Exchange Act; and (ii) if a material change occurs in the information published or sent or given to security holders, the offeror complies with the dissemination requirements of Rule 13e-4(e)(3) or Rule 14d-4(b) under the Securities Exchange Act in disseminating information about the material change to security holders, including the minimum periods during which the offer must remain open (with withdrawal rights) after notice of the change is provided to security holders.

To commence an exchange offer early (i.e., before the effectiveness of the registration statement), the offeror must file with the SEC a registration statement for the securities offered and include in the preliminary prospectus all information, including pricing information, necessary for investors to make an informed investment decision. The preliminary prospectus may not omit information under Rule 430 or Rule 430A under the Securities Act. The offeror must also disseminate the preliminary prospectus and related letter of transmittal to all security holders and file a tender offer statement with the SEC before the exchange offer can commence. The initial 20-business-day offering period required by the US Tender Offer Rules will commence on such dissemination and filing.

S-K. Exchange offers for these types of transactions cannot commence until the registration statement is declared effective and a prospectus complying with Section 10(a) of the Securities Act is delivered to investors. See Securities Exchange Act Rules 13e-4(e)(2) and 14d-4(b).

Early commencement is at the option of the offeror. Exchange offers can commence as early as the filing of the registration statement, or on any later date selected by the bidder up to the date of effectiveness. If the offeror does not commence its exchange offer before effectiveness of the registration statement, then the exchange offer must commence on or shortly after effectiveness. If the offeror commences its exchange offer early, it must disseminate a preliminary prospectus to all security holders and, in addition, deliver a preliminary prospectus supplement to security holders if there are any material changes in the information previously disclosed, whether as a result of staff review or otherwise. Depending on the significance of the change, exchange offers must remain open for a minimum period of time after a supplement is sent to security holders containing the new information. This is to permit security holders to react to the information by tendering securities or withdrawing securities already tendered.

Rules 14d-4(d) and 13e-4(e)(3) under the Securities Exchange Act specify the minimum time periods necessary for the dissemination of a prospectus supplement (or a revised prospectus) that contains material changes to a preliminary prospectus used to commence an exchange offer early. Exchange offers that commence early must remain open for at least: (i) five business days for a prospectus supplement that contains a material change other than a change in the number of securities sought; (ii) ten business days for a prospectus supplement that contains a change in price, the number of securities sought, the dealer's soliciting fee, or other similarly significant changes; (iii) ten business days for a prospectus supplement that is included as part of a post-effective amendment; and (iv) twenty business days for a revised prospectus when the initial prospectus was materially deficient (e.g., because it failed to comply with the going-private rules or because it was a "shell" document filed solely to trigger commencement and staff review). If a material change in the information previously disseminated to security holders occurred shortly before the expiration of the offer, a prospectus supplement would need to be disseminated to security holders and the offer extended for the appropriate length of time. The SEC believes that the above time periods represent general guidelines that should be applied uniformly to all tender offers, including those tender offers for debt securities that are subject only to Regulation 14E under the Securities Exchange Act.[276]

[276] See *Regulation M-A Adopting Release*, Securities Exchange Act Release No. 42,055 (October 22, 1999).

Under Rule 162(b) under the Securities Act, exchange offers that commence early are exempt from the final prospectus delivery requirement in Section 5(b)(2) of the Securities Act. While an offeror that commences its exchange offer early need not deliver a final prospectus to security holders, it must file a final prospectus with the SEC. In addition, for exchange offers that commence early (as well as exchange offers that commence on or after effectiveness), all brokers and dealers participating in the distribution of securities must comply promptly with the written request of any person for a copy of the final prospectus.

3.3 Liability in registered exchange offers

Liability for disclosure deficiencies in public offerings of securities offered in exchange offers is based on a number of statutory provisions of the Securities Act, the Securities Exchange Act, and the rules and regulations promulgated thereunder. The most important of these provisions are Sections 11, 12(a)(2), and 17(a) of the Securities Act and Rule 10b-5 under the Securities Exchange Act. In connection with material misstatements or omissions relating to the tender offer element of the exchange offer, liability is also based on Section 14(e) of the Securities Exchange Act.

Under Section 11 of the Securities Act, issuers have virtually absolute liability to purchasers of registered securities for any material misstatement in, or material omission from, the registration statement filed under the Securities Act in connection with the relevant offering of securities. Section 11(a) of the Securities Act provides an express private right of action for damages to any purchaser of a security if the registration statement (which includes the prospectus), when it became effective, contained a false statement of material fact or omitted a material fact required to be included in the registration statement (or necessary to make the statements in the registration statement not misleading).

The materiality of any particular statement or omission will depend on the particular facts and circumstances. A fact will be considered material if there is a substantial likelihood that a reasonable investor would consider it important in making an investment decision. Those who may be held liable under Section 11 are: (i) those who signed the registration statement; (ii) directors of (or persons performing similar functions) or partners in the issuer when the part of the registration statement as to which their liability is asserted is filed; (iii) those named in the registration statement (with their consent) as being or about to become directors (or persons performing similar functions) or partners; (iv) underwriters;

(v) accountants, engineers, appraisers, and others who consent to be named as experts in the registration statement; and (vi) persons who control any of the above (including controlling shareholders).

Liability for misstatements or omissions under Section 11 of the Securities Act covers statements made in a registration statement at the time it became effective, and does not cover other documents that are not considered part of a registration statement, such as research reports or free writing prospectuses not filed as part of the registration statement, or apply to oral statements made, for example, in a road show. A claim under Section 11 can be brought against each person who signed the registration statement, the issuer, the issuer's board of directors, the issuer's auditors (for audited financial statements), and each underwriter.

Under Section 12(a)(2) of the Securities Act, any person who offers or sells a security by means of a "prospectus or oral communication," including in connection with a registered exchange offer, which contains a material misstatement, or fails to state a material fact that is "necessary in order to make the statements, in the light of the circumstances under which they were made, not misleading" is liable to a purchaser of such security for damages. Whether any particular statement or omission is material will depend on the facts and circumstances in question; information is, however, considered to be material if "there is a substantial likelihood that a reasonable shareholder would consider it important" in making an investment decision.[277] For a fact to be deemed to be material, there must be a substantial likelihood that such fact "would have been viewed by the reasonable investor as having significantly altered the 'total mix' of information made available."[278] Section 12(a)(2) covers oral statements, including those made in road shows, free writing prospectuses, and statements in a statutory prospectus. Under Section 12(a)(2), a person who buys securities in a registered exchange offer on the basis of a prospectus or oral representation that contains a material misstatement or omission can rescind the sale and recover his or her purchase price (plus interest), and if the investor no longer owns the securities, he or she can recover damages equal to the difference between the purchase and sale price of the securities.

Unlike Section 11 of the Securities Act, which establishes liability for a range of offering participants, liability under Section 12(a)(2) of the Securities Act is expressly limited to those who offer or sell the securities in question. Someone is a seller for the purposes of Section 12(a)(2) if such person has been both an immediate and direct seller of the securities to the

[277] See *TSC Industries, Inc.* v. *Northway, Inc.*, 426 U.S. 438, 449 (1976). [278] Ibid.

plaintiff.[279] Thus, a person who merely participated in the preparation of the registration statement is not considered to be a seller for the purposes of Section 12(a)(2) unless he or she was also an immediate and direct seller of the securities to the plaintiff. Even substantial involvement in the preparation of registration and offering materials will not create liability unless there is also active involvement in the negotiations leading to the sale in question.[280] Rule 159A under the Securities Act clarifies that for purposes of Section 12(a)(2), in a primary offering of securities, the "seller" will always include the issuer of the securities sold as part of the initial distribution of such securities, if the securities are offered by means of a preliminary, final, or supplementary prospectus, any free writing prospectus, and any other communication that is an offer made by the issuer to such person. Other offering participants, however, including the underwriters, and the directors, officers, and principal shareholders of the issuer, will only be subject to Section 12(a)(2) liability if they have been both immediate and direct sellers of the securities sold or have been actively involved in the negotiations leading to such sale. As in Section 11, a plaintiff attempting to rely on Section 12(a)(2) is not required to establish that the defendant acted with fraudulent intent or that the plaintiff relied upon the misstatements or omissions in making his or her purchase. Plaintiffs must only establish the existence of a material misstatement or omission and that they had no actual knowledge of such misstatements or omissions.[281] A seller has an affirmative defense to liability under Section 12(a)(2) if he or she can show that he or she "did not know, and in the exercise of reasonable care could not have known," of the untrue statement or omissions.

Section 17(a) of the Securities Act is the broad anti-fraud provision of the Securities Act, which closely mirrors the language of Rule 10b-5 under the Securities Exchange Act. It provides that it is unlawful for any person in the offer or sale of any securities to (i) employ any device, scheme, or artifice to defraud, (ii) obtain money or property by means of untrue statements or material omissions, or (iii) engage in any transaction, practice, or course of business which operates or would operate as fraud or deceit upon the purchaser. False statements or material omissions in connection with the offer or sale of securities in registered exchange offers, whether

[279] See *Pinter* v. *Dahl*, 486 U.S. 622, 108 S. Ct. 2063, 100 L. Ed. 2d 658 (1988).

[280] See *In re Infonet Services Corp. Securities Litigation*, 310 F. Supp. 2d 1080, 1101 (C.D. Cal. 2003).

[281] See *Mid-Am. Federal Savings & Loan Assoc.* v. *Shearson/Am.Express, Inc.*, 886 F.2d 1249, 1256 (10th Cir. 1989).

made in writing or in oral representations, are within the scope of Section 17(a) and, unlike Rule 10b-5, mere negligence in disclosure suffices to substantiate a violation thereof. The majority of the courts have held, however, that Section 17(a) does not establish a private cause of action and is therefore only an administrative enforcement remedy that can be used by the SEC or criminal proceedings instituted by the Department of Justice. It is not therefore available to investors.

The anti-fraud provisions of Section 10(b) of the Securities Exchange Act and its accompanying Rule 10b-5 have become the most significant remedy against any person making a false or misleading statement of material fact or omitting to state a material fact in connection with the sale or purchase of securities, including statements in written materials, oral representations, and road shows. A cause of action under Rule 10b-5 requires, however, a showing on the part of the plaintiff that the defendant acted with intent to defraud, deceive, or manipulate, or with deliberate recklessness. This is a significantly higher burden of proof than the burden of proof required under Sections 11 or 12(a)(2) of the Securities Act.

Finally, Section 14(e) of the Securities Exchange Act is a broad anti-fraud prohibition that is remarkably similar to the anti-fraud provisions of Rule 10b-5 under the Securities Exchange Act.[282] The section prohibits factual misrepresentations, omissions of material fact, or other fraudulent, manipulative, or similar practices. Section 14(e) of the Securities Exchange Act applies to statements of a material fact (or omissions thereof) or deceptive or manipulative acts or practices, in each case "in connection with" any tender offer or request or invitation for tenders or solicitations of security holders in opposition to or in favor of any such offers, requests, or invitations. The section applies to any tender offer (including any exchange offer) for any type of securities subject to the Securities Exchange Act[283] (other than exempted securities[284]) regardless of whether or not they are equity securities, debt securities, or hybrid

[282] Regarding Section 14(e), see generally Mark J. Loewenstein, "Section 14(e) of the Williams Act and Rule 10b-5 Comparisons," 71 *Georgetown Law Journal* 1311 (1983) (hereinafter, "Loewenstein").

[283] The term "security" is defined in Section 3(a)(10) of the Securities Exchange Act for the purposes of that statute. The definition is virtually identical to the definition of "security" for purposes of the Securities Act.

[284] Securities that are exempt from the scope of application of the Securities Exchange Act are outside the scope of application of Section 14(e) thereof. A long list of "exempted securities" is set forth in Section 3(a)(12) of the Securities Exchange Act.

securities and regardless, further, of whether or not they are required to be registered under the registration requirements of the Securities Act.[285] Furthermore, Section 14(e) makes no distinction between a tender offer by the issuer of the tender securities, by an affiliate of the issuer, or by an unaffiliated third party nor does it treat differently a tender offer supported by the management of the issuer of the tender securities compared to a "hostile" tender offer that is not so supported.

Consequently, Section 14(e) covers a broad range of transactions that are outside the scope of application of Section 14(d) and the provisions of the Williams Act that apply solely to equity securities registered under Section 12 of the Securities Exchange Act, including, without limitation: (i) a tender offer where the tender offeror owns, after the consummation of the tender offer, 5 percent or less of the class of securities to which the tender offer relates; (ii) a tender offer for securities that are not equity securities, such as debt securities; (iii) a tender offer for securities that are not registered under Sections 12 or 15 of the Securities Exchange Act; and (iv) a tender offer for non-cash consideration. A necessary predicate to claim under the protective provisions of Section 14(e) is the existence (imminent, pending, or recent) of a tender offer.[286] Section 14(e) is not available in privately negotiated transactions[287] or other offers or solicitations that are not "tender offers" within the meaning of Sections 14(d) and 14(e) of the Securities Exchange Act.[288] Furthermore, persons who sold their securities prior to the tender offer or the alleged tender offer do not have any remedies under the protective provisions of Section 14(e).[289] The application of Section 14(e) is not limited to an actual tender offer; it covers pre-offer statements so long as the tender offeror has made public a clear intention to make a tender offer; it also covers false or misleading statements published before any announcement is made if the tender offer is likely, probable, or imminent.[290] Misrepresentations or material omissions made after a proposed tender offer is announced are also actionable where it is likely that the proposed tender offer will become

[285] See Rule 14d-1 (a) under the Securities Exchange Act. See also *E. H. I. of Florida, Inc.* v. *Insurance Co. of North America*, 499 F. Supp. 1053 (E.D. Pa. 1980), aff'd, 652 F.2d 310 (3d Cir. 1981).

[286] See *John Labatt Ltd.* v. *Onex Corp.*, 890 F. Supp. 235 (S.D.N.Y. 1995) (hereinafter, "*Labatt*").

[287] See *Astronics Corp.* v. *Protective Closures Co., Inc.*, 561 F. Supp. 329 (W.D.N.Y. 1983).

[288] We discuss the definition of a "tender offer" within the meaning of Sections 14(d) and 14(e) of the Securities Exchange Act, as well as the rules and regulations adopted by the SEC thereunder, in Chapter 2.

[289] See *Johnston* v. *Wilbourn*, 682 F. Supp. 879 (S.D. Miss. 1988).

[290] See *Pullman-Peabody Co.* v. *Joy Mfg. Co.*, 662 F. Supp. 32, 34 (D.N.J. 1986) and cases cited.

effective.[291] Section 14(e) is therefore applicable when a fraud is committed in connection with (i) a tender offer; (ii) a request for tenders; (iii) an invitation for tenders; (iv) any solicitation of security holders in opposition to a tender offer, request, or invitation; or (v) any solicitation of security holders in favor of a tender offer, request, or invitation.

The anti-fraud provisions of Section 14(e) of the Securities Exchange Act are discussed in detail in Chapter 7.

4 Section 3(a)(9) exchange offers

The Securities Act requires registration of the offer and sale of securities in the United States unless an exemption from such registration is available. Section 3(a)(9) of the Securities Act provides an exemption from the registration and prospectus delivery requirements of the Securities Act for "any security exchanged by the issuer with its existing security holders exclusively when no commission or other remuneration is paid or given directly or indirectly for soliciting such exchange." Congress determined that the Section 3(a)(9) exemption was appropriate and necessary to permit issuers of securities to effect certain voluntary adjustments and modifications of their securities without the delay, expense, and public disclosure requirements of registration under the Securities Act. The rationale was that prohibiting paid solicitation in Section 3(a)(9) exchanges would be a safeguard against the abuse of Section 3(a)(9) to evade the registration and prospectus delivery requirements of Section 5 of the Securities Act.[292]

4.1 Introduction

The exemption under Section 3(a)(9) of the Securities Act is part of the list of "exempted securities" of Section 3 of the Securities Act, not the "exempted transactions" of Section 4 of the Securities Act. A more careful consideration of the genuine exempted securities of Section 3 (e.g., interests in a railroad equipment trust of Section 3(a)(6)) will immediately reveal that Section 3(a)(9) should not have been placed under Section 3 but under Section 4 of the Securities Act because it does not describe exempted securities, but an exempted transaction.

There is nothing peculiar about the securities issued in a Section 3(a)(9) offering, or the issuers of such securities, that would justify their

[291] Ibid.

[292] See generally Allen E. Throop and Chester T. Lane, "Some Problems of Exemptions under the Securities Act of 1933," 4 *Law and Contemporary Problems* 89 (1937).

exemption from the registration and prospectus delivery requirements of the Securities Act. The exemption was created because of the circumstances surrounding the particular offering and, as such, it would have been more appropriate to list the exemption as part of the "exempted transactions" of Section 4 of the Securities Act. The distinction between "exempted securities" and "exempted transactions" is not one of academic purity but of great practical importance. If Section 3(a)(9) is to be read literally as the statutory basis for creating securities that are exempt from the registration and prospectus delivery requirements of the Securities Act, then offers and sales of such securities by affiliates of the issuer would also be exempt from Section 5 of the Securities Act. Nevertheless, the SEC has always taken the position that secondary distributions of securities issued in a Section 3(a)(9) exchange offer are not exempt from Section 5 of the Securities Act because Section 3(a)(9) establishes a transaction exemption.[293] Thus, if the securities to be surrendered in the exchange offer are unrestricted securities, the security holders acquire new securities that are also unrestricted within the meaning of Rule 144 under the Securities Act even where the exempted Section 3(a)(9) transaction is nonpublic in nature.[294] Similarly, if securities to be surrendered in a Section 3(a)(9) exchange are *restricted securities*, the new securities issued in the exchange will also be *restricted securities* and subject to the resale limitations applicable to such "restricted securities." Rule 144(d)(3)(ii) under the Securities Act provides that if the securities sold were acquired from the issuer solely in exchange for other securities of the same issuer, the newly acquired securities shall be deemed to have been acquired at the same time as the securities surrendered for conversion or exchange, even if the securities surrendered were not convertible or exchangeable by their terms.

4.2 *Reasons for Section 3(a)(9) exchange offers*

Section 3(a)(9) permits issuers to issue new securities in exchange for existing securities outside the limitations of the registration and prospectus delivery requirements of the Securities Act. The exchange offer may be desirable or necessary for one or more of the following reasons: (i) to comply with covenants or other contractual obligations or in order to honor the terms of a contractual agreement (for example, an issuer may rely on Section 3(a)(9) to issue cash and promissory notes or other debt securities to holders of options under employee stock ownership

[293] See, e.g., SEC, *Securities Act Release 33–4434* (December 6, 1961).
[294] See, e.g., *Carlton, Inc.*, SEC No-Action Letter (September 30, 1991).

plans);[295] (ii) to eliminate outstanding securities that carry burdensome interest, dividend, mandatory redemption, or voting rights, or to replace debt securities with equity securities; to replace voting equity securities with non-voting equity securities or debt securities; to simplify a complicated capital structure; to extend short-term debt obligations, or to reduce high administrative and/or accounting or reporting expenses relating to the maintenance of the outstanding securities; (iii) to modify the terms of existing securities;[296] (iv) to make corrections to otherwise desirable outstanding securities;[297] and (v) to reduce the number of existing securities.[298]

Section 3(a)(9) exchange offers present several advantages compared to other types of exchange offers and restructuring offers. They:

- can be completed without much delay because there is no registration required under the Securities Act and, therefore, no SEC staff review;
- are flexible to the extent that the newly issued securities may have any terms and conditions deemed desirable from a commercial and financial perspective;
- do not require cash on hand;
- do not trigger liability under Section 11 of the Securities Act; and
- can be combined with a consent solicitation.

The main disadvantages are the limited ability to engage and compensate an investment bank or other third parties in connection with the exchange offer, and the requirement for the new securities to be issued by the same issuer, which reduces the structural flexibility often required in a complex restructuring transaction.

4.3 Methods of Section 3(a)(9) exchange offers and types of consideration offered by issuer

Section 3(a)(9) is available in *exchange offers* and in *exchange agreements*. An exchange offer by the issuer to existing security holders allows the security holders to assess the merits of the exchange and either reject the offer and continue holding the outstanding security or accept the issuer's

[295] See, e.g., *Miller Enterprises, Inc.*, SEC No-Action Letter (June 20, 1977).

[296] See, e.g., *Allied-Carson Corp.*, SEC No-Action Letter (February 12, 1976); *Peabody Galeon Corp.*, SEC No-Action Letter (August 16, 1973); *Earth Sciences, Inc.*, SEC No-Action Letter (August 20, 1979); *Magic Marker Corp.*, SEC No-Action Letter (June 30, 1971).

[297] See *Metagraphic Sys., Inc.*, SEC No-Action Letter (April 1, 1975).

[298] See *Roy F. Weston, Inc.*, SEC No-Action Letter (September 21, 1979).

offer and become holders of the new securities issued in exchange of the old securities. This type of exchange offer forces the security holder to evaluate the relative merits of the securities involved and obviously involves the making of a new investment decision. Alternatively, Section 3(a)(9) is also available in exchange agreements, which reduce or eliminate the uncertainty associated with the making of a new investment decision by the security holders when presented with an exchange offer by the issuer.

Two different forms of exchange agreement have been used in connection with Section 3(a)(9): (i) the issuer may agree with the security holders when originally issuing securities, under the terms of the original stock purchase agreement or indenture, that the issued securities will be exchanged in the future for another class of securities under certain circumstances defined in the exchange agreement;[299] and (ii) the issuer and the security holders may agree on an amendment to the issuer's charter or similar corporate constitutional document or the contract under which the securities were originally issued to authorize and approve the exchange of the original securities for newly issued securities.[300]

Regardless of the method employed in accomplishing a Section 3(a)(9) exchange, an issuer may not require its security holders to exchange anything other than the issuer's own securities. For example, the security holders may not be asked to deliver securities and cash. This limitation does not apply to the issuer, however, which may employ a variety of techniques to realize a successful exchange. The most common exchange involves the issuance of a single new security that may, or may not, be different from the outstanding security it purports to replace. The issuer may also choose to exchange an existing security with two or more different securities, an existing security with two or more new securities and cash, or a combination of debt securities, equity securities, cash, and another form of non-cash consideration.[301]

[299] See *Foster Wheeler Corp.*, SEC No-Action Letter (July 2, 1973); *Squibb Corp.*, SEC No-Action Letter (June 3, 1971).

[300] See, e.g., *Varco International, Inc.*, SEC No-Action Letter (February 24, 1986). The articles of incorporation of the company were amended to permit the payment of dividends on the company's cumulative convertible preferred shares in shares of the company's common stock or in cash, at the option of the company.

[301] See, e.g., *WECO Development Corp.*, SEC No-Action Letter (January 24, 1973); see also *Seaman Furniture Co., Inc.*, SEC No-Action Letter (October 10, 1989) (the issuer offered a package of new subordinated debentures and shares of common stock for existing subordinated debt); *Mortgage Investors of Washington*, SEC No-Action Letter (September 8, 1980), relating to an exchange offer from subordinated notes into a package containing

Neither Section 3(a)(9) itself, nor administrative interpretations of it, require that the securities issued in the exchange are identical or share similar characteristics with the outstanding securities they replace. All of the following types of exchanges are available to issuers considering voluntary Section 3(a)(9) exchanges:

- equity securities for equity securities;
- equity securities for debt securities;
- debt securities for equity securities;
- debt securities for debt securities;
- debt securities for warrants; and
- equity securities for warrants.

4.4 Statutory conditions of Section 3(a)(9) exchange offers

As applied by the SEC and the US federal courts, the following requirements must be met for the Section 3(a)(9) exemption to apply: (i) *identity of the issuer* – the issuer of the new security must be the same as the issuer of the old security for which the new security is exchanged; (ii) *exclusivity of the exchange* – the new security received in exchange must be exchanged only, not sold; i.e., security holders do not pay additional consideration for the new security; and (iii) *absence of remunerated solicitation* – no party may receive compensation for encouraging security holders to accept the exchange, whether that acceptance comes about through individual exchange decisions or through majority acceptance of a related restructuring.

a more attractive subordinated note and a share of beneficial interest; *Comprehensive Communities Corp.*, SEC No-Action Letter (May 14, 1975), relating to an exchange offer from $1,000 face amount of convertible debentures into $50 in cash, 133 shares of common stock, and a $500 convertible note. Although the cash component to the issuer's exchange plan typically comes from the issuer, in at least one plan of recapitalization, the cash was provided by an affiliate. See *Caroline Wholesale Florists, Inc.*, SEC No-Action Letter (August 17, 1976). The exchange offer may also include cash and debt securities from the issuer and common stock issued by a wholly owned subsidiary of the issuer. See, e.g., *LeBlond, Inc.*, SEC No-Action Letter (June 19, 1981); exchange of preferred stock into a combination of cash or, at the shareholder's option, voting preferred stock is also permitted; see, e.g., *American Can Co.*, SEC No-Action Letter (April 10, 1980). See also *WestMarc Communications, Inc.*, SEC No-Action Letter (November 20, 1989) (cash in lieu of fractional shares); *Radyne Corp.*, SEC No-Action Letter (February 6, 1990) (either new debentures or a combination of new debentures and common stock in lieu of old debentures); *International Controls Corp.*, SEC No-Action Letter (August 6, 1990) (an exchange of debt securities with a combination of cash, new debt securities, and warrants to purchase common stock).

In addition to satisfying the conditions set forth above, issuers and their counsel must be concerned about whether a Section 3(a)(9) exchange offer might be integrated into another offering of securities by the issuer that is being conducted simultaneously or in timing proximity to the exchange offer and, if so, whether any of the conditions set forth above would be violated by the conduct of any such concurrent and integrated securities offering.

A concurrent public or private offering of securities for cash to other groups of investors would likely eliminate the availability of the Section 3(a)(9) exemption to the issuer's existing security holders. Issuers and counsel conducting Section 3(a)(9) exchange offers must ensure that, after an independent integration analysis of the exchange offer with any other securities offerings conducted at the same time, the three conditions of Section 3(a)(9) identified above have been satisfied. In practice, the issuer and counsel must be satisfied that the exchange offer is "exclusively" with the existing security holders and is not integrated with concurrent or simultaneous offers to other groups of investors. The determination of whether the exchange offer is separate from another concurrent offer will depend upon a consideration of various factors concerning the methods of sale and distribution employed to effect the offerings and the disposition of the proceeds. If the offerings may be segregated into separate blocks, as evidenced by material differences in the use of the proceeds, in the manner and terms of distribution, and in similar related details, each offering will be a separate offering of securities.[302] The SEC takes into account five factors that relate to the single issue requirement: (i) are the offerings part of a single plan of financing? (ii) do the offerings involve issuance of the same class of security? (iii) are the offerings made at or about the same time? (iv) is the same type of consideration to be received? and (v) are the offerings made for the same general purpose?[303]

Restricting an exchange offer to existing security holders does not mean that the offer must be made to all the existing security holders. An exchange offer under Section 3(a)(9) may be limited to certain classes of existing security holders meeting certain conditions.[304]

[302] See *In The Matter Of Unity Gold Corporation*, 3 SEC 618, 1938 WL 1293 (July 19, 1938).

[303] See *Securities Act Release No. 33–4424*, fn 294 above. The same factors are set forth in Preliminary Note 3 to Rule 147 under the Securities Act.

[304] See Letter of SEC General Counsel relating to Sections 3(a)(9) and 4(1) of the Securities Act, *Securities Act Release No. 35–2029* (August 8, 1939); see also *Systemedics, Inc.*, SEC No-Action Letter (January 19, 1976); *Frier Indus., Inc.*, SEC No-Action Letter (October 16, 1975).

We will examine each of the relevant conditions in turn.

Identity of the issuer. The issuer of the new security must be the same as the issuer of the old security for which the new security is exchanged. Section 3(a)(9) exempts any security exchanged by the issuer with "its" security holders. The SEC has interpreted this provision as requiring that both the security issued and the security surrendered in the exchange are securities issued by the same issuer.[305] This construction does not create problems for obvious internal corporate transactions such as stock splits or amendments of the terms and conditions of existing securities. The SEC has adopted a strict interpretation of the "same issuer" requirement, even in circumstances in which the issuer changes legal form, issues new securities in exchange for old securities, and continues substantially the same business.[306] When an issuer with outstanding securities disappears in a merger, consolidation, or transfer of substantially all of the assets, the successor issuer, or its affiliate, usually replaces the outstanding securities with newly issued securities. Because two different issuers are involved in these types of transactions (whether between affiliates or unaffiliated entities), Section 3(a)(9) is not available.

The fact pattern set forth above must be distinguished from a situation in which the issuer of outstanding securities disappears into a new entity which assumes all the obligations of the disappearing issuer and subsequently exchanges such obligations with newly issued securities. For example, an issuer may issue debt securities to several investors. The issuer is subsequently acquired by another company, which assumes all liabilities and obligations relating to the outstanding debt securities and subsequently exchanges the outstanding debt securities with newly issued debt securities convertible into the issuer's common stock. The SEC granted the no-action request in this situation, relying on Section 3(a)(9).[307] Although the debt securities were securities originally issued by the disappearing issuer, the staff reasoned that the obligations ceased to exist upon the merger, and new securities with identical characteristics had been issued by the acquiring entity when it assumed all liability and

[305] See *Securities Act Release No. 646* (February 3, 1936); *Securities Act Release No. 2029* (August 8, 1939).

[306] See also *Koolau Farmers Cooperative Ltd.*, SEC No-Action Letter (October 14, 1986), where the SEC noted the absence of identity between the predecessor entity and the issuer of the securities in the reorganization in denying relief.

[307] See *Heritage Bancorporation*, SEC No-Action Letter (January 15, 1973); *AutoFinance Group, Inc.*, SEC No-Action Letter (December 3, 1991), relating to an exchange offer of common stock for debt securities of a predecessor; see also *Grand Metropolitan Public Limited Company*, SEC No-Action Letter (April 14, 1998).

obligation on them. Therefore, holders of the replaced debt securities were considered the acquiring entity's "existing security holders." The SEC generally permits a person seeking Section 3(a)(9) relief to make an exempt exchange offer for obligations it did not originate but for which it subsequently assumed primary or joint liability.[308]

A merger of affiliates may be effected in order to change an issuer's domicile or corporate seat without, however, altering the business, assets, and capital structure of the original issuer. The question then is whether two separate legal persons that are economically and functionally identical may be considered to be "the issuer" for purposes of Section 3(a)(9). Under Rule 145(a)(2) of the Securities Act, this type of transaction is deemed not to involve an offer or sale of securities and, therefore, registration under Section 5 of the Securities Act is unnecessary. If Rule 145(a)(2) is not technically available, Section 3(a)(9) may provide the necessary relief. The SEC has provided no-action relief on the basis that (i) the new company is to have exactly the same certificate of incorporation, including the same authorized capital, as the old company, (ii) the terms and rights of the new securities were to be exactly the same as those of the old securities, (iii) the new company was to adopt the same bylaws of the old company and would mirror it in all respects, and (iv) no commission or other remuneration was to be paid or given for soliciting the exchange.[309] A parent company may also use Section 3(a)(9) to exchange its own securities for securities originally issued by one of the subsidiaries of the parent company but only if the parent company assumes all the obligations and conditions of the securities issued by the subsidiary.[310]

[308] See *Pacesetter Fin. Corp.*, SEC No-Action Letter (January 23, 1974): two different banks with certain convertible debt securities outstanding formed Pacesetter as a holding company to acquire the two banks. Two phantom banks, wholly owned subsidiaries of Pacesetter, were going to be created to receive the two predecessor banks under the consolidation agreements. Each consolidation agreement was to be a three-party contract under which Pacesetter would agree to issue its common stock to the shareholders of the old bank pursuant to Rule 133 under the Securities Act. The phantom bank subsidiaries and Pacesetter were to assume joint and several liability for the due payment of the principal and interest of the convertible debt securities of the old bank, and Pacesetter was to agree to exchange its common stock upon any conversion of the debt securities.

[309] See *Liquid Air Corporation*, SEC No-Action Letter (August 20, 1986).

[310] See, e.g., *Pan American World Airways, Inc.*, SEC No-Action Letter (May 28, 1975), relating to an exchange offer of convertible debentures issued by a wholly owned subsidiary of Pan Am outside the United States. When the foreign issuer was liquidated in 1974, Pan Am expressly assumed the obligations and conditions of the former subsidiary, including the obligation of issuing shares of its common stock upon conversion of the debentures. The SEC staff agreed that Section 3(a)(9) would exempt the conversion of debentures into common stock.

The issuance of a guarantee in a transaction raises additional complications. For example, assume that a company (the *parent guarantor*) guarantees the securities of its wholly owned subsidiary at the time the securities were issued to the public. The guarantee of the parent guarantor is itself a separate security and, consequently, two securities are issued to the investing public in the original transaction: the debt securities and the parent guarantee. If subsequently the subsidiary offers to exchange the existing securities with new securities that will be guaranteed by the parent company, then Section 3(a)(9) is available without any difficulty. Two issuers (i.e., the subsidiary and the parent guarantor) are exchanging their original securities (the debt securities and the parent guarantee) for new securities. The issue becomes complicated where only one of the two persons involved in the original transaction, either the parent guarantor or the issuer of the guaranteed securities, offers to exchange a new security, or where only one of the persons was involved in the original transaction, but both participate in the exchange transaction. The SEC has permitted the conversion of exchangeable guaranteed securities issued by a subsidiary of the parent company (guaranteed by the parent company) and convertible into the common stock of the parent company. Because the parent company is the issuer of the guarantee, its issuance of the shares upon the conversion of the guaranteed debt securities should be exempt under Section 3(a)(9). This conclusion reflects economic reality to the extent that the issuer of the debt securities is usually a corporate financing subsidiary, without separate material assets.[311] The SEC also permits Section 3(a)(9) to exempt the issuance of new securities that are joint and several obligations of the parent and subsidiary, in exchange for convertible debentures that are joint and several obligations of the

[311] See, e.g., *Timken Co.*, SEC No-Action Letter (December 19, 1985), where the staff agreed that Section 3(a)(9) was available for the conversion of exchangeable guaranteed debentures issued by a subsidiary of the guarantor and convertible into common stock of the guarantor. See also *Dynalectron Corp.*, SEC No-Action Letter (October 10, 1986). In taking such a position with respect to an exchange involving outstanding debt obligations, the SEC noted that (i) the indentures pursuant to which the convertible securities were issued did not require the issuer to, and the issuer did not, solicit the consent or vote of the holders of the convertible securities with respect to the subject transaction, the guarantee of the convertible securities, or the adjustment of the conversion feature, (ii) the indenture under which the convertible securities were issued permitted the issuer and the trustee to execute a supplemental indenture to guarantee the convertible securities without the consent or vote of the holders of the convertible securities, and (iii) no commission or other remuneration was paid or given, directly or indirectly, in connection with the conversion of the convertible securities. See also *Weatherford International, Inc.*, SEC No-Action Letter (June 25, 2002).

parent and subsidiary as to both principal and interest.[312] If a subsidiary has outstanding a class of debt securities guaranteed by its parent, Section 3(a)(9) will not be available to the offering of a new debt security in exchange for the guaranteed debt securities if the new debt security will not be similarly guaranteed by the parent.[313] If the security holder of an outstanding debt security is asked to accept a guarantee of a different issuer as part of the exchange offer package, the SEC takes the view that Section 3(a)(9) is not available. Consider, for example, the investor who is asked to exchange a 10 percent debt security for 5 percent debt securities issued by the same issuer and guaranteed by a separate issuer. Assuming that the 5 percent debt securities have value, the investor is required to consider the financial prospects of two different issuers, one of which may be unknown to him or her. The SEC denies the availability of the Section 3(a)(9) exemption in these circumstances.[314] The issuance of securities by a finance subsidiary, guaranteed fully and unconditionally by the parent company of the finance subsidiary, is a different matter. Assessing the economic reality of the transaction, the SEC has provided no-action letter relief under Section 3(a)(9) for an exchange of guaranteed debt securities issued by a finance subsidiary for the securities of the parent guarantor.[315] Insofar as the finance subsidiary is established by the parent company to finance the activities of the parent company and has only *de minimis* assets and liabilities tied only to the issuance of debt securities, there is "identity of issuer" for purposes of Section 3(a)(9). The SEC has also agreed to provide no-action relief in the event there is an exchange of a new parent company security for an outstanding parent company security supported by one or more upstream guarantees from the parent company's wholly owned subsidiaries.[316]

[312] See *First Liberty Financial Corporation*, SEC No-Action Letter (July 23, 1991).

[313] See SEC Division of Corporation Finance, *Compliance and Disclosure Interpretations*, Question 125.05 (November 26, 2008).

[314] See *Gulf and Western Industries, Inc.*, SEC No-Action Letter (August 4, 1976).

[315] See *Echo Bay Resources, Inc.*, SEC No-Action Letter (May 18, 1998).

[316] See *Upstream Guarantees*, SEC No-Action Letter (January 13, 2010). It is interesting to follow the logic and rationale of the no-action letter request. The availability of Section 3(a)(9) for such exchanges presents itself on a regular basis typically in one of the two following fact patterns: (i) *convertible notes* – frequently issued with guarantees by one or more of the issuer's 100 percent-owned subsidiaries. These convertible securities are typically debt securities of the parent that are convertible at the option of the holder into common stock of the parent. The subsidiary guarantees are included to protect the convertible note holder against structural subordination to claims of the subsidiaries' creditors. The subsidiary guarantees play an integral role in defining the effective seniority

Exclusivity of the exchange. The SEC takes the view that Section 3(a)(9) does not permit existing security holders to deliver any consideration

of the convertible notes; and (ii) *exchange offers* by issuers seeking to de-lever and equitize their balance sheets. These exchange offers typically involve the issuance of a new parent security (whether debt or equity) in exchange for the parent's outstanding convertible or non-convertible debt security that is guaranteed by one or more of the parent's 100 percent-owned subsidiaries. As with the convertible notes described above, the subsidiary guarantees were included to protect against structural subordination. Section 3(a)(9) of the Securities Act provides an exemption from registration for "any security exchanged by the issuer with its existing security holders exclusively where no commission or other remuneration is paid or given directly or indirectly for soliciting such exchange." Where a single issuer is involved, without any third-party guarantees, the requirement of Section 3(a)(9) that the exchange of securities be between the issuer and its existing security holders (the *identity of issuer* requirement) is clearly met. In essence, in enacting Section 3(a)(9), Congress concluded that investors in an enterprise could agree to its reorganization, and the resulting exchange of different types of investments in that enterprise, without the benefit of SEC registration, so long as no one was paid a commission to induce them to do so. Section 3(a)(9) is available in certain situations where a security of an issuer with a *downstream* guarantee from its parent is exchangeable for a newly issued security of such parent. These fact patterns have involved: (i) securities issued by a finance subsidiary and guaranteed by its parent that are exchangeable for a parent security (see e.g., *The Warnaco Group, Inc.*, SEC No-Action Letter (August 7, 1998) and *Echo Bay Mines, Ltd*, SEC No-Action Letter (May 18, 1998)); (ii) reorganizations, where an issuer reorganizes to create a holding company and the new parent guarantees the outstanding securities of the issuer, which are thereafter exchangeable for a parent security (for example, *Kerr McGee Corporation*, SEC No-Action Letter (July 31, 2001)); and (iii) acquisitions, where the acquirer guarantees the outstanding securities of the acquired company, which are thereafter exchangeable for securities of the acquirer (for example, *Grand Metropolitan Public Limited Company*, SEC No-Action Letter (April 14, 1998)). In each of these fact patterns the common theme was that although two or more issuers were involved, as a practical matter, the investor regarded the exchange of the outstanding parent security for a new parent security as the substance of the conversion or exchange. The first fact pattern, a finance subsidiary, is the most straightforward, because there is no economic substance to the finance subsidiary and clearly the investor is looking solely to the parent guarantee. In the reorganization and acquisition contexts there is meaningful economic substance to the subsidiary issuer, but as an economic matter, the investor is not looking at multiple investments in different issuers, but instead at a single investment in an *indivisible business* with varying degrees of structural subordination. An investor holding debt that is issued only by the parent will have a claim on the assets of the indivisible business ranking ahead of equity of the parent, but junior to secured debt of the parent or debt issued by the parent that is, through a guarantee, also an obligation of subsidiaries. Where the issuers and guarantors are parents and 100 percent-owned subsidiaries, the presence or absence of guarantees affects the holder's relative ranking among other stakeholders, not the essence of the investment. This is not dissimilar from the change in contractual or structural subordination that results in an exchange by a single issuer of its senior notes for its senior subordinated notes, secured debt for unsecured debt, or its debt for its equity for which Section 3(a)(9) clearly is available (and was intended). Nevertheless, all the fact patterns where the SEC staff had taken a no-action position had involved downstream guarantees (i.e., situations in which the parent guaranteed a security issued in the exchange other than the existing securities. If, for example, an issuer offers to exchange new securities upon the security holder's exercise of warrants (thus requiring cash payments), the exemption is not available.[317]

The requirement for a clean exchange of an old security, but nothing more than that, for a new security does not mean that the security holders must always receive something of equivalent economic value. An issuer may replace existing warrants or debt securities with newly issued warrants or debt securities having greater market value.[318] The pertinent question is whether any new consideration is moving from the existing security holders to the issuer (other than the surrendered securities to be replaced), and not whether security holders have lost economic value that might have been recovered from the issuer.[319] If the exchange offer requires a security holder to deliver his or her old security and to perform certain services or, in addition, deliver some other security or cash, Section 3(a)(9) would not be available.[320]

The prohibition against the presence of additional consideration in a Section 3(a)(9) offer is subject to two limited exceptions. Rule 149 under the Securities Act permits the security holder in a Section 3(a)(9) exchange to make whatever cash payments may be necessary "to effect an equitable adjustment, in respect of dividends or interest paid or payable on the securities involved in the exchange, as between such security holder and other security holders of the same class accepting the offer of exchange." Furthermore, Rule 150 under the Securities Act allows an issuer to make payments to its security holders "in connection with an exchange of securities for outstanding securities, when such payments are part of the

by one or more of its subsidiaries) as opposed to *upstream* guarantees (i.e., situations in which one or more subsidiaries guaranteed a security issued by the parent). The no-action letter request submitted, however, that this was a distinction without a difference. Economic reality should dictate the result. As an economic matter, the investor is not looking at multiple investments in different issuers, but instead at a single investment in an indivisible business with varying degrees of structural subordination. Where the issuers and guarantors are parents and 100 percent-owned subsidiaries, the presence or absence of guarantees affects the holder's relative ranking among other stakeholders, not the essence of the investment.

[317] See *Allied Leisure Industry, Inc.*, SEC No-Action Letter (September 4, 1979).

[318] See, e.g., *Wright Air Lines, Inc.*, SEC No-Action Letter (August 23, 1973) (an exchange of common stock for subordinated notes that were in default and planned to rely upon Section 3(a)(9)).

[319] See *First Pa. Mortgage Trust*, SEC No-Action Letter (February 4, 1977).

[320] Additional consideration that is prohibited by Section 3(a)(9) is not only cash but could also be securities. See, e.g., *F&M Schaefer Corp.*, SEC No-Action Letter (August 23, 1977).

terms of the offer of exchange." So long as cash payments in an exchange offer structured for a Section 3(a)(9) exemption do not come from security holders, except as permitted under Rule 149 under the Securities Act, it should not matter that they come from an affiliate of the issuer.[321]

In summary, the security holders cannot make cash payments to the issuer except where necessary to achieve an "equitable adjustment" under Rule 149 under the Securities Act or for the purpose of combining fractional interests into whole interests under Rule 152a under the Securities Act. They are permitted to waive rights to accrued but unpaid dividends or interest and the issuer is free to include additional cash payments (together with the issuance of the new securities in exchange for the old securities).[322]

No commission or other remuneration. Section 3(a)(9) is available only in exchanges where "no commission or other remuneration is paid or given directly or indirectly for soliciting such an exchange." The restriction does not limit solicitation itself, but rather prohibits payment or compensation for soliciting activities. More than any other condition of Section 3(a)(9), this requirement significantly restricts the successful conduct of unregistered exchange offers and leads market participants to structure exchange offers subject to the registration requirements of the Securities Act.

The phrase "commission or other remuneration" does not prohibit an issuer from compensating those agents who incur ordinary transaction expenses in connection with a Section 3(a)(9) exchange offer. The dividing line, however, lies between payments that are in essence for soliciting or promotional activity as distinguished from payments that cover the expenses incident to the exchange procedure. In addition to engraving and clerical costs, these expenses could include a payment to third parties for services in connection with effecting, but not promoting, such an exchange. An issuer contemplating a Section 3(a)(9) transaction may, consequently, retain a financial advisor to assist it in planning and carrying out the exchange offer. Payments to such an advisor should generally be structured as a flat fee which is not contingent upon the success or failure of the offer.[323] The range of services which such an advisor can

[321] See, e.g., *The News Corporation Limited*, SEC No-Action Letter (May 15, 1992) and *Carolina Wholesale Florists, Inc.*, SEC No-Action Letter (August 17, 1976).

[322] See SEC Division of Corporation Finance, *Compliance and Disclosure Interpretations: Securities Act Sections*, Question 125.04 (November 26, 2008).

[323] A contingent fee arrangement is viewed as providing an incentive for solicitation and financial advisory fees are therefore structured as fixed-fee arrangements.

provide is strictly limited and it is crucial that any assistance provided by a financial advisor not be construed as promotional or constitute solicitation. Accordingly, a financial advisor to an issuer making a Section 3(a)(9) exchange offer may not give any advice or make any recommendations to the offerees as to the exchange, nor may it solicit the offerees' acceptance.[324] Moreover, the SEC has objected to any direct contact with security holders if the financial advisor has given a *fairness opinion* with respect to the transaction.[325] Financial advisors may, however, render services that are mechanical or ancillary to the procedural operation of the transaction. The SEC appears to view the neutrality of any communication from a financial advisor to an issuer's security holders as the critical factor for distinguishing mechanical services from solicitation.

There is a distinction between activities permitted to financial advisors in connection with advising the issuer over the course of a Section 3(a)(9) transaction and activities permitted to financial advisors in connection with their interaction with offerees. The SEC has not objected to the following activities undertaken by issuers' financial advisors in the course of helping the issuer to design the structure of the transaction: (i) formulating the offer or advising the issuer with regard to the possible terms of the offer, including any financial analysis relating thereto;[326] (ii) assisting the issuer in the preparation of the offering materials;[327] (iii) advising the issuer on procedures to be used in connection with conversations with offerees concerning the offer;[328] (iv) being named in the offering circular as financial advisor; and (v) rendering a fairness opinion.[329]

The SEC appears to focus greater attention on the interaction of financial advisors and offerees. Financial advisors have been permitted to contact offerees for the following purposes: (i) to confirm that offerees have received the offering materials; (ii) to confirm the addresses of the offerees;[330] (iii) to confirm that offerees understand the mechanics of accepting or rejecting the offer; (iv) to answer offerees' questions as to the mechanics of the offer; (v) to instruct offerees who ask for advice to seek

[324] See, e.g., *Stokely-Van Camp, Inc.*, SEC No-Action Letter (April 29, 1983).

[325] See, e.g., *Dean Witter & Co.*, SEC No-Action Letter (February 24, 1975).

[326] See *Calton, Inc. and Subsidiaries*, SEC No-Action Letter (September 30, 1991); *International Controls Corporation*, SEC No-Action Letter (August 6, 1990).

[327] See *Calton, Inc. and Subsidiaries*, fn 327 above; *International Controls Corporation*, fn 327 above.

[328] See *SunTrust Banks, Inc.*, SEC No-Action Letter (July 16, 1999); *Petroleum Geo-Services ASA*, SEC No-Action Letter (June 8, 1999).

[329] See *Dean Witter & Co.*, fn 326 above.

[330] See *SunTrust Banks, Inc.*, fn 329 above; *Petroleum Geo-Services*, fn 329 above.

advice from their own investment counselors or to contact appropriate officers of the issuer;[331] (vi) to answer offerees' substantive questions solely by referring to the appropriate portion of the offering materials; (vii) to ascertain what action offerees plan to take (and subsequently convey this information to the issuer);[332] (viii) to remind offerees of all appropriate deadlines;[333] (ix) to present the issuers' proposal to legal counsel and financial advisors of committees representing security holders, and receiving and discussing the committees' counter-proposals;[334] (x) to present the issuers' proposals directly to financially sophisticated security holders, and receiving and discussing the security holders' counter-proposals;[335] and (xi) to communicate with the back office personnel of brokers, banks, and other nominees who hold the securities for the benefit of the offerees to verify that the offering materials are being forwarded promptly and to request that back office personnel contact the beneficial owners to inquire whether they have received the offering materials and understand the mechanics of the offer.[336]

Under no circumstances may the financial advisor make any recommendation, either directly or indirectly through the communication of selective facts or information, regarding acceptance or rejection of the exchange offer. The SEC declined to take a no-action position, for instance, when Dean Witter & Co. proposed to telephone offerees and answer their questions about the offer (confining its answers to material contained in the offering circular) after having rendered a fairness opinion.[337] Dean Witter subsequently asked the SEC to advise it on whether the Section 3(a)(9) exemption would be available if it (i) rendered the opinion, and described the opinion in the offering materials, but refrained from telephoning the offerees, or (ii) rendered the opinion, did not disclose in the offering materials that it had rendered such opinion, and thereafter telephoned the offerees.[338] The SEC did not object to the former proposal, but did not believe that the exemption would be available if Dean Witter pursued the latter course, explaining that there would be an inconsistency on the surface in the proposition that representatives of a firm which has expressed an opinion (whether publicly stated or not) on the fairness of a proposed exchange may initiate contacts with security holders voting on

[331] Ibid. [332] Ibid. [333] See *Petroleum Geo-Services ASA*, fn 329 above.

[334] See *International Controls Corporation*, fn 327 above.

[335] See *Calton, Inc. and Subsidiaries*, fn 327 above.

[336] *SunTrust Banks, Inc.*, fn 329 above; *Petroleum Geo-Services ASA*, fn 329 above.

[337] See *Dean Witter & Co.*, SEC Reply to Letter of Inquiry (December 23, 1974).

[338] See *Dean Witter & Co.*, fn 326 above.

the exchange and express wholly impartial views on questions raised by these security holders.[339]

Beyond those activities expressly permitted, the SEC places less emphasis on any single activity of the issuer's financial advisor than on the impression created by the sum of all its activities. As the Dean Witter example illustrates, the SEC is concerned that certain activities or combinations of activities may amount to an oblique and indirect, yet nonetheless impermissible, recommendation or solicitation to offerees. Thus, the SEC has recognized that the use of a financial advisor or similar agents to conduct an exchange transaction is instrumental in an issuer's attempt to preserve its financial health and has taken *no-action* positions in a number of cases where it could be demonstrated that the financial advisor and other agents of the issuer would perform activities that do not constitute paid "solicitations" (e.g., activities that are only designed to "effect" but not "promote" the exchange).[340] In summary, the permitted activities of a financial advisor are the following: (i) the financial advisor may be named as dealer manager in the exchange offer documents; (ii) the financial advisor may consult with and advise the issuer as to the terms of the exchange offer and the security that may be issued pursuant to the exchange offer; it may engage with the issuer to perform the financial analysis for the issuer, create or assist in the creation of a restructuring proposal for the approval of the issuer, which could include setting out the capital structure of the issuer following the restructuring, the organization and timing of the restructuring proposal, the proposed terms of the new securities, the proposed terms and mechanical procedures of the exchange, the preparation of the exchange offer documents, and the instructions to employees of the issuer relating to the procedures to be used in communicating with the security holders; (iii) the financial advisor may render, under certain conditions, a formal opinion as to the fairness of the exchange offer to security holders from a financial point of view; (iv) any and all contact with any security holders by the financial advisor or agents should be undertaken with great care and must be closely supervised; the financial advisor may engage in certain specific services in order to convey information in the exchange offer documents to security holders, including obtaining a list of the holders of the relevant securities from the issuer and confirming the accuracy of the addresses of such holders,

[339] Ibid.

[340] See *International Controls Corporation*, fn 327 above; *Seaman Furniture Company, Inc.*, fn 302 above.

mailing or otherwise assisting in the distribution of the exchange offer documents, maintaining records on the exchange, contacting nominees holding the securities and ascertaining the number of the exchange offer documents for each brokerage house, delivering the appropriate amount of exchange offer documents to brokerage houses, trust officers, other banks, and nominees, and mailing duplicate copies of the exchange offer documents to holders of the securities who appear to have lost or mislaid those originally sent to them; the financial advisor or agents may also contact the security holders for the primary purpose of facilitating an understanding of the issuer's financial condition or structure of the exchange offer, and providing any clarifications that may be required on the procedures for participation in the exchange offer, if required, or to remind them of the relevant deadlines; in the event that an advisor or agent is contacted by an unsolicited security holder for investment advice regarding the exchange offering, the advisor should direct the security holder to directors and officers of the issuer or to the exchange offer documents; the financial advisor may also perform tasks that are permitted to be performed by investor relations firms (e.g., ascertaining what action individual security holders intend to take with respect to the exchange offer and communicating that information to the issuer); (v) the financial advisor or agents may advise the issuer and its employees with respect to procedures to be used in conversations with security holders; (vi) it may consult with and advise the issuer in connection with the preparation of various communications from the issuer to its security holders; (vii) the financial advisor and agents may participate in meetings and telephonic conferences prior to the commencement of the exchange offer, between representatives of the issuer, on the one hand, and the legal and financial advisors to any committee of security holders, on the other hand; and (viii) the financial advisor may receive and discuss counter-proposals of the legal and financial advisors to any security holder committee prior to the commencement of the exchange offer.

On the other hand, the following activities must be considered prohibited activities in the context of a Section 3(a)(9) exchange offer: (i) the financial advisor or agents must not solicit acceptances of the exchange offer; (ii) the issuer's financial advisor or agents must not make any recommendations to the security holders or any advisor or representative of the security holder regarding the acceptance or rejection of the exchange offer; (iii) they must not convey management's views or recommendations regarding the exchange offer or discuss the merits of the exchange, even if those views and recommendations are contained in the exchange offer materials; (iv) when communicating with security holders, the financial advisor or agents must provide no information other than that which is included in the materials sent by the issuer to the security holders, such as the prospectus, the letter of transmittal, the cover letter, and any other exchange offer documents; and (v) the financial advisor or agents must not express views as to the value of the securities to be issued in the exchange offer. If any security holder or any advisor or representative of any security holder asks the financial advisor a question concerning a characteristic of the exchange related to making any investment decision, the financial advisor must direct the holder of the securities to contact the appropriate employee of the issuer.

Officers, directors, and employees of the issuer may act on the exchange offer but they too are subject to limitations. According to the SEC, officers, directors, and employees in a continuing employment relationship with an issuer are naturally permitted to solicit and even recommend a Section 3(a)(9) exchange, but only so long as they are not rewarded with a bonus or special commission. To avoid any inference of special compensation for soliciting the exchange, the employees involved should receive only their regular salaries and maintain their usual duties.[341]

Investor relations or proxy solicitation firms may be hired to act as information or tender offer agents to perform certain ministerial and logistical tasks in connection with the exchange offer. Such tasks may include (i) notifying the security holders of all details of the exchange offer, (ii) confirming the accuracy of the contact details of the security holders, (iii) ascertaining whether the security holders have received the exchange offer materials and understand the procedures for participating in the exchange offer, (iv) ascertaining what action the security holders plan to take and communicating such information to the company, and (v) reminding security holders of appropriate deadlines and communicating with back-office personnel to make sure the exchange offer is administered properly.[342] Nevertheless, the SEC objected to an issuer

[341] See *Chris-Craft Industries, Inc.*, SEC No-Action Letter (September 8, 1972), where the SEC concurred with the view that since the company could act only through its officers, directors, and employees, so long as these individuals received no special compensation in connection with the exchange offer, Section 3(a)(9) permitted their communicating with security holders. The corporation also believed that Section 3(a)(9) "permits officers and directors affirmatively to recommend to bondholders that they accept the Exchange Offer." See also *Paine Webber Retail Property Investments, Inc.*, SEC No-Action Letter (July 9, 1993).

[342] See *Varco Int'l*, SEC No-Action Letter (March 24, 1986) (corporation's agents may obtain the corporation's list of security holders to confirm the accuracy of security holders'

relying on Section 3(a)(9) for an exchange offer where an investor relations firm was hired, among other things, to inform security holders of "management's recommendation" with respect to the proposal as such recommendation was set forth in the proxy statement.[343]

4.5 Relationship with the Trust Indenture Act

Securities issued under Section 3(a)(9) of the Securities Act are not exempt from the provisions of the Trust Indenture Act of 1939 (the "Trust Indenture Act").[344] Consequently, the requirements of Section 306(c) of the Trust Indenture Act apply and the securities issued in the Section 3(a)(9) transaction must be qualified under the Trust Indenture Act. In this respect, the view of the SEC is that, in the absence of an exemption from the Trust Indenture Act, a solicitation relating to an offer of debt securities exempt from registration pursuant to Section 3(a)(9) of the Securities

addresses); *ECL Indus. & Norlin Corp.*, SEC No-Action Letter (December 16, 1985) (corporate agents may ascertain whether security holders understand the mechanics of the exchange transaction); *Boston Futures Mgmt. Corp.*, SEC No-Action Letter (October 22, 1984) (corporate agents may contact security holders to confirm their receipt of materials received in the exchange): *Hershey Foods Corp.*, SEC No-Action Letter (October 12, 1984) (corporate agents may mail or assist in the distribution of materials used in the exchange); *Trans-Sterling, Inc.*, SEC No-Action Letter (June 16, 1983) (corporate agents may maintain records on the Section 3(a)(9) exchange); *Time, Inc.*, SEC No-Action Letter (April 19, 1979) (corporate agent may deliver the necessary volume of exchange materials for distribution to security holders used in the exchange); *Barnett Mortgage Trust*, SEC No-Action Letter (June 9, 1978); *Shareholder Communications Corp.*, SEC No-Action Letter (July 6, 1977); *Valhi, Inc.*, SEC No-Action Letter (February 17, 1977); *The Carter Org.*, SEC No-Action Letter (April 7, 1975) (corporate agents may remind back-office personnel to confirm with security holders corporate deadlines and that the exchange offer is correctly forwarded); *Dominion Mortgage & Realty Trust*, SEC No-Action Letter (October 29, 1975) (corporate agent may contact security holders to estimate the quantity of materials needed for transmittal in the exchange); *Frier Indus.*, SEC No-Action Letter (November 17, 1975); *UniCapital Corp.*, SEC No-Action Letter (November 4, 1974) (corporate agent may answer questions about the procedure of the exchange transaction); *Infotronics Corp.*, SEC No-Action Letter (April 3, 1972).

[343] See *Valhi, Inc.*, SEC No-Action Letter (February 17, 1977) ("The investor relations firm will be instructed that it may not make any recommendation regarding approval or disapproval of the Exchange Offer and that if it is asked for advice by a stockholder, it will respond that it is not authorized to give investment advice and that the stockholder should obtain such advice from his own advisors or contact appropriate officers of the Company."); *Accord, Mortgage Investors*, SEC No-Action Letter (September 8, 1980); *Dominion Mortgage & Realty Trust*, SEC No-Action Letter (October 30, 1975); *Carter Organization, Inc.*, SEC No-Action Letter (March 5, 1975).

[344] See Section 304(a) of the Trust Indenture Act.

Act may commence when an application for qualification of an indenture has been filed under the Trust Indenture Act.

4.6 Other US federal securities laws applicable to Section 3(a)(9) exchange offers

There are no specific disclosure, registration, or filing requirements for offers or issuances of securities within the scope of Section 3(a)(9) of the Securities Act. However, Section 3(a)(9) does not provide an exemption from the anti-fraud provisions of the US federal securities laws, including Rule 10b-5 under the Securities Exchange Act. Section 3(a)(9) provides an exemption from registration under Section 5 of the Securities Act but does not exempt the transaction from filing or registration requirements under other securities laws. If the new securities to be issued are debt securities subject to the Trust Indenture Act, the issuer must meet the substantive and qualification requirements of the Trust Indenture Act. If the exchange offer is also a tender offer for the securities to be surrendered, the issuer must comply with the applicable US Tender Offer Rules under Section 14(e) and, if equity securities are surrendered, Section 14(d) of the Securities Exchange Act. In an exchange of debt securities for equity securities, the law of incorporation of the issuer will determine the corporate formalities to be complied with in relation to the issuance of the newly issued equity securities in exchange of the old debt securities.

5 Section 3(a)(10) exchange offers

Section 3(a)(10) of the Securities Act provides an exemption from the registration and prospectus delivery requirements of Section 5 of the Securities Act in connection with offers and sales of securities in specified exchange transactions that are administered and supervised by a judicial or administrative body. The exemption applies in a situation where a

> security . . . is issued in exchange for one or more bona fide outstanding securities, claims or property interests, or partly in such exchange and partly for cash, where the terms and conditions of such issuance and exchange are approved, after a hearing upon the fairness of such terms and conditions at which all persons to whom it is proposed to issue securities in exchange shall have the right to appear, by any court, or by any official or

> agency of the United States, or by any State or Territorial banking or insurance commission or other governmental authority expressly authorized by law to grant such approval.[345]

The exemption is used in three broad areas: the settlement of litigation; bankruptcy, or similar proceedings; and business combinations and reorganizations outside of bankruptcy. There are two main policy considerations behind Congress's decision to include an exemption for certain reorganizations that meet the requirements of Section 3(a)(10): First, business reorganizations that include an exchange of securities can take many forms, some of which do not conform to the procedures for distributing securities that are contemplated by the Securities Act. Second, and probably most important, in the case of the reorganizations contemplated by the exemption, the purposes of the Securities Act could be achieved without additional regulation as long as the fairness of the transaction was supervised by a governmental or administrative body. According to the SEC:

> the whole justification for the exemption afforded by Section 3(a)(10) is that the examination and approval by the body in question of the fairness of the issue in question is a substitute for the protection afforded to the investor by the information which would otherwise be made available to him through registration.[346]

Before the issuer can rely on the exemption, the following conditions must be met:[347] (i) the securities must be issued in exchange for securities, claims, or property interests; they cannot be offered for cash; (ii) a court or authorized governmental entity must approve the fairness of the terms and conditions of the exchange; (iii) the reviewing court or authorized governmental entity must: (a) find, *before approving the transaction*, that the terms and conditions of the exchange are fair to those to whom securities will be issued; and (b) be advised before the hearing that the issuer will rely on the Section 3(a)(10) exemption based on the court's or authorized governmental entity's approval of the transaction; (iv) the court or authorized governmental entity must hold a hearing before approving the fairness of the terms and conditions of the transaction; (v) a governmental entity must be expressly authorized by law to hold the hearing, although it is not necessary that the law require the hearing;

[345] See Section 3(a)(10) of the Securities Act.

[346] See *Securities Act Release No. 312* (March 15, 1935).

[347] See *SEC Staff Legal Bulletin* No. 3 (July 25, 1997).

(vi) the fairness hearing must be open to everyone to whom securities would be issued in the proposed exchange; (vii) adequate notice must be given to all those persons; and (viii) there cannot be any improper impediments to the appearance by those persons at the hearing.[348] The Section 3(a)(10) exemption is available without any action by the SEC. It is, however, common that issuers that are unsure of whether the exemption is available for a specific contemplated transaction seek the SEC's views by requesting a "no-action" position from the relevant division of the SEC.[349] If there is any desire to seek SEC no-action relief, it is important to bear in mind that the SEC will not issue a no-action response *after* the fairness hearing has been held.[350] A no-action request must be submitted *before* the fairness hearing and in plenty of time in advance to allow the SEC to consider the issues presented and respond before the fairness hearing.[351]

5.1 *Approval of the exchange's terms and conditions by a court*

If a court is approving the exchange, the court must be authorized by statute: (i) to hold a hearing on the transaction, although it is not necessary that the statute require the hearing; and (ii) to approve the fairness of the exchange's terms and conditions.[352] In this analysis, the statute must require the entity to conclude affirmatively that the exchange is fair to the *security holders participating in the exchange.*[353] For example, the statute must require the governmental entity to conclude that the terms and conditions of the exchange are *in the best interest of shareholders* or *fair* to shareholders, *not* that the exchange is *not unfair, not unreasonable, not prejudicial,* or "not counter to the best interest of shareholders." Moreover, the governmental entity must find the terms and conditions to be fair both procedurally and substantively.

If there is a question as to whether the statute authorizes the governmental entity to hold a hearing on the transaction and to approve the fairness of the exchange's terms and conditions, it may be clear from the actual practice of the authorized governmental entity. For example, in *State Mutual Life Assurance Company* (March 23, 1995), the SEC relied on an opinion from counsel to the Division of Insurance of the Commonwealth of Massachusetts that the relevant statute authorized the Massachusetts Insurance Commissioner to make the requisite fairness determination. Analogous relief is available in the case of foreign courts.[354]

[348] Ibid. [349] Ibid. [350] Ibid. [351] Ibid. [352] Ibid. [353] Ibid. [354] Ibid.

The term "any court" in Section 3(a)(10) may include a foreign court.[355] It is clear from a long line of SEC no-action letters that the same requirements that apply to exchanges approved by US courts must be met by the relevant procedures of a foreign court. In addition, based on the no-action practice of the SEC, it is prudent that the issuer seeks opinion of competent foreign counsel that passes upon the following matters: (i) under applicable law, the court cannot approve the exchange unless it finds the transaction to be fair to the persons who will receive the securities; (ii) those persons will receive notice of, and have the right to appear at, the fairness hearing; and (iii) the issuer will advise the court *before* the hearing that it will rely on the Section 3(a)(10) exemption and not register the exchange under the Securities Act based on the court's approval of the exchange.

5.2 *Fairness hearing*

The court or authorized governmental entity[356] must: (i) hold a hearing to determine whether the proposed exchange's terms and conditions are fair to all those who will receive securities in the exchange; and (ii) approve the fairness of the terms and conditions of the proposed exchange. The hearing must be open to everyone to whom securities would be issued in the proposed exchange. The issuer must provide appropriate notice of the hearing in a timely manner. For example, if the securities are held in bearer form, there must be adequate publicity and publication of notices well in advance. Section 3(a)(10) does not specify the information that must be included in the required notice. The notice must, however, contain sufficient information to adequately advise those who are proposed to be issued securities in the exchange of their right to attend the hearing; and give them the information necessary to exercise that right in an informed manner.

5.3 *Section 3(a)(10) and schemes of arrangement*

The SEC has blessed the use of Section 3(a)(10) in a fair number of exchange offers by UK companies effected through a scheme of arrangement. A good example is offered by the exchange offer of Williams plc, a

[355] See, e.g., *SanDisk Corp.*, SEC No-Action Letter (September 21, 2006); *AngloGold Ltd.*, SEC No-Action Letter (January 15, 2004); *Constellation Brands, Inc.*, (January 29, 2003); *Galen Holdings PLC*, SEC No-Action Letter (August 7, 2000); *Lucas Industries plc*, SEC No-Action Letter (August 20, 1996); *Symantec Corp.*, SEC No-Action Letter (November 22, 1995); and *Orbital Sciences Corp.*, SEC No-Action Letter (October 13, 1995).

[356] Ibid.

public limited company organized under the laws of England and Wales ("Williams"). Based on the following facts, the SEC issued a no-action letter, which recognized the availability of Section 3(a)(10) in the circumstances described below.

In connection with a business combination transaction involving Williams, a UK court (the "Court") was asked to approve under Sections 135 or 425 of the Companies Act of 1985 (the "Companies Act") among others, the following transaction: a scheme of arrangement (the "Scheme") providing in two parts for (i) the conversion of all outstanding cumulative convertible redeemable preferred shares of Williams into ordinary shares of Williams, and (ii) the cancellation of all ordinary shares of Williams in exchange for ordinary shares of newco. Overall, the entire business combination transaction (the "Transaction") required three hearings (one for the cancellation of the outstanding preference shares and their conversion into ordinary shares of Williams, one for the cancellation of the ordinary shares of Williams in exchange for ordinary shares of newco, and one for the reduction of share capital of newco through the cancellation of a portion of the ordinary shares of newco).

The SEC agreed with the application of Section 3(a)(10) based on Williams's commitment to take all the following procedural and substantive steps in response to the requirements of Section 3(a)(10) as described above: (i) Williams applied to the High Court of Justice in England for permission to convene meetings of the holders of its convertible shares and ordinary shares to consider the Scheme and related transactions. The application was to be supported by an affidavit sworn by a director of Williams to the following effect:

> If the terms and conditions of the Scheme and related Reduction of Capital are approved by the Court, no registration of the securities to be issued to the holders of shares issuable in the Demerger transaction will be required under the United States Securities Act of 1933 in relation to holders of the shares in the United States of America. The exemption from registration is provided by Section 3(a)(10) of the Securities Act on the basis that the sanction of the Scheme and related Reduction of Capital by the Court is relied upon as an approval of the Scheme and related Reduction of Capital following a hearing on their fairness to holders of shares of Williams.

(ii) Pursuant to the application, the Court issued an order directing convening of the shareholders' meetings to approve the transactions necessary to implement the business combination. (iii) The Court also approved the form of circular and notice of the meeting to be sent to shareholders. (iv) After distribution of the circular and notice of meeting, the appropriate shareholders' meetings were held to approve the Scheme and related reduction of capital pursuant to the Court order and the requirements of the Companies Act, as required under Sections 135 and 426. (v) After the necessary majorities were obtained, the Court was petitioned to hold final hearings to approve the cancellation of the preference shares; to sanction the Scheme, including both the conversion of Williams's convertible shares into ordinary shares and the exchange of shares pursuant to which Newco became the holding company of Williams; and the reduction of capital pursuant to which a portion of the ordinary shares of Newco was cancelled. (vi) At this stage, the Court was delivered an affidavit demonstrating that all shareholders were sent a copy of the circular and an affidavit by Williams's chairman requesting that the Court sanction the cancellation of the preference shares, implementation of the two-part Scheme and the confirmation of the reduction of capital. (vii) Following the circulation of announcement announcing the date of the final hearings, the Court held final hearings and entered the orders described above.

6 Section 4(2) exchange offers

One of the most significant exceptions to the registration requirements of the Securities Act is the exception contained in Section 4(2) thereof, which exempts "transactions by an issuer not involving any public offering," i.e., private placements. Consequently, in a Section 4(2) exchange offer, the issuer issues new securities in a transaction not involving any public offering in accordance with the requirements of Section 4(2) of the Securities Act. The exemption from registration under Section 4(2) is based on the fact that investors in the private placement market are the type of investors who do not need the protection of the registration provisions of the Securities Act as a result of their ability to obtain from the issuer the information needed for their investment decisions.

6.1 Advantages and disadvantages of a Section 4(2) exchange offer

A Section 4(2) exchange offer has several advantages and disadvantages compared to a registered exchange offer. The advantages of a Section 4(2) exchange offer are the absence of publicity, the ability to pay an agent to solicit acceptances of the exchange offer, and the lower costs associated with a transaction that is not registered with the SEC and does not have to meet the substantial financial expense of SEC registration fees and other related expenses. In relation to publicity, a Section 4(2) exchange offer will not be publicized and, consequently, may allow the issuer to solicit tenders or commitments to tender before the security holders have an opportunity to organize and block a restructuring or liability management proposal.

The disadvantages of a private place pursuant to Section 4(2) of the Securities Act are also well known. In a Section 4(2) exchange offer, participating holders receive unregistered securities that may not be freely transferred without registration under the Securities Act or an exemption. The issuer may have to offer registration rights in order to get holders to tender. Furthermore, the Section 4(2) exchange offer is limited to sophisticated holders, accredited investors, or other holders who may be issued securities in a private placement. As a result, it may not be an appropriate technique for a debt issue that is widely held (including by retail investors). Moreover, if the exchange offer requires an *exit* amendment that eliminates or negatively affects covenants and other protections in the indenture governing the old securities, the inability in a Section 4(2) exchange offer to permit all holders to participate (in effect forcing certain holders to accept negative changes with no opportunity to accept the tender) may be regarded as fundamentally unfair. Finally, like all exchange offers, a Section 4(2) exchange offer is voluntary and (except for exit amendments) is not binding upon a non-tendering holder. Thus, it offers a holder who can successfully *hold out* of a troubled debt liability management transaction a potential windfall at the expense of other holders who tender and make concessions.

6.2 Structuring a Section 4(2) exchange offer

In order to decide whether a transaction is a private placement, the SEC traditionally applies five criteria:[357] (i) the type of offerees involved, including their financial capability to bear the economic risk of the investment and their degree of sophistication as investors; (ii) the number of offerees; (iii) the absence of any general solicitation or advertisement concerning the placement; (iv) the access of potential investors to relevant information concerning the issuer; and (v) resale restrictions.

In order to facilitate the application of Section 4(2), and in certain ways to expand it, in 1982 the SEC adopted Regulation D,[358] which provides a

[357] See, e.g., Release No. 285 (1935); 4552 (1962); *SEC* v. *Ralston Purina Co.*, 346 U.S. 119 (1953); *Hill York Corp.* v. *American International Franchises, Inc.*, 448 F.2d 680 (5th Cir. 1971); *SEC* v. *Continental Tobacco Co.*, 453 F.2d 137 (5th Cir. 1972); *Doran* v. *Petroleum Management Corp.*, 545 F.2d 893 (5th Cir. 1977).

[358] See Release No. 33–6389 (March 8, 1982). Regulation D consists of six Rules (Rules 501 to 506).

safe harbor exemption from registration if the offering satisfies certain enumerated conditions. Even if an issuer should decide not to come within the terms of the safe harbor under Regulation D, it is generally advisable to comply with the basic conditions of the regulation since they are considered by the SEC and the courts in interpreting Section 4(2).

Under traditional private placement theory, the SEC applies a doctrine known as *integration*, pursuant to which the issuer's other transactions are analyzed in order to determine whether any securities sold outside the private placement should be integrated with the private placement, thereby potentially destroying eligibility for the exemption. Under Regulation D, integration would occur if separate sales (i) are part of a single plan of financing, (ii) involve a single class of security, (iii) are carried out at or about the same time, (iv) involve the same type of consideration, and (v) are made for the same general purpose. Regulation D states that there is no integration if an offering is made more than six months before or after a private placement. A public offering on a foreign market and a concurrent private placement in the United States raises the question of integration affecting the exemption from registration of the private placement in the United States. Generally, the SEC has taken the view that such offerings need not be integrated.

Because there is no requirement to register with the SEC, a private placement under Section 4(2) or Regulation D is traditionally faster to accomplish than a registered offering. The issuer or its investment bank drafts a private placement memorandum which does not require filing with or review by the SEC. The securities are offered on the basis of a purchase agreement that includes not only the issuer's undertakings and warranties but also, in order to avoid an indirect public offering, the purchasers' undertaking to resell the securities only under certain conditions. Where investment banks are involved as placement agents, their relations with the issuer are governed by a placement agreement. In equity offerings, the placement agreement may be similar in scope to an underwriting agreement, with the addition of covenants by the banks as to how the placement will be conducted. In debt offerings, the placement agreement may be more in the nature of an engagement letter. The investment banks play a central role in insuring that the conditions for private placements are followed, particularly with respect to the characteristics and number of potential investors and the absence of general solicitation or advertising.

6.3 *Conditions for a Section 4(a)(2) exchange offer*

A private placement of exchange securities "not involving a public offering" pursuant to Section 4(a)(2) of the Securities Act must generally meet the following conditions:

Absence of general solicitation or advertising. Rule 502(c) of Regulation D provides that there must be no advertising or other general solicitation in the United States for the securities. Sales activity should not exceed that reasonably necessary to complete the private placement. This restriction applies equally to Section 4(a)(2) private placements. This restriction in the manner of sale, as well as on who the investors are, is not always easily understood. For instance, placing an ad for the offering in a financial publication, or doing a general mailing to stockholders, stating that only certain types of investors need apply, would itself invalidate the exemption.

Number and type of investors. Under Rule 506 of Regulation D the securities may be offered to an unlimited number of *accredited* investors and up to thirty-five other purchasers who have sufficient knowledge and experience in financial and business matters to assess (possibly with the help of third parties) the merits and risks of the investment. Regulation D does not provide any criteria for judging whether an investor has the requisite level of expertise. The highly technical definition of "accredited" investor includes banks, insurance companies, investment companies, employee benefit plans, trusts, the issuer's directors, executives or partners, corporations over a certain size, and certain individuals with high incomes or net worth. The theoretical ability under Regulation D to have an unlimited number of accredited investors (subject to the no general solicitation requirement) was a major departure from traditional private placement theory. A private placement under Section 4(a)(2) may only be extended to a limited number of experienced investors who are able to bear the economic loss of the investment – they must be wealthy and sophisticated. Offerees are counted as well as purchasers. In a Section 4(a)(2) offering, it is advisable not to offer the securities to more than the number of potential investors necessary to complete the offering up to several hundred purchasers, assuming a very large offering. To ensure the right type of offeree, it is also advisable to confine the offering to institutions and not to individuals. In order to ensure that purchasers lacking the requisite qualifications will not take part in private placements under Section 4(a)(2), it is common practice to set a minimum level of investment of $100,000 to $500,000. The potential investor is asked to confirm its status in an investor's letter that it countersigns and returns to the issuer or placement agent.

Disclosure requirements. There is no specific disclosure requirement for private placements under Rule 506 of Regulation D when the only investors are accredited investors. However, Rule 502(b) requires that the information specified by the rule (which is not fundamentally different from that required for registration under the Securities Act) be supplied to all unaccredited purchasers. For this reason, Regulation D offerings would normally be limited to accredited investors. Under Regulation D or Section 4(a)(2) placements, potential investors must have the ability to ask questions of the issuer concerning the terms and conditions of the offering and to request additional information from the issuer. The information provided must be sufficient to allow investors to make an informed investment decision. Whether an offering memorandum is prepared or publicly available information is used will depend on marketing considerations, the type of placement (debt or equity, size), and how well the issuer is known. In both Regulation D and Section 4(a)(2) placements, any issuer giving information that contains material misstatements or omissions is subject to liability under the Securities Act.

Restrictions on resale. Traditionally, private placees have taken securities for investment, without a view to resale. This means they are end-investors and not distributors in a broader distribution. Whatever the form of private placement, the securities can only be resold if they are registered at the time of resale or if the reoffer and resale are exempt from registration. The initial investor has to be informed that the securities may not be freely resold and investors are generally asked to sign a written acknowledgment to that effect as part of the investor's letter. In addition, the certificates representing the securities typically have a legend describing the restrictions on resale; under Regulation D, the legend is required. Privately placed securities of foreign issuers may, however, be immediately resold outside the United States to non-US persons or across certain foreign exchanges outside the United States.

Form D. For a placement under Regulation D the issuer must file a relatively simple form, Form D, with the SEC, giving certain details about the offering. No filing is necessary for a private placement under Section 4(a)(2).

Investor letter. As noted above, one of the traditional indicia of a private placement is a letter signed by investors. In this, investors represent as to their status, acknowledge that they had sufficient information to make an investment decision, acknowledge that they are able to evaluate the investment and bear the economic loss, and agree to resale restrictions. Because the form of letter is sent out to investors and then sent back signed by them, a signed letter has become known as a *two-way* letter. A *one-way* letter would in effect simply be notice to investors of the same information. The question arises in investment banks conducting private placements of whether a *one-way* letter is sufficient, as it is in Rule 144A under the Securities Act offerings to QIBs. That Rule requires certain notices to be given to QIBs but does not require anything back. The answer is that unlike in Rule 144A offerings there is no rule in a private placement that permits a simple notice. Also, the type of purchasers may be much broader than QIBs. As an evidentiary matter it is generally desirable to get two-way letters in most private placements. In a placement to a very small number of large QIBs that the bank knows well, it may, however, be acceptable to send out one-way letters.

7 Offshore exchange offers

Under Section 5 of the Securities Act, registration of securities offered to the public is required when the means of US interstate commerce are used in the offering. The term "interstate commerce" is defined broadly enough under the Securities Act to include any transaction or communication between the United States and a foreign country. As a result, the registration requirements of the Securities Act would technically apply to offerings being conducted outside the United States when the means of interstate commerce had been used, for instance, where the issuer is a US company or where the issuer is a non-US company but where there are some sales into the United States.

In Release No. 33–4708, adopted in 1964, the SEC stated that the purpose of the Securities Act registration requirements was to protect US investors. Securities offered outside the United States to non-US persons did not need to be registered, provided that procedures were implemented that were reasonably designed to ensure that the securities came to rest outside the United States.[359] Release 4708 dates back to the early days of the euromarkets, and its requirements proved to be increasingly difficult to apply to international transactions. In particular, many non-US issuers

[359] See Release No. 33–4708 (July 9, 1964) (hereinafter, "Release 4708"). For foreign private issuers, see also *Vizcaya International N.V.*, SEC No-Action Letter (April 4, 1973) and *Republic of Ireland*, SEC No-Action Letter (March 19, 1971); for investment companies, see Release No. 33–5068 (June 23, 1970).

had, since the promulgation of Release No. 4708, created US listings and markets for their securities and, as a result, found themselves subject to Release No. 4708 procedures for non-US offerings. Major US institutional investors found themselves shut out of foreign offerings in which they wanted to participate because of Release No. 4708 procedures. The SEC was criticized for its regulatory "imperialism" at a time when markets and investors had become increasingly global. Consequently, in Regulation S under the Securities Act, the SEC codified and redefined the principles for applying the registration requirements contained in Section 5 of the Securities Act to international securities transactions.

As a result, foreign private issuers issuing securities to holders outside the United States have been able to structure debt exchange offers in exclusively offshore transactions outside the United States and outside the scope of application of the US federal securities laws. These *offshore exchange offers* are structured as a combination of (i) an exclusionary offshore tender offer outside the scope of Section 14(e) of the Securities Exchange Act, and (ii) an offshore offering of new securities pursuant to Regulation S under the Securities Act.

7.1 Offshore tender offers for debt securities outside the scope of Section 14(e)

Federal courts in the United States have long accepted that Section 14(e) of the Securities Exchange Act does not apply to tender offers outside the United States that exclude security holders in the United States and where the relevant offer neither solicits nor accepts tenders by security holders in the United States.[360] Section 14(e) is designed to ensure that holders of securities confronted with a tender offer have adequate and accurate information on which to base their decision on whether or not to tender their shares.[361] A necessary predicate to a claim under Section 14(e) is therefore the existence (either imminent, pending, or recent) of a tender offer. Absent the existence of a tender offer, there can be no fraud "in connection with" a tender offer. Where security holders are "never presented with th[e] critical decision" of whether or not to tender, "a vital element of a § 14(e) claim" is missing. Outside the jurisprudence of the federal circuits, the SEC has long encouraged offerors to extend cross-border

[360] Ibid.

[361] See *Piper* v. *Chris-Craft Indus., Inc.*, 430 U.S. 1 (1977); *Rondeau* v. *Mosinee Paper Corp.*, 422 U.S. 49 (1975).

tender offers to US holders, particularly where the subject class of securities is registered under Section 12 of the Securities Exchange Act and the percentage of target securities held by US holders is not small. The SEC recognizes, however, that there are legitimate reasons for making exclusionary offers and provides that if they are made, appropriate measures must be implemented to avoid the US jurisdictional means implicating the application of the US Tender Offer Rules. In Release No. 33–8957, the SEC summarized the measures that would be required to avoid such jurisdiction means: (i) offer materials should clearly state that the offer is not available to US holders; (ii) obtain adequate information to identify US holders; (iii) obtain representations from tendering holders that the investor tendering the securities is not a US holder; and (iv) avoid mailing offer materials into the United States.[362] Even if such procedures are implemented, bidders must take notice of indications that a tendering holder may be a US holder. A more detailed discussion of exclusionary tender offers is set forth in Chapter 7.

7.2 Offshore transactions pursuant to Regulation S under the Securities Act

In April 1990 the SEC adopted Regulation S, which takes as its starting point the principle of territorial application of Section 5 of the Securities Act. Regulation S relates only to the application of the registration requirements of the Securities Act. It does not limit the scope or extraterritorial application of the other provisions of the federal securities laws, particularly the anti-fraud provisions.

Regulation S was accompanied by a 90-page interpretive release which attempted to clarify the application of the regulation to various situations. In April 1998, the SEC adopted amendments to Regulation S which were designed to prevent perceived abusive practices in connection with offerings of equity securities, including convertible securities, of US issuers purportedly made in reliance on Regulation S. Absent a showing of abusive practices in offerings under Regulation S by foreign issuers, the SEC determined not to extend the amendments to equity securities of foreign issuers. However, the SEC remains concerned with the potential for abuse by foreign issuers and regularly monitors practices in this area.

[362] A legend or a disclaimer stating that the offer is not being made into the United States, or that the offer materials may not be distributed there, is not likely to be sufficient in this respect.

Regulation S consists of a general statement on the scope of the registration requirements contained in Section 5 of the Securities Act, an issuer safe harbor and a resale safe harbor. Pursuant to the general statement, offers and sales made outside the United States will not trigger the registration requirements of the Securities Act.

Offerings that satisfy the conditions of the issuer safe harbor are not required to be registered under the Securities Act. The issuer safe harbor applies to offers and sales by issuers, distributors, their respective affiliates (other than certain affiliated officers and directors to whom the resale safe harbor applies), and persons acting on behalf of any of the foregoing. Offerings relying on the issuer safe harbor are subject to different conditions depending on the type of issuer and transaction; however, all offerings must comply with two general conditions.

General conditions. The two general conditions that must be satisfied for any offering complying with the issuer safe harbor are that (i) each offer or sale is made in an *offshore transaction*, and (ii) no *directed selling efforts* are made in the United States.

Qualifying an offer and sale as an offshore transaction for purposes of the issuer safe harbor requires that (i) the offer not be made to a person located in the United States, and (ii) when the buy order is originated the buyer is, or the seller reasonably believes that the buyer is, outside the United States or the transaction is executed in, on, or through a physical trading floor of an established foreign securities exchange that is located outside the United States. Registered offers and sales to US persons, or offers and sales made pursuant to an exemption such as Rule 144A under the Securities Act, do not jeopardize the issuer's reliance on Regulation S for offshore offers and sales.

Directed selling efforts include activities, such as promotional seminars or advertisements in the United States, that are undertaken for the purposes of, or that reasonably could be expected to result in, the conditioning of the US market for the securities offered. Directed selling efforts are selling efforts in relation to securities being sold in reliance on Regulation S. Selling efforts for a concurrent offer of securities under Rule 144A or another exemption or in a regulated US offering would not be considered directed selling efforts for purposes of Regulation S as long as they were legitimately required for the selling of the securities being sold in the United States.

Directed selling efforts do not include offshore press activity permitted by Rule 135e under the Securities Act, advertisements that are required to be published under US or foreign law, certain tombstone advertisements, visits of prospective investors to facilities located in the United States, or press releases that comply with Rule 135 in the case of a concurrent registered offering or Rule 135c in the case of a concurrent unregistered offering.

Specific conditions. The issuer safe harbor establishes three categories of offerings, each with applicable restrictions, based upon such factors as nationality and the reporting status of the issuer, the degree of US market interest in the issuer's securities, the type of offering, and the type of security being offered. Category 1 requires only compliance with the general conditions. Category 2 and Category 3 require, in addition to the general conditions, offering restrictions to be implemented and certain transactional restrictions to be followed. An issuer may choose the least restrictive category available for its particular offering.

Category 1. Foreign issuers may use Category 1 where there is no substantial US market interest ("SUSMI") in their securities. As stated above, there are no offering restrictions imposed other than the general conditions. SUSMI is defined separately for debt and equity securities. SUSMI for equity securities is determined on a class by class basis, while SUSMI for debt securities is determined in the aggregate. In each case, the issuer need only have a reasonable belief that there is no SUSMI with respect to the appropriate class of equity or of debt securities at the commencement of an offering. SUSMI exists with respect to a class of a foreign issuer's equity securities where, at the commencement of the offering, either (i) stock exchanges and inter-dealer quotation systems in the United States in the aggregate constitute the single largest market for the securities of that class over the prior fiscal year, or (ii) 20 percent or more of the trading in the securities of that class took place in, on, or through the facilities of stock exchanges and inter-dealer quotation systems in the United States and less than 55 percent of such trading took place in, on, or through the facilities of securities markets of a single foreign country over the prior fiscal year. SUSMI exists with respect to a foreign issuer's debt securities where, at the commencement of the offering, at least 300 US persons are record-holders (including securities held through voting arrangements, deposit agreements, or similar arrangements) of $1 billion or more in principal amount of the issuer's debt securities and 20 percent or more of the issuer's debt securities outstanding worldwide. Commercial paper that qualifies for the exemption provided by Section 3(a)(3) of the Securities Act is not considered in determining SUSMI. Hence, the thresholds for SUSMI are quite high, and most foreign issuers will not have SUSMI in either debt or equity.

Offers of securities directed into a single country (other than United States) to the residents thereof and that are made in accordance with local laws, customary practices, and documentation, securities backed by the full faith and credit of a foreign government, and securities offered and sold to employees of the issuer other than US residents pursuant to an employee benefit plan established and administered in accordance with the law of a country other than the United States, also fall into Category 1.

Category 2. Category 2 of the issuer safe harbor is available where the securities being distributed in reliance on the issuer safe harbor are (i) equity securities of a Securities Exchange Act reporting foreign issuer, or (ii) debt securities (including asset-backed securities and non-participating preferred stock) of any Securities Exchange Act reporting issuer or of a non-reporting foreign issuer. Category 2 requires offering restrictions to be implemented and certain transactional restrictions to be observed. The offering restrictions under Category 2 require that distributors agree in writing that all offers and sales of the securities made prior to forty days following the closing (referred to as the *distribution compliance period*) be made only in accordance with the issuer safe harbor or the resale safe harbor, or pursuant to registration under the Securities Act or an applicable exemption therefrom. In addition, all offering materials and documents (other than press releases) used in connection with offers and sales of the securities prior to the end of such period must include a statement to the effect that the securities have not been registered under the Securities Act and may not be offered or sold in the United States or to US persons unless the securities are registered under the Securities Act or an exemption from registration is available. The transactional restrictions under Category 2 prohibit, prior to the end of the forty-day distribution compliance period, offers and sales to US persons or for the account or benefit of US persons and require a confirmation to be sent to purchasers who are dealers stating that the purchaser is subject to the same restrictions on offers and sales that apply to distributors.

Category 3. Category 3 is a residual category available for offers and sales of any security and by any issuer. Category 3 is the only category available for offerings of equity securities of reporting and non-reporting US issuers, debt securities of non-reporting US issuers, and equity securities of non-reporting foreign issuers with SUSMI. In addition to the general conditions, the most restrictive offering restrictions are imposed by Category 3, designed to prevent unregistered distributions in the United States under circumstances where the likelihood of the offering inadvertently extending to the United States is greatest and/or Securities Exchange Act information is unavailable to protect investors. The restrictions on equity are more stringent than for debt. The Category 3 restrictions were previously applicable only to sales of equity securities of non-reporting issuers. Following the amendments to Regulation S in 1998, they now apply to offerings of equity securities by all reporting as well as non-reporting US issuers. Like Category 2, Category 3 requires that offering restrictions be implemented and that certain transactional restrictions be observed. The offering restrictions required to be implemented for Category 3 are the same as outlined above with respect to Category 2 except that, for equity securities, distributors must agree to observe a *one-year* restricted period and that, in respect of equity securities of US issuers, they will not engage in hedging transactions prior to the expiration of the distribution compliance period unless in compliance with the Securities Act. For equity securities of US issuers, the offering materials must also state that hedging transactions may not be conducted unless in compliance with the Securities Act. The transactional restrictions vary according to whether the securities issued are debt or equity. With respect to debt securities, Category 3 transactional restrictions are the same as Category 2 but also require that the securities be represented initially by a temporary global security which is exchangeable for definitive securities only after the expiration of the forty-day distribution compliance period and upon certification of non-US beneficial ownership.

With respect to equity securities, Category 3 transactional restrictions impose a one-year distribution compliance period on sales to US persons and confirmation delivery requirements, and during the one-year period additionally require that each purchaser certifies as to non-US beneficial ownership and agrees to resell such securities only in accordance with the provisions of Regulation S or pursuant to registration or another exemption, and to engage in hedging transactions only in compliance with the Securities Act. The securities of domestic issuers must contain a legend to the foregoing effect. Additionally, the issuer must be required by contract or a provision in its bylaws or charter to refuse to register transfers of the securities not made in accordance with the resale restrictions. While the forty-day lock-up for Category 3 debt securities is in accordance with market expectations, the one-year distribution compliance period and the related certification requirements mean that Category 3 is a less useful option for equity. In the release relating to the 1998 amendments, the SEC acknowledged the practical difficulties associated with the new transactional restrictions but noted that the potential for abuse was so great that US issuers would have to deal with these practical difficulties or not rely on Regulation S in making offshore offerings, instead either registering the equity securities under the Securities Act or offering them offshore pursuant to the Section 4(2) or Regulation D private placement exemptions. For a domestic US Securities Exchange Act reporting company, the sensible way to offer additional equity securities, whether or not the offering is offshore, would be to register the entire offer under the Securities Act.

7.3 Abuse of the offshore transaction exemptions

In 1995, the SEC published a release entitled "Problematic Practices Under Regulation S" that described a number of transactions which, while in technical compliance with Regulation S, would be viewed by the SEC as transactions in which the economic or investment risk never shifted to the offshore purchaser; thus, as a substantive matter, the subject securities never left the United States or remained offshore for less than the distribution compliance period. Examples of such transactions described in the release include the use of non-recourse notes as consideration – or recourse notes from an entity with minimal assets – where the expectation is that the repayment will be made from the proceeds of resales of the offered securities in the United States, and short-selling or hedging transactions where the purchasers transfer the benefits and burdens of ownership back to the United States during the distribution compliance period.

Regulation S may not be used for transactions which, although in technical compliance with the regulation, are part of a plan or scheme to evade the registration provisions of the Securities Act. Any transaction that results in a substantial flow-back of securities into the United States, either immediately after the distribution or immediately after the end of the applicable distribution compliance period, may be regarded as an abusive transaction which does not qualify for the Regulation S exemption.

8 Other securities laws affecting exchange offers

A debt exchange offer is subject to additional legal requirements, including the federal US Tender Offer Rules of Section 14(e) of the Securities Exchange Act and the rules and regulations promulgated thereunder, the Trust Indenture Act and the general anti-fraud provisions of Rule

10b-5 and, in Europe, the rules and regulations under the Market Abuse Directive.

8.1 US Tender Offer Rules under Regulation 14E

An exchange offer for debt securities is subject to the US Tender Offer Rules adopted in the form of Regulation 14E under the Securities Exchange Act for the part of the exchange offer that constitutes a tender offer for the securities that are the subject of the exchange offer. Regulation 14E under the Securities Exchange Act comprises several rules,[363] all reasonably designed to prevent fraudulent, deceptive, or manipulative acts or practices within the meaning of Section 14(e) of the Securities Exchange Act.[364] Section 14(e) was introduced as part of the Williams Act and its legislative purpose and motivation (i.e., the prevention of fraudulent or abusive practices in connection with tender offers) are extensively covered in Chapter 1.[365] The detailed discussion of the provisions of Regulation 14E applicable to tender offers for debt securities is set forth in Chapter 3.

8.2 The Trust Indenture Act

The Trust Indenture Act applies to the sale of debt securities and interests therein if the means of US interstate commerce are used. Any security subject to the Trust Indenture Act must be issued under an indenture, absent an exemption. A guarantee of indebtedness or a participation in a guarantee is covered by the Trust Indenture Act unless the security being guaranteed is exempt under Section 304 of the Act. In the case of securities subject to the Trust Indenture Act and required to be registered under the Securities Act, the SEC may not permit the registration statement to become effective if the security to which the registration statement relates has not been or is not to be issued under an indenture, or the trustee is ineligible to serve.

[363] See fn 107 above. [364] See Rule 14e-1 under the Securities Exchange Act.

[365] Pursuant to the House Report, the proposed subsection (e) of Section 14 of the Securities Exchange Act was intended to affirm the fact that persons engaged in making or opposing tender offers or otherwise seeking to influence the decision of investors or the outcome of the tender offer are under an obligation to make full disclosure of material information to those with whom they deal. See H.R. Rep. No. 1711, 90th Cong., 2d Sess. 11 (1968); quoted in *U.S.* v. *Chestman*, 947 F.2d 551, 559.

In certain cases, the Trust Indenture Act also applies to the sale of securities that are not required to be registered under the Securities Act. Section 304 of the Trust Indenture Act exempts numerous securities and transactions from the provisions of that Act, and many of the exemptions overlap with those provided in the Securities Act. The most commonly used exemptions from the Securities Act that are not also found in the Trust Indenture Act are those provided by Sections 3(a)(9) (exchange offers with the issuer's security holders) and 3(a)(10) (certain exchange offers approved after a fairness hearing) of the Securities Act. In such cases, the securities must be issued under a qualified indenture even though the securities are exempt from Securities Act registration.

With regard to the Trust Indenture Act implications of Regulation S under the Securities Act, the SEC has taken the position that it would not take any enforcement action under the Trust Indenture Act where an offer and sale of securities is made otherwise than under a qualified indenture, if the offer and sale is made in compliance with the provisions of Regulation S under the Securities Act.[366]

Application of the Trust Indenture Act to debt exchanges. In a registered debt exchange offer involving the issuance of new debt securities, the indenture under which such securities will be issued must be qualified under the Trust Indenture Act. Any security subject to the Trust Indenture Act must be issued under an indenture, absent an exemption.[367] In the case of securities required to be registered under the Securities Act, the SEC must issue an order prior to the effectiveness of the registration statement denying effectiveness if the security to which the registration statement relates has not been or will not be issued under an indenture, or with one exception discussed below, any person designated to act as trustee is ineligible to serve as such. The indenture is filed with the registration statement or by pre-effective amendment together with an eligibility statement of the trustee, usually on SEC Form T-1. The indenture is an exhibit to the registration statement, as is Form T-1. The indenture is deemed to be *qualified* when the subject securities are registered under the Securities Act.[368] In the case of securities *not* registered under the Securities Act that are subject to the Trust Indenture Act because no exemption is available – such as debt securities issued pursuant to Sections 3(a)(9) and 3(a)(10) of the Securities Act – the securities must be issued under an

[366] See SEC Division of Corporation Finance, *Offshore Offers and Sales* (April 24, 1990).

[367] See Sections 305 and 306 of the Trust Indenture Act.

[368] See Section 309(a)(1) of the Trust Indenture Act.

indenture and "an application for qualification . . . as to such indenture" must become effective.[369] If the Trust Indenture Act applies, the issuer must comply with the qualification provisions, including the requirement of using an indenture and an eligible trustee even though the securities are exempt from Securities Act registration. The application is filed on SEC Form T-3, which elicits information designed to show primarily whether the trustee is eligible under Section 310(a) or subject to a conflict of interest under Section 310(b). Form T-3 also requires certain information relating to the availability of the exemptions provided for by Sections 3(a)(9) and 3(a)(10) of the Securities Act if either of those exemptions is being claimed. The trust indenture to be qualified is an exhibit to the Form T-3. The indenture is qualified when the application for qualification of the indenture becomes effective pursuant to Section 307 of the Trust Indenture Act which incorporates by reference procedures from the Securities Act. Specifically, the application for qualification becomes effective pursuant to the provisions of Section 8 of the Securities Act. Generally, the application on Form T-3 will be filed at the commencement of the exchange offer. Unless a delaying amendment is filed, the Form T-3 becomes effective on the twentieth day after the date of filing.[370]

8.3 Anti-fraud protection in debt exchange offers

Section 14(e) of the Securities Exchange Act is a broad anti-fraud prohibition that is remarkably similar to the anti-fraud provisions of Rule 10b-5 under the Securities Exchange Act.[371] Section 14(e) applies in relation to tender offers, while Rule 10b-5 applies generally in connection with the purchase or sale of any securities, including in relation to tender offers and exchange offers. Section 14(e) prohibits factual misrepresentations or omissions of material fact or other fraudulent, manipulative,

[369] See Section 306(a) of the Trust Indenture Act.

[370] Rule 7a-9 under the Trust Indenture Act specifies a form of delaying amendment that is deemed to be filed on such dates as may be necessary to delay the effective date of an application for qualification of an indenture pursuant to Section 307(a) of the Trust Indenture Act. The form and content of the delaying amendment are specified in Rule 7a-9(a) and filing procedures are specified in Rule 7a-9(b). Rule 7a-9 under the Act specifies a form of delaying amendment that is deemed to be filed on such dates as may be necessary to delay the effective date of an application for qualification of an indenture pursuant to Section 307(a). Cf. Rule 473 under the Securities Act. The form and content of the delaying amendment are specified in Rule 7a-9(a) and filing procedures are specified in Rule 7a-9(b).

[371] Regarding Section 14(e), see generally Loewenstein, fn 283 above.

or similar practices. Section 14(e) of the Securities Exchange Act applies to statements of a material fact (or omissions thereof) or deceptive or manipulative acts or practices, in each case in connection with any tender offer or request or invitation for tenders, or solicitations of security holders in opposition to or in favor of any such offers, requests, or invitations. In line with the legislative purpose of the Williams Act, Section 14(e) protects all the holders of the tender securities, both those who intend to tender the relevant securities and those who do not. Both groups must be assured full, fair, and adequate disclosure so that their decision to tender or retain their securities will be predicated upon a knowledgeable and informed evaluation of the alternatives as well as full and fair disclosure.[372] Non-tendering holders have standing to sue for violations of Section 14(e) if they show that untrue statements or omissions of statements of material fact in connection with the tender offer injured such non-tendering holders by leading them to retain the securities instead of selling them at the price offered by tender offeror.[373] Conversely, non-tendering holders who are not misled by alleged misrepresentations in the course of a tender offer and who consequently do not rely on them are not able to sue under Section 14(e) for injury caused by successful completion of the tender offer.[374] Section 14(e) of the Securities Exchange Act and the applicable insider trading and market abuse regulations in the European Union are examined elsewhere in this book.

[372] See *Commonwealth Oil Refining Co., Inc.* v. *Tesoro Petroleum Corp.*, 394, F. Supp. 267 (S.D.N.Y. 1975); *Gunter* v. *Ago Intern. B. V.*, 533 F. Supp. 86 (N.D. Fla. 1981).

[373] See *Horowitz* v. *Pownall*, 582 F. Supp. 665 (D. Md. 1984).

[374] See *Hundahl* v. *United Benefit Life Ins. Co.*, 465 F. Supp. 1349 (N.D. Tex. 1979).

6

Debt repurchases in the open market and privately negotiated transactions

1 Introduction

As we saw in Chapter 1, if a corporate or sovereign issuer of outstanding debt securities (or, in the case of a corporate issuer, the broader consolidated corporate group of which the issuer is part) has excess cash from operating revenues, fresh borrowings, or the sale of assets and wishes to reduce the principal amount (and debt service obligations) of its outstanding indebtedness, it may purchase the relevant debt securities from the holders thereof, either directly or through a subsidiary or affiliate. If at the time of the repurchase by the issuer (or its affiliate) the relevant debt securities are trading in the open market at a price lower than the nominal value of the principal amount of such securities, or if the privately negotiated price agreed with the seller of the securities is lower than the nominal value of the principal amount of the securities subject to the sale (*below par*), the repurchase of those securities at the then current market price would lead to a greater reduction of the issuer's consolidated indebtedness than the reduction that the issuer would otherwise achieve with the same amount of cash through the partial redemption of the relevant debt securities at their nominal par value. This type of debt repurchase by the issuers (or their affiliates) is a popular method of debt liability management by corporate groups and sovereign issuers at times of financial stress when the market price of the relevant subject securities has declined considerably due to concerns over the solvency or liquidity of the relevant issuer. The issuer may also wish to retire debt securities with inappropriate or problematic covenants.

There are four possible transaction structures available to issuers considering a repurchase of their own debt securities: (i) a repurchase of the subject securities by the issuer of those securities; (ii) a repurchase of the subject securities by a parent company of the issuer; (iii) a repurchase of the subject securities by a subsidiary of the issuer; and (iv) a repurchase of the subject securities by a person (other than a parent company or a subsidiary of the issuer) that is an *affiliate*[375] of the issuer. The repurchase of outstanding debt securities by the issuer (or an affiliate of the issuer), in whole or in part, can be effected in a single, privately negotiated transaction between the seller and the purchaser of the debt securities. Alternatively, the issuer (or an affiliate of the issuer) may initiate a series of repurchases of outstanding debt securities in the open market with the assistance of a broker or dealer that will solicit or procure interested sellers of the relevant securities. The issuer or the purchasing affiliate may negotiate the purchase price directly with the selling security holder or it may purchase the securities in the secondary market. The issuer may also engage a broker or dealer to identify potential sellers of the relevant securities or the issuer may agree with the broker or dealer to purchase the debt securities from such broker or dealer.

2 The application of the US Tender Offer Rules to debt repurchases

If the purchase of debt securities in the open market or in privately negotiated transactions, in a single transaction or a series of related transactions, is deemed to constitute a tender offer, it will be subject to the US Tender Offer Rules and the transaction, among other requirements, will be required to remain open for at least twenty business days and will be subject to other restrictions.

As shown in Chapter 2, the Wellman test[376] listed eight factors or conditions that may indicate the existence of a tender offer that is subject to the anti-fraud US Tender Offer Rules: (i) an active and widespread solicitation of public security holders for the securities of an issuer; (ii) a solicitation made for a substantial percentage of the issuer's securities; (iii) an offer to purchase made at a premium over the prevailing market price; (iv) the terms of the offer being firm rather than negotiable; (v) the offer being contingent on the tender of a fixed number of securities, often subject to a fixed maximum number or amount of securities to be purchased; (vi) the offer being open to holders of securities only for a limited time and expiring thereafter; (vii) the offeree being subject to pressure to sell the relevant securities; and (viii) rapid accumulation of large amounts of target's securities, preceded by a public announcement of purchases of such securities. The courts have applied these eight factors flexibly, sometimes finding tender offers even if a

[375] See fn 8 above for a definition of terms.

[376] See generally Chapter 2.

number of factors are not satisfied, and giving greater or lesser weight to different factors, depending on the circumstances. The alternative Hanson test does not examine any specific factors but takes into account the totality of circumstances and more specifically if there appears to be a likelihood that, unless the procedural and substantive protections of the US Tender Offer Rules are followed, there will be a substantial risk that investors being solicited will lack information needed to make a carefully considered appraisal of the proposal put before them. In *SEC* v. *Carter Hawley Hale Stores, Inc.*,[377] the court applied the eight-factor Wellman test and reached the conclusion that the repurchase by the company of its own ordinary shares was not a tender offer subject to the US Tender Offer Rules. Because the repurchase plan involved the purchase of ordinary shares at available market prices, without any premium, and set no firm deadline for the holders of the shares to respond, the court concluded that the holders experienced only market pressure, not any form of coercion by the offeror, which the Williams Act was not designed to prohibit.

In light of all the factors considered above, purchases of debt securities in the open market by the issuer (or an affiliate of the issuer) are not usually found to be tender offers within the meaning of the term under the provisions of the Williams Act. Courts and legal practitioners reach this conclusion under both the eight-factor Wellman test and the *totality of circumstances* Hanson test.[378]

We discussed in Chapter 2 how a purchase of debt securities in the open market, directly by the purchaser or through a dealer, is probably not a solicitation of the relevant securities, certainly not an active and widespread solicitation; there are no fixed terms, no premium involved, no conditionality on acquiring a certain amount of securities, no limited time period, no pressure to sell, and no publicity of the offer. For debt securities offered and sold in the institutional debt markets (to QIBs or

[377] See *SEC* v. *Carter Hawley Hale Stores, Inc.*, 760 F.2d 945 (9th Cir. 1985).

[378] See, e.g., *Hanson Trust PLC* v. *SCM Corp.*, 774 F.2d 47, 56 (2d Cir. 1985); *Panter* v. *Marshall Field & Co.*, 646 F.2d 271, 286 (7th Cir. 1981); *City Investing Co.* v. *Simcox*, 633 F.2d 56, 61 (7th Cir. 1980); *E.ON AG* v. *Acciona, S.A.*, 468 F. Supp. 2d 559, 581(S.D.N.Y. 2007); *In re General Motors Class E Stock Buyout Securities Litigation*, 694 F. Supp. 1119, 1129 (D. Del. 1988); *Energy Ventures, Inc.* v. *Appalachian Co.*, 587 F. Supp. 734, 739, 740–42 (D. Del. 1984); *Liberty Nat. Ins. Holding Co.* v. *Charter Co.* (N.D. Ala. 1982), aff'd, 734 F.2d 545 (11th Cir. 1984), aff'd, 734 F.2d 545 (11th Cir. 1984); *Ludlow Corp.* v. *Tyco Laboratories, Inc.*, 529 F. Supp. 62, 67 (D. Mass. 1981); *Freedom Nat. Bank of New York* v. *Daniels & Bell, Inc.*, 528 F. Supp. 680, 683 (S.D.N.Y. 1981); *LTV Corp.* v. *Grumman Corp.*, 526 F. Supp. 106, 1094 (E.D.N.Y. 1981) (January 18, 1967).

other types of sophisticated investors), the sophistication of the likely sellers of those securities, especially for securities issued and traded in the high-yield market, precludes the finding that the holders of the relevant securities are likely to require the protections of the US Tender Offer Rules in making an informed selling decision. Thus, the conclusion that open market purchases of debt or other securities are not tender offers applies to purchases that result in the accumulation of a large percentage of the relevant outstanding amount of the securities,[379] purchases representing a large portion of the daily trading volume of the relevant class of securities,[380] purchases at a premium to the then current market price,[381] purchases following a public announcement,[382] purchases made after the offeror formed the intention to make a tender offer,[383] purchases by one competing tender offeror during a tender offer by another competing tender offeror,[384] or purchases from market-makers, or on the securities exchange's floor.[385]

A typical privately negotiated purchase of debt securities is also not usually a tender offer, as discussed in Chapter 2.[386] When a potential purchaser of debt securities approaches one or more potential buyers of debt securities with a view to negotiating a purchase or series of related purchases, there is usually no active and widespread solicitation and no premium is offered; the terms are not fixed and firm, but negotiable; the purchases are not conditional on the acquisition of a set

[379] See *SEC* v. *Carter Hawley Hale Stores, Inc.*, 760 F.2d 945, 952 (9th Cir. 1985) (over 50 percent); Exchange Act Release No. 24976, § I. (October 1, 1987).

[380] See *Kennecott Copper Corp.* v. *Curtiss-Wright Corp.*, 449 F. Supp. 951, 961 (S.D.N.Y. 1978), judgment aff'd in part, rev'd in part, 584 F.2d 1195 (2d Cir. 1978), judgment aff'd in part, rev'd in part, 584 F.2d 1195 (2d Cir. 1978) (on seventeen of forty-three trading days, exceeded 50 percent of volume).

[381] See *Mid-Continent Bancshares, Inc.* v. *O'Brien*, 1981 WL 1404 (E.D. Mo. 1981). Contra, Exchange Act Release No. 16385, § A. (November 29, 1979) (proposed, but never adopted, rule).

[382] See *SEC* v. *Carter Hawley Hale Stores, Inc.*, fn 380 above.

[383] Ibid., at 948–53.

[384] See *Luptak* v. *Central Cartage Co.*, 1979 WL 1280 (E.D. Mich. 1979).

[385] See *Water & Wall Associates, Inc.* v. *American Consumer Industries, Inc.*, 1973 WL 383 (D.N.J. 1973); *Chromalloy American Corp.* v. *Sun Chemical Corp.*, 474 F. Supp. 1341, 1346–347 (E.D. Mo. 1979), judgment aff'd, 611 F.2d 240 (8th Cir. 1979), judgment aff'd, 611 F.2d 240 (8th Cir. 1979); *Nachman Corp.* v. *Halfred, Inc.*, 1973 WL 457 (N.D. Ill. 1973).

[386] See *Pin* v. *Texaco, Inc.*, 793 F.2d 1448, 1454–455 (5th Cir. 1986); *In re General Motors Class E Stock Buyout Securities Litigation*, 694 F. Supp. 1119, 1129 (D. Del. 1988); *Rand* v. *Anaconda-Ericsson, Inc.*, 623 F. Supp. 176, 187–88, Bus. Disp. Guide (CCH) 6173 (E.D.N.Y. 1985), judgment aff'd, 794 F.2d 843, R.I.C.O. Bus. Disp. Guide (CCH) 6303, 1986–1 Trade Cas. (CCH) 67183 (2d Cir. 1986).

amount of securities; no time limit is imposed; no publicity surrounds the transaction; and the sellers are likely to be well informed and sophisticated.[387]

As a result of both of the Wellman and Hanson tests, companies repurchase large amounts of equity and debt securities through open market and privately negotiated purchases conducted outside the scope of the Williams Act and the US Tender Offer Rules. To our knowledge, there is no case law addressing the specific issue of repurchases of debt securities in the open market or in privately negotiated transactions. Given the nature of debt securities and the sophisticated investor base of the international bond markets, debt repurchases should be deemed to constitute tender offers only in limited circumstances where the facts and the policy rationale of the Williams Act require regulatory protection.

Companies are generally advised to keep both open market and privately negotiated purchases from falling into the trap of becoming subject to the US Tender Offer Rules. To achieve this objective, it is important to ensure that (i) the repurchase transactions should be made over an extended period of time without a firm deadline for completion, (ii) the direct offers to repurchase securities should be made to a limited number of potential sellers, (iii) each negotiation is independent of any other, (iv) each seller is sophisticated, (v) no attempt is made to impose the same terms on all sellers or to set any fixed deadline for responding (a record of negotiation is helpful) but the repurchase should be at different prices and on different terms, preferably negotiated individually with each seller, and (vi) the offerees should not be coerced (e.g., telling the debt security holder that the security will subsequently become very illiquid).

[387] See *In re General Motors Class E Stock Buyout Securities Litigation*, 694 F. Supp. 1119, 1130 (D. Del. 1988); *Beaumont* v. *American Can Co.*, 621 F. Supp. 484, 502 (S.D.N.Y. 1985), opinion aff'd, 797 F.2d 79 (2d Cir. 1986), opinion aff'd, 797 F.2d 79 (2d Cir. 1986); *Astronics Corp.* v. *Protective Closures Co., Inc.*, 561 F. Supp. 329, 335 (W.D.N.Y. 1983); *Kennecott Copper Corp.* v. *Curtiss-Wright Corp.*, 449 F. Supp. 951, 961 (S.D.N.Y. 1978), judgment aff'd in part, rev'd in part, 584 F.2d 1195 (2d Cir. 1978), judgment aff'd in part, rev'd in part, 584 F.2d 1195 (2d Cir. 1978); *Financial General Bankshares, Inc.* v. *Lance*, 1978 WL 1082 (D.D.C. 1978), on reconsideration, 1978 WL 1102 (D.D.C. 1978); *D-Z Inv. Co.* v. *Holloway*, 1974 WL 440 (S.D.N.Y. 1974); *Nachman Corp.* v. *Halfred, Inc.*, 1973 WL 457 (N.D. Ill. 1973) (small and powerful group of investors). Sophistication is relevant because sophisticated sellers are less likely to be pressured; *Stromfeld* v. *Great Atlantic & Pac. Tea Co., Inc.*, 484 F. Supp. 1264, 1273 (S.D.N.Y. 1980), aff'd, 646 F.2d 563 (2d Cir. 1980), aff'd, 646 F.2d 563 (2d Cir. 1980).

3 Disclosure requirements in connection with purchases of debt securities

3.1 Rule 10b-5 and repurchases of debt securities

Purchases as well as sales of debt securities by the issuer of the securities (or an affiliate of the issuer) are subject to the disclosure and anti-fraud rules of Rule 10b-5 under the Securities Exchange Act. While the rule has many different applications, its most important function in connection with purchases of debt securities is the proscription of such purchasers while the purchaser (whether an insider or an outsider) is in possession of *material non-public information.*[388]

Rule 10b-5, patterned closely after Section 17(a) of the Securities Act, prohibits the use of any means of interstate commerce to (i) employ any device, scheme, or artifice to defraud, (ii) make material misstatements or omissions, or (iii) engage in any course of business that operates as a fraud against any person, *in connection with the purchase or sale* of any security or securities-based swap agreement.

In connection with purchasing securities while in possession of material non-public information, the rule is clear. It is unlawful for an insider, such as an officer, a director, a majority shareholder, or the issuer of the securities, to purchase the securities from existing holders of such securities without disclosing material facts affecting the value of the securities, known to the purchaser of such securities by virtue of his or her inside position but not known to the existing holders of the securities and the general public, which information would have affected the judgment of the sellers.[389] Judge Leahy in the leading *Transamerica* insider trading

[388] Indeed, Rule 10b-5 was adopted as a random response in a fraudulent series of purchases of securities. This is the account given by one of the writers of Rule 10b-5, Milton V. Freeman, of the creation of the rule: "It was one day in the year 1942, I was sitting in my office in the SEC building in Philadelphia and I received a call from Jim Treanor who was then the Director of the Trading and Exchange Division. He said, 'I have just been on the telephone with Paul Rowen,' who was then the SEC Regional Administration in Boston, 'and he has told me about the president of some company in Boston who is going around buying up the stock of his company from his own shareholders at $4 a share, and he has been telling them that the company is doing very badly, whereas, in fact, the earnings are going to be quadrupled and will be $2 a share for this coming year. Is there anything we can do about it?' So he came upstairs and I called in my secretary and I looked at Section 10(b) and I looked at Section 17, and I put them together, and the only discussion we had there was where 'in connection with the purchase or sale' should be, and we decided it should be at the end." See ABA Section of Corporate, Banking and Business Law, "Conference on Codification of the Federal Securities Laws," 22 *Business Lawyer* 793, 921–23 (1967).

[389] See *Speed* v. *Transamerica Corp.*, 71 F. Supp. 457 (D. Del. 1947) (hereinafter, "*Transamerica*").

case had the following to say against the purchase of securities by persons while in possession of material non-public information:

> The duty of disclosure stems from the necessity of preventing a corporate insider from utilizing his position to take unfair advantage of the uninformed [holders]. It is an attempt to provide some degree of equalization of bargaining position in order that the [holders] may exercise an informed judgment in any such transaction. One of the primary purposes of the Securities Exchange Act was to outlaw the use of inside information by corporate officers and principal stockholders for their own financial advantage to the detriment of uninformed public security holders.[390]

That having been said, it is well established that, strictly speaking, Rule 10b-5 does not create an independent duty to disclose all material non-public information in connection with the sale or purchase of a security in all circumstances. Such duty exists only if the disclosure of the non-public and material information is necessary to avoid another statement from being misleading or if the person owes the other party a fiduciary duty or other similar relation of trust and, as a result of such duty, full disclosure of all material non-public information is essential.[391] In connection with open market sales and/or purchases of securities, the duty to disclose arises when one party has information that the other party is entitled to know because of a fiduciary or other similar relation of trust and confidence between them and not merely from one's ability to acquire information because of his or her position in the market.[392] To reach this conclusion, the Supreme Court in *Chiarella* examined the language and the legislative history of Section 10(b) of the Securities Exchange Act and the SEC's and federal courts' interpretations of it. Because the statute is silent and the legislative history provides no guidance as to whether silence constituted a manipulative or deceptive device within the meaning of Section 10(b) of the Securities Exchange Act, the Supreme Court

390 Ibid., at 99 F. Supp. at 828–29; see also *Kolher* v. *Kolher Co.*, 319 F.2d 634, 638 (7th Cir. 1963).

391 When an allegation of fraud is based upon non-disclosure, "there can be no fraud absent a duty to speak." *Chiarella* v. *United States*, 445 U.S. 222, 235, 100 S. Ct. 1108, 63 L. Ed. 2d 348 (1980) (hereinafter "*Chiarella*"). "Such a duty does not arise from the mere possession of material, nonpublic information." *Alexandra Global Master Fund, Ltd.* v. *Ikon Office Solutions, Inc.*, No. 06 Civ. 5383, 2007 WL 2077153, at *4 (S.D.N.Y. July 20, 2007) (hereinafter "*Alexandra*"). "Rather, a duty to disclose or abstain arises only from a fiduciary or other similar relationship of trust and confidence between the parties to the transaction." *United States* v. *Chestman*, 947 F.2d 551, 565 (2d Cir. 1991) (hereinafter "*Chestman*").

392 See *Chiarella*, ibid., at 228.

turned to case law and found that it supported the imposition of liability for fraud "premised upon a duty to disclose arising from a relationship of trust and confidence between parties to a transaction."[393]

Generally, courts look to securities fraud action precedents and the common law in determining whether a relationship carries a "fiduciary or other similar relation of trust" that imposes a duty to speak and disclose all material non-public information to the counter-party.[394] Certain fiduciary relationships, such as those between corporate insiders and shareholders, require that the fiduciary corporate insider disclose material non-public information to the shareholders in connection with securities trading or abstain from trading. In *Alexandra*,[395] the defendant contended that the relationship between a corporate issuer and its convertible note holders was not a fiduciary or other similar relationship of trust and confidence but simply a contractual relationship governed by the terms of the debt instrument. Thus, it submitted to the court that the plaintiff cannot establish that the defendant had any duty to disclose non-public information about its future plans when entering into the securities transactions in question. The court, in its opinion, agreed that corporations do not have a fiduciary relationship with their unsecured creditors, including debt security holders. The relationship is contractual rather than fiduciary and cited a number of precedents in support of that view.[396] Absent

[393] See *In re Enron Corp. Securities, Derivative & ERISA Litigation*, 610 F. Supp. 2d 600 (S.D. Tex., 2009); See also *Cady, Roberts & Co.*, 40 SEC 907, 1961 WL 60638 (1961) (holding that a corporate insider must abstain from trading in shares of his own corporation unless he has first disclosed the material information known to him, not because of the relationship between the buyer and seller, but because of the relationship of trust and confidence between the shareholders and the insider, who obtained the confidential information by reason of his position with that corporation; that relationship gives rise to a duty to disclose because of the need to prevent the insider from taking unfair advantage of the uninformed minority stockholders); and *Affiliated Ute*, 406 U.S. at 152–53, 92 S. Ct. 1456 ("Court recognized that no duty of disclosure would exist if the bank merely had acted as a transfer agent. But the bank also had assumed a duty to act on behalf of the shareholders and the Indian sellers had relied upon its personnel when they sold their stock," and thus its employees "could not act as market makers inducing the Indians to sell their stock without disclosing the existence of the more favorable non-Indian market.").

[394] See *Chestman*, fn 392 above, at 568.

[395] *Alexandra Global Master Fund, Ltd.* v. *Ikon Office Solutions, Inc.*, fn 392 above.

[396] *Lorenz* v. *CSX Corp.*, 1 F.3d 1406, 1417 (3d Cir. 1993) (New York law); *Page Mill Asset Mgmt.* v. *Credit Suisse First Boston Corp.*, 98 Civ. 6907, 2000 WL 335557, at *11 (S.D.N.Y., 2000) (New York law); *Metro. Secs.* v. *Occidental Petroleum Corp.*, 705 F. Supp. 134, 141 (S.D.N.Y. 1989) (New York law); *Simons* v. *Cogan*, 549 A.2d 300, 303–04 (Del. 1988) (Delaware law), aff'g 542 A.2d 785 (Del. Ch. 1987) (Allen, C.); see also *Metro. Life Ins.*

a positive duty to disclose, the court concluded, the issuer's silence about its future financing plans was not fraudulent.

This is not to say that issuers conducting purchases or tender offers of their debt securities should be relaxed about insider trading violations or would not be under a duty to disclose all material non-public information or abstain from trading. A duty to disclose could be founded on any other statement made public by the issuer, in press releases or filings, which would be misleading unless the issuer disclosed additional material information. A duty may also be established if the issuer, through its directors and officers, makes representations or discloses certain facts during the negotiations for the repurchase of the debt securities that would be misleading in the absence of additional disclosure of material non-public information.

In general, a cause of action under Rule 10b-5 includes the following elements: (i) a false statement or an omission of a material fact; (ii) with scienter, i.e., intentional fraud or recklessness; (iii) in connection with the purchase or sale of a security; (iv) upon which the plaintiff justifiably relied; and (v) which proximately caused the plaintiff's economic loss.

Rule 10b-5 limits liability to the material omission of facts or misrepresentation. The leading case on materiality is *TSC Industries, Inc.* v. *Northway, Inc.*, which defined a *material fact* as one to which there is a substantial likelihood that a reasonable investor would attach importance in making a decision because the fact would significantly alter the *total mix* of available information. Generally, a finding of materiality will be based on the total mix of information available to investors. This is an important concept. Relying on this "total mix" concept, for example, courts have held that omissions of fact are not material as long as the market possessed the correct information from other sources; and cautionary language in offering documents was sufficient to render alleged omissions not material. Information that is generally circulated through the media or other publicly available information will be considered in its entirety in assessing the total mix of information available to potential investors in connection with the purchase or sale of a security. The test of materiality is whether a reasonable investor would have considered

Co. v. *RJR Nabisco, Inc.*, 716 F. Supp. 1504, 1524–25 (S.D.N.Y. 1989) (finding that a New York court would agree with Simons that corporations do not owe fiduciary duties to debt holders); see also Harvey L. Pitt and Karl A. Groskaufmanis, "A Tale of Two Instruments: Insider Trading in Non-Equity Securities," 49 *Business Lawyer* 187 (1993), at 213: ("[T]he prevailing notion of debt securities expressly rules out the fiduciary relationship that gives rise to a duty to abstain or disclose.").

the matter significant; it is not sufficient to show that a bondholder or shareholder might have found the information to be of interest.

Based on existing case law, the following list includes, without limitation, facts which, if omitted, will likely be considered material to investors in debt securities in connection with the purchase of debt securities by the issuer, an affiliate of the issuer, or a corporate insider from an unsuspecting and uninformed holder of those securities: a new contract to sell the company's assets at a very attractive price;[397] a several-fold increase in the value of the company's inventory or assets;[398] the discovery of a rich mineral reserve or resource;[399] a substantial undisclosed increase in earnings; a substantial understatement of revenue; disclosures relating to corporate control and changes to the board of directors, e.g., failure to disclose the existence of a group of investors or executive officers that could exercise control over the company; failure to disclose a pending public offering or a probable acquisition or disposition of a significant asset; failure to disclose an upgrade of the company's credit rating; failure to disclose that the company had been awarded a substantial contract;[400] failure to disclose improved sales, earnings, and productive capacity, and the projection of the very favorable effect of additional capital;[401] and failure to disclose an offer or likely offer from a third person to pay a higher price.[402] Information need not be market-moving in order to be material. Material non-public information can include information regarding negotiations leading to financial restructuring, potential mergers, and acquisitions or other significant transactions, projections, business plans, or other information about business performance that has not yet been publicly released.

There is no doubt that the general rule of disclosure under Rule 10b-5 applies in the event of the purchase of debt securities by the issuer or an affiliate of the issuer: the issuer should not purchase such securities if the issuer possesses material information to which a reasonable investor would attach importance in making an investment decision in the debt securities, which material information is not publicly available. The issuer must disclose all material non-public information prior to purchasing the debt securities or should otherwise refrain from engaging in the relevant transaction. Any information that is *material* information within the

[397] See *Kardon* v. *National Gypsum Co.*, 73 F. Supp. 798, 800 (E.D. Pa. 1947).

[398] See *Transamerica*, above fn 390.

[399] See *SEC* v. *Texas Gulf Sulphur Corp.*, 401 F.2d 833 (2d Cir. 1968).

[400] See *Lerner & Co.*, Sec. Ex. Act. Rel. 7721 (1965).

[401] See *Van Alstyne, Noel & Co.*, 43 SEC 1080 (1969).

[402] See *SEC* v. *Fruit of the Loom, Inc.*, Litig. Rels. 1923, 1938 (S.D.N.Y. 1961).

meaning of Rule 10b-5 should be disclosed in connection with the repurchases of the relevant debt securities prior to the occurrence of such repurchases.

It is possible that there is a conflict between the Rule 10b-5 duty to disclose the material non-public information and some other duty that the company or the corporate insider may have, under the terms of a non-disclosure agreement or otherwise, to keep the relevant information confidential. In that case, the issuer or the relevant corporate insider has no viable alternative but to abstain from purchasing the relevant securities.[403] As it was aptly put in *Cady, Roberts & Co.*, if disclosure prior to effecting a purchase or sale would be improper or unrealistic under the circumstances, the alternative is to forgo the transaction.[404] The principle is clear: in connection with the purchase of any securities, Rule 10b-5 overrides any conflicting duty of silence and requires anyone in possession of material non-public information either to disclose it to the investing public or, if he or she is disabled from disclosing it in order to protect a corporate confidence, or he or she chooses to do so, abstain from trading.[405]

In *United States* v. *Royer*, the Supreme Court construed the term *public* for trading purposes to mean "readily available, broadly disseminated information, or the like."[406] The time required for the market to digest the relevant information so that the information is considered readily available and broadly disseminated varies with the circumstances.[407] Before insiders may act upon material information, such information must have been effectively disclosed in a manner sufficient to ensure its availability to the investing public.[408]

3.2 The Market Abuse Directive and purchases of debt securities

In the European Union, the Market Abuse Directive provides comparable protection from fraudulent behavior in connection with the purchase of debt securities by the issuer or an affiliate of the issuer.

The Market Abuse Directive prohibits three types of activities:[409] any primary insider or any secondary insider acquiring or disposing or attempting to acquire or dispose of financial instruments on the basis of *inside information*; any primary insider or secondary insider disclosing inside information to any other person unless such disclosure is made in the normal course of the exercise of his or her employment, profession,

403 See *Oliver* v. *Oliver*, 45 S.E. 232, 234 (Ga. 1903). 404 40 SEC 907, 911 (1961).
405 See *Texas Gulf Sulphur*, fn 400 above. 406 549 F.3d 886, 897 (2d Cir. 2008).
407 Ibid. 408 Ibid. 409 Market Abuse Directive, Articles 1–3.

or duties; and any primary insider or secondary insider recommending or inducing another person, on the basis of inside information, to acquire or dispose of financial instruments to which that information relates.

As discussed in Chapter 4, for purposes of the prohibitions introduced by the Market Abuse Directive, *inside information* means (i) information of a precise nature, (ii) which has not been made public, (iii) relating, directly or indirectly, to one or more issuers of financial instruments or to one or more financial instruments, and (iv) which, if it were made public, would be likely to have a significant effect on the prices of those financial instruments or on the price of related derivative financial instruments.[410]

The Market Abuse Directive does not contain a precise definition of what is non-public information. It is generally accepted that information that has been disclosed to the public is no longer non-public information. Other information based on publicly available information, including research, projections, and analysis, should also not be regarded as non-public information. Information relating to the issuer of a security or to one or more series of securities includes information on the operations and financial results of the issuer, recent developments, the composition of the board of directors or shareholders, corporate policy, dividend policy, litigation, potential mergers or acquisitions, the development of new technologies, and other facts and developments relating to operations, financial profile, corporate structure, or personnel. Information that directly relates to one or more series of securities includes decisions regarding the status and marketability of the financial instruments of an issuer, decisions and information relating to purchases, offers to purchase, repurchases, redemptions, or repayments of securities, which directly affect relevant financial instruments. For the purposes of applying the prohibition of the Market Abuse Directive, information shall be deemed to be of a precise nature if it indicates a set of circumstances that exists or may reasonably be expected to come into existence or an event that has occurred or may reasonably be expected to do so and if it is specific enough to enable a conclusion to be drawn as to the possible effect of that set of circumstances or event on the prices of financial instruments or related derivative financial instruments.[411]

Inside information is only *price-sensitive information*. Price-sensitive information is information which, if it were made public, would be likely

[410] See Market Abuse Directive, Article 1(1).

[411] Directive on Public Disclosure, Section 1(1), fn 223 above.

to have a significant effect on the prices of those financial instruments or on the price of related derivative financial instruments. In other words, information is price sensitive if a reasonable investor would be likely to use it as part of the basis of his or her investment decisions. In its guidance to the markets, CESR clarifies that market participants have to be able to assess beforehand whether the information is price sensitive, in order to be able to act accordingly, regarding the duties of confidentiality, prompt disclosure, and the prohibition on entering into transactions.[412] This means that this assessment has to take into consideration the market impact, which would be foreseeable at the moment when the information has not yet been disclosed and the market impact is not yet measurable. Therefore *ex-ante* factors have to be found in order to guide market participants in their decisions. In order to perform this *ex-ante* analysis, any (relevant) information available at the time has to be taken into account. A piece of information could be considered as likely to have a significant effect on the prices of financial instruments even though, when the piece of information is published, this does not actually produce any such effect.[413]

3.3 Special disclosure issues in repurchases of debt securities

A slightly different question is whether the fact that the issuer or the affiliate of the issuer is preparing to repurchase debt securities is itself material non-public information that should be disclosed in advance of commencement of the relevant transactions. For a holder selling its debt securities for cash, the identity of the purchaser of the securities (whether it is the issuer of the securities itself, an affiliate of the issuer, or a third party) should not be deemed to be material information for purposes of Rule 10b-5 under the Securities Exchange Act.

The repurchase of the debt securities may, however, cause adverse or positive effects on the results of operations, financial condition, and liquidity of the issuer. These effects can be, depending on the facts and circumstances, material information for the holders of the debt securities and other persons seeking to purchase the debt securities in the open market. For example, the potential reduction in the issuer's cash, coupled with the reduction of the outstanding amount of indebtedness, may

[412] See generally CESR, *Advice on Level 2 Implementing Measures for the Proposed Market Abuse Directive*, p. 15, December 2002, available at www.esma.europa.eu/system/files/02_089d.pdf. Accessed June 11, 2013.

[413] Ibid.

represent an improvement in the financial condition of the issuer such that holders of the debt securities (including the seller of the securities) may argue that they would not have sold at the relevant price or at all if they had known that the financial condition of the business would have so improved. Furthermore, the reduction of the debt by the issuer may cause taxable income and trigger material tax liabilities. Other aspects of the debt repurchase program may also be material. The materiality of the repurchase transactions must also be assessed by reference to the impact it may have on the trading market and general liquidity of the debt securities that will remain outstanding following the completion of the repurchases. For example, the amount of the securities to be repurchased may constitute a substantial part of the entire outstanding principal amount of the securities and, following the completion of the transaction, the remaining outstanding principal amount may be too small to support any meaningful trading activity. Whether the repurchase amount is such that it requires disclosure will not only depend on the size of the transaction but also on the overall profile of the debt securities that will remain outstanding after the completion of the repurchase transactions. The repurchase of 30 percent of the principal amount of a $150 million debt issuance will have very different impact on the liquidity of the remaining outstanding principal amount compared to the repurchase of 30 percent of the principal amount of a $900 million debt issuance. If the remaining outstanding principal amount is still sufficient from a trading liquidity perspective (as is obviously the case in our second example of a $900 million issue that goes down to $600 million following the completion of the debt repurchase program), then the debt repurchase program shall not be deemed to be itself material non-public information to be disclosed to the market. It goes without saying that each case is different and the relevant determination will always be highly fact-specific.

If disclosure of a debt repurchase program to the markets is required, the issuer may disclose the summary of the program to the markets through any available means of public communication, including a press release or other public announcement that is reasonably designed to achieve the public dissemination of the relevant information. It is often suggested to issuers that it may be a good idea to include a statement in their periodic public reports to investors to the effect that the relevant issuer, in the context of their financial policies and liquidity management, may from time to time seek to retire, redeem, repurchase, or refinance its outstanding debt securities through purchases of such securities in the open market, in privately negotiated transactions, or through redemptions or refinancings.

A related question that may affect the disclosure obligations of the issuer or an affiliate of the issuer is what the specific plan is with respect to the debt securities that will remain outstanding after the completion of the debt repurchase. If, for example, the issuer or an affiliate of the issuer considers the repurchase of the debt securities to be the first step in a series of transactions that will ultimately lead to the retirement of the entire issue (e.g., by launching a tender offer for or effecting a mandatory redemption of the securities not purchased on the open market or in privately negotiated transactions), then potential disclosure questions will have to be addressed.

3.4 Regulation FD

Private discussions or negotiations between the issuer or an affiliate of the issuer and the holders of the issuer's debt securities may trigger disclosure or other obligations under Regulation FD under the Securities Exchange Act. Regulation FD provides that when an issuer, or a person acting on its behalf, discloses material non-public information to certain enumerated persons (in general, securities market professionals and holders of the issuer's securities who may well trade on the basis of the information), it must make public disclosure of that information.[414] The timing of the required public disclosure depends on whether the selective disclosure was intentional or unintentional; for an intentional selective disclosure, the issuer must make public disclosure simultaneously; for an unintentional disclosure, the issuer must make public disclosure promptly.[415] Under the regulation, the required public disclosure may be made by filing or furnishing the relevant information with the SEC, or by another method or combination of methods that is reasonably designed to effect the broad, non-exclusionary distribution of the information to the public.[416] In the case of private negotiations between the issuer or an affiliate of the issuer and the holders of the issuer's debt securities, the fact that the discussions are taking place may be considered material non-public information in and of itself, or the discussions may be conducted within the overall framework of a restructuring of the issuer's debt obligations. Although such discussions are commonly accompanied by the disclosure

[414] Regulation FD, Rule 100 (a). [415] Ibid. [416] Ibid.

of material information about the issuer's financial condition, issuers usually avoid the obligation to disclose such information to the market because the person receiving the information is either under a duty of confidentiality or expressly agrees to keep the information confidential by means of a confidentiality agreement.

3.5 Regulation M

Regulation M under the Securities Exchange Act ("Regulation M") was adopted by the SEC in 1996 and was intended to preclude manipulative conduct by persons with an interest in the outcome of an offering. Rule 102 of Regulation M covers activities by issuers and selling security holders during a distribution of securities. Rule 102 makes unlawful, in connection with a distribution of securities effected by or on behalf of an issuer or a selling security holder, for such person or any affiliated purchaser of such person, directly or indirectly, to bid for, purchase, or attempt to induce any person to bid for or purchase a *covered security* during the applicable restricted period. Thus, if an issuer engages in a distribution of securities while at the same time completing repurchases of its debt securities, the issuer will be subject to Regulation M and must ensure compliance with its requirements. Investment-grade non-convertible debt securities and asset-backed securities are excepted securities not subject to the limitations of Regulation M. Also, if the distribution of the securities complies with the requirements of Rule 144A under the Securities Act, then the simultaneous repurchases will not be prohibited by Regulation M. The prohibition applies to covered securities, i.e., any security that is the subject of a distribution or any *reference security* (i.e., any security into which a security that is the subject of a distribution may be converted, exchanged, or exercised or which under the terms of the subject security may in whole or in significant part determine the value of the subject security).[417]

4 Transaction structures of repurchases of debt securities

Purchases of debt securities in the open market are accomplished through a broker, dealer, or agent and require the purchaser to pay a market price. The parties involved in an open market purchase are not aware of one another's identity. In a privately negotiated transaction, the buyer (acting

[417] See Regulation M under the Securities Exchange Act, Rule 100.

either directly or indirectly through an agent) approaches holders of the debt securities and negotiates a specified purchase price. Both types of transaction do not carry significant documentation or transaction costs.

The issuer of the debt securities or an affiliate of the issuer considering the repurchase of the debt securities should also consider covenant and other contractual restrictions in the relevant documentation governing the debt securities or other documentation (including intercreditor arrangements) that may contain limitations on the ability of the issuer or its affiliates to repurchase their own (or their affiliates') debt securities. All the necessary credit agreements, indentures, intercreditor agreements, and deeds must be carefully reviewed to ensure that these agreements do not contain any restrictions on the issuer's or the affiliate's ability to purchase the issuer's debt securities. Generally, it would be unlikely for a typical New York law-governed indenture or English trust deed to prohibit repurchases of debt securities issued under that instrument but there are always exceptions to the rule and the position must be thoroughly checked by counsel. Senior credit facilities and other senior financing documents may often contain limitations on the ability of the borrower group to repurchase debt obligations in the absence of special baskets and similar provisions that can be used for that purpose. If the debt securities in question are subordinated in right of payment to other senior debt securities issued by the same issuer (or the parent company or a subsidiary of the same issuer), then the repurchase of the relevant *subordinated* debt securities will probably be deemed for purposes of the indenture or trust deed of the *senior* debt securities to constitute *restricted payments*. Intercreditor agreements among the borrower group, senior lenders, senior bondholders, and subordinated bondholders contain similar provisions, and thus the ability to repurchase subordinated debt in the open market or in negotiated transactions is commonly subject to restrictions. In this case, the repurchase cannot be completed without the consent of the relevant creditors pursuant to the provisions of the underlying credit documentation. Moreover, if the issuer or the affiliate of the issuer needs to borrow the funds that will finance the repurchase of the securities, it must consider the covenant restrictions in relation to the incurrence of indebtedness.

There are three main alternative structures for the repurchase of debt securities by the issuer or an affiliate of the issuer: a repurchase of the debt securities by the issuer; a repurchase of the debt securities by the parent company of the issuer; and a repurchase of the debt securities by a subsidiary of the issuer.

5 Corporate law matters relating to repurchases of debt securities

The corporate law of the issuer's jurisdiction of incorporation and the issuer's constitutional documents (including the articles and memorandum of association) must also be reviewed in respect of potential statutory limitations or restrictions affecting the repurchase by the issuer of the relevant debt securities. Different jurisdictions restrict in various degrees the ability of an issuer of debt securities to repurchase the relevant debt securities with cash when the repurchase would be reasonably expected to impair the issuer's share capital or constitute preferential treatment of one class of creditors over another class of creditors during the issuer's insolvency or *suspect period* prior to insolvency. For example, pursuant to Section 548 of the US Federal Bankruptcy Code, a purchase by an issuer of its securities within one year before the filing of a bankruptcy petition is voidable by the trustee if such purchases were made with actual intent to hinder, delay, or defraud creditors, or the issuer received less than a reasonably equivalent value in exchange and either was insolvent at the time or was rendered insolvent thereby, was left with unreasonably small capital for the transaction of its business, or intended or expected to incur debt beyond its ability to repay such debt. Similar restrictions exist in virtually every other major commercial legal system.

Companies in certain industries (e.g., utilities) are further subject to notification and filing requirements in connection with the purchase by them of their own securities. Other corporate actions required include amendments to constitutional documents to the extent such documents (e.g., the charter or articles of association) restrict the ability of the issuer to effect repurchases of debt securities and shareholder meetings in the event that shareholders must authorize the relevant action. Moreover, the board of directors should consider its general fiduciary obligations to the issuer and its shareholders when determining the price of the relevant repurchases. A derivative shareholder action for waste of corporate assets and breach of fiduciary duty if the price is too high could be successful, especially if the securities are purchased from affiliates of the issuer or any of the directors in the issuer's board of directors.

6 Tax issues relating to repurchases of debt securities

The repurchase of debt obligations by the issuer of those obligations or a person related to or affiliated with the issuer is likely to have tax consequences. In the United States, in general, the purchase at a discount of a solvent borrower's debt, by either the borrower or a person related to the borrower, generates taxable income for the borrower in the form of cancellation of indebtedness ("COD") income. This COD income equals the excess of the amount owed on the purchased debt over the price paid for such debt by the issuer or the related person. Other countries have similar provisions. From time to time, tax laws come into effect that provide temporary relief from the tax effects of the recognition of income due to the COD at a discount, especially in times of crisis. For example, the American Recovery and Reinvestment Act of 2009 provided temporary relief from the COD rules by allowing borrowers to defer the recognition of such taxable income, thus making the refinancing and restructuring of corporate debt liabilities more attractive and efficient from a tax perspective. The same spirit of encouraging corporate rescues underlies the provisions of the Finance Act 2010 in the United Kingdom, which provides an exemption to the general rule that forgiveness of debt leads to taxable income in the case of a change of ownership associated with the forgiveness of debt if it is reasonable to assume that, but for the change in ownership, the issuer would be subject to insolvency arrangements within a twelve-month period. A detailed review of the relevant tax issues is outside the scope of this book.

7

Anti-fraud protection in debt tender offers

Section 14(e) of the Securities Exchange Act, case law, and market practice

1 Introduction

Tender offer regulations are anti-fraud regulations. They purport to protect investors from fraudulent or deceptive practices by tender offerors, the issuers of the tender securities, the financial institutions acting on behalf of such offerors or issuers, their affiliates, or their instrumentalities in connection with the commencement, conduct, and settlement of tender offers for securities held by the investing public.

In the United States, Congress enacted the Williams Act and thereby introduced Section 14(e)[418] of the Securities Exchange Act as one of the principal legislative responses to fraudulent, abusive, and/or deceptive practices in connection with tender offers for securities. Further, it empowered the SEC "by rules and regulations, [to] define, and prescribe means reasonably designed to prevent, such acts and practices as are fraudulent, deceptive, or manipulative."[419]

Pursuant to this rule-making power, and in connection with tender offers for all types of securities (equity securities, debt securities, and hybrid securities), the SEC adopted Regulation 14E comprising several rules,[420] all reasonably designed to prevent fraudulent, deceptive,

418 15 U.S.C.A. § 78n(e).

419 See Securities Exchange Act, Section 14(e). Senator Williams, the sponsor of the Williams Act, explained during the Congressional hearings that under Section 14(e) all relevant and important facts concerning the person or group making the tender offer would be disclosed. In this way, corporations, the holders of the securities, and potential investors could adequately evaluate a tender offer or its potential effects. In addition, he underlined that the bill, while protecting investors, would not place undue burdens on honest and fairly conducted business transactions. He used the Securities Act and the Securities Exchange Act as examples that full disclosure was not an impediment, but an aid, to such transactions. See Hearings before the Subcommittee on Securities of the Committee on Banking and Currency, US Senate, 19th Congress, First Session, March 21 and 22, and April 4, 1967, Federal Register, volume 32, number 54, March 21, 1967, pp. 4301–36.

420 See fn 107 above.

or manipulative acts or practices within the meaning of Section 14(e) of the Securities Exchange Act.[421] Section 14(e) was introduced as part of the Williams Act, and its legislative purpose and motivation (i.e., the prevention of fraudulent or abusive practices in connection with tender offers) are extensively covered in Chapter 1.[422]

The anti-fraud rules adopted by the SEC pursuant to the Congressional mandate enshrined in Section 14(e) of the Securities Exchange Act are not exclusive. Since the adoption of the Williams Act, federal and state courts in the United States have developed an expanding body of jurisprudence relating to acts, omissions, and general conduct that violate the anti-fraud provisions of Section 14(e) of the Securities Exchange Act through the interpretation of the following provisions of Section 14(e):

> It shall be unlawful for any person to make any untrue statement of a material fact or omit to state any material fact necessary in order to make the statements made, in the light of the circumstances under which they are made, not misleading, or to engage in any fraudulent, deceptive, or manipulative acts or practices, in connection with any tender offer or request or invitation for tenders, or any solicitation of security holders in opposition to or in favor of any such offer, request, or invitation.

In this chapter, we will examine the anti-fraud provisions of Section 14(e) with the assistance of the many federal and state court cases that have analyzed the relevant provisions against specific facts and circumstances relating to tender offers.

2 Scope of application of Section 14(e) of the Securities Exchange Act

Section 14(e) is a broad anti-fraud prohibition that is remarkably similar to the anti-fraud provisions of Rule 10b-5 under the Securities Exchange Act.[423] Section 14(e) prohibits factual misrepresentations and omissions of material fact as well as other fraudulent, manipulative, and similar practices. Section 14(e) of the Securities Exchange Act applies to statements of

[421] See Rule 14e-1 under the Securities Exchange Act.

[422] Pursuant to the House Report, the proposed subsection (e) was intended to affirm the fact that persons engaged in making or opposing tender offers or otherwise seeking to influence the decision of investors or the outcome of the tender offer are under an obligation to make full disclosure of material information to those with whom they deal. See H.R. Rep. No. 1711, 90th Cong., 2d Sess. 11 (1968); quoted in *U.S.* v. *Chestman*, 947 F.2d 551, 559.

[423] Regarding Section 14(e), see generally Loewenstein, fn 283 above.

a material fact (or omissions thereof) or deceptive or manipulative acts or practices, in each case "in connection with" any tender offer or request or invitation for tenders or solicitations of security holders in opposition to or in favor of any such offers, requests, or invitations.

2.1 General application

The section applies to any tender offer (including any exchange offer) for any type of securities subject to the Securities Exchange Act[424] (other than exempted securities[425]) regardless of whether or not they are equity

424 The term "security" is defined in Section 3(a)(10) of the Securities Exchange Act for the purposes of that statute. The definition is virtually identical to the definition of "security" for purposes of the Securities Act. "The term 'security' means any note, stock, treasury stock, security future, bond, debenture, evidence of indebtedness, certificate of interest or participation in any profit-sharing agreement, collateral-trust certificate, preorganization certificate or subscription, transferable share, investment contract, voting-trust certificate, certificate of deposit for a security, fractional undivided interest in oil, gas, or other mineral rights, any put, call, straddle, option, or privilege on any security, certificate of deposit, or group or index of securities (including any interest therein or based on the value thereof), or any put, call, straddle, option, or privilege entered into on a national securities exchange relating to foreign currency, or, in general, any interest or instrument commonly known as a 'security,' or any certificate of interest or participation in, temporary or interim certificate for, receipt for, guarantee of, or warrant or right to subscribe to or purchase, any of the foregoing." Section 2(a)(1) of the Securities Act.

425 Securities that are exempt from the scope of application of the Securities Exchange Act are outside the scope of application of Section 14(e) thereof. A long list of "exempted securities" is set forth in Section 3(a)(12) of the Securities Exchange Act, pursuant to which the term "exempted security" or "exempted securities" includes government securities, municipal securities, or any interest or participation in any common trust fund or similar fund that is excluded from the definition of the term "investment company" under Section 3(c)(3) of the Securities Exchange Act, any interest or participation in a single trust fund, or a collective trust fund maintained by a bank, or any security arising out of a contract issued by an insurance company, which interest, participation, or security is issued in connection with a qualified plan as defined, any security issued by or any interest or participation in any pooled income fund, collective trust fund, collective investment fund, or similar fund that is excluded from the definition of an "investment company" under Section 3(c)(10)(B) of the Securities Exchange Act, solely for purposes of Sections 12, 13, 14, and 16 of the Securities Exchange Act any security issued by or any interest or participation in any church plan, company, or account that is excluded from the definition of an "investment company" under Section 3(c)(14), and such other securities (which may include, among others, unregistered securities, the market for which is predominantly intrastate) as the SEC may, by such rules and regulations it deems consistent with the public interest and the protection of investors, either unconditionally or upon specified terms and conditions or for stated periods, exempt from the operation of any one or more provisions of this title which by their terms do not apply to an exempted security or to exempted securities.

securities, debt securities, or hybrid securities and regardless, further, of whether or not they are required to be registered under the registration requirements of the Securities Act.[426]

Furthermore, Section 14(e) makes no distinction between a tender offer by the issuer of the tender securities, by an affiliate of the issuer, or by an unaffiliated third party nor does it treat differently a tender offer supported by the management of the issuer of the tender securities compared to a *hostile* tender offer that is not so supported.

Consequently, Section 14(e) covers a broad range of transactions that are outside the scope of the application of Section 14(d) and the provisions of the Williams Act that apply solely to equity securities registered under Section 12 of the Securities Exchange Act, including, without limitation: (i) a tender offer where the tender offeror owns, after the consummation of the tender offer, 5 percent or less of the class of securities to which the tender offer relates; (ii) a tender offer for securities that are not equity securities, such as debt securities; (iii) a tender offer for securities that are not registered under Sections 12 or 15 of the Securities Exchange Act; and (iv) a tender offer for non-cash consideration.

As discussed in Chapter 5, a necessary predicate to a cause of action under the protective provisions of Section 14(e) is the existence (imminent, pending, or recent) of a tender offer.[427] Section 14(e) is not available in privately negotiated transactions[428] or other offers or solicitations that are not "tender offers" within the meaning of Sections 14(d) and 14(e) of the Securities Exchange Act.[429] Furthermore, persons who sold their securities prior to the tender offer or the alleged tender offer do not have any remedies under the protective provisions of Section 14(e).[430] The application of Section 14(e) is not limited to an actual tender offer; it covers pre-offer statements so long as the tender offeror has made public a clear intention to make a tender offer; it also covers false or misleading statements published before any announcement is made if the tender offer

[426] See Rule 14d-1(a) under the Securities Exchange Act. See also *E. H. I. of Florida, Inc.* v. *Insurance Co. of North America*, 499 F. Supp. 1053 (E.D. Pa. 1980), aff'd, 652 F.2d 310 (3d Cir. 1981).

[427] See *Labatt*, fn 287 above.

[428] See *Astronics Corp.* v. *Protective Closures Co., Inc.*, 561 F. Supp. 329 (W.D.N.Y. 1983).

[429] We discuss the definition of a "tender offer" within the meaning of Sections 14(d) and 14(e), as well as the rules and regulations adopted by the SEC thereunder, in Chapter 2.

[430] See *Johnston* v. *Wilbourn*, 682 F. Supp. 879 (S.D. Miss. 1988).

is likely, probable, or imminent.[431] Misrepresentations or material omissions made after a proposed tender offer is announced are also actionable where it is likely that the proposed tender offer will become effective.[432] Section 14(e) is therefore applicable when a fraud is committed (i) in connection with a tender offer, (ii) a request for tenders, (iii) an invitation for tenders, (iv) any solicitation of security holders in opposition to a tender offer, request, or invitation, *or* (v) any solicitation of security holders in favor of a tender offer, request, or invitation.

In line with the legislative purpose of the Williams Act, Section 14(e) protects all the holders of the tender securities, both those who intend to tender the relevant securities and those who do not. Both groups must be assured full, fair, and adequate disclosure so that their decision to tender or retain their securities will be based on a knowledgeable and informed evaluation of the alternatives as well as full and fair disclosure.[433] Non-tendering holders have standing to sue for violations of Section 14(e) if they show that untrue statements or omissions of statements of material fact in connection with tender offer injured such non-tendering holders by leading them to retain the securities instead of selling them at the price offered by tender offeror.[434] Conversely, non-tendering holders who are not misled by alleged misrepresentations in the course of a tender offer and who consequently do not rely on them are not able to sue under Section 14(e) for injury caused by successful completion of the tender offer.[435]

2.2 Application in "offshore" or "exclusionary" tender offers

Section 14(e) does not contain the typical *jurisdictional means* wording (unlike Section 14(d) of the Securities Exchange Act and Rule 10b-5 under the Securities Exchange Act, which both apply only to conduct, acts, or omissions made "by the use of any means or instrumentality of interstate commerce"). It is, however, generally accepted that the remedies of Section 14(e) are not available in connection with tender offers if there is no use of

[431] See *Pullman-Peabody Co.,* v. *Joy Mfg. Co.,* 662 F. Supp. 32, 34 (D.N.J. 1986) and cases cited.

[432] Ibid.

[433] See *Commonwealth Oil Refining Co., Inc.* v. *Tesoro Petroleum Corp.,* 394 F. Supp. 267 (S.D.N.Y. 1975); *Gunter* v. *Ago Intern. B.V.,* 533 F. Supp. 86 (N.D. Fla. 1981).

[434] See *Horowitz* v. *Pownall,* 582 F. Supp. 665 (D. Md. 1984).

[435] See *Hundahl* v. *United Benefit Life Ins. Co.,* 465 F. Supp. 1349 (N.D. Tex. 1979).

jurisdictional means or another basis for federal regulation.[436] In the same vein, Section 14(e) does not apply to tender offers outside the United States that exclude security holders in the United States and where the relevant offer neither solicits nor accepts tenders by security holders in the United States.[437]

Federal courts in the United States have long accepted that Section 14(e) of the Securities Exchange Act does not apply to tender offers outside the United States that exclude security holders in the United States and where the relevant offer neither solicits nor accepts tenders by security holders in the United States.[438] Section 14(e) is designed to insure that holders of securities confronted with a tender offer have adequate and accurate information on which to base their decision on whether or not to tender their shares.[439] A necessary predicate to a claim under Section 14(e) is therefore the existence (either imminent, pending, or recent) of a tender offer.[440] Absent the existence of a tender offer, there can be no fraud "in connection with" a tender offer.[441] Where security holders are "never presented with th[e] critical decision" of whether or not to tender, "a vital element of a § 14(e) claim" is missing.[442]

In *Labatt*, a tender offer by a foreign private issuer to holders of securities outside the United States, expressly excluding US holders, the court found that neither of the defining characteristics of a tender offer was present insofar as US holders were concerned. Under the terms of the offer, tenders were not being solicited from US residents and tenders were not going to be accepted from or on behalf of US residents. Each holder accepting the offer had to certify that he or she was not a US person who would be excluded from the offer. The court found that where, as

[436] For example, in Exchange Act Release No. 16384, the SEC notes that "Section 14(e) is not limited by its language to matters subject to federal jurisdiction, that is, acts or practices committed through the use of the mails or the facilities of interstate commerce. However, such an essential jurisdictional predicate for federal rule-making has been read into that section."

[437] See *Labatt*, fn 287 above. [438] Ibid.

[439] See *Piper* v. *Chris-Craft Indus., Inc.*, 430 U.S. 1, 35, 97 S. Ct. 926, 946, 51 L. Ed. 2d 124 (1977); *Rondeau* v. *Mosinee Paper Corp.*, 422 U.S. 49, 58, 95 S. Ct. 2069, 2076, 45 L. Ed. 2d 12 (1975).

[440] See *Stromfeld* v. *Great Atlantic & Pacific Tea Co.*, 496 F. Supp. 1084, 1088–89 (S.D.N.Y.) ("Section 14 is simply not applicable" where the plaintiff is neither confronted with a tender offer nor required to respond to one), aff'd, 646 F.2d 563 (2d Cir. 1980).

[441] See *Lewis* v. *McGraw*, 619 F.2d 192, 195 (2d Cir.), cert. denied, 449 U.S. 951, 101 S. Ct. 354, 66 L. Ed. 2d 214 (1980).

[442] See *Panter* v. *Marshall Field & Co.*, 646 F.2d 271, 283–84 (7th Cir.), cert. denied, 454 U.S. 1092, 102 S. Ct. 658, 70 L. Ed. 2d 631 (1981).

in that case, a tender offer is totally foreign and neither solicits nor will accept tenders by US holders, it is not a tender offer directed to US holders and the threshold jurisdictional requirement of Section 14(e) is not met.[443] The court also addressed the point of references to the foreign tender offer in press materials in the United States. The conclusion was that nothing in the US securities laws requires a foreign tender offeror to exclude US press coverage in order to avoid US regulation of its foreign offer. As the court stated in *Plessey*,[444] in refusing to apply the Williams Act to a foreign tender offer even though publicity about the transaction had appeared in *The Wall Street Journal*:

> [W]here a foreign bidder has steadfastly avoided American channels in its pursuit of a foreign target, the American interest in extensive disclosure appears minimal. Where the only acts within the United States are second hand news accounts not directly attributable to the bidder, the American contact which would justify an exercise of jurisdiction is relatively small and counsels against its use.
>
> (628 F. Supp. at 495)

When the plaintiff in *Labatt* argued that Section 14(e) should nevertheless apply because, despite the exclusion of US persons from the tender offer, the offer might influence such persons to sell their shares in the open market, the court was unsympathetic because the Second Circuit had rejected that very argument in earlier case. The argument had also been rejected by the Seventh Circuit in *Panter*,[445] which held that "the sole purpose of Section 14(e) is protection of the investor faced with the decision to tender or retain his shares," and that whatever the factors are that might influence a shareholder to retain or sell on the open market outside a tender offer, they are not "the proscribed pressures the Williams Act was designed to alleviate."

Outside the jurisprudence of the federal circuits, the SEC has long encouraged offerors to extend cross-border tender offers to US holders, particularly where the subject class of securities is registered under Section 12 of the Exchange Act and the percentage of target securities held by US holders is not small. The SEC recognizes, however, that there are legitimate reasons for making exclusionary offers and provides that if they are made, appropriate measures must be implemented to avoid

[443] See *Plessey Co. plc* v. *General Electric Co. plc*, 628 F. Supp. 477 (D. Del. 1986) (refusing to apply Section 14(e) to a tender offer in Great Britain involving two British companies, even though the offer was open to US shareholders).

[444] Ibid. [445] See fn 443 above.

the US jurisdictional means implicating the application of the US Tender Offer Rules. In Release No. 33–8957, the SEC summarized the measures that would be required to avoid such jurisdictional means: (i) offer materials should clearly state that the offer is not available to US holders; (ii) information adequate to identify US holders must be obtained; (iii) representations from tendering holders that the investor tendering the securities is not a US holder must be obtained; and (iv) avoid mailing offer materials into the United States.[446] Even if such procedures are implemented, bidders must take notice of indications that a tendering holder may be a US holder. For example, an investor may indicate that it is unable to provide the representations mentioned earlier, receipt of payment may be drawn on a US bank, a US taxpayer identification number may be provided, and the form of acceptance may be included in an envelope with a US postmark. On the basis of this guidance, market participants have developed procedures and market practices for the conduct of tender offers exclusively outside the United States and, as a result, outside the scope of application of Section 14(e) of the Securities Exchange Act. We are also aware that the SEC has offered informal telephonic guidance to counsel on the appropriate procedures to be followed in transactions structured as exclusionary offers outside the scope of application of the US Tender Offer Rules.

Although the SEC has, to date, offered general guidance on the substantive and procedural conditions for the conduct of exclusionary tender offers by foreign private issuers outside the United States, we are not aware of an affirmative approval by the SEC or the federal courts of exclusionary offers by US-based issuers.[447] While our view is that, for the same reasons discussed above, Section 14(e) of the Securities Exchange Act should not apply to tender offers by US-based issuers outside the United States that exclude security holders in the United States and where the relevant offer neither solicits nor accepts tenders by security holders in the United States, the absence of affirmative judicial or regulatory authority on this point would not allow counsel to give a clean opinion (i.e., an opinion that is not a reasoned opinion) on the applicability of Section 14(e) in this instance.

[446] A legend or a disclaimer stating that the offer is not being made into the United States, or that the offer materials may not be distributed there, is not likely to be sufficient in this respect.

[447] We are aware that the SEC has offered informal telephonic guidance accepting exclusionary offers by domestic US special purpose vehicles but not, to our knowledge, in the case of domestic US issuers with operations and senior management based in the United States.

From a practical standpoint, however, if the parties take steps to ensure that a proposed exclusionary offer is not targeted at US persons and prevent general participation in the offer by US persons, the risk that the SEC will consider such proposed non-US tender offer as being within the scope of application of Section 14(e) of the Securities Exchange Act is, as a practical matter, small. Similarly, the risk that a holder of tender securities (whether inside or outside the United States) would establish a cause of private action for fraud under Section 14(e) of the Securities Exchange Act solely for the failure of the offeror to comply with the US Tender Offer Rules is also, as a practical matter, small for the following reasons.

First, the same considerations relating to the legislative intent of Section 14(e) that apply to exclusionary offers by foreign private issuers are also directly relevant in exclusionary offers by US-based issuers. In offers by both foreign private issuers and US-based issuers, neither of the defining characteristics of a tender offer is present insofar as US holders are concerned. Under the customary terms of an exclusionary offer, tenders are not being solicited from US residents and tenders cannot be accepted from or on behalf of US residents. Each holder accepting the offer must certify that he or she is not a US person who would be excluded from the offer. The different status of a US-based offeror in a non-US offer (compared to the foreign private issuers in the existing case law) should not undermine the legal basis of exclusionary offers, i.e., that so long as a tender offer neither solicits nor will accept tenders by US holders, it is not a tender offer directed to US holders and the threshold jurisdictional requirement of Section 14(e) is not met. While the courts and the SEC have not affirmatively confirmed the position in relation to US-based issuers, they have not made an express distinction between foreign private issuers and US-based issuers either. Nor is there any statement in the case law or the positions of the SEC that would undermine this conclusion. Second, if the proposed non-US tender offer is limited to a percentage only of the outstanding principal amount of the tender offer securities and, based on the estimated principal amount of tender offer securities held by US persons, it is not necessary to include US holders in the offer to ensure the success of such offer, this is a helpful fact in the relevant analysis. This is one of the factors that the SEC takes into account when considering the validity of exclusionary offers. Third, when the tender offer securities are initially offered in the United States to QIBs within the meaning of Rule 144A under the Securities Act in large minimum denominations, the need to invoke the protections of the Williams Act diminishes. Consequently, it is unlikely that the types of sophisticated investors in the United States holding the tender offer securities at the time of the tender offer will be found to require the protections of the Williams Act in this set of circumstances.

3 Relationship between Section 14(e) and Rule 10b-5

The similarities between the anti-fraud provisions of Section 14(e) and those of Rule 10b-5 are obvious. They are both anti-fraud rules, prohibiting misrepresentations and omissions of material fact and other types of manipulative, fraudulent, or deceptive practices, schemes, or devices, except that, under Section 14(e), violations must be "in connection with" tender offers whereas, under Rule 10b-5, the relevant violations must be in connection with the purchase or sale of securities.[448] Moreover, Section 14(e) allows non-tendering holders and issuers of tender securities to sue for violations of anti-fraud requirements which would not be possible under the anti-fraud provisions of Rule 10b-5.[449]

In addition to imposing a duty on a tender offeror to disclose material information, the Williams Act expanded the class of persons protected under the federal securities laws. In other words, prior to the passage of the Williams Act, a party defrauded in connection with a tender offer had to seek relief under Rule 10b-5. Rule 10b-5 prohibits any fraudulent activity connected with the purchase or sale of securities. Since Rule 10b-5 contains a *purchaser–seller* requirement, holders of securities who did not tender securities or whose securities were not purchased did not have causes of action under the federal securities statutes. Section 14(e) is therefore virtually identical to Rule 10b-5, except that Section 14(e) does not contain a purchaser-seller requirement but covers all persons who have suffered economic loss caused by fraudulent conduct in connection with a tender offer. Federal courts in the United States have endorsed this view.

In *Dyer* v. *Eastern Trust & Banking Co*,[450] the court accepted that the intention of Congress in enacting Section 14(e) was to make available to those defrauded in connection with tender offers the full arsenal of remedies available under Section 10(b) of the Securities Exchange Act and Rule 10b-5 thereunder, providing defrauded holders of securities, including

[448] See *In re Gulf Oil/Cities Service Tender Offer Litigation*, 725 F. Supp. 712 (S.D.N.Y. 1989).
[449] See *GAF Corp.* v. *Milstein*, 324 F. Supp. 1062 (S.D.N.Y. 1971).
[450] 336 F. Supp. 890 (D. Me. 1971).

non-sellers and non-purchasers, with a federal cause of action.[451] In *Schreiber* v. *Burlington Northern, Inc.*,[452] analyzing the legislative history of Section 14(e), the court found that Section 14(e) was directed at ensuring full disclosure in connection with the trading of securities being the target of a tender offer.[453] Section 14(e) was viewed as a "broad antifraud prohibition" modeled on the anti-fraud provisions of Section 10(b) of the Securities Exchange Act and Rule 10b-5 thereunder.

The federal courts have on numerous occasions held that the two provisions are virtually identical (except in relation to the "in connection" wording) and should be construed in *pari materia*.[454] The effect of *pari materia* interpretation generally is that, when a statute is ambiguous, its meaning may be determined in light of other statutes on the same subject matter and, as a result, Section 14(e) must be interpreted in light of the jurisprudence on the anti-fraud provisions of Rule 10b-5 under the Securities Exchange Act. This guiding principle applies to all the elements of Section 14(e), including the requirements of fraud and manipulation, the requirement of materiality, and the requirement of scienter.

4 Untrue statements and misleading omissions of material fact in tender offers

4.1 Introduction

Section 14(e) prohibits two broad types of conduct in connection with a tender offer (or a request for tenders *or* an invitation for tenders *or* any solicitation of security holders in opposition to a tender offer, request, or invitation *or* any such solicitation in favor of a tender offer, request, or invitation): first, to make any untrue statement of a material fact ("material misrepresentation") or to omit to state any material fact necessary in order to make the statements made, in the light of the circumstances under which they are made, not misleading ("misleading material omission"); and second, to engage in any fraudulent, deceptive, or manipulative acts or practices. In this subsection, we will examine the first prong of Section

451 See *Lowenschuss* v. *Kane*, 520 F.2d 255 (2d Cir. 1975); *H.K. Porter, Inc.* v. *Nicholson Tile Co.*, 482 F.2d 421 (lst Cir. 1973).

452 472 U.S. 1, 11, 105 (1985) (hereinafter, "*Schreiber*").

453 H.R. Rep. No. 1711, 90th Cong., 2nd Sess. 11 (1968); S. Rep. No. 550, 90th Cong., 1st Sess. 11 (1967) U.S.Code Cong. & Admin. News 1968, 2811.

454 See *American Carriers, Inc.* v. *Baytree Investors, Inc.*, 685 F. Supp. 800 (D. Kan. 1988).

14(e), i.e., the prohibition on *material misrepresentations* and *misleading material omissions.*

Securities lawyers familiar with the wording of Rule 10b-5 under the Securities Exchange Act will not fail to recognize that the wording of the prohibition of material misrepresentations and misleading material omissions in Section 14(e) is identical to that of Rule 10b-5. Consequently, as the federal courts have repeatedly confirmed in tender offer litigation under Section 14(e), the legal analysis of what constitutes an untrue statement of a material fact or a misleading omission of a material fact in connection with a tender offer is identical to the legal analysis under Rule 10b-5 in connection with the sale or purchase of securities, *mutatis mutandis* for the different factual context of the various types of transactions subject to Section 14(e) and Rule 10b-5, as the case may be.

As a general matter, a material misrepresentation is an untrue statement of a material fact. It is a factual statement, either oral or in writing, that is not true. It is also a statement that conveys a false impression to a reasonable investor.

The concept of a misleading material omission is more complex and nuanced. An omission is, by definition, not an express statement. It is the absence of an express statement, an act of silence, or non-verbal conduct, which misleads a reasonable investor. A misleading material omission also includes a *half truth.* A half truth is a statement which accurately discloses some facts, but misleads the listener or reader by concealing other data necessary for a true understanding of the information that is expressly included in the relevant oral or written statement.[455] Certainly, the demarcation line between a material misrepresentation and a material half truth is not always clear. Complete silence or omission to say anything at all is also actionable under Section 14(e) and Rule 10b-5 to the extent the omission to speak renders other information included in the statements made misleading.

4.2 Materiality in Section 14(e)

Assuming there is a misleading statement of fact or a misleading omission to state a fact, there is no prohibition and no remedies are available under Section 14(e) if the relevant fact is not *material* within the meaning of Section 14(e). The term "material" for these purposes is identical

455 See *Abell* v. *Potomac Ins. Co.*, 858 F.2d 1104, 1119.

to the standard of materiality under the federal jurisprudence in Rule 10b-5 cases.

In *TSC Indus., Inc.* v. *Northway, Inc.*,[456] the court, ascertaining the meaning of Rule 14e-3 under the Securities Exchange Act in connection with a tender offer, held that information is material whenever there is a substantial likelihood that a reasonable investor would consider it important in deciding how to invest. The materiality of information was deemed to be a mixed "question of law and fact, where the legal component depends on whether the information is relevant to a given question in light of the controlling substantive law and the factual requires an inference as to whether the information would likely be given weight by a person considering that question."[457] To be material, the information need not be such that a reasonable investor would necessarily change the investment decision based on it. It is sufficient that a reasonable investor viewed it as significantly altering the *total mix* of information available to the investing public. More specifically, material facts include those "which affect the probable future of the company and those which may affect the desire of investors to buy, sell or hold the company's securities"[458] or any fact which in reasonable and objective contemplation by a reasonable investor might affect the value of the corporation's stock or other securities.[459] The well-known materiality case *SEC* v. *Texas Gulf Sulphur Co.*[460] added an extra factor in determining whether information is material: the importance attached to the information by the persons who knew about it.[461] From another perspective, in *Basic, Inc.* v. *Levinson*,[462] the Supreme Court noted that the materiality of information, with respect to contingent or speculative information or events, depended upon a balancing of both the indicated probability that the acquisition would occur and the magnitude of this acquisition in light of the totality of the company's activity.

In relation to misrepresentations or misleading omissions of facts in connection with tender offers or any solicitation of security holders in opposition to such offers, the condition of materiality focuses on importance of the misstated or omitted fact in a reasonable investor's decision

456 426 U.S. 438, 449 (1976).
457 See *SEC* v. *First Jersey Sec., Inc.*, 101 F.3d 1450, 1466 (2d Cir. 1996).
458 See *SEC* v. *Texas Gulf Sulphur Co.*, 401 F.2d 833, 849 (2d Cir. 1968).
459 See *List* v. *Fashion Park, Inc.*, 340 F.2d 457, 462 (2d Cir. 1965).
460 See fn 459 above.
461 Ibid. 462 485 U.S. 224 (1988).

to buy or sell. The key question is whether a prototype reasonable investor would have relied on such statement or omission. The legal assessment takes into account all surrounding circumstances to determine whether the facts under consideration are of such significance that a reasonable investor would weigh them in connection with a decision to tender or not.[463] Stated differently, Section 14(e) and the other anti-fraud remedies of the Williams Act do not require that the tender offeror disclose all information that it possesses about itself or the securities to which the tender offer relates, but only those material, objective, factual matters which a reasonable security holder would consider important in deciding whether to tender its securities or not. For purposes of Section 14(e), facts are deemed to be material if there is reasonable likelihood that a reasonable investor would consider them important or significant in making an investment decision in connection with the tender offer.[464] The standard of materiality requires that omissions or misstatements in a tender offer have a significant propensity to affect a decision, i.e., there must be a substantial likelihood that, under all the circumstances, an omission or misstatement would have assumed actual significance to a reasonable security holder evaluating a tender offer.[465] The focus is always on the effect of such misleading misrepresentation or misleading omission of fact on a reasonable investor's decision to tender or not the relevant securities subject to the tender offer.[466]

For the purposes of the Williams Act, the distinction between materiality and reliance is one of degree. Inquiry as to materiality in the tender offer context is whether there exists a substantial likelihood that a reasonable security holder would consider a particular fact important in deciding what to do with the relevant tender offer securities. The element of reliance essentially concerns whether the misrepresentation or omission actually induced the plaintiff to act differently than he or she would have acted in his or her investment decision. In general, a plaintiff must demonstrate both materiality and reliance in securities fraud cases.[467]

[463] See generally *Chris-Craft Industries, Inc.* v. *Piper Aircraft Corp.*, 430 F.2d 341 (2d Cir. 1973).

[464] See *Koppers Co., Inc.* v. *American Exp. Co.*, 689 F. Supp. 1371 (W.D. Pa. 1988).

[465] See *In re TransOcean Tender Offer Securities Litigation*, 427 F. Supp. 1211 (C.D. Ill. 1977); *Prudent Real Estate Trust* v. *Johncamp Realty, Inc.*, 599 F.2d 1140 (C.A.N.Y. 1979); *Riggs Nat. Bank of Washington D. C.* v. *Allbritton*, 516 F. Supp. 164 (D.D.C. 1981).

[466] See *A & K Railroad Materials, Inc.* v. *Green Bay & W.R.R. Co.*, 437 F. Supp. 636 (W.D. Wis. 1977).

[467] See *Berman* v. *Gerber Products Co.*, 454 F. Supp. 1310 (W.D. Mich. 1978).

Viewed from a different perspective, a certain misleading misrepresentation or omission will not be sufficient for the purposes of an action under Section 14(e) if, based on the specific facts and circumstances, the relevant fact is *immaterial*. Courts have found various types of fact to be immaterial for a number of reasons: (i) the fact is insignificant, vague, or trivial in light of the circumstances;[468] (ii) the fact is obvious, already public, or common knowledge;[469] (iii) it is only tangentially related to the relevant question and therefore unnecessary for an investment decision;[470] and (iv) the information is stale or the plaintiff knows that the statement is false or probably false.[471]

Whether the relevant fact is material or not is measured at the time that the alleged violation occurred. Later developments or information that is revealed after the time of the alleged violation cannot be used to convert an immaterial fact into a material fact and, consequently, nondisclosure of a fact that did not exist at the time of the alleged violation cannot be an omission of a material fact nor can a material fact become immaterial due to facts occurring after the relevant violation.[472] The correct time in a silence case is when disclosure should have been made.[473]

A series or combination of facts that are individually immaterial may be regarded as material in the aggregate. For example, if one misstatement or omission influences another, the totality of the statements made in the aggregate could be "material."[474] After a further development of the facts, it may become apparent that although some or all of the alleged misstatements or omissions are only slightly inaccurate or misleading, the combination of these misstatements would amount to misleading disclosure of material facts.

Materiality is often confused with reliance and causation. Although the three concepts are closely related, they are not the same. Reliance and causation will be discussed later. Materiality also should be distinguished

[468] See *Firestone Tire & Rubber Co.* v. *MDC Corp.*, Fed. Sec. L. Rep. 97,680, at 90,342 (E.D. Pa. 1981).

[469] See *In re Clearly Canadian Securities Litigation*, 875 F. Supp. 1410, 1418 (N.D. Cal. 1995).

[470] See *Cohen* v. *Ayers*, 449 F. Supp. 298, 315 (N.D. Ill. 1978).

[471] See *Rand* v. *Cullinet Software, Inc.*, 847 F. Supp. 200, 210 (D. Mass. 1994); *Picard Chem. Inc. Profit Sharing Plan* v. *Perrigo Co.*, 940 F. Supp. 1101, 1123 (W.D. Mich. 1996).

[472] See *Ehrler* v. *Kellwood Co.*, 521 F.2d 1347, 1350, Fed. Sec. L. Rep. 95271 (8th Cir. 1975).

[473] See *Rogen* v. *Ilikon Corp.*, 361 F.2d 260, 266–67 (1st Cir. 1966).

[474] See *Newgard* v. *Electro-Nucleonics, Inc.*, Fed. Sec. L. Rep. 95,805, at 90,920 (S.D.N.Y. 1976).

from the misleading nature of a statement. A statement can be misleading because it conveys a false impression to a reasonable investor, and yet not be material either because the relevant fact at issue was immaterial or because the fact, while material, was so obviously false that no reasonable person would be influenced by it. Materiality also differs from scienter, i.e., the required state of mind of an actionable defendant in any actions under Rule 10b-5 and Section 14(e).

4.3 Potential violators of Section 14(e) of the Securities Exchange Act

A prohibited misrepresentation or misleading omission of material fact in connection with a tender offer, actionable under Section 14(e) of the Securities Exchange Act, is likely to be made by one of three groups of persons involved in the commencement, completion, and settlement of a tender offer: (i) the person making the offer to purchase the relevant securities (the "tender offeror") or an affiliate of the tender offeror; (ii) the issuer of the relevant securities that are the subject of the tender offer (the "issuer"), a director or executive officer of the issuer, or any other person that is an affiliate of the issuer; and (iii) a third party participating in the tender offer as an agent, representative, or advisor of the tender offeror or the issuer (including a broker or dealer acting as a financial advisor or manager of the tender offer, a solicitation agent, legal counsel, or an accounting firm acting as a representative of any direct participant in the tender offer).

It should be noted that, depending on the structure and specific circumstances of the tender offer, in an issuer tender offer (i.e., an offer by the issuer or an affiliate of the issuer for the purchase of securities issued by the issuer) the tender offeror and the issuer are the same person, whereas in a third-party tender offer (i.e., an offer by a person not affiliated with the issuer for the securities of the issuer), the tender offeror is neither controlled by nor controlling the issuer of the relevant securities and, as a result, statements or omissions of material fact follow very different fact patterns in third-party tender offers compared to issuer tender offers. Through the prism of the jurisprudence of US federal courts, the following sections will set forth examples of misrepresentations or misleading omissions in connection with tender offers of securities made by the tender offeror (or its affiliates), the issuer, its directors, executive officers, and other affiliates and persons acting as representatives, agents, or advisors of the main participants in a tender offer.

4.4 Misrepresentations in tender offer documents and other public announcements

In relation to statements actually made by the tender offeror or the issuer of the relevant securities in a tender offer, the prohibition of Section 14(e) is rather simple: such statements, in the tender offer documentation, any press release or other publication used to commence the tender offer, any press release or other publication used to update the market about new developments or facts relating to the tender offer, or any other statement (oral or in writing) in connection with the tender offer, shall not be untrue, false, or misleading.

A tender offeror commencing a tender offer (whether or not the person is the issuer of the securities subject to the tender offer (the "tender securities"), an affiliate of the issuer, or a third party) will make statements in connection with the tender offer in the tender offer documentation (comprising, usually, a press release announcing the tender offer, an offering memorandum relating to the tender offer, press releases, or other announcements following the commencement of the tender offer, which usually update the market on new events or developments or communicate changes to the terms and conditions of the tender offer, and (less frequently) other types of public communications, made in writing or orally, such as statements made by directors or executive officers in conferences, the press, industry or business publications, and electronic media (including social media)).

If the person commencing the tender offer is not the issuer of the tender securities, then the issuer of the tender securities is required to publish, send, or give to the holders of the relevant tender securities a statement disclosing the position of the issuer of the relevant securities in relation to the tender offer: whether the issuer recommends acceptance or rejection of the tender offer; whether it expresses no opinion and is remaining neutral towards the tender offer; or whether it is unable to take any position with respect to the tender offer.[475] If any material change occurs in the disclosure made by the issuer of the tender securities, the issuer must then promptly publish, send, or give a statement disclosing such material change to the holders of the tender securities.[476] Issuers of tender securities are required to publish *at least* the statements regarding their positions under the provisions of Rule 14e-2, but they are not prohibited from

[475] See Rule 14e-2(a) under the Securities Exchange Act.

[476] See Rule 14e-2(b) under the Securities Exchange Act.

making other statements in connection with the tender offer, and many issuers of tender securities (as well as their directors and executive officers) often make additional statements to the press, their employees, or in special communications to their security holders in connection with the relevant tender offer. In all cases, under the anti-fraud provisions of the Section 14(e) of the Securities Exchange Act, any statement published or otherwise made in connection with a tender offer by the issuer of the tender securities or the tender offeror in the relevant tender offer must be true and not misleading.

Statements made in tender offer documentation, press materials, or otherwise in connection with a tender offer must also be clear and complete. What is "clear and complete" disclosure will always depend on the facts and circumstances. For example, statements of material fact must be prominent in the relevant documentation and satisfy the requirement of clarity in the disclosure required under the Securities Exchange Act. If there is a substantial likelihood that a reasonable holder of the tender securities would consider a set of facts important in evaluating the terms of the tender offer, disclosure of those facts in the tender offer documentation must be complete, clear, and complete and published prominently in the relevant documentation.[477]

Statements of fact must be distinguished from statements that are not statements of historical fact, but represent estimates, predictions of future events and developments, opinions, intentions, present expectations, and beliefs ("forward-looking statements"). Neither the tender offeror nor the issuer of the tender securities is required to make statements that are not statements of fact but subjective views or opinions in connection with a tender offer.[478] These forward-looking statements are introduced by words such as "believe," "estimate," "expect," "intend," "anticipate," and similar expressions that reflect views and opinions in relation to, for example, the tender offeror's intentions, expectations, and plans with respect to the tender securities, as opposed to "hard" facts. Consequently, they are not subject to the same standard of scrutiny if they turn out, based on future events and developments, to be untrue for purposes of Section 14(e) of the Securities Exchange Act. To the extent that the views expressed by the person making the statements are honestly held and made in good faith, such statements are not "untrue" statements of material fact for purposes of Section 14(e).

[477] See *Blanchette* v. *Providence & Worcester Co.*, 428 F. Supp. 347 (D. Del. 1977).

[478] See *Berman* v. *Gerber Products Co.*, fn 468 above.

If an untrue statement of fact is made in connection with a tender offer, the person making the statement shall correct the untrue statement by making appropriate disclosure of the correct and true statement and ensuring the dissemination of the correcting statement to all holders of the tender securities.[479] Depending on the structure of the tender offer, a press release or other type of public announcement containing the relevant correction, update, or amendment is sufficient to protect the person making the untrue statement from liability under Section 14(e) so long as such correction, update, or amendment is published or sent to the holders of the tender securities in sufficient time prior to the expiration of the tender offer (i.e., the time by which holders of the tender securities must communicate their offer to tender the tender securities to the tender offeror). Receiving the correcting information in sufficient time prior to their making an investment decision in connection with the tender offer enables the holders of the tender securities to absorb and assess the relevant information on time.

4.5 Misleading omissions of material fact by tender offerors

4.5.1 Introduction

Not surprisingly, Section 14(e) of the Securities Exchange Act is more relevant (and more commonly invoked by plaintiffs) in relation to material facts that are withheld or concealed from holders of tender securities and other tender offer participants than in relation to statements actually made by tender offer participants during a tender offer. Securities lawyers who are familiar with anti-fraud litigation under Rule 10b-5 under the Securities Exchange Act in connection with the sale or purchase of securities should find the following statement unremarkable: more often than not, fraud or deception in securities transactions is based on the concealment of important information from the investing public (be it the other "half" of some misleading half-true statement or some other fact or development that would be essential in making the actual disclosure made not misleading) than the disclosure of blatantly untrue information in the relevant documentation. Fraud and deception in tender offers are not different in that respect.

Under the relevant provision of Section 14(e) of the Securities Exchange Act it is unlawful to omit to state, in connection with a tender offer, any

[479] See *Scientific Computers, Inc.* v. *Edudata Corp.*, 599 F. Supp. 1092 (D. Minn. 1984).

material fact necessary in order to make the statements made, in the light of the circumstances under which they are made, not misleading. It is not an omission of material fact that is actionable under Section 14(e). Section 14(e) does not create a duty to disclose all material information in connection with a tender offer. It requires the disclosure of all material information necessary to make the statements actually made, in the light of the circumstances under which they are made, not misleading. If the omitted material fact does not render the statements actually made in the relevant tender offer documentation misleading, i.e., because, e.g., the statements actually made are consistent in all material respects with the information that would have been conveyed if the omitted fact had been included, then there is no actionable conduct under Section 14(e).

Both the tender offeror and the issuer of the tender securities are capable of making misleading omissions of material fact in connection with the tender offer. If the tender offeror is also the issuer of the tender securities (or an affiliate of the issuer), misleading material omissions of the tender offeror may relate to: (i) the terms and conditions of the tender offer; (ii) the plans and intentions of the tender offeror; or (iii) the business, operations, financial results, or prospects of the issuer of the tender securities.

If the tender offeror is not the issuer of the tender securities (or the affiliate of the issuer), then the tender offeror is likely to omit material information regarding the terms and conditions of the tender offer or the plans and intentions of the tender offeror in relation to the tender securities but the tender offeror, not being the issuer or an affiliate of the issuer, is not capable of omitting any material information relating to the business, operations, financial results, or prospects of the issuer of the tender securities (unless the tender offeror has access to material non-public information, which is covered in Chapter 6, section 3.1). In the case of an exchange offer, the tender offeror will issue new securities in consideration, in whole or in part, of the purchase of the tender securities and, consequently, a misleading omission of material fact regarding the business, financial position, prospects, or operations of the tender offeror (as issuer of the exchange securities to be offered to holders tendering the tender securities) is also actionable under Section 14(e) or, indeed, Rule 10b-5 under the Securities Exchange Act.

Section 14(e) does not require a specific form of disclosure or filing requirement. If the information is already made available to holders of the tender securities (either through statements made in the tender offer memorandum, in a press release, or otherwise), there is no separate duty to include the information (whether it relates to the tender offeror, the terms of the tender offer, or the tender securities).[480] Section 14(e) does not require disclosures of forward-looking information or predictions of future behavior unless they are necessary to make any statements made in connection with the tender offer not misleading.[481]

4.5.2 Misleading omissions by tender offerors

Persons commencing a tender offer must disclose all material facts necessary in order to make the statements made in connection with the tender offer, in the light of the circumstances under which they are made, not misleading. Such disclosure of all material facts is usually made with a tender offer disclosure document (a "tender offer memorandum" or an "offer to purchase"), which aims to provide a comprehensive description of the terms of the tender offer (including the tender offer consideration, the expiration of the tender offer, provisions relating to the termination, withdrawal or amendment of the tender offer, any applicable withdrawal rights, the settlement date, and other relevant mechanics), the tender securities, the expected timetable of the tender offer, information about the tender offeror and the rationale for the tender offer, the source and amount of funds required to pay for the tendered securities, risk factors and other considerations to be taken into account by the holders of the tender securities, the applicable material income tax consequences of the tender offer, market and trading information relating to the tender securities, sources of further information relating to the tender offer, the applicable procedures for tendering securities in the tender offer, any applicable offer and distribution restrictions, and other relevant material information. The tender offer memorandum or offer to purchase is commonly accompanied by a summary publication of the tender offer and the applicable terms and conditions in the printed and electronic media to ensure the prompt dissemination of the relevant information to the investing public.

If any new material facts or developments must be disclosed to the holders of the tender securities, a supplement to the tender offer memorandum or a press release must be published in accordance with the

[480] See *Gulf & Western Industries, Inc.* v. *Great Atlantic & Pac. Tea Co., Inc.*, 356 F. Supp. 1066 (S.D.N.Y. 1973).

[481] See *Riggs Nat. Bank of Washington D. C.* v. *Allbritton*, 516 F. Supp. 164 (D.D.C. 1981).

procedures that are usually described in the tender offer memorandum commencing the tender offer. All material facts must be disclosed at the latest by the earliest time at which the securities can be permissibly tendered. If the tender offer period does not commence until a period of time has lapsed from the announcement of the offer, then it is not a material omission to withhold material information so long as such information is available at the earliest time investors can tender.[482] If the tender offer period has commenced but new material facts must be disclosed to the holders of the tender offer securities after the commencement of the tender offer, then the tender offer must remain open for a reasonable period of time following the disclosure of the new material facts, and any holders of tender securities must have the right to withdraw their tender before the expiration of the tender offer period.[483]

In this section, we will discuss the most significant types of actionable misleading omissions of material fact for purposes of Section 14(e) of the Securities Exchange Act. It goes without saying that materiality is a mixed question of law and fact, and whether a misleading omission of certain fact is material or not will always depend on the specific facts and circumstances. Consequently, while the following examples from the jurisprudence of the US federal courts are indicative of the types of facts that have been considered to be material, that determination was made in connection with the specific facts and circumstances of the particular case and is not necessarily indicative of the position of the courts in other, similar situations.

Terms and conditions of the tender offer. A full and accurate description of the contractual terms and conditions of the tender offer (the time of commencement, a description of tender offer consideration, a description of the tender securities, the existence or not of withdrawal rights, and other similar material terms of the tender offer) is essential not only under the anti-fraud provisions of Section 14(e) but also as a means of establishing a contractual agreement between the tender offeror and the tendering holders of the tender securities. The tender of securities by a holder in accordance with the terms and conditions of the tender offer as described in the tender offer document is a contractual offer, the acceptance of which by the tender offeror following the expiration of the tender offer period leads to the formation of a contract for the sale and purchase of the tender

[482] See *Billard* v. *Rockwell Intern. Corp.*, 683 F.2d 51 (C.A.N.Y. 1982).

[483] See, for example, Rule 14e-1(b) under the Securities Exchange Act, discussed extensively in Chapter 3.

securities. It is, however, important for tender offer documents to describe accurately and prominently all the applicable terms, conditions, and tendering procedures relating to the tender offer and not to misrepresent or omit to state any such term, condition, or procedure (e.g., the expiration date of withdrawal rights). The circumstances under which the tender offer may be terminated by the tender offeror must also be disclosed[484] or any possibility of delay in the consummation of the tender offer.[485] Any such omission would be actionable under Section 14(e).[486] If additional payments are made to certain holders of the tender securities that are not extended in equal measure to all the holders of the tender securities or two different groups of holders of tender securities will be treated differently, this additional consideration or discriminatory treatment must also be disclosed.[487] If the acceptance of the tender offer by the tender offeror is subject to conditions, the tender offeror must disclose all the circumstances under which the tender offeror would be prepared to waive any of the acceptance conditions.[488]

Tax consequences of the tender offer. It is common market practice to include in the tender offer documents a summary of certain income tax consequences of the relevant tender offer to holders of tender securities in the United States and other relevant jurisdictions. If any such summary is included in the tender offer documents, the tender offeror is obligated under the anti-fraud provisions of Section 14(e) of the Securities Exchange Act to make full and complete disclosure of all relevant and material facts relating to such tax consequences in order to make the disclosure of the summary, in light of the specific circumstances of the tender offer, not misleading.[489] The tender offeror may of course decide not to include any disclosure of the tax consequences of the tender offer and merely refer the holders of the tender securities to their own independent tax advisors. So long as there is no misleading statement in the tender offer

[484] See *Symington Wayne Corp.* v. *Dresser Industries, Inc.*, 383 F.2d 840, 842–43 (2d Cir. 1967).

[485] See *Time Inc.* v. *Paramount Communications Inc.*, Fed. Sec. L. Rep. 94,505, at 93,218–93,219 (S.D.N.Y. 1989).

[486] See *Macfadden Holdings, Inc.* v. *JB Acquisition Corp.*, 802 F.2d 62 (2d Cir. 1986).

[487] See *Biechele* v. *Cedar Point, Inc.*, 747 F.2d 209, 214 (6th Cir. 1984); *Securities and Exchange Commission* v. *Texas Intern. Co.*, 498 F. Supp. 1231, 1251 (N.D. Ill. 1980).

[488] See *Feder* v. *MacFadden Holdings, Inc.*, 698 F. Supp. 47 (S.D.N.Y. 1988).

[489] See *Commonwealth Oil Refining Co., Inc.* v. *Tesoro Petroleum Corp.*, 394 F. Supp. 267 (S.D.N.Y. 1975).

documentation, Section 14(e) does not require any specific tax disclosure in connection with the tender offer of securities.

Purpose and rationale of tender offer; plans and status of tender offeror. The purpose and rationale of the tender offer is a material fact and the omission to disclose fully and fairly why the tender offeror is commencing the tender offer is a misleading omission under Section 14(e). If, for example, the purpose of the tender offer is the ultimate acquisition of corporate control, this is a fact that ought to be disclosed to the holders of the tender securities.[490] It is also a material misleading omission to fail to disclose substantial impediments and risk factors to achieving the stated purpose of the tender offer, including, without limitation, any legal proceedings, regulatory requirements, or litigation that must be overcome before the stated purpose of the tender offer is completed.[491] An accurate description of the tender offeror, and any other persons controlling the tender offeror, must also be disclosed in the tender offer documentation. The financial resources of the tender offeror and its ability (or inability) to pay for the tender offer consideration or its otherwise poor financial condition are also material facts to be disclosed.[492] If the tender offeror purchased the tender securities in the open market recently, the prices paid by the tender offeror in such open market purchases must also be disclosed.[493] For purposes of Section 14(e), the person in control of the tender offeror commencing a tender offer must be identified in the tender offer documentation and so must any other person who would be able, under existing contractual agreements or otherwise, to exercise control over the tender offeror in the near future.[494] If any directors and/or officers of the tender offeror are holders of the tender securities and are set to profit from the tender offer when tendering their securities, the tender offer documentation should also disclose that fact.[495] The tender offeror must also disclose to holders of the tender securities any other competing

[490] See *Gulf & Western Industries, Inc.* v. *Great Atlantic & Pac. Tea Co., Inc.*, 476 F.2d 687, 695–97 (2d Cir. 1973).

[491] See *Alaska Interstate Co.* v. *McMillian*, 402 F. Supp. 532 (D. Del. 1975); *Boyertown Burial Casket Co.* v. *Amedco, Inc.*, 407 F. Supp. 811 (E.D. Pa. 1976).

[492] See *IU Intern. Corp.* v. *NX Acquisition Corp.*, 840 F.2d 220, 221–22 (4th Cir. 1988); *Pacific Realty Trust* v. *APC Investments, Inc.*, 685 F.2d 1083, 1088 (9th Cir. 1982).

[493] See *Pacific Ins. Co. of New York* v. *Blot*, 267 F. Supp. 956, 957 (S.D.N.Y. 1967).

[494] See *Boyertown Burial Casket Co.* v. *Amedco, Inc.*, fn 493 above; *Ronson Corp.* v. *Liquifin Aktiengesellschaft*, 370 F. Supp. 597 (D.N.J. 1974).

[495] See *Kramer* v. *Time Warner Inc.*, 937 F.2d 767 (2d Cir. 1991).

offers for the tender securities that the tender offeror is aware of,[496] or whether or not the tender offeror is intending to purchase tender securities in the open market during the tender offer period.[497]

Other material facts. Other material facts relating to tender offers that must be disclosed under the anti-fraud provisions of Section 14(e) can be the following: the impact of applicable laws on the legality (substantive or procedural) of the tender offer or the ability of the tender offeror to consummate the tender offer;[498] that the financial condition and prospects of the issuer of the tender securities is better than that which is disclosed to the general public;[499] and injunctions and similar proceedings against the tender offeror in connection with the tender offer.[500]

4.6 Misleading omissions in exchange offers

Section 14(e) applies to tender offers in which the consideration paid by the tender offeror for the securities tendered, in whole or in part, consists of securities issued by the tender offeror to the holders of the tender securities. In addition, an exchange offer is also subject to Rule 10b-5 under the Securities Exchange Act. Consequently, the tender offeror is subject to liability under both Section 14(e) and Rule 10b-5 for false statements or misleading omissions in connection with the offer and sale of the newly issued securities, and any broker or dealer facilitating the distribution of the newly issued securities is also subject to disclosure liability for false statements or misleading omissions. Since the tender offeror in the exchange offer is also the issuer of the exchange securities, the disclosure regarding the tender offeror must be identical to the required disclosure in connection with a securities offering by the tender offeror, including in relation to the business, financial results, operations, management, and other material facts that are likely to be considered by a reasonable investor in connection with an investment in the tender offeror.[501]

[496] See *Berman* v. *Gerber Products Co.*, fn 468 above.

[497] See *Pacific Ins. Co. of New York* v. *Blot*, 267 F. Supp. 956, 957 (S.D.N.Y. 1967).

[498] See *MAI Basic Four, Inc.* v. *Prime Computer, Inc.*, Fed. Sec. L. Rep. 94,317, at 92,082 (D. Mass. 1988), aff'd, 871 F.2d 212 (1st Cir. 1989).

[499] See *Feder* v. *Harrington*, 52 F.R.D. 178, 180–81 (S.D.N.Y. 1970).

[500] See *Raybestos-Manhattan, Inc.* v. *Hi-Shear Industries, Inc.*, 503 F. Supp. 1122, 1127 (E.D.N.Y. 1980).

[501] See *Berman* v. *Gerber Products Co.*, fn 468 above.

Furthermore, exchange offers for debt securities are predominantly liability management transactions of companies in financial distress or companies seeking to make changes to their capital structure and financial profile, reduce their overall debt burden or interest expense associated with their debt position, extend maturities, restructure the terms and conditions of their debt obligations, or effect any combination of the foregoing. Consequently, the courts have used Section 14(e) to scrutinize the rationale, purpose, plans, and intentions of tender offerors in connection with an exchange offer and improve the disclosure of information regarding the benefits, adverse consequences, conflicts of interests, ulterior motives, and other similar factors relating to the liability management of debt obligations. In that respect, facts and circumstances that have been regarded as material in connection with exchange offers, particularly in connection with liability management transactions, the omission of which would be a misleading omission, include: personal benefits and conflicting interests of directors and officers of the tender offeror in connection with the exchange offer;[502] the future plans of the tender offeror following the liability management transaction;[503] the financial prospects and credit rating of the tender offeror following the liability management transaction;[504] that the delisting of the tender securities and reduced liquidity would be the result of the exchange offer;[505] and that certain current holders of tender securities would be given special treatment in the allocation of the newly issued securities.[506]

4.7 Misleading omissions of material fact by issuers of tender securities

If the issuer of the tender securities is not the tender offeror commencing the tender offer (or an affiliate of the tender offeror), which can only occur in a third-party tender offer for the issuer's securities, Section 14(e) does not impose any independent duty on the issuer to make any disclosures in connection with the tender offer.[507] If, however, the issuer of the tender securities decides to respond to the tender offer or make any public statement in connection with the tender offer, then

[502] See *Blanchette* v. *Providence & Worcester Co.*, fn 478 above, at 355.

[503] See *Berne St. Enterps., Inc.* v. *American Export Isbrandtsen Co.*, Fed. Sec. L. Rep. at 99, 132 (S.D.N.Y. 1970).

[504] See *Anaconda Co.* v. *Crane Co.*, 411 F. Supp. 1210, 1217 (S.D.N.Y. 1975).

[505] See *Berne St. Enterps., Inc.* v. *American Export Isbrandtsen Co.*, fn 505 above.

[506] See *Chris-Craft Industries, Inc.* v. *Piper Aircraft Corp.*, fn 464 above.

[507] See *Berman* v. *Gerber Products Co.*, fn 468 above.

such response, disclosure, or statement must not be false and not misleading, and must not omit any material fact that is necessary to make the statements or disclosures made not misleading in light of the specific facts and circumstances.[508] For example, it has been held that the issuer of the tender securities responding to a tender offer (or any director or executive officer of the issuer) must disclose any conflict of interest that arises in connection with the tender offer that is likely to affect the response of the issuer of the tender securities to the tender offer made by the tender offeror.[509]

Other indicative examples of material facts concealed by the directors or officers of the issuer of tender securities when responding to a tender offer by a third-party tender offeror include: that a better offer has become or will or is likely to become available to the holders of the tender securities;[510] that the directors and officers of the issuer will receive certain benefits if they recommend the offer and the offer is successfully completed;[511] that the internal non-public projections of management show substantial increases of future earnings or cash flows;[512] that directors or executive officers hold tender securities and whether their intention is to tender or not in connection with their personal holdings;[513] that the directors or officers of the issuer had prior dealings or outstanding contractual relationships with the tender offeror;[514] that another offer for the tender securities was imminent;[515] any other material non-public information that is likely to make the response of the issuer of the tender securities misleading (e.g., a recommendation to tender the securities if material non-public information available to the issuer but not to the holders of the tender securities shows that the financial prospects of the issuer will substantially improve; or a recommendation not to tender the securities if material non-public information available to the issuer but not the holders of the tender securities shows that the financial prospects

[508] Ibid. See also the obligation imposed on the issuers of tender securities by Rule 14e-2 to disclose their position with respect to the tender offer for the tender securities, as more fully discussed in Chapter 3.

[509] See *A & K Railroad Materials, Inc.* v. *Green Bay & W.R.R. Co.*, fn 467 above.

[510] See *Flamm* v. *Eberstadt*, 814 F.2d 1169, 1173 (7th Cir. 1987).

[511] See *Royal Indus., Inc.* v. *Monogram Indus., Inc.*, Fed. Sec. L. Rep. 95,863, at 91,140 (C.D. Cal. 1976).

[512] See *Berman* v. *Gerber Products Co.*, fn 468 above.

[513] See *Were* v. *Mack*, Fed. Sec. L. Rep. 92,956 at 90,524–90,525 (S.D.N.Y. 1971).

[514] See *Missouri Portland Cement Co.* v. *Cargill, Inc.*, 498 F.2d 851, 873 (2d Cir. 1974).

[515] See *Flamm* v. *Eberstadt*, fn 512 above.

of the issuer will substantially worsen);[516] that the tender offer consideration is lower or higher than the tender offer consideration offered in a previous tender offer for the same tender securities;[517] that the tender offer consideration is higher or lower than the current market price of the tender securities;[518] that the tender offer is likely to have adverse tax consequences for all or certain categories of holders of tender securities;[519] and that the tender offer consideration is inadequate or lower than a competing proposal or lower than the value suggested by financial advisors.[520]

Finally, under the anti-fraud provisions of Section 14(e), corporate insiders of the issuer of the tender securities are prohibited from participating in the tender offer while in possession of material non-public information[521] and, as a result, their participation in the tender offer is predicated on the prior disclosure to the market of all such material non-public information.

4.8 Misleading statements or omissions of material fact by brokers or dealers

Brokers or dealers assisting tender offerors or issuers of tender securities in connection with a tender offer are also subject to the obligation to avoid false statements or misleading omissions of material facts in connection with the tender offer in communications with the holders of the tender securities or the investing public at large. Whether the brokers or dealers advise holders of tender securities to tender or not tender the relevant securities, solicit tenders, or make general statements in connection with the prospects of the tender offeror or the tender offer, the general duty to avoid false statements and misleading omissions of material fact under Section 14(e) applies.[522]

516 See *Berman* v. *Gerber Products Co.*, fn 468 above.

517 See *Gulf & Western Industries, Inc.* v. *Great Atlantic & Pac. Tea Co., Inc.*, 356 F. Supp. 1066, 1071 (S.D.N.Y. 1973).

518 See *Berman* v. *Gerber Products Co.*, fn 468 above.

519 See *Anaconda Co.* v. *Crane Co.*, fn 506 above, at 1216.

520 See *Plaza Securities Co.* v. *Fruehauf Corp.*, 643 F. Supp. 1535, 1544 (E.D. Mich. 1986).

521 See *O'Connor & Associates* v. *Dean Witter Reynolds, Inc.*, 529 F. Supp. 1179 (S.D.N.Y. 1981).

522 See *Iroquois Indus., Inc.* v. *Syracuse China Corp.*, Fed. Sec. L. Rep. 92,301, at 99,433 (W.D.N.Y. 1968), aff'd 417 F.2d 963 (2d Cir. 1969), cert. denied, 399 U.S. 909 (1970).

5 Other fraudulent, deceptive, or manipulative acts in connection with tender offers

The second type of conduct prohibited by the anti-fraud provisions of Section 14(e) is any fraudulent, deceptive, or manipulative act or practice in connection with a tender offer (or any request or invitation for tender, or any solicitation of security holders in opposition to or in favor of any such offer, request, or invitation).[523] Pursuant to the actual wording of Section 14(e), the prohibition on fraudulent, deceptive, or manipulative practices is a separate prohibition from the prohibition on untrue statements and misleading omissions of a material fact. The disjunctive "or" separating the two prongs of the Section appears to create two separate causes of action under Section 14(e): the first, against persons making untrue statements of a material fact or omitting to state material facts necessary in order to make the statements made, in the light of the circumstances under which they are made, not misleading; and the second, against those persons engaging in fraudulent, deceptive, or manipulative acts or practices.

The term "manipulative" was discussed by the Supreme Court in the context of a Rule 10b-5 claim in *Ernst & Ernst* v. *Hochfelder.*[524] There the Court found that the term "manipulate" is "a term of art" that "connotes intentional or willful conduct designed to deceive or defraud investors by controlling or artificially affecting the price of securities." Thus, manipulative conduct in securities transactions consisted of three elements: (i) "intentional or willful conduct" (ii) "designed to deceive or defraud investors" by (iii) "controlling or artificially affecting the price of securities."

Despite the literal meaning of the disjunctive "or," the Supreme Court concluded in the seminal case *Schreiber.*[525] that the term "or" should not be read disjunctively, concluding that in connection with Section 14(e):

> All three species of misconduct, i.e., "fraudulent, deceptive or manipulative," listed by Congress are directed at failures to disclose. The use of

[523] "It shall be unlawful for any person to make any untrue statement of a material fact or omit to state any material fact necessary in order to make the statements made, in the light of the circumstances under which they are made, not misleading, *or to engage in any fraudulent, deceptive, or manipulative acts or practices,* in connection with any tender offer or request or invitation for tenders, or any solicitation of security holders in opposition to or in favor of any such offer, request, or invitation." See Section 14(e) of the Securities and Exchange Act. (Emphasis added.)

[524] 425 U.S. 185, 199 (1976).

[525] See fn 453 above.

> the term "manipulative" provides emphasis and guidance to those who must determine which types of acts are reached by the statute; it does not suggest a deviation from the section's facial and primary concern with disclosure or Congressional concern with disclosure which is the core of the Act.[526]

The *Schreiber* case serves as the controlling judicial precedent for the position that fraudulent, deceptive, and manipulative practices in connection with a tender offer will only give rise to a Section 14(e) claim if they involve a misrepresentation of a material fact or a misleading omission of a material fact. Consequently, full and fair disclosure of all the relevant acts and circumstances relating to a tender offer, even when the tender offeror or the issuer of the tender securities purports to manipulate the price of the tender securities or otherwise treats the holders of the tender securities unfairly will suffice to protect a potential defendant from causes of action under Section 14(e) of the Securities Exchange Act.[527] Any other interpretation of the anti-fraud provisions of Section 14(e) has been held to constitute an unwarranted extension of the Williams Act.[528]

Drawing from *Schreiber*, federal courts have repeatedly emphasized that the purpose of the Williams Act is to require disclosure to permit holders of tender securities to make informed decisions in connection with tender offers; the Williams Act was not intended to impose substantive restrictions on the actual terms of tender offers or other fairness requirements. Congress expressly disclaimed an intention to provide a weapon for management to discourage takeover bids (in connection with tender offers for equity securities) or impose other substantive requirements in connection with the terms of liability management transactions in the form of tender or exchange offers for debt securities.[529] Section 14(e) requires full and fair disclosure in connection with tender offers, not the fairness of the terms and conditions or aspects of particular transactions. It does not create fiduciary duties or expectations of fairness absent a false statement of a material fact or a misleading omission of a material fact.[530]

526 Ibid.

527 On the *Schreiber* case and the meaning of "manipulative" in Section 14(e), see Norman S. Poser, "Stock Market Manipulation – Corporate Control Transactions," 40 *University of Miami Law Review* 671 (1986).

528 See *Buffalo Forge Co.* v. *Ogden Corp.*, 717 F.2d 757, 760 (2d Cir.), cert. denied, 104 S. Ct. 550 (1983).

529 See *Newmont Min. Corp.* v. *Pickens*, 831 F.2d 1448 (9th Cir. 1987).

530 See *Abella* v. *Universal Leaf Tobacco Co., Inc.*, 546 F. Supp. 795 (D. Va. 1982); *Berman* v. *Gerber Products Co.*, fn 468 above.

Section 14(e), furthermore, does not, in and of itself, grant a right of access to a list of the issuer's security holders. The issuer of the relevant securities is not required to automatically turn over its security holder list to any tender offeror, even when the tender offer is expected to be beneficial to the holders of the tender securities. Mere refusal on the part of a corporate defendant to allow plaintiffs to inspect its security holder list is not, in itself, a "manipulative practice" in violation of statutory prohibition against a material misstatement or omission concerned with a tender offer.[531]

6 Other elements of a cause of action under Section 14(e)

A successful claim under Section 14(e) requires the satisfaction of the following conditions: (i) a tender offer; (ii) an untrue statement of a material fact or a misleading omission of a material fact; (iii) connection with a tender offer; (iv) materiality; (v) the required mental state in the breach of the basic prohibition; (vi) reliance; (vii) causation; (viii) injury; and (ix) standing to sue.

We have already examined elements (i), (ii), and (iv). In the following pages, we will examine the remaining elements (iii), (v), (vi), (vii), (viii), and (ix).

6.1 Required state of mind

Section 14(e) is substantially identical to Rule 10b-5. Mere negligence without an intention to defraud or, at least, a reckless disregard for the prohibition of Section 14(e) is not sufficient. A violation of Section 14(e) of the Securities Exchange Act, making it unlawful to engage in any fraudulent, deceptive, or manipulative acts or practices in connection with a tender offer, requires "scienter," i.e., a showing that there has been a material misstatement or omission concerned with a tender offer and that such misstatement or omission was sufficiently culpable to justify granting relief to injured party.[532] The term "scienter" as an essential element of a cause of action under Rule 10b-5 and Section 14(e) is defined as the mental state embracing intent to deceive, manipulate, or defraud, knowledge of the falsity of a statement or reckless disregard of the truth. Mere negligent conduct is insufficient to establish culpability for a material

[531] See *A & K Railroad Materials, Inc.* v. *Green Bay & W.R.R. Co.*, fn 467 above.

[532] See *Cauble* v. *White*, 360 F. Supp. 1021 (E.D. La. 1973).

misstatement or omission concerned with a tender offer.[533] If the tender offeror is an outsider (in the event of a third-party tender offer), the outsider status is one factor to be considered in determining whether an omission of fact violated Section 14(e).[534] The scienter requirement for purposes of Section 14(e) is identical to the scienter requirement for purposes of Rule 10b-5 under the Securities Exchange Act.

6.2 Reliance

A plaintiff bringing an action under Section 14(e) for false statements or misleading omissions of a material fact in connection with a tender offer must prove the reliance of such plaintiff on such statement or omission. Reliance for purposes of Section 14(e) is identical to reliance for purposes of Rule 10b-5 under the Securities Exchange Act. All the significant cases on the element of reliance relate to claims under Rule 10b-5.

According to the cases, there are three alternative tests of reliance, not all of which are available in all sets and circumstances:[535] (i) constructive reliance; (ii) subjective reliance (including the "fraud on the market" theory); and (iii) justifiable reliance. *Constructive reliance* is the presumption of reliance in cases of misleading omissions of a material fact. When the Section 14(e) claim relates to a failure to disclose a material fact, positive proof of reliance is not a prerequisite to recovery. All that is necessary is that the facts withheld be material in the sense that a reasonable investor might have considered them important in making this decision.[536] *Subjective reliance* exists if the plaintiff believes the misleading statement to be true or the plaintiff would have been influenced to act differently than he or she did in connection with a tender offer if the defendant had disclosed the true statement.[537] This is a difficult test. The Supreme Court held that requiring a plaintiff to prove a speculative state of facts (such as how he or she would have acted if the omitted information had been disclosed or if a misrepresentation had not been made) would place an unnecessarily

533 See *A & K Railroad Materials, Inc.* v. *Green Bay & W.R.R. Co.*, fn 467 above; *In re Commonwealth Oil/Tesoro Petroleum Corp. Securities Litigation*, 467 F. Supp. 227 (W.D. Tex. 1979).

534 See *Flynn* v. *Bass Bros. Enterprises, Inc.*, 456 F. Supp. 484 (D. Pa. 1978).

535 See *Janus Capital Group, Inc.* v. *First Derivative Traders*, 564 U.S. 131 (2011).

536 See *Affiliated Ute Citizens of Utah* v. *U.S.*, 406 U.S. 128, 153–54 (1972); accord, *Stoneridge Inv. Partners, LLC* v. *Scientific-Atlanta*, 552 U.S. 148 (2008); *Basic, Inc.* v. *Levinson*, fn 463 above.

537 See *List* v. *Fashion Park, Inc.*, fn 460 above.

unrealistic evidentiary burden on a plaintiff who traded on an impersonal market.[538] Consequently, the Supreme Court accepts the "fraud on the market" theory on reliance, which is based on the hypothesis that, in an open and developed securities market, the price of a company's security is determined by the available material information regarding the company and its business. Misleading statements will therefore defraud purchasers of securities even if the purchasers do not directly rely on the misstatements and, consequently, reliance is presumed and need not be specifically proven.[539] Thus, fraud on the market is available when (i) the defendant makes a public statement containing a misrepresentation or non-disclosure of a fact, (ii) the fact is material, (iii) the securities are traded on an open and developed securities market, and (iv) the plaintiff trades between the time the public statement is made and the time the truth is revealed.[540] A plaintiff accordingly can invoke the fraud on the market theory and establish reliance for purposes of Section 14(e) even though he or she does not rely on the misleading corporate statement, does not read it, and does not know it was issued.[541] Fraud on the market reliance is a rebuttable presumption and can be rebutted if there is any fact or development that severs the link between the alleged misrepresentation and either the price received (or paid) by the plaintiff, or his or her decision to trade at a fair market price.[542] The use of *justifiable reliance* is not consistent in the case law. It requires a showing by the plaintiff that a reasonable man or woman would have believed that a false statement made to the plaintiff was true. Some cases do demand this form of reliance, while others dismiss it.

6.3 Causation

Causation in fact is an essential element of a private cause of action brought under Section 14(e), just as it is for Rule 10b-5 actions.[543] In order to prevail, a plaintiff must demonstrate a causal nexus between the defendant's wrongful conduct and his or her loss, i.e., the loss must be shown to have been caused by the wrongful conduct. In connection with a tender offer, the requisite causation exists to the extent that either the

[538] See *Basic, Inc.* v. *Levinson*, fn 463 above. [539] Ibid.

[540] See *Steiner* v. *Southmark Corp.*, 734 F. Supp. 269, 277 (N.D. Tex. 1990).

[541] See *In re Gulf Oil/Cities Service Tender Offer Litigation*, 725 F. Supp. 712, 752 (S.D.N.Y. 1989).

[542] See *Basic, Inc.* v. *Levinson*, fn 463 above.

[543] See *Fridrich* v. *Bradford*, 542 F.2d 307, 318 (6th Cir. 1976), cert. denied, 429 U.S. 1053, 97 (1977).

plaintiff is misled into retaining the tender securities when he or she could have sold them on the market at a higher price or the plaintiff is misled into tendering the tender securities in the tender offer in circumstances resulting in an economic loss.[544] Causation in tender offer cases cannot be based on statements made after tender securities are purchased in a tender offer.[545] Also, causation cannot be based on hedging activities undertaken in response to a misrepresentation in the tender offer materials when the security holder would have lost even more money hedging his or her position had the tender offer materials been accurate.[546]

6.4 *Injury*

A plaintiff suing under Section 14(e) and seeking damages must prove he or she was injured. Injury for purposes of Section 14(e) is identical to injury in Rule 10b-5 cases. The injury suffered is either tendering securities or failing to tender securities in a tender offer, in each case based on misleading disclosure and resulting in economic loss. There is no injury if the seller sells the securities before the tender offer commences and, unremarkably, there is no injury if the tender offer consideration is too low or too high.[547]

6.5 *Standing to sue*

Who are the potential plaintiffs and defendants in a Section 14(e) action? At the outset, we should clarify that much of the wealthy case law relating to the right to sue under Rule 10b-5 is also applicable to Section 14(e) cases. Nevertheless, Rule 10b-5 allows purchasers and sellers of securities to sue "in connection with the purchase or sale of any security," while Section 14(e) applies in connection with any tender offer or request or invitation for tenders or any solicitation of security holders in opposition to or in favor of any such offer, request, or invitation. There is no limit to the number of sellers or purchasers of securities.

The Supreme Court uses a number of criteria in determining whether or not a person has standing to sue under a federal statute. The seminal case in

544 See *Berman* v. *Gerber Products Co.*, fn 468 above; *Hundahl* v. *United Benefit Life Ins. Co.*, 465 F. Supp. 1349, 1369 (N.D. Tex. 1979).

545 See *Petersen* v. *Federated Development Co.*, 416 F. Supp. 466, 474–75 (S.D.N.Y. 1976).

546 See *Pryor* v. *U.S. Steel Corp.*, 591 F. Supp. 942, 959 (S.D.N.Y. 1984), judgment aff'd in part, rev'd in part, 794 F.2d 52 (2d Cir. 1986).

547 See *Hanover* v. *Zapata Corp.*, Fed. Sec. L. Rep. 93,904, 1973 WL 376 (S.D.N.Y. 1973).

relation to tender offers and lawsuits under Section 14(e) of the Securities Exchange Act is *Piper* v. *Chris-Craft Industries, Inc.*,[548] which examined the question of whether a competing tender offeror could bring a claim under Section 14(e). According to *Piper*, private enforcement under the anti-fraud provisions of Section 14(e) is a necessary supplement to official SEC enforcement. Based on the legislative history of the anti-fraud remedy, the Supreme Court accepted that the sole purpose of anti-fraud remedies in connection with tender offers was the protection of investors who are confronted with a tender offer and, as a result, refused to recognize a competing tender offeror as a person having standing to sue under Section 14(e). Classes of persons with standing to sue are: first, holders of tender securities, either tendering or refusing to tender in connection with the tender offer; and, second, persons trading in the market during a tender offer (after the tender offer is commenced). Potential defendants are the tender offeror, the issuer of the tender securities, their respective senior management teams, and any broker, dealer, or other advisor involved in the tender offer.

6.6 *"In connection with" a tender offer*

A sale or purchase of a security is not one of the essential elements of a Section 14(e) cause of action. It suffices that the false statement, the "half truth" or the misleading material omission has occurred "in connection with" a tender offer or request or invitation for tenders, or any solicitation of security holders in opposition to or in favor of any such offer, request, or invitation.

The plain meaning of the words "in connection with" suggests that the actionable wrongful conduct must have a connection with a tender offer. What constitutes a "connection" with a tender offer and when such connection exists is commonly reviewed by reference to three distinct periods of time: (i) the period before a tender offer is announced; (ii) the period commencing on the announcement of the tender offer and ending on the termination of the tender offer; and (iii) the period following the termination of the tender offer.

6.6.1 Pre-announcement period

If the public announcement by the tender offeror of a tender offer for the purchase of the issuer's securities discloses for the first time the existence

[548] See *Piper* v. *Chris-Craft Industries, Inc.*, 430 U.S. 1 (1977).

of a tender offer to the market, the tender offeror's preparations for the tender offer and the knowledge of the tender offeror that the future commencement of a tender offer is probable are likely to precede the announcement of the tender offer, often by a considerable period of time. The question then is whether public statements made by the tender offeror or purchases or sales of tender securities by the tender offeror while in possession of material non-public information prior to the announcement of the tender offer are subject or not to the anti-fraud provisions of Section 14(e) of the Securities Exchange Act.

The SEC has clarified the point in the affirmative.[549] Since the scope of Section 14(e) applies to acts or practices in connection with any tender offer, the SEC believes that the statutory protection was intended to cover any wrongful conduct occurring prior to the date of commencement of, as well as during, a tender offer. According to the SEC, trading in the tender securities while in possession of material non-public information or false statements made prior to the commencement of a tender offer can result in the same abuses and cause the same detrimental effects as trading during a tender offer.[550] The period of time prior to the announcement of a tender offer that is covered by Section 14(e) depends on the specific facts and circumstances. While it is always difficult to draw a straight line, wrongful conduct when a tender offer is imminent, likely, or probable will be actionable under the anti-fraud provisions of Section 14(e).[551] If, on the other hand, the pre-announcement wrongful conduct is never followed by the announcement of a tender offer, there is no actionable conduct under Section 14(e).

[549] See generally SEC Release 15,548, February 5, 1979.

[550] The SEC cited the following views of Senator Bennett and an official of the New York Stock Exchange, respectively, in supporting the application of the anti-fraud prohibition during the pre-announcement stage: "I am more concerned with the situation which makes it possible for insiders to take advantage of their knowledge that the pending offer is coming and therefore get a quick profit by buying stock with the sure knowledge that they are going to have a market for it"; and "[C]urrently, to insure secrecy and avoid leaks and rumors . . . tender offers are normally made to stockholders immediately after a decision to make the offer is reached and a price has been determined. In spite of all precautions, there have been cases where tender offers have been preceded by leaks and rumors which caused abnormal market problems." See SEC Release 15,548, February 5, 1979 at p. 45. See also *Applied Digital Data Systems, Inc.* v. *Milgo Electronic Corp.*, 425 F. Supp. 1145 (S.D.N.Y. 1977).

[551] See *Pullman-Peabody Co.* v. *Joy Mfg. Co.*, 662 F. Supp. 32, 34 (D.N.J. 1986); Exchange Act Release No. 15,548, Proposed Rule 14d-10: Solicitation/Recommendation Statements With Respect to Certain Tender Offers (February 5, 1979).

6.6.2 Period after announcement of the tender offer

Section 14(e) applies during the period following the announcement of the tender offer, even if the tender offer period has not yet commenced. Section 14(e) obviously applies after the commencement of the tender offer. The public announcement itself, if misleading or false, is actionable under Section 14(e). There is no additional requirement that the tender offer be effective or consummated. Wrongful conduct in connection with a tender offer is actionable under Section 14(e) even when the tender offer is subsequently terminated. Section 14(e) is also applicable when a tender offer is commenced and becomes effective, but the tender offeror withdraws or terminates the offer before any tender securities are actually tendered or purchased.

6.6.3 Period after termination of the tender offer

A tender offer may be terminated at the termination time set by the tender offeror. The tender offeror will also reserve the right to terminate the tender offer prematurely at its discretion by providing notice to the holders of the tender securities. If, following the termination of the tender offer, the tender offeror accepts for purchase any or all of the securities tendered in the tender offer, the tender offer will be consummated on the settlement date through the delivery of the accepted tender securities to the tender offeror and the payment by the tender offeror of the tender offer consideration to the tendering holders of the tender securities whose tendered securities were accepted for purchase by the tender offeror. There is no doubt that wrongful conduct during the period of the tender offer ending on the date that the tender offer is terminated in accordance with its terms or prematurely at the election of the tender offeror or, if accepted, at the settlement date will be "in connection" with a tender offer and within the scope of Section 14(e). The termination of the tender offer (with or without consummation of purchases of tender securities) marks the end of the application of Section 14(e). We have used the term "termination" of a tender offer here more broadly than its technical meaning of the time after which tender securities may not be tendered. Section 14(e) extends to the period from the time after which tender securities may no longer be tendered and ends on the day of settlement, i.e., when the securities to be purchased by the tender offeror are delivered to the tender offeror in exchange for the payment of the tender offer consideration.

7 Transactions in securities on the basis of material non-public information in the context of tender offers

One of the most significant aspects of the anti-fraud prohibition of Section 14(e) of the Securities Exchange Act is the prohibition of trading in the tender securities while in possession of material non-public information in connection with the tender offer. Rule 14e-3 under the Securities Exchange Act, adopted by the SEC pursuant to Section 14(e) of the Securities Exchange Act, treats as a fraudulent, deceptive, or manipulative act or practice within the meaning of Section 14(e) for any person who is in possession of material non-public information relating to the tender offer to purchase or sell any tender securities while the relevant information remains non-public information during the period following the commencement of a tender offer or the taking of a substantial step or steps to commence a tender offer. We discussed trading in tender securities while in possession of material non-public information and the provisions of Rule 14e-3 in Chapter 3.

8

The law and practice of consent solicitations

1 Introduction

The solicitation of consents to make changes to the terms of debt securities is often necessary for the success of a debt restructuring or other liability management transaction. In a consent solicitation, the *issuer* solicits consents from the holders of the *subject securities* to amend or supplement the terms of the securities[552] or the provisions of the indenture, trust deed, or other similar instrument governing the subject securities.[553] Depending on the terms of the indenture relating to amendments, supplements, or modifications, a consent solicitation may be a necessary condition for the entering into a valid *supplemental indenture.* With or without the consent of the holders of the subject securities (depending on the topic and the materiality of the amendments), a supplemental indenture may add new provisions to the existing provisions of the subject securities, may change the existing provisions in any manner, or may eliminate altogether any of the existing provisions or modify the rights of the holders of the subject securities. To maximize holder participation, the issuer frequently pays a consent fee to consenting holders. Depending on the facts and circumstances of a specific capital-raising or debt restructuring effort, consent

[552] Once duly executed and delivered by the parties thereto (pursuant to the execution and delivery formalities of the relevant applicable law), the indenture is a contract enforceable in accordance with its terms and binding on all of the parties thereto.

[553] Section 303(7) of the Trust Indenture Act defines an "indenture" as "any mortgage, deed of trust, trust or other indenture, or similar instrument or agreement (including any supplement or amendment to any of the foregoing) under which securities are outstanding or are to be issued, whether or not any property, real or personal, is, or is to be, pledged, mortgaged, assigned, or conveyed thereunder." Generally, the indenture establishes and regulates the rights, obligations, and duties of the parties to the indenture, i.e., the issuer of the securities, any guarantors, the trustee acting for the holders of the securities, the paying agent, the registrar, the transfer agent, and any other intermediaries performing an administrative function such as the security agent and/or any escrow agent appointed to act in connection with the issuance of the subject securities.

solicitations are often combined with tender offers for the purchase of the subject securities by the issuer or an affiliate of the issuer or with the issuance of new securities.

The consent of the holders of the subject securities is required when the amendments, additions, or eliminations of the provisions of the indenture that the issuer is seeking to complete affect the rights of the holders of the subject securities and, consequently, the indenture expressly requires such consent to be obtained before any such amendment, addition, or elimination can be effected. The issuer may desire to amend the terms and conditions of the subject securities for a variety of reasons. The issuer may be experiencing financial difficulties and, as a result, be unable to comply with one or more covenants in the indenture. The issuer may also desire to complete a single transaction or series of transactions that would have violated the terms of the indenture but for the making of the relevant amendments (e.g., a sale of assets, the granting of security, the incurrence of indebtedness, a merger or similar business combination transaction, a transaction with an affiliate, a dividend payment, or any combination thereof, which would have violated the relevant restrictive covenants of the indenture unless such covenants were amended with the consent of the holders of the subject securities).

In addition to consent solicitations facilitating certain transactions that would otherwise violate the terms of the relevant indenture, consent solicitations are often employed by issuers of debt securities and their financial and legal advisors in combination with tender offers for the purchase of the subject securities or exchange offers of the subject securities for newly issued securities. In a combined tender offer and consent solicitation, the issuer is asking the holders of the subject securities to tender the securities for purchase by the issuer for cash. In addition, under the terms of the tender offer, the issuer deems automatically the tendering of subject securities by the holders as the holders' express consent to amendments of the indenture, which normally affect adversely the rights or interests of the holders. In this structure, the purpose of the consent solicitation is to induce the holders to tender the securities in the tender offer in the knowledge that, if they do not tender (*hold out*), they will be forced to hold securities that will remain outstanding after the completion of the tender offer with amended terms as adversely amended through the consent of the tendering holders.

The rationale for an exchange offer combined with a consent solicitation is similar. The issuer is asking the holders of the subject securities to tender the relevant securities in the exchange offer for purchase by the issuer in consideration for the issuance of new securities. The purpose of the relevant consent solicitation is also to induce participation in the exchange offer by reducing the attractiveness of the terms of the outstanding subject securities. The effectiveness of this strategy is increased when issuers condition the completion of the relevant tender offer or exchange offer on the receipt of the requisite consents to effect the relevant amendments pursuant to the terms of the indenture. Because the consents are delivered by the holders of the securities as they tender their securities to the issuer, these types of consent solicitations are commonly known as *exit consent solicitations.*

Changing the terms of a contract with the consent of the parties thereto is a routine transaction. More specifically in relation to debtor–creditor relationships, amendments of the terms of the credit or loan agreements are frequent: it is not a rare event to see a debtor, experiencing a change in circumstances, requesting the consent of its creditors to amendments of the credit agreement. What makes consent solicitations in connection with debt securities an interesting topic for discussion is the different nature of the debtor–creditor relationship in capital markets compared to bilateral or multi-lateral debtor–creditor relationships in the bank market. It is argued that voluntary amendments of the terms of debt securities with the consent of the holders of such securities can be inherently unfair due to the dispersed composition of the creditor group in a capital markets instrument and the absence of coordination among the holders. Dispersed and uncoordinated holders of debt securities in the capital markets, unlike lenders in bilateral credit arrangements, can be subject to issuer strategies and/or tactics that are coercive or abusive in nature due to the dispersed and diffused nature of the creditor–borrower relationship.[554]

2 Amendments, indentures, and the Trust Indenture Act

An amendment of the terms of the indenture governing debt securities will be effected pursuant to the terms of the indenture being amended. The indenture itself will contain a separate chapter or section regulating

554 For a complete review of the various tactics used by issuers of debt securities to take advantage of the dispersed composition of creditor classes in debt securities traded in the capital markets, see Victor Brudney, "Corporate Bondholders and Debtor Opportunism: In Bad Times and Good," 105 *Harvard Law Review* 1821 (1992). The article advances an argument for tighter regulatory and judicial control over consent solicitations that seek to achieve tactical advantages over holders of debt securities in capital markets.

amendments and modifications of its own terms and the terms of any securities issued thereunder.

Indentures for non-convertible debt securities governed by New York law usually provide for three types of amendments: (i) technical or ministerial amendments that would not require any prior consent from the holders of the relevant securities; (ii) amendments of the basic or fundamental economic terms of the securities that would require the consent of every holder of the relevant securities (the *unanimous consent principle*);[555] and (iii) all other amendments that are neither technical nor ministerial in nature nor affect any fundamental economic rights, which would normally require the consent of holders representing more than 50 percent[556] of the principal amount of securities outstanding.

2.1 *Amendments without consent*

The ability of the issuer to amend the indenture without the consent of the holders of the subject securities is very limited. If the investment decision made by the investors is based on a specified set of terms and conditions governing the relevant securities, it follows that the holders of the securities should not be deprived of their right to determine, through their vote in a collective decision-making process, on whether the indenture may be amended by the issuer. Unilateral amendments by the issuer, without the consent of the holders, must be limited to terms and conditions that are, beyond any doubt, technical in nature and immaterial from an investment or economic perspective. From a contract law perspective, it goes without saying that the amendment to the indenture will still need to be effected by all of the parties thereto (including the trustee for the

[555] In recent years, issuers, underwriting banks, investors, and experienced counsel have determined that it is often undesirable to demand the consent of every holder of the relevant securities as a condition to the amendment of basic or fundamental economic rights due to a perceived risk that an absolute requirement may render otherwise economically rational and viable debt restructurings virtually impossible to accomplish. Thus, some indentures, especially outside the United States, permit the amendment of basic or fundamental economic rights with the consent of holders representing 90 percent or 95 percent of the principal amount outstanding without any of the terms of the indenture being subject to the unanimous consent principle. This is obviously not possible in relation to certain fundamental rights protected by the Trust Indenture Act in the case of indentures that are subject to the provisions of the Trust Indenture Act, especially Section 316(b); see section 2.3 of this chapter.

[556] Sometimes, the threshold is raised to holders representing more than two-thirds of the principal amount outstanding. The 50 percent standard has become virtually unexceptional in recent years.

benefit of the relevant holders), which will be executing a supplemental indenture containing the relevant amendments.

Common changes that are effected without the consent of any of the holders of the relevant securities include: (i) amendments or supplements to cure ambiguities, defects, or inconsistencies in the indenture,[557] which are all legal concepts interpreted very narrowly by the courts of the State of New York; (ii) amendments or supplements to give effect to provisions already embedded in the indenture (e.g., an amendment required to release any guarantee or securities pursuant to the terms of the indenture or providing for the assumption of the issuer's obligations under the indenture by a successor entity in the case of a merger of the issuer into another person, that other person being the surviving entity succeeding the issuer in its rights and obligations under the indenture); (iii) amendments or supplements that would provide for additional rights or benefits to the holders[558] or that would not adversely affect the legal rights of the holders under the indenture; or (iv) amendments or supplements required to conform the text of the indenture to the description of the indenture in the offering memorandum delivered to the holders during the marketing period of the relevant securities.

2.2 Amendments of basic or fundamental economic terms

At the other end of the spectrum, certain amendments, supplements, or modifications sought by the issuers of debt securities affect such fundamental investment terms that the relevant amendment cannot be effected unless consented to by every holder of the relevant securities or, as indicated above in footnote 557, by holders representing at least a very high percentage of the aggregate principal amount of the then outstanding securities (usually set at the 90 percent or 95 percent level).

Some of the most common terms that are subject to the unanimous consent principle include: (i) amendments reducing the principal amount of debt securities; (ii) reducing the principal amount of securities the holders of which must consent to an amendment, supplement, or waiver;

[557] The purpose of this provision is to correct ambiguities discovered subsequent to the execution of the original indenture that are inconsistent with the intention of the parties as clearly evidenced elsewhere in the indenture.

[558] For obvious reasons, this clause is rarely invoked because the issuer ordinarily would not seek to add covenants for the benefit of the holders or surrender any of its rights under the indenture except as part of an arrangement in which the issuer, experiencing, perhaps, financial difficulties, agrees to enter into additional covenants in exchange for some other benefit received by the issuer.

(iii) changing the fixed maturity of the relevant securities or altering the provisions with respect to the redemption of the relevant securities; (iv) adversely changing the ranking in right of payment of the securities; (v) reducing the rate of interest payable by the issuer; (vi) the currency of the securities; (vii) impairing the right of any holder to receive payment of principal of and interest on the relevant securities on or after the due dates therefor or to institute suit for the enforcement of any such payment; (viii) waiving a default in the payment of principal of, or interest on, any securities; (ix) releasing the issuer or any guarantor from any of their obligations under the indenture or the guarantee; (x) releasing any collateral granted for the benefit of the holders of the securities; and (xi) making any change in the amendment or waiver provisions of the indenture.

These clauses partly reflect the provisions of Section 316(b) of the Trust Indenture Act. Pursuant to Section 316(b), notwithstanding any other provision of the indenture,

> the right of any holder . . . to receive payment of the principal of and interest on such security, on or after the respective due dates expressed in such security, or to institute suit for the enforcement of any such payment on or after such respective dates shall not be impaired or affected without the consent of such holder.

Although Section 316(b) of the Trust Indenture Act applies only to indentures that are qualified pursuant to the Trust Indenture Act, the protective provisions of Section 316(b) are commonly incorporated into indentures for corporate securities that are not subject to the statute.

2.3 Unanimous consents for material terms and Section 316(b) of the Trust Indenture Act

The Trust Indenture Act was enacted to protect the interests of investors against abusive or fraudulent practices in the corporate debt securities markets. The necessity for federal legislation became apparent after years of judicial conflict over the duties of trustees to bondholders and the lack of financial protection afforded even to secured bondholders in the chaos that followed the 1929 stock market crash. The Trust Indenture Act goes beyond disclosure and imposes regulation over the substance of corporate and other private debt securities.[559]

[559] See generally George W. Shuster, "The Trust Indenture Act and International Debt Restructurings," 14 *American Bankruptcy Institute Law Review* 431 (2006).

The Trust Indenture Act applies to all types of debt securities, including notes, bond, debentures, evidences of indebtedness, and certificates of interest or participation in any of them.[560] A guarantee of indebtedness or a participation in a guarantee is also subject to the Trust Indenture Act unless the security being guaranteed is exempt under the Act.[561] For debt securities required to be registered under the Securities Act, the SEC will not permit the registration statement to become effective if the relevant security has not been issued under an indenture or the trustee is ineligible to serve.[562] Although, generally, securities and transactions exempt from the Securities Act are exempt from the Trust Indenture Act, in certain cases the Trust Indenture Act requires an indenture where the Securities Act does not apply (e.g., exchange offers solely with the issuer's security holders or exchange offers approved after a fairness hearing, which are exempt from registration under the Securities Act under Sections 3(a)(9) and (10)).[563]

Section 316(b) of the Trust Indenture Act is one of the central investor protection provisions required to be included in trust indentures by the Trust Indenture Act.[564] Section 316(b) provides that a holder's right to

[560] Section 302(2) of the Trust Indenture Act.

[561] Section 304(a)(7) of the Trust Indenture Act.

[562] Sections 305(b)(1) and (2) of the Trust Indenture Act.

[563] See Section 304(a)(4) of the Trust Indenture Act. Consequently, although debt securities issued in a reorganization or exchange with existing security holders are exempt from registration under the Securities Act by Sections 3(a)(10) and 3(a)(9) of the Securities Act, respectively, any securities exempted under these sections must still be issued under an indenture, and an application for qualification under the Trust Indenture Act as to the indenture must be filed with the SEC. If an application for qualification of the indenture is not effective, the sale of any such securities is prohibited under Sections 306 and 307 of the Trust Indenture Act. However, Section 306 of the Trust Indenture Act does not apply to exchange offers that are exempt from Securities Act registration under Section 3(a)(9) where the offering does not exceed $5 million and Section 304(a)(8) of the Trust Indenture Act and Rule 4a-1 thereunder otherwise are available. See SEC Trust Indenture Act Interpretations, at Question & Answer 207.01 (last updated March 30, 2007; website says last updated May 3, 2012), www.sec.gov/divisions/corpfin/guidance/tiainterp.htm. Accessed June 11, 2013.

[564] The full text of Section 316(b) provides: "Notwithstanding any other provision of the indenture to be qualified, *the right of any holder of any indenture security to receive payment of the principal of and interest on such indenture security*, on or after the respective due dates expressed in such indenture security, *or to institute suit for the enforcement of any such payment on or after such respective dates, shall not be impaired or affected without the consent of such holder*, except as to a postponement of an interest payment consented to in paragraph (2) of subsection (a) of this section, and except that such indenture may contain a provision limiting or denying the right of any such holder to institute any such suit, if and to the extent that the institution or prosecution thereof or

payment of principal and interest cannot be altered absent that individual holder's consent. As an exception to Section 316(b), Section 316(a)(2) allows the holders of 75 percent of the principal amount of the subject securities to consent to a postponement of interest for up to three years. Notwithstanding the foregoing, Section 316(b) also provides that an indenture may include a provision limiting a holder's right to institute an action for recovery of its principal and interest where such action would impair any lien or security interest available under the indenture.

Section 316(b) of the Trust Indenture Act was designed to protect investors against abusive practices, seen in the markets in the years leading to the adoption of the Act, whereby certain holders, often controlled by insiders, could form a majority of the outstanding principal amount and agree to amendments to an indenture, which would adversely affect the rights of other holders.[565] In certain circumstances, existing

the entry of the judgment therein would, under applicable law result in the surrender, impairment, waiver, or loss of the lien of such indenture upon any property subject to such lien." (Emphasis added.)

[565] See *In re Bd. of Dirs. of Multicanal S.A.*, 307 B.R. 384, 388 (Bankr. S.D.N.Y. 2004): "The Trust Indenture Act of 1939 sets forth certain requirements relative to indentures. One purpose of the statute was to regulate and reform prior practice whereby indentures contained provisions that permitted a group of bondholders, often controlled by insiders, to agree to amendments to the indenture that affected the rights of other holders – so-called 'majority' or 'collective' action clauses. See Sec. and Exch. Comm'n., Report on the Study and Investigation of Protective and Reorganization Committees, Parts I–VIII (1937–1940); Section 316(a) of the TIA provides that a qualified indenture may contain certain limited collective action clauses. Section 316(b) then declares that '[n]otwithstanding any other provision of the indenture to be qualified,' the right of any holder to institute suit for principal or interest on the holder's bonds or debentures cannot be impaired without consent." Also, see *UPIC & Co. Kinder-Care Learning Centers, Inc.*, 793 F. Supp. 448, 452 (S.D.N.Y. 1992) (hereinafter, "*UPIC*"): "Section 316(b) . . . proscribes certain . . . 'majority action clauses' . . . [and] expressly prohibits use of an indenture that permits modification by majority security holder vote of any core term of the indenture, *i.e.*, one affecting a security holder's right to receive payment of the principal of or interest on the indenture security." Also, "all holders of notes that are absolute promises to pay have contract rights against the issuer that cannot be impaired without consent. This is true whether the note is issued in a series under a TIA-qualified indenture, under an indenture not qualified under the Trust Indenture Act, or issued directly by the borrower to the lender without any indenture at all. Assuming there is no limitation in the applicable note as to the right of the holder to sue, each holder has a contractual right to principal and interest and to commence a lawsuit if these are not paid when due. For holders of notes issued under a qualified indenture, this right is protected against impairment through the mechanism of a collective action clause. See § 316(b) of the Trust Indenture Act, whose interlocutory clause is, '[n]otwithstanding any other provision of the indenture to be qualified . . . .' More fundamentally, the right against impairment is also protected, as to all holders (whether under a qualified indenture

shareholders, officers, directors or their affiliates, and other insiders could use the provisions permitting changes to the terms of the securities with the consent of the holders of the majority of principal amount to the detriment of other holders. In response to those practices, which were considered unacceptable, Congress enacted Section 316(b), which prohibits an indenture from allowing the holders of a majority of principal amount to modify core economic terms of the indenture such as the payment of principal or interest, while allowing certain other amendments and waivers under Section 316(a).[566] Thus, a bondholder's right to receive payments of principal and interest outside bankruptcy proceedings on a debt security cannot be impaired except with the consent of that individual holder. Collective action based on a majority of other holders is completely ineffectual. This is true even when other provisions of the indenture may permit the indenture trustee acting for the benefit of the holders to pursue remedial proceedings on behalf of the holders.

In *Continental Bank & Trust Co. of N.Y.* v. *First National Petroleum Trust*,[567] the court found that the mandatory provisions of Section 316(b) of the Trust Indenture Act overrode the provision in the same indenture allowing for a majority of holders to direct the indenture trustee's pursuit of remedial proceedings. The court ruled that the specific language of Section 316(b) controlled regardless of any contrary provisions in the indenture. Section 316(b) therefore protects the basic economic rights of each individual holder under an indenture against the ability of the majority of holders to make fundamental changes. It protects each holder against the desires of the issuer of the securities as well as the desires of its fellow holders acting in concert. It determines the fundamental economic characteristics of the securities which cannot be changed even if the majority of holders, acting democratically and forming a strong majority, agree to effect the relevant changes.

In *UPIC & Co.* v. *Kinder-Care Learning Centers, Inc.*,[568] the district court ruled that Section 316(b) grants holders an unfettered right to

or otherwise), by the Constitutional prohibition against the impairment of contracts. U.S. Const. Art. I, §10. Section § 316(b) does not create rights against impairment of contractual obligations that are already imbedded in the Constitution; it places a further gloss on such rights by restricting the use of collective action clauses." See *In re Bd. of Dirs. of Multicanal S.A.*

566 Ibid. See also *UPIC & Co.* v. *Kinder-Care Learning Ctrs., Inc.*, 793 F. Supp. 448, 452 (S.D.N.Y. 1992); Mark J. Roe, "The Voting Prohibition in Bond Workouts," 97 *Yale Law Journal* 232 (1987), at 251–52; see also generally James Gadsden, "Introduction to the Annotated Trust Indenture Act," 67 *Business Lawyer* 979 (2012).

567 67 F. Supp. 859 (D.R.I. 1946).

568 See fn 567 above.

bring an action to enforce the payment of principal and interest due on securities issued in connection with an indenture, notwithstanding how the principal becomes due or the practical effect of subordination provisions on the recovery to the holders. The issuer had argued that even if Section 316(b) mandated that the holders have a procedural right to bring a suit against the obligor for recovery on the securities, such section did not override the subordination provisions of the indenture requiring that any recoveries to the holders be paid over to certain senior indebtedness until such senior indebtedness is paid in full. The court agreed that Section 316(b) did not override subordination provisions but ruled that the holders of the subordinated notes were nevertheless entitled to bring an action against the issuer for repayment, even if such ultimate recoveries would be paid over to holders of senior indebtedness under the effect of the contractual subordination provisions.[569] In *Envirodyne Industries, Inc.* v. *Connecticut Mutual Life Co.* (*In re Envirodyne Industries, Inc.*),[570] the court ruled that Section 316(b) grants holders an absolute right to institute an action, including the filing of an involuntary bankruptcy proceeding, seeking payment of overdue principal and interest, notwithstanding the requirements of a *no action* clause in an indenture, which would otherwise restrict the ability of holders to bring such suits. The no action clause in question prevented lawsuits by holders under the indenture unless (i) such holder had first notified the trustee of a default, (ii) 25 percent of the holders in the aggregate principal amount of the securities outstanding had made a request to the trustee to institute such action and had offered reasonable indemnity to the trustee, and (iii) the trustee had neglected or refused such request for action despite the foregoing. Notwithstanding the existence of such provision in the indenture, the court was categorical that, under Section 316(b), holders were not prohibited from commencing an involuntary bankruptcy proceeding against the obligor without first complying with the requirements of the no action clause.[571]

The *due dates* for the payment of principal and/or interest are not necessarily limited to the initial stated maturity of the relevant securities. In the *UPIC* case, the issuer was required to repurchase notes, at the holders' option, during buyback periods associated with certain fixed dates. The court rejected the argument that Section 316(b) should not apply to

[569] Ibid., at 457–58. [570] 174 B.R. 986, 992 (Bankr. N.D. Ill. 1994).

[571] Ibid. See also *Great Plains Trust Co.* v. *Union Pac. R.R. Co.*, 492 F.3d 986, 991 (8th Cir., 2007).

that repurchase obligation.[572] The court noted that the securities did not contain any limitation on what would qualify as a payment of principal for purposes of the Trust Indenture Act, and that the securities simply provided alternative mechanisms (the repurchase provision and the provision for payment at the maturity date) pursuant to which the principal may become payable. The court concluded that the repurchase right was essentially a demand obligation in favor of the holder to be exercised at fixed dates at the holder's sole discretion, and thus qualified as a right to receive payment of the principal after a due date to which Section 316(b) of the Trust Indenture Act would apply.[573] In so concluding, the court noted that the legislative history and commentary "tends to evince Congress' intent to have Section 316(b) interpreted so as to give effect to the absolute and unconditional nature of the right to payment it affords a security holder."[574] If the due date has not been fixed but remains conditional on the occurrence of some other event, the protection of Section 316(b) is not available. Thus, it is generally accepted that removing the change of control covenant, which establishes the holders' conditional right to offer their securities for purchase by the issuer, would not impair the legal right that Section 316(b) seeks to protect.

Section 316(b) does not apply in situations where the relevant amendments to the terms of the indenture adversely affect the practical prospects of recovery of principal or interest without, however, impairing any legal rights given the holders under the terms of the indenture. In *YRC Worldwide*,[575] the trustee had argued that the elimination of the merger covenant from the relevant indenture would result in the issuer's ability to merge or transfer its assets without assumption of the payment obligation by the transferee entity. The trustee argued that the holders would then be denied direct recourse against the transferee for payment on the notes, thus impairing the practical prospects of recovery of the holders' rights for the payment of interest and/or principal.[576] The court did not agree. Citing the earlier *Magten* case,[577] the court ruled that Section 316(b) applied to the holders' legal rights but not to the holders' practical rights to recover principal and interest. So long as the legal rights are not impaired, diminishing the prospects of recovery through amendments of other provisions

[572] See fn 567 above, at 454–56. [573] Ibid., at 456. [574] Ibid., at 455.

[575] *YRC Worldwide Inc.* v. *Deutsche Bank Trust Co. Americas*, not reported in F. Supp. 2d, 2010 WL 2680336 (D. Kan. 2010).

[576] Ibid., at 7.

[577] *Magten Asset Management Corp.* v. *Northwestern Corp.*, 313 B.R. 595 (Bankr. D. Del. 2004).

in the indenture does not violate Section 316(b); there is no guarantee against default under the Trust Indenture Act. Accordingly, the fact that the deletion of the merger covenant from the indenture might make it more difficult for holders to receive payment directly from the plaintiff does not mean that the deletion without unanimous consent violates Section 316(b) of the Trust Indenture Act.

2.4 Consents of holders in all other circumstances

For supplemental indentures effecting amendments of the indenture (other than those requiring the consent of every holder or those that can be effected without the consent of any holder), the consent of the holders representing more than the majority of the outstanding principal amount (or, in some older indentures, more than two-thirds of the outstanding principal amount) is required generally. This is the default mechanism for effecting indenture amendments except in cases where the amendments are either immaterial or, at the other end of the spectrum, fundamentally affecting the value of the holders' investment by affecting adversely key economic rights.

The ability of the holders representing the majority of the outstanding principal amount to effect amendments to the terms of the securities, which upon effectiveness are binding on the holders who find themselves in the dissenting minority, introduces a strong element of collective action governance in the relationship between the holders and the issuer of the subject securities, as well as the relationship among the different holders of the subject securities acting as a class. These collective decision-making provisions of the indenture are intended to allow the holders acting collectively as a class to implement their collective will in the handling of an exchange offer, a consent solicitation, or another form of debt restructuring. Stated differently, the provisions that empower the majority to bind the minority are designed to prevent a small minority from undermining a collective debt restructuring.

When majority-action clauses first began to appear in a limited number of American bonds in the late nineteenth century, they were intended to allow the issuer and its majority creditors an alternative to liquidation of the debtor in bankruptcy should the need arise.[578] In exercising

[578] See generally a historical review of collective action clauses in corporate and sovereign bonds in Lee C. Buchheit and G. Mitu Gulati, "Sovereign Bonds and the Collective Will," 51 *Emory Law Journal* 1317 (2002).

their powers under these clauses, however, the majority creditors were assumed, in the past, to have a duty to act in the best interests of all the bondholders. The leading case of this era was *Hackettstown National Bank* v. *D.G. Yuengling Brewing Co.*[579] In *Hackettstown*, the court invalidated an attempt to use a majority-action clause to postpone payments due on a corporate bond in light of what the court construed as "a corrupt and unwarranted exercise of the power of the majority" bondholders. The perceived fiduciary duty of good faith, owed by the majority bondholders to the dissenting minority, was gradually eroded and ultimately abandoned in recent years due to the hostility of modern-era courts to recognizing duties of good faith and fiduciary protection owed by bondholders to one another, particularly in complex debt securities issued and held by sophisticated commercial parties who can protect themselves with expert legal advice. It is now good law that no intercreditor duty of good faith exists between investors or financial institutions when such investors or institutions are creditors under the same instrument unless such fiduciary duty is created expressly by the terms of the agreement.[580]

3 Consent solicitations for debt securities under the US federal securities laws

Consent solicitations in connection with debt securities are subject, under certain conditions, to certain requirements under the US federal securities laws. Section 14(a)(1) of the Securities Exchange Act provides that it shall be unlawful for any person, by the use of the mails or by any means or instrumentality of interstate commerce, or of any facility of a national securities exchange, or otherwise, in contravention of such rules and

[579] 74 F. 110, 114 (2d Cir. 1896).

[580] See *Banque Arabe et International D'Investissement* v. *Maryland National Bank*, 819 F. Supp. 1282, 1296 (S.D.N.Y. 1993): "[I]n the case of arms length transactions between financial institutions, no fiduciary duty exists unless one was created in the agreement . . . [and] there is no automatic, status-based fiduciary duty created [in] the transaction." For similar language, see also *Yucyco, Ltd.* v. *Republic of Slovenia*, 984 F. Supp. 209, 221 (S.D.N.Y. 1997) (no duty of the facility agent owed to the minority to declare an event of default and accelerate the debt, in circumstances in which the facility agreement required consent from the majority creditors to accelerate and such consent was lacking); *New Bank of New England* v. *Toronto-Dominion Bank*, 768 F. Supp. 1017, 1021–22 (S.D.N.Y. 1991) (no implied duty of the majority lenders to accelerate the agreement as a result of an "implied obligation of good faith" to a fellow lender where a majority of the lenders did not vote to accelerate the debt despite the occurrence of an event of default).

regulations as the SEC may prescribe as necessary or appropriate in the public interest or for the protection of investors, to *solicit* or to permit the use of his or her name to solicit any proxy or *consent* or authorization *in respect of any security* (other than an exempted security) registered pursuant to Section 12 of the Securities Exchange Act. Regulation 14A under the Securities Exchange Act, comprising Rules 14a-1 to 14a-21 and Schedule 14, provides the detailed disclosure requirements for the conduct of consent solicitations in relation to securities registered under Section 12 of the Securities Exchange Act.

Debt securities traded in the over-the-counter markets are outside the scope of the federal laws regulating proxy and consent solicitations. Debt securities listed on US national security exchanges are also generally exempt from federal proxy and consent solicitation regulation,[581] except that the following Securities Exchange Act rules continue to apply to consent solicitations for listed debt securities: Rule 14a-1; Rule 14a-2(a); Rule 14a-9; Rule 14a-13; Rule 14b-1; Rule 14b-2; Rule 14c-1; Rule 14c-6; and Rule 14c-7. Furthermore, although debt securities issued by foreign private issuers are also completely outside the scope of application of the federal proxy and consent solicitation regulations, foreign private issuers (and their counsel) are well advised to apply by analogy as many of the substantive provisions of Regulation 14A that apply to domestic US issuers as possible, and many actually do, taking into account the differences between debt securities and equity securities, and the purpose of the relevant consent and proxy solicitations.

3.1 The definition of "consent solicitation" in Regulation 14A under the Securities Exchange Act

The Securities Exchange Act and the rules promulgated by the SEC thereunder[582] set forth regulatory requirements with respect to the solicitation of *proxies* from holders of securities registered under Section 12 of the Securities Exchange Act. Because the reach of the federal regulatory regime extends to every solicitation of a proxy with respect to securities registered under the Securities Exchange Act (subject to certain exemptions), the definitions of the terms "proxy" and "solicitation" are especially important.

[581] See Rule 3a12-11 under the Securities Exchange Act.

[582] Section 14(a) of the Securities Exchange Act and Regulation 14A thereunder.

If a communication of the issuer with the holders of securities registered under the Securities Exchange Act is deemed to be the "solicitation of a proxy," the issuer becomes subject to the rigorous regulatory regime of proxy regulation found in Regulation 14A under the Securities Exchange Act. These regulatory provisions specify the information required to be disclosed to security holders prior to or at the time of a proxy solicitation, the presentation of such information, the form of proxies, and the treatment of proposals made by security holders. The regulations further prohibit certain types of solicitations and false or misleading statements in connection with solicitations. While foreign private issuers are generally exempt from the entire regulatory regime relating to proxy solicitations,[583] the requirements of Regulation 14A under the Securities Exchange Act relating to proxy solicitations, as interpreted or applied by the courts and the SEC, provide useful interpretative guidance for the structuring of consent solicitations relating to debt securities generally in a way that is in line with the public interest and the protection of investors.

Rule 14a-1(f) under the Securities Exchange Act defines the term "proxy" broadly to include "every proxy, consent or authorization," including when the consent or authorization takes the form of a failure to object to a course of action or to dissent to a course of action.[584] Therefore, the term "proxy" includes any form of express or implicit consent granted by a holder of a security in relation to such security. There is no requirement that such consent follow a particular form. The consent may be oral or written. There is no requirement that there be a formal vote or security holders' meeting or certain procedure to be followed. The significant factor is whether there is any proposal relating to the subject securities that requires collective or representative action by the holders of the relevant securities. The solicitation by the issuer of securities of an authorization to change the terms of any outstanding securities is certainly the solicitation of a proxy that would be within the scope of the federal regulatory regime, if the issuer was not an exempt foreign private issuer and if the securities were registered under Section 12 of the Securities Exchange Act.

The SEC's definition of what constitutes a "solicitation" of security holders is equally broad. The determination of whether a solicitation exists for purposes of Regulation 14A is a question of fact that depends on the

583 Rule 3a12-3 under the Securities Exchange Act provides that securities registered by "foreign private issuers," as defined in Rule 3b-4 of the Securities Exchange Act, are exempt from Sections 14(a), (b), (c), and (f) and Section 16 of the Securities Exchange Act.

584 See Rule 14a-1(f) in combination with Section 14(a) of the Securities Exchange Act.

nature of the communication and the circumstances under which it was transmitted. Pursuant to Rule 14a-1(1)(1) under the Securities Exchange Act, the terms "solicit" and "solicitation" include any request for a proxy, consent, or authorization (oral or written), any request (oral or written) to execute or not to execute, or to revoke a proxy, consent, or authorization; and the furnishing of a form of proxy, consent, or authorization or a card requesting a proxy, consent, or authorization or other communication, written or oral, to holders of the relevant securities under circumstances that are reasonably calculated to foster the submission or execution of a proxy, consent, or authorization.

The broad nature of the SEC's basic definition of "solicitation" (and "proxy") is illustrated by the court's decision in *Studebaker Corp.* v. *Gittlin.*[585] In *Gittlin*, a shareholder wished to obtain the shareholder list to solicit his fellow shareholders and, for that purpose communicated with forty-two other shareholders in an attempt to form a group that would own enough securities to satisfy the statutory requirement. The Second Circuit held that Gittlin's communications with the other shareholders were a "solicitation" because they were a part of a continuous plan ending in a solicitation and which prepared the way for the solicitation's success. Over the years, the courts have identified other factors relevant in determining whether a communication to the holders of the issuer's securities by the issuer is a "solicitation." The timing of a communication is an important factor. The closer a communication is to a holders' meeting or action by written consent, the more likely the courts are to find the communication to be a "solicitation." In contrast, communications in the ordinary course of corporate business do not usually constitute a solicitation of proxies. Communications to persons who are not security holders are not considered solicitations if there is a bona fide purpose for the communication and it is not solely an effort to evade the application of Regulation 14A. That the communication may facilitate a proposed solicitation does not necessarily raise compliance issues with Regulation 14A unless one can show there is no bona fide purpose for the communication or that it is an attempt to evade the requirements of Regulation 14A.

3.2 The content of consent solicitation statements

The most important disclosure document addressed to the holders of the relevant securities, whose consent is being sought in the relevant consent solicitation, is the *consent solicitation statement.* Rule 14a-3 under

[585] 360 F.2d 692 (2d Cir. 1966).

the Securities Exchange Act provides generally that no solicitation can be made unless each holder of securities solicited has been sent or is concurrently provided a publicly filed preliminary proxy (including consent) statement or a definitive written proxy or consent statement containing the information required by Schedule 14A of Regulation 14A.

Rule 14a-3 does not dictate the use of a particular format for the consent solicitation statement so long as the document contains all the required items of information. Issuers are, however, encouraged to use tables, charts, graphs, and any other appropriate method to present all necessary information in an understandable fashion. If the relevant securities are listed on a stock exchange or some other organized securities market, the consent solicitation statement must be filed with the exchange and if the relevant indenture or other legal instrument governing the terms of the securities requires other methods of dissemination of any communication to the holders of the relevant securities, those publicity and dissemination requirements must also be complied with. Applying by analogy Rule 14a-3, which permits delivery of the relevant materials to the security holders in an electronic medium, issuers conducting consent solicitations in respect of debt securities will often disseminate electronic, not hard, copies of the relevant consent solicitation statements. If electronic distribution methods are used, the issuer must satisfy the legibility requirements by "presenting all required information in a format readily communicated to investors."[586]

Rule 14a-4 sets forth form requirements with which the consent solicitation statement must comply. The form of the consent must clearly and impartially set forth each matter that the soliciting party agrees to or intends to act on and must allow the solicited security holders to express their intention regarding the consent solicitation clearly and unambiguously. Rule 14a-5 requires that the information in a consent or proxy solicitation statement be "clearly presented" and logically organized by subject matter.[587] Rule 14a-5(d)(2) provides that the legibility requirements can be satisfied in proxy or consent solicitation statements delivered electronically "by presenting all required information in a format readily communicated to investors." The first page of the proxy statement must set forth the complete mailing address for the principal executive offices of

[586] See SEC, Exchange Act Release No. 34–37183 (May 9, 1996).

[587] Rule 14a-5(d)(1) under the Securities Exchange Act provides that the type of the text must be Roman and at least as large as 10-point modern type (footnotes and financials can use smaller type if demanded for ease and clarity of presentation).

the soliciting party and the approximate date of distribution of the proxy statement to security holders. If the proxy statement includes information relating to the terms of securities or any other matter which from a practicable standpoint must be determined in the future, the preparer must state the information in terms of present knowledge and should limit seeking authority to that reasonably needed.

Rule 14a-3(a) requires that every holder being solicited receive a publicly filed preliminary or a definitive written proxy statement containing the information specified by Schedule 14A. Schedule 14A sets forth the minimum disclosure requirements to be included in all proxy and consent solicitation statements. Obviously, a lot of the disclosure requirements relate to proxy contests among the issuer's shareholders and are not relevant in the case of consent solicitations for the modification of the terms of outstanding debt securities. It is, however, important for issuers structuring liability management transactions and their counsel to understand the regulatory framework and the comprehensive disclosure requirements of Regulation 14A and draw guidance when drafting consent solicitation statements for amendments of the terms of debt securities.

Schedule 14A does not preclude additional information or disclosures. It also does not dictate the format of the document or specific language. The SEC, however, does look for documents that can be readily understood by a security holder. Unduly complex, lengthy, or wordy documents may encounter problems in a SEC review or violate the letter and spirit of Rule 14a-6 relating to filing requirements. In addition, Schedule 14A does require that standardized disclosure items be segregated into self-contained sections with appropriate headings.

The following paragraphs briefly describe the standardized disclosure items set forth in Schedule 14A that would be relevant in a consent solicitation for amendments of the terms of debt securities.

- *Item 1: Basic information.* This item requires disclosure of basic information, including the date, time, and place of the security holders' meeting (if any), and the complete mailing address of the soliciting party's principal executive headquarters.
- *Item 2: Revocability of consent.* Item 2 provides that the proxy or consent statement must state whether or not a proxy or consent can be revoked by the security holders and the manner of revocation.
- *Item 4: Persons making the solicitation.* Item 4 requires disclosure of the identity of the persons making a solicitation and the method to be employed for the solicitation if other than the use of the mails or the

use of the Internet pursuant to Rule 14a-16. The statement must also indicate the names of the persons who will directly or indirectly bear the cost of solicitation. The statement must also disclose the total expenses to date plus the estimated cost of the completed solicitation. Expenses include professional fees (e.g., lawyers, accountants, and proxy solicitors) and litigation costs. The issuer must also disclose whether any director has expressed an intention to oppose any action to be presented at the meeting. The identity of the director does not have to be disclosed.

- *Item 5: Interest of certain persons in matters to be acted upon.* This item requires disclosure of any substantial interest, direct or indirect, of each participant in the solicitation (and if the solicitation is made on behalf of the registrant, of each director or senior officer of the issuer) and any associates of the foregoing in any matter to be presented for security holder action. If, for example, a member of the board of directors is going to benefit personally from the consent that is the subject of the consent solicitation, this matter should be disclosed.
- *Item 6: Voting securities and principal holders thereof.* Item 6 requires disclosure with respect to each class of voting securities of the issuer entitled to be voted or participate in the consent, including the number of shares or principal amount outstanding. In addition, the statement must disclose the record date, if any, of the solicitation.
- *Item 12: Modification or exchange of securities.* Item 12 concerns self-tender offers or issuer exchange offers for its own securities as well as offers that would modify the terms of an outstanding class of securities. Item 12 calls for a complete description of the proposed action, the purposes for the transaction, and any transaction that prompted or required the modification or exchange.
- *Item 18: Matters not required to be submitted.* Item 18 provides that if action is to be taken on any matter that is not required to be submitted to the security holders, the registrant must disclose both its reasons for submitting the matter to the security holders and its intentions as to how it will act if the matter is not approved.

In addition to the disclosure items set forth above, the consent solicitation statement should include all other material information relating to the consent solicitation, including information on the commencement and expiration time of the solicitation, the payment of the consent solicitation fee, how the issuer may effect changes or amend, extend, or terminate the consent solicitation, the professional advisors advising the issuer in the relevant consent, the settlement date of the consent, the time of effectiveness of the amendments being sought in the consent, risk factors and other investor considerations relating to the consent, tax consequences, voting procedures, public announcements relating to the consent solicitation, the requisite number of consents being sought and the consequences of the failure to obtain such consents, the applicable procedures for consenting, and contact information where investors may obtain further information in relation to the consent.

3.3 Regulation 14A and consent solicitations for debt securities listed on US exchanges

While debt securities of domestic US issuers listed on US securities exchanges have been exempted from most of the regulatory requirements of Regulation 14A under the Securities Exchange Act, the following proxy and consent solicitation rules continue to apply to listed debt securities of domestic US issuers and, often by analogy, to consent solicitations for other types of securities in the interest of investor protection: Rule 14a-1 (definitions); Rule 14a-2(a) (further exemptions); Rule 14a-9 (false or misleading statements); Rule 14a-13 (communications with beneficial owners); Rule 14b-1 (obligations of brokers or dealers in connection with communications); Rule 14b-2 (obligations of banks and other fiduciaries in connection with communications); Rule 14c-1 (further definitions); Rule 14c-6 (false or misleading statements); and Rule 14c-7 (providing copies of materials for certain beneficial owners).

Rule 14a-9 under the Securities Exchange Act. Rule 14a-9 under the Securities Exchange Act (together with Rule 14c-7) contains the basic anti-fraud rule applicable to all proxy and consent solicitation and consent solicitation statements for securities registered under Section 12 of the Securities Exchange Act. Other anti-fraud provisions of the federal securities laws (e.g., Rule 10b-5) as well as state statutory provisions and common law may be applicable as well. Rule 14a-9 prohibits any solicitation that is false or misleading with respect to any material fact, or any solicitation that omits any material fact that is necessary to make any statement not false or misleading. To succeed in a cause of action under Rule 14a-9, a private plaintiff must show the existence of a misrepresentation or omission of a misleading statement of material fact. In the *Sharon Steel Corporation* No-Action Letter,[588] the SEC found that with

[588] See *Sharon Steel Corporation*, SEC No-Action Letter, 1981 SEC No-Action File LEXIS 3664.

respect to a proposed consent solicitation to be made without compliance with the proxy rules under the Securities Exchange Act or the registration requirements of the Securities Act, its no-action position did not preclude application of the anti-fraud provisions of Section 17(a) of the Securities Act or Section 10(b) of the Securities Exchange Act, and the rules and regulations thereunder, to the proposed transaction. It is primarily for this reason that counsel and issuers preparing consent solicitation statements should prepare and distribute to all security holders a consent solicitation statement that complies in all material respects with the substantive disclosure provisions of the proxy rules in Regulation 14A under the Securities Exchange Act insofar as those rules are relevant for a consent solicitation in connection with debt securities.

Rule 14a-13 under the Securities Exchange Act. Rule 14a-13 establishes very detailed rules regarding the obligation of the issuer to provide information to the beneficial owners of the securities that are the subject of a consent solicitation by furnishing appropriate and timely soliciting materials to the record-holders.

Rule 14b-1 and Rule 14c-7 under the Securities Exchange Act. Rule 14b-1 and Rule 14c-7 establish detailed requirements that a broker or dealer must comply with when disseminating certain communications to beneficial owners or when providing beneficial owner information to issuers in connection with consent solicitations.

Rule 14b-2 under the Securities Exchange Act. Rule 14b-2 establishes detailed requirements that a bank, custodian, or other fiduciary must comply with when disseminating certain communications to beneficial owners in connection with consent solicitations.

4 Registration under the Securities Act: the "New Security" Doctrine

Securities lawyers have long considered the question of whether the solicitation of consents to the execution and delivery of a supplemental indenture effecting changes to the terms of the subject securities amounts to an "offer" or "sale" of a "security" as such terms are defined in the Securities Act and, consequently, triggers the application of the registration and prospectus delivery requirements of Section 5 of the Securities Act and other consequences triggered by the offer and/or sale of securities within the meaning of the US federal securities laws.

This question is generated by the fact that the issuer of a security is offering to pay cash or some other consideration to the holders of its outstanding securities in exchange for their consent to the elimination or amendment of certain provisions contained in the indenture governing those securities. To the extent that the changes being sought in the consent solicitation affect the terms of the securities in a material way, the transaction is equivalent to the issuance and sale of a *new security* for value, thus requiring the protection of the registration and prospectus delivery requirements of Section 5 of the Securities Act. If a consent solicitation is deemed to constitute an issuance and sale of a new security, then the Trust Indenture Act will also require the qualification of the relevant indenture prior to the sale of any securities issued thereunder.

Whether the amendments to the terms of the securities resulting from a consent solicitation create a new security is not void of practical consequences.[589] If a new security is offered and sold, the offer and sale would require the filing and effectiveness of a registration statement under the Security Act and relevant filings and qualifications under the Trust Indenture Act. These filings will invite regulatory review, with timing and other adverse consequences for the company and the structure of the proposed transaction. The offer and/or sale of the new security would also be subject to the strict communication rules applicable during the pre-filing and quiet period and would further prevent the issuer from having negotiations or other discussions with its security holders prior to the filing of the registration statement. In addition, if a registration statement is used, the issuer of the securities (as well as any statutory underwriter involved in the sale of the new security and the issuer's officers and directors) would be subject to the strict liability regime of Section 11 of the Securities Act. From the perspective of the holders of the relevant securities, the creation of a new security will determine if the relevant holder could invoke the protection of the anti-fraud remedies of the US federal securities laws (primarily Rule 10b-5 under the Securities Exchange Act) because one of the requisite elements of standing pursuant

[589] In the case of *equity securities*, Rule 145 under the Securities Act extends the protection of the registration requirements of the Securities Act and finds that an "offer," "offer to sell," "offer for sale," or "sale" of a security occurs when there is submitted to the holders of equity security a plan or agreement pursuant to which such holders are required to elect, on the basis of what is in substance a new investment decision, whether to accept a new or different security in exchange for their existing security. If the voting or the consent leads to a plan or arrangement resulting in a merger, consolidation, transfer of assets, or reclassification of the relevant equity securities, then a new security would be offered, requiring compliance with the registration requirements of the Securities Act. See Rule 145 under the Securities Act.

to Rule 10b-5 is the existence of a purchase or sale "of a security."[590] In the absence of anti-fraud protection under the US federal securities laws, any cause of action arising from the consent solicitation would only be based on applicable contract law.

Whether the amendments result in the creation of a new security that is being offered and/or sold to the existing security holders is a difficult question, and the answer will normally depend on the types of amendments being considered in the light of the facts and circumstances. The case law, or at least most of it, discusses the question in situations that are unrelated to the Securities Act. Most of the guidance on this topic is sourced from SEC no-action letters (which are discussed below), academic literature,[591] and the views of leading counsel when structuring securities transactions.

4.1 Case law

In determining whether the amendment of a security or the indenture governing the security constitutes the offer and sale of a new security, thus requiring registration under the Securities Act and qualification under the Trust Indenture Act, the generally accepted test in the case law is whether the amendment has substantially affected the legal rights and obligations of the holders of the outstanding securities, thus creating a

[590] See *Blue Chip Stamps* v. *Manor Drug Stores*, 421 U.S. 723 (1975); *Birnbaum* v. *Newport Steel Corp.*, 193 F.2d 461 (2d Cir. 1952). Whether or not a new security is created, for that limited class of securities subject to Section 14(a) of the Securities Exchange Act, the relief provided by Rule 14a-9 thereunder would be available. If, however, the solicitation is "in connection with any tender offer," Section 14(e) of the Securities Exchange Act would also be applicable. See also *Schreiber* v. *Burlington Northern, Inc.*, 472 U.S. 1 (1985).

[591] On the new security doctrine, see generally Louis Loss and Joel Seligman, *Securities Regulation*, 4th edn (Wolters Kluwer Law and Business: New York, 2007), at p. 1148; Philip P. McGuigan and William P. Aiken, Jr., "Amendment of Securities," 9 *Review of Securities Regulation* 935 (1976), at p. 939 ("whether the rights of security holders have been so substantially affected by the particular change in the terms of the outstanding security that it becomes a new security") and at 935 ("In determining whether the amendment of a security constitutes the sale . . . of a new security, the generally accepted test is whether the alteration has substantially affected the legal rights and obligations of the holders of the outstanding securities"); Ronald R. Adee, "Creating a New Security," 3 *Insights, Corporate and Securities Law Advisor* 23 (1989); Nicholas P. Saggese, Gregg A. Noel and Michael A. Mohr, "A Practitioner's Guide to Exchange Offers and Consent Solicitations," 24 *Loyola L.A. Law Review* 527 (1991), at pp. 602–7; Bryant B. Edwards and Jon J. Bancone, "Modifying Debt Securities: The Search for the Elusive 'New Security' Doctrine," 47 *Business Lawyer* 571 (1992).

new investment for those holders.[592] The federal courts have accepted that significant changes in the rights of a security holder can result in the purchase or sale of a new security if there is such a significant change in the nature of the investment or in the investment risks as to amount to a new investment.[593] The basic economic terms of fixed-income securities, including the payment of the principal amount, the interest rate, the redemption schedule and premium, the maturity of the obligation, the place of payment, the currency in which obligations are payable, and the right to institute suit for any default are generally regarded as the fundamental economic terms of the securities, the amendment or modification of which would reasonably result in the offering of a new security.[594]

If the relevant changes in the terms and conditions of the securities were contemplated by the holders of the securities at the time of the initial investment or the relevant change represented a mere adjustment in the relevant terms that would not amount to a new investment or investment risk, then the amendment would not create a new security.[595] For example, in *Freschi* v. *Grand Coal Venture*,[596] the investor invested in a joint venture in coal-mining leases. When the venture exchanged a lease

592 See generally *Keys* v. *Wolfe*, 709 F.2d 413 (5th Cir. 1983): "before changes in the rights of security holder can qualify as the purchase of a new security under Section 10b-5 of the Securities Exchange Act and Rule 10b-5, there must be a 'significant change in the nature of the investment or in the investment risks as to amount to a new investment'."

593 See, for example, *Abrahamson* v. *Fleschner*, 568 F.2d 862, 868 (2d Cir. 1977), cert. denied, 436 U.S. 913, 98 S. Ct. 2253, 56 L. Ed. 2d 414 (1978); *Smith* v. *Cooper/T. Smith Corp.*, 846 F.2d 325, 327 (5th Cir. 1988) (modifying a stock purchase agreement involved the purchase or sale of a new security within the meaning of Section 10(b) under the Securities Exchange Act); *Keys* v. *Wolfe*, see fn 594 above (allegation that the modification of management contracts in connection with growing trees and orchards in a pecan plantation constituted such a change in investment as to amount to the purchase of a new investment contract, was sufficient to state a claim under Section 10(b)); *Ahern* v. *Gaussoin*, 611 F. Supp. 1465, 1478–79 (D. Or. 1985) (exchange of terms of notes after a corporate restructuring was such a significant change in the nature of investment as to constitute a new investment).

594 These provisions have been referred to as the terms defining the "basic nature," the "essence of" and the "intrinsic rights" of the relevant securities. See *Leasco Corp.*, SEC No-Action Letter (September 22, 1982) (no-action position taken on the basis that the proposed amendments would "not affect the provisions of the Indenture relating to payment of principal and interest, interest rate, interest payment date, maturity date, redeemability or the sinking fund provisions"); also, *Magic Marker Corp.*, SEC No-Action Letter (June 30, 1971).

595 See *Sanderson* v. *Roethenmund*, 682 F. Supp. 205 (S.D.N.Y. 1988); *Freschi* v. *Grand Coal Venture*, 551 F. Supp. 1220 (S.D.N.Y. 1982); *Browning Debenture Holders' Committee* v. *DASA Corp.*, Fed. Sec. L. Rep. 95,071 (S.D.N.Y. 1975).

596 Ibid., at 551 F. Supp. 1220 (S.D.N.Y. 1982).

on an unproductive property in one state for a lease on a property in another state, the investor argued that the new lease constituted the purchase of a new security. The court reviewed the substance of the transaction and, on the basis that the substitution of property at the option of the issuer of the security was provided for in the original agreement, dismissed the argument that the change of lease created a new security.[597]

In the seminal case *SEC* v. *Associated Gas & Electric Co.*,[598] the issuer proposed to pay a percentage of the principal amount owed on certain investment certificates and to extend the maturity date of the remaining balance for a period of up to five years. In consideration for the security holders' consent to such change, an additional payment of 2 percent was offered. The extended maturity date of the investment certificates was held to involve the sale of a new "security" within the meaning of the Public Utility Holding Company Act of 1935[599] (now defunct). The court observed that the holders would surrender their right to have the certificate paid in full on November 15, 1938 and, in its place, they would receive 20 percent in cash and acquire the right to payment of the remaining 80 percent within a period of one or five years later, not on the original maturity date. The court emphasized the economic essence of the transaction, i.e., that there would be a legal consideration for the new obligation, and disregarded the fact that the same piece of paper would contain the earlier and later obligation as "quite immaterial."[600] The court analyzed the economic essence of the transaction and concluded that the investors were, in effect, making a further investment when the maturity of the debt securities was extended and, consequently, the stamping of the certificates with a new date extending their maturity, when accepted by the owner of the certificate, constituted the "sale" of a security. For purposes of registration under the Securities Act and qualification under the Trust Indenture Act, the "sale" was deemed to have occurred upon effectiveness of the proposed amendments to the indenture.[601] Other courts, using a similar *substantive investment* test, have concluded

597 Ibid. at 209. 598 99 F.2d 795 (2d Cir., 1938).

599 Although the case was decided for the purposes of the Public Holding Company Act, it is generally accepted that its rationale applies equally to the determination of the issuance of new securities for purposes of the Securities Act and the Securities Exchange Act. See, e.g., *Bradford* v. *Moench*, 809 F. Supp. 1473 (D. Utah 1992).

600 See *Associated Gas*, fn 600 above, at 797.

601 Ibid. See also *United States* v. *Riedel*, 126 F.2d 81, 83 (7th Cir., 1942) (confirming that an exchange of an outstanding security for a new security is a "sale" within the meaning of the Securities Act).

that a new security has been created if the modification of the terms of the indenture alters substantially the nature and terms of an investor's involvement in a business enterprise through the creation of new rights or obligations.[602]

While the terminology used by the circuit and district courts is not necessarily identical from case to case, the "new security" jurisprudence has focused primarily on whether a modification is "substantial" or "significant" so as to change the nature of the relevant investment (often by reference to the "basic" or "fundamental" economic terms of the securities such as principal amount, interest rate, maturity, redemption features, right to sue, ranking, subordination, and currency). It is fair to observe that a substantive modification of the terms of the indenture in a way that is both material and adverse to the security holders is one of the principal factors that a court will take into account when assessing if a new security has been issued.

4.2 *The position of the SEC*

In relation to specific facts and circumstances presented to them within the framework of their no-action letter practice, the staff of the SEC considered, especially in the 1970s and the 1980s, amendments and/or modifications of the terms of debt securities or the indenture governing such securities and provided no-action relief that those amendments did not or would not constitute sales of new securities for purposes of the federal securities laws.[603] Only in a very small number of cases,

[602] See, e.g., *United States* v. *Wernes*, 157 F.2d 797 (7th Cir. 1946).

[603] From a long line of SEC no-action letters on this point, see *PLM Companies, Inc.*, SEC No-Action Letter (September 14, 1987); *Electronic Memories and Magnetics Corp.*, SEC No-Action Letter (November 15, 1984); *Wilson Foods Corporation*, SEC No-Action Letter (August 6, 1984); *Continental Telephone Co. of Upstate New York, Inc.*, SEC No-Action Letter (March 24, 1983); *Time, Inc.*, SEC No-Action Letter (December 9, 1983); *Continental Telephone Co.*, SEC No-Action Letter (June 17, 1983); *Aristar, Inc.*, SEC No-Action Letter (July 8, 1982); *Alabama Gas Corporation*, SEC No-Action Letter (April 9, 1982); *Northwestern Mutual Life Mortgage Realty Investors*, SEC No-Action Letter (December 22, 1982); *Macmillian, Inc.*, SEC No-Action Letter (February 22, 1982); *Leasco Corporation*, fn 596 above; *NCNB Corporation*, SEC No-Action Letter (March 11, 1982); *Purex Corporation*, SEC No-Action Letter (September 6, 1982); *The Limited Stores*, SEC No-Action Letter (May 12, 1982); *Motorola, Inc.*, SEC No-Action Letter (March 5, 1982); *Sharon Steel Corporation*, fn 590 above; *Southern Railway Co.*, SEC No-Action Letter (September 14, 1981); *Eaton Corp.*, SEC No-Action Letter (May 22, 1980); *Wickes Cos., Inc.*, SEC No-Action Letter (September 2 and 15, 1980); *J. Ray McDermott & Co., Inc.*, SEC No-Action Letter (September 10, 1979); *The Susquehanna*

in which the requested amendments and/or modifications required the consent of every holder affected by those changes, did the staff of the SEC conclude that the relevant amendments and/or modifications resulted in the issuance of a new security for purposes of the Securities Act.[604]

One may distinguish a number of different categories of amendments, modifications, or supplements to terms of outstanding securities that the SEC staff has considered eligible for no-action relief and responded favorably to such no-action request.

In certain cases, the relevant amendments seek to reorganize the business and operations of the issuer through a merger of the issuer into a successor entity that assumes the rights and obligations of the issuer under the terms of the relevant indenture.[605] The transaction is effected without the consent of the holders of the debt securities. The issuer's business, fiscal year, capitalization, charter, bylaws, consolidated results of operations and financial position, directors, officers, and employees remain the same. While the applicable corporate law may require that shareholders vote on the transaction, the staff of the SEC has taken the view that such an intracorporate reorganization does not involve the making of a new investment decision and does not trigger the application of the registration and other requirements of the Securities Act applicable to the issuance and sale of new securities.[606]

Corporation, SEC No-Action Letter (June 29, 1979); *Sunderling Broadcasting Corp.*, SEC No-Action Letter (March 23, 1979); *Sheraton Corp.*, SEC No-Action Letter (November 24, 1978); *Work Wear Corp.*, SEC No-Action Letter (March 11, 1977); *Tennessee Forging Steel Corp.*, SEC No-Action Letter (January 21, 1977); *San Diego Gas & Electricity Co.*, SEC No-Action Letter (April 3, 1975); *Lockheed Aircraft Corp.*, SEC No-Action Letter (August 10, 1976); *IDS Realty Trust*, SEC No-Action Letter (May 17, 1976); *Envirodyne, Inc.*, SEC No-Action Letter (July 26, 1976); *National Mortgage Fund*, SEC No-Action Letter (April 11, 1975); *Daitch Crystal Dairies, Inc.*, SEC No-Action Letter (November 13, 1972); and *Mississippi River Corporation*, SEC No-Action Letter (October 28, 1971).

604 See Bryant B. Edwards and Jon J. Bancone, fn 593 above, at 595; only two out of sixty no-action letters surveyed by the author concluded that a new security would be issued and sold in light of the facts and circumstances presented to the staff.

605 See, for example, *SAIC, Inc.*, SEC No-Action Letter (April 27, 2012); *GP Strategies Corporation*, SEC No-Action Letter (October 4, 2011); *Newmont Mining Corp.*, SEC No-Action Letter (March 15, 2000); *Newmont Mining Corp.*, SEC No-Action Letter (April 27, 2000); *Lexmark Int'l Group, Inc.*, SEC No-Action Letter (March 14, 2000); *Union Carbide Corporation*, SEC No-Action Letter (March 2, 1994); and *Union Carbide Corporation*, SEC No-Action Letter (April 15, 1994).

606 For example, see *Union Carbide*, and *SAIC, Inc.*; we note that the staff has granted no-action relief in business reorganization transactions, including holding company formations and re-incorporations, completed both with and without shareholder approvals.

In other cases, the issuer proposes to modify or eliminate restrictive covenants that would otherwise apply under the terms of the indenture. Based on no-action relief granted in numerous such cases, it is fair to conclude that if the proposed amendment does not change fundamental economic terms of the securities (such as the dates of the maturity of the notes, the interest rate payable, or other fundamental terms), the proposed amendment would not be equivalent to the creation of a new security for purposes of the Securities Act or the Trust Indenture Act. It is clear that the staff carries out a factual determination of the significance of the changes and only provides no-action relief if the relevant amendments to the terms do not adversely affect the holders of the securities or materially alter the nature of the relevant securities or the investment risks associated with them.[607] Moreover, a careful review of the relevant no-action letters and specific facts and circumstances often reveals that the SEC staff takes into account, in addition to the nature of the relevant amendments, broader investor protection considerations served by the registration requirements of the Securities Act. If, for example, the changes are extensive but not adverse to the holders in any material respect, or if the purposes of the Securities Act are served by extensive disclosure in the consent solicitation or proxy materials used in connection with the relevant transaction, then the staff is more likely to grant the relevant no-action relief.[608]

Amendments that have been granted no-action relief as "not fundamental" include the following amendments: eliminating a covenant

See, for example, *Mentor Corporation*, SEC No-Action Letter (September 25, 2008); *Dollar Tree Stores, Inc.* (February 20, 2008); *Energy West, Incorporated*, SEC No-Action Letter (January 15, 2008); *Transocean, Inc.*, SEC No-Action Letter (September 25, 2007); *Roper Industries, Inc.*, SEC No-Action Letter (July 19, 2007); *Mercer International, Inc.*, SEC No-Action Letter (December 12, 2005); *The News Corporation Limited*, SEC No-Action Letter (November 3, 2004); *AngloGold Limited*, SEC No-Action Letter (January 15, 2004); *Nabors Industries, Inc. and Nabors Industries Ltd.*, SEC No-Action Letter (April 29, 2002); *Reliant Energy, Incorporated*, SEC No-Action Letter (December 21, 2001); *NUI Corporation*, SEC No-Action Letter (December 22, 2000); *T. Rowe Price Associates, Inc.*, SEC No-Action Letter (April 28, 2000); *El Paso Natural Gas Company*, SEC No-Action Letter (May 21, 1998); *Payless ShoeSource, Inc.*, SEC No-Action Letter (April 20, 1998); *Idaho Power Company*, SEC No-Action Letter (March 16, 1998); *Consolidated Edison Company of New York, Inc.*, SEC No-Action Letter (October 31, 1997); *Rouge Steel, Inc.* (April 22, 1997); *Boston Edison Company* (February 24, 1997); *Halliburton Company* (December 11, 1996); and *Toys "R" Us, Inc.* (December 1, 1995).

607 See, for example, *The Continental Group*, SEC No-Action Letter (March 15, 1978); *Wilson Foods Corporation*, fn 605 above (August 6, 1984).

608 See, for example, *Lockheed Aircraft Corporation*, SEC No-Action Letter (July 14, 1975).

requiring compliance with state and federal law;[609] changes to covenants providing more operational flexibility in light of adverse business developments;[610] the elimination of covenants restricting payment of dividends and/or repurchases of certain types of subordinated securities;[611] the elimination of covenants requiring the maintenance of a certain minimum level of financial net worth;[612] the elimination of covenants requiring compliance with applicable tax laws;[613] changes relaxing certain financial covenants in the indenture, coupled with a corresponding increase of the interest rate payable to the holders;[614] the elimination of covenants relating to the amount of debt that the issuer may incur, limitations on the payment of dividends, the disposition of shares of certain subsidiaries and the transfer of manufacturing plants in sale and leaseback transactions;[615] the elimination of covenants restricting the payment of dividends or the making of investments to the parent company;[616] modifications to the covenant relating to the incurrence of indebtedness;[617] and amendments to the indenture as necessary to allow a specific reorganization, merger, or spin-off transaction.[618]

While the facts and circumstances described in each of the foregoing requests for no-action relief differ materially from one another, they share a number of common underlying features. First, the amendments being sought in each case did not affect the fundamental economic terms of the relevant securities (i.e., maturity, principal amount, currency, or rate of interest). Second, the amendments taken as a whole and/or the specific transaction that the amendments facilitated (whether

[609] See *Columbus and Southern Ohio Electric Company*, SEC No-Action Letter (March 12, 1973).

[610] See *San Diego Gas & Electric Company*, SEC No-Action Letter (April 3, 1975).

[611] See *Lockheed Aircraft*, fn 610 above.

[612] See *Tennessee Forging Steel Corporation*, SEC No-Action Letter (January 21, 1977).

[613] See *IDS Realty Trust*, fn 605 above.

[614] See *The Continental Group*, fn 609 above; *J. Ray McDermott & Co., Inc.*, SEC No-Action Letter (October 9, 1979).

[615] See *Eaton Corporation*, fn 605 above.

[616] See *The Sheraton Corp.*, fn 605 above.

[617] See *Reliance Financial Services Corporation*, SEC No-Action Letter (August 7, 1978).

[618] See *Sonderling Broadcasting Corporation*, SEC No-Action Letter (March 23, 1979). The staff's position in this instance was based by the same reasoning in the No-Action Letters issued to *Work Wear Corporation* (March 11, 1977 and December 17, 1976), the No-Action Letters issued to *Lockheed Aircraft Corporation* (February 14, 1975, July 14, 1975, and September 10, 1976) as well as the No-Action Letters issued to *IDS Realty Trust* (May 17, 1976) and *National Mortgage Fund* (available May 12, 1975). See also *Envirodyne, Inc.*, SEC No-Action Letter (July 26, 1976).

financial restructuring, merger, or a combination thereof) was viewed by the SEC staff as beneficial to the holders. Third, the justification put forward that registration under the Securities Act was not required focused on the rather insubstantial effect of the proposed amendments on the interests of the holders. Fourth, the relevant amendments were capable of being effected, unexceptionally, with the consents of the holders of the majority of the principal amount of securities outstanding and not with the consent of each individual holder (which is required for amendments of fundamental economic terms). The SEC staff accepted the view that, for purposes of registration under the Securities Act, the proposed indenture modifications did not create new securities if the modifications did not exceed the scope of the original investment agreement among the parties or materially increase the investment risks incurred by security holders.[619] Changes to the definitions and covenants that do not affect the basic financial terms are deemed to be adjustments to the contractual rights embedded in the indenture governing the debt securities and not new securities requiring registration under the Securities Act.[620]

The voting procedures in the relevant indenture are good indicators of whether a term is a *basic financial term* the amendment of which is likely to result in the creation of new security for purposes of the Securities Act or the Securities Exchange Act: if the amendment of the relevant term requires the consent of each holder of the relevant securities,[621] then any amendment effected with the unanimous consent of all the relevant holders is likely to result in the creation of a new security.[622] In the *Magic Marker* No-Action Letter,[623] the issuer proposed an amendment that would have extended the stated maturity date of the securities by up to ten years, increased the interest rate, and decreased the conversion price of the issuer's convertible debt securities. The relevant amendments required the consent of every holder affected thereby. In its no-action

[619] See, e.g., *Work Wear Corporation*, fn 620 above (amendment of restrictive covenant's subordination provisions, in connection with a merger); *Lockheed Aircraft Corp.*, fn 620 above (amendment of indenture to permit mandatory and optional redemptions, retirements, and dividend payments in connection with the financial restructuring of the issuer).

[620] See, for example, *Continental Telephone Company of Upstate New York*, SEC No-Action Letter (June 17, 1983).

[621] In some indentures, the unanimous consent of the holders of the securities has been replaced with the consent of the holders holding at least 90 percent or 95 percent. The changes of the basic financial terms can be effected even when a small minority of bondholders (no more than 5 percent or 10 percent) does not consent.

[622] See section 2.3 above.

[623] See *Magic Marker*, fn 596 above.

letter request, the issuer argued, in the alternative, that the transaction did not involve the sale of a new security under the Securities Act or, if it were deemed to involve the sale of a new security, the transaction would still be exempt from registration thereunder pursuant to Section 3(a)(9) of the Securities Act. In its response, the SEC staff stated that it would not recommend enforcement action if the consent solicitation and the related amendment were conducted in compliance with the requirements of Section 3(a)(9), thus expressing by negative inference the view that the transaction involved the sale of a new security in the first instance. A similar position in relation to an amendment extending stated maturity was taken by the staff in the *Allied-Carson* No-Action Letter.[624]

The no-action letter responses that have considered amendments and/or modifications of economic terms favorable to the holders, which under the relevant indentures can be made without any consent from the holders, have also taken the position that the improvement of the economic terms does not result in the offer or sale of a new security because the improvements can be made without any further consents and, for that reason, they are within the scope of the original investment decision.[625] The facts and granted no-action relief in the *Wilson Foods* No-Action Letter[626] probably offer the strongest support yet for the view that amendments that can be effected with less than the consent of every holder of the relevant security do not involve the sale of a new security for purposes of the Securities Act.

In the *Wilson Foods* No-Action Letter, the issuer sought the consent of the relevant bondholder majority to advance the stated maturity date of the debentures. The advancement of the maturity date (as opposed to an extension of the maturity date) was one of the changes that did

[624] See *Allied-Carson*, SEC No-Action Letter (February 12, 1976).

[625] See *PLM Co.*, fn 605 above (increase in interest rate by up to fifty basis points in consideration of waiver of merger covenant); *Alabama Gas Corp.*, SEC No-Action Letter (August 9, 1982) (increase in interest rate by up to 100 basis points in consideration of relaxation of covenants regarding replenishment of collateral); *NCNB Corp.*, SEC No-Action Letter (February 10, 1982) (increase in interest rate by fifty basis points in consideration of modifications of certain financial covenants); *Macmillian, Inc.*, fn 605 above (increase in interest rate by 1.4 percent in consideration of waiver of certain dividend and restricted payments tests); *Eaton Corp.*, fn 605 above (increase in interest rate by fifty basis points and addition of cross-default provision in consideration of elimination of covenants restricting funded debt, other indebtedness, and sales of shares of restricted subsidiaries and modification of covenant restricting asset sales).

[626] See fn 605 above.

not require the consent of every holder but could be completed with the requisite majority bondholder consent. Counsel argued that registration under the Securities Act should not be required on the facts because the relevant modifications did not exceed the scope of the original investment agreement among the parties or materially increase the investment risks incurred by the holders. Counsel specifically argued that the relevant indentures permitted the modifications sought by the issuer with the consent of the requisite majority and, consequently, those changes "represented contractual adjustments of the indentures," approved with a higher vote than would have been required under the indentures' own provisions regarding modification. Crucially, counsel argued that the advancement of the maturity date by the issuer and the holders was substantially different in nature from an extension of the maturity date. Indentures typically provide that the security's maturity date cannot be extended without the consent of each affected holder. Because such an extension is thus beyond the scope of the original agreement between the issuer and the trustee, it requires in essence a new investment agreement and, accordingly, the SEC has required in those circumstances that an issuer proposing such an extension register the securities under the Securities Act. By contrast, when an indenture clearly permits the advancing of the maturity date by majority holder consent, and such modification is proposed to be made with the requisite majority, the modification is in accordance with, not an alteration of, the original investment.[627]

The view that amendments that do not require the consent of every holder do not create a sale of new securities for purposes of the Securities Act is not without exception. Despite the arguments to the contrary,[628] a transaction that combines certain amendments which, individually, do not require the consent of every holder may still be regarded by the staff of the SEC as involving the sale of new securities if, in light of the totality of circumstances and the impact of the transaction on the investment position of the holders, the transactions involve such

[627] The same rationale was offered by counsel in other cases of no-action relief which the SEC staff agreed to provide, namely the changes being sought in the no-action relief were made pursuant to the relevant investment contract through the amendment provisions. See, for example, *Sonderling Broadcasting Corp.*, fn 620 above; *Lockheed Aircraft Corp.*, fn 620 above; *Work Wear Corp.*, fn 620 above; *Tennessee Forging Steel Corp.*, fn 614 above; *IDS Realty Trust*, fn 605 above; *San Diego Gas & Electric Co.*, fn 612 above; and *Columbus and South Ohio Electric Co.*, fn 611 above.

[628] See Bryant B. Edwards and Jon J. Bancone, fn 593 above.

fundamental changes as to involve the sale of a new security. In the *Gulf & Western Industries* No-Action Letter,[629] the staff refused to offer no-action relief in a series of amendments to an indenture pursuant to which all the protective covenants would be eliminated (including the covenant to provide separate financial statements of the issuer) in return for a guarantee issued by the parent company of the issuer. In effect, the transaction would involve a wholly owned subsidiary of the parent terminating the provision of separate financial statements to the holders of its debt securities and the elimination of all the other protective covenants in return for the benefit of a new parent guarantee. It is difficult to argue how the transaction did not involve the exchange of an investment in the credit of the subsidiary for a new investment in the credit of the parent company, especially in light of the change of control transaction (i.e., the acquisition of the subsidiary by the parent) that immediately preceded the request for no action. Consequently, even though each of the related transactions could be consummated with amendments of the relevant indenture that did not require the consent of each holder of the relevant securities, viewed as a series of related transactions leading to an investment in a new credit group (that of the parent company of the original issuer), the transactions involved a new investment decision and the creation of a new security.

The SEC's position is now codified in the summary of disclosure and telephonic interpretations which provides that a transaction may be deemed to involve the issuance of a new security if it represents a fundamental change in the nature of the holder's investment.[630] What constitutes a "fundamental change" is not defined but, in light of the consistent SEC staff positions on this point, it is safe to conclude that modifications and/or amendments that can be effected without any consent of the holders or with the consent of the holders of the majority of the principal amount (i.e., other than amendments that require the consent of every holder or a super-majority of holders, such as 90 percent or 95 percent) would not represent a fundamental change in the nature of the holder's investment.

[629] See *Gulf & Western Industries, Incorporated*, SEC No-Action Letter (September 6, 1976).

[630] See *SEC Compliance and Disclosure Interpretations*, para. 24 (Securities Act Sections, July 1997; last updated March 4, 2011). These Compliance and Disclosure Interpretations comprise the SEC staff's interpretations of the provisions of the Securities Act and are revised by the staff from time to time. They often codify preexisting views of the staff that may not have been previously communicated to the public.

5 "Exit" consent solicitations

One of the most important techniques for liability management and debt restructuring, as well as one of the most controversial,[631] is the exchange offer combined with a consent solicitation. The technique is simple and effective. Most indentures for corporate (as well as sovereign) debt securities protect a small number of fundamental bondholder rights (for example, the right to collect principal and interest when due, the currency of payments, and the ranking of the right of payment) which cannot be amended without the consent of every holder of the relevant securities. All the other provisions of the indenture may be amended by the holders of the simple (50 percent) or increased (66.6 percent) majority of principal amount of debt securities outstanding. Consequently, the requisite majority of holders may accept to tender their securities to the issuer for purchase by the issuer at an agreed price or exchange their securities for new securities issued by the issuer and, simultaneously, with their consent (an "exit consent"),[632] make such changes to the terms of the

[631] See generally, for an overview of the topic, Roe, fn 568 above, at 248–49; George W. Shuster, "The Trust Indenture Act and International Debt Restructurings," 14 *American Bankruptcy Institute Law Review* 431 (2006), at 434; Lee C. Buchheit and G. Mitu Gulati, "Exit Consents in Sovereign Bond Exchanges," 48 *UCLA Law Review* 59 (2000); See, e.g., Bryant B. Edwards and Jon J. Bancone, fn 593 above, at 571–72; John C. Coffee, Jr. and William A. Klein, "Bondholder Coercion: The Problem of Constrained Choice in Debt Tender Offers and Recapitalizations," 58 *University of Chicago Law Review* 1207 (1991), at 1241–42. For a critique of exit consents as coercive, see Victor Brudney, "Corporate Bondholders and Debtor Opportunism: In Bad Times and Good," 105 *Harvard Law Review* 1821 (1992), at 1833–34; Coffee and Klein, above, at 1212–33; Zohar Goshen, "Controlling Strategic Voting: Property Rule or Liability Rule?" 70 *Southern California Law Review* 741 (1997), at 785–88. There is also an interesting line of academic literature that seeks to perform an economic analysis of the behavior of holders of debt securities when presented with consent solicitations proposed by debtors (either sole consent solicitations or combined with exchange or tender offers). See, e.g., Royce De R. Barondes, "An Economic Analysis of the Potential for Coercion in Consent Solicitations for Bonds," 63 *Fordham Law Review* 749 (1994), with extensive bibliography annotated in the footnotes.

[632] In a case that attracted a lot of attention in global capital markets and the professionals acting in those markets, the English High Court of Justice, Chancery Division, recently issued an opinion on the legality of exit consents. In that opinion, the court defined "exit consents" for debt securities as follows: "[t]he issuer wishes to persuade all the holders of a particular bond issue to accept an exchange of their bonds for replacement bonds on different terms. The holders are all invited to offer their bonds for exchange, but on terms that they are required to commit themselves irrevocably to vote at a bondholders' meeting for a resolution amending the terms of the existing bonds so as seriously to damage or, as in the present case substantially destroy, the value of the rights arising from those existing bonds." See *Assenagon Asset Management SA* v. *Irish Bank Resolution*

existing securities, including eliminating covenants, as to make such existing securities unattractive as investments to any holder who may consider not accepting the terms of the new securities (in an exchange offer) or the cash payment agreed by the majority (in a tender offer). Through their consent to the amendments sought by the issuer, the requisite simple or increased majority of holders exercises its power to amend the outstanding securities and, through this exit consent, creates an incentive for all other holders to join them in the main transaction (an exchange offer or a tender offer for cash).

Issuers use *exit consent solicitations* as a technique that aims to maximize the prospects of success of the main liability management transaction. The financial terms of the new security (in an exchange offer) or the cash payment and the new capital structure of the issuer following the repayment of the outstanding securities through the tender offer will be designed to reflect the issuer's expected future debt-servicing capacity. The transaction will have been structured on the basis of certain assumptions, including in relation to the maximum participation of the existing creditors in the exercise. Any significant deviation from the fundamental economic assumptions regarding the principal amount of the debt securities to be exchanged or tendered is likely to prove fatal to the success of the transaction. The holders of the existing securities must be incentivized to participate. In addition, it is often the case that the terms of the new securities in an exchange offer are in conflict with or violate the covenants of the "old" securities that are being offered for exchange. A consent solicitation of participating holders consenting to eliminate all the covenants that may potentially conflict with the desirable terms of the new securities is the only way to complete the transaction.

An exit consent solicitation is effective because it uses an obvious element of coercion.[633] Existing holders are encouraged to participate in

Corp. Ltd (formerly Anglo Irish Bank Corp. Ltd), 2012 WL 2923062, Chancery Division (July 27, 2012) (hereinafter, "[*Irish Bank*]").

633 The coercive nature of exit consents is said to be obvious in the common transaction structure in which the issuer combines the exit consent with a tender or exchange offer, requiring participating holders to consent to the elimination of protective covenants from the relevant indenture or other investment contract. The result is that holders feel compelled to participate or, alternatively, continue to hold debt securities without any protective covenants. If holders representing the requisite principal amount of the outstanding debt securities (as required by the indenture) agree to the amendments, the entire class of debt securities (including those debt securities held by "dissenting" holders) will be modified pursuant to the accepted amendments. The coercion is thought to originate in part in the individual holder's concern that unless the holder participates

the main transaction because the terms of the debt securities that will remain outstanding if the unattractive amendments are effected will be much worse than the terms of the securities (or the cash payments) that are being offered to them. Without the threat of being left holding a debt security lacking any protective covenant, the minority holders may not have otherwise found the exchange or tender offer attractive. Using their ability under the indenture to effect changes to the terms with the consent of a simple or increased majority of holders, issuers ensure that, through the exit consent technique, minority holders are not going to ruin the transaction for everybody. Whether minority holders are unable to see the benefits of the exchange offer presented to them (benefits that are obvious to the majority holders who are happy to consent to the relevant amendments) or opportunistically holding out in the hope of better recovery in the future, their ability to threaten the success of the exchange or tender offer is diminished if it becomes clear to them, through the coercive effects of the exit consent solicitation, that their only option is to participate.[634]

5.1 The legality of exit consents

Exit consent solicitations, combined with exchange or tender offers for debt securities, have thus far withstood claims of illegality. Critics of exit consent solicitations have not had an easy task. After all, when a debt security contains terms permitting certain types of amendments to be

in the tender or exchange offer, the relevant securities, devoid of any protective covenants and other protections and experiencing liquidity problems, will be worth substantially less than the relevant market price of those securities prior to the tender or exchange offer, especially in the event of bankruptcy or insolvency. Therefore, the exit consent, the priority and more attractive features of the new securities issued in the exchange offer, the likelihood of insolvency, and the elimination of protective covenants are thought to create a coercive environment in which the pressure to participate in the tender or exchange offer is too great. In these circumstances, issuers may find it value-enhancing (for the value of the equity) to force holders into accepting coercive offers (even when a rational investor would not have participated in such offer absent the coercive exit consent). Put in different words, the offer is coercive if the offer price (in the tender or exchange offer) would be lower than the value of the existing securities in the event of a failure of the tender or exchange offer. See generally Lewis S. Peterson, "Who's Being Greedy? A Theoretical and Empirical Examination of Holdouts and Coercion in Debt Tender and Exchange Offers," 103 *Yale Law Journal* 505 (1993).

634 See generally a wealth of academic commentary on this point in Roe, fn 568 above; Shuster, fn 633 above; Buchheit and Gulati, fn 633 above; Bryant B. Edwards and Jon J. Bancone, fn 593 above; Coffee and Klein, fn 633 above.

made to the security or the relevant indenture with the consent of the holders of a certain agreed principal amount of the securities, it is difficult to see what the complaint can be against the issuer of those securities seeking the consent of the holders to effect any and all of the changes permitted to be made with such consent. All the holders of the relevant securities accepted, at the time of their original investment, that the terms of such securities permitted a majority (simple or increased) of the holders to effect changes to the terms, including some very unattractive changes, which once made, would be binding on all the holders without exception.

What triggers some pause in the case of the exit consent is entirely the "exit" element, not the power and effectiveness of collective action: the holders consenting to the relevant amendments are not the holders whose investment is going to be adversely affected by the relevant changes; they are "out" but the amendments will affect someone else's investment security. When a holder who has consented to the adverse changes to the terms of an investment security has made a commercial decision to dispose of that security, an obvious question of bad faith is raised.

The leading case on exit consent solicitations is *Katz* v. *Oak Industries, Inc.* (hereinafter, "*Katz*"),[635] a Delaware case. Oak Industries ("Oak") was in deep financial difficulties and had agreed, in a distressed sale, to sell one of its operating divisions, plus a percentage of its common stock, to a corporate buyer for cash. Crucially, the transaction was conditional on the repurchase by Oak, through an exchange offer, of not less than 85 percent of the outstanding principal amount of its debt securities. Pursuant to the terms of the agreement, Oak made an offer to holders of its debt securities to exchange such securities for a specified amount of common stock plus rights entitling the holders to a future cash payment of a certain percentage of the principal amount of the exchanged securities from the proceeds from the sale of Oak's operating division. Crucially for the legal analysis that follows, the cash payment was going to be higher than the then current market prices of Oak's debt securities. Holders of Oak's debt securities tendering their securities in the exchange offer were required to consent simultaneously to amendments of the indentures eliminating all protective covenants. The *exit amendments* were clearly and unambiguously going to remove significant negotiated protections for the benefit of the holders and would have adverse consequences to debt holders who elected not to participate in the exchange offer. One of the holders filed an application to enjoin the consummation

[635] 508 A.2d 873 (Del. Ch. 1986).

of the exchange offer on the grounds that the offer was "coercive" and violated the issuer's obligation to act in good faith with respect to its bondholders.

In a seminal 1986 opinion of Chancellor Allen, the Delaware Court of Chancery refused to grant the injunction and found that: (i) the relationship between a corporation and its holders of debt securities is contractual in nature;[636] implicit fiduciary obligations on the part of the corporations should not and would not be read into the relationship by the courts;[637] (ii) even if the terms of the issuer's exchange offer could be characterized as "coercive," this characterization alone was of limited analytical utility and not relevant unless the coercion was wrongful; (iii) the appropriate legal test for determining whether the issuer breached an obligation to

636 This was neither controversial nor ground-breaking but consistent with a long line of earlier and contemporaneous cases. What follows is a small sample of earlier cases that had confirmed the contractual, arm's length, and not fiduciary, relationship between the holders of the debt securities and the issuer of those securities. "It has now become firmly fixed in our law that among the duties owed by directors of a Delaware corporation to holders of that corporation's debt instruments there is no duty of the broad and exacting nature characterized as fiduciary duty." *Simons* v. *Cogan*, 452 A.2d 785, 786 & n.1 (Del. Ch. 1987) (citing *Katz* among an extensive list of cases), aff'd, 549 A.2d 300 (Del. 1988) (hereinafter, "*Simons*"). The Delaware Chancery Court, in *Simons*, stated that "courts of this state have consistently recognized that neither an issuer of debentures nor a controlling shareholder owes to holders of the company's debt securities duties of the special sort characterized as fiduciary in character." Ibid., at 788. See also to the same effect, *Shenandoah Life Ins. Co.* v. *Valero Energy Corp.*, No. 9032, slip op. at 10 n.2 (Del. Ch. June 21, 1988); *Continental Ill. Nat'l Bank & Trust Co.* v. *Hunt Int'l Resources Corp.*, No. 7888, slip op. at 9 (Del. Ch. February 27, 1987) ("the relationship between a corporation and its directors and debenture holders is contractual, not 'fiduciary,' in nature is well settled in this state"); *Eastern Air Lines*, Nos. 8700, 8701, 8711, slip op.; *Norte & Co.* v. *Manor Healthcare Corp.*, Nos. 6827, 6831, slip op. at 10–11 (Del. Ch. November 21, 1985); See also *MacAndrews & Forbes Holdings* v. *Revlon, Inc.*, 506 A.2d 173, 1982 (Del. 1986).

637 The primary rationale for the absence of a fiduciary duty in this context is that "[u]nlike shareholders, to whom such [fiduciary] duties are owed, holders of debt may turn to documents that exhaustively detail the rights and obligations of the issuer, the trustee under the indenture, and the holders of the securities." See *Simons*, fn 638 above, at 786. Consequently, "courts traditionally have directed bondholders to protect themselves against . . . self-interested issuer action with explicit contractual provisions. Holders of senior securities, such as bonds, are outside the legal model of the firm for protective purposes: a heavy black-letter line bars the extension of corporate fiduciary protections to them." Ibid., at 78; Chancellor Allen in *Simons* concluded that "[t]o introduce the powerful abstraction of 'fiduciary duty' into the highly negotiated and exhaustively documented commercial relationship between an issuer of convertible securities and the holders of such securities would, or so it now appears to me, risk greater insecurity and uncertainty than could be justified by the occasional increment of fairness that might be hoped for." Ibid. at 791.

deal fairly and in good faith with its bondholders was whether the parties who negotiated the terms of those instruments, had they foreseen the exchange offer and consent solicitation the issuer eventually made, would have forbidden such an action; (iv) in this case, the parties to the underlying indentures, had they foreseen the issuer's offer, may well not have prevented the issuer from making an offer to all bondholders that returned in cash to participating holders more than the then current market price of the securities; and (v) the issuer's board of directors, in approving these arrangements, may have reasonably concluded that this represented "the last good chance to regain vitality for the enterprise."

Whether US courts will always dismiss complaints against exit consents is uncertain. After all, the offer presented to the bondholders in *Katz*, the leading case on the topic, included a cash payment to holders above the then market value of the debt securities sought to be exchanged. Although inherently coercive, the exchange offer and consent solicitation in *Katz* sought to implement a restructuring plan that made economic sense and offered above-market returns for the holders of the debt securities. US courts have yet to opine on the use of exit consents in situations where the exit consent is being used to implement an unreasonable restructuring plan.[638]

Subsequent Delaware and New York courts have repeatedly cited Chancellor Allen's opinion in *Katz* with approval.[639] Since *Katz* was decided in the Delaware courts in 1986, exit consents have been the subject of considerable academic debate but the technique has been repeatedly used to this day in corporate debt restructurings without successful legal challenge. It is now firmly established in the judicial authorities that, absent extraordinary circumstances, the holders of debt securities are protected solely by the contractual protections reflected in the terms of the securities and the relevant indenture.[640]

638 See Buchheit and Gulati, fn 633 above; it is not clear that US courts will always, in every case, uphold the legality of exit consents; see also Hal S. Scott, "A Bankruptcy Procedure for Sovereign Debtors," 37 *International Lawyer* 103 (2003), at 118.

639 See, for example, *GAF Union Carbide*, 624 F. Supp. 1016, 1021, 1031–32 (S.D.N.Y. 1985) (dictum implicitly approving exit consents).

640 See *Harris Trust and Savings Bank* v. *E-II Holdings, Inc.*, 926 F.2d 636, 641 (7th Cir. 1991), cert. denied, 112 S. Ct. 192 (1991) (observing that there was "no cognizable legal basis" upon which relief might be available, the Seventh Circuit refused to imply a covenant to provide financial information not expressly set forth in the indenture); see also *Metropolitan Life Ins. Co.*, 906 F.2d at 890 ("[a]ny suggestion that RJR bargained for and obtained a period to cure of longer than the period expressly and unambiguously provided in the indentures is wrong as a matter of law"); *Carson* v. *Long-Bell Lumber Corp.*,

5.2 *Exit consents and the federal securities laws*

There is no rule or regulation under the Securities Exchange Act (including Section 14(e) and the rules and regulations thereunder in relation to tender and exchange offers), the Trust Indenture Act, or the Securities Act that precludes issuers from soliciting exit consents.[641] The SEC has also not taken a view against the practice of exit consents despite voices, including investor groups, calling for regulatory intervention in this area.[642]

73 F.2d 397, 402 (8th Cir. 1934), cert. denied, 294 U.S. 707 (1935) ("[i]t is elementary that a simple contract creditor, without having reduced his claim to judgment, and without having exhausted his remedy at law, or having acquired some lien upon the property transferred, cannot maintain a suit to set aside such transfer"); *American Express Travel Related Services Co.* v. *Washington Public Power Supply System*, 488 U.S. 805 (1988) ("bondholders' rights are created and protected by contracts between the bondholders and issuers"); *Hazzard* v. *Chase National Bank of City of New York*, 287 N.Y.S. 541 at 566–67 (1936), aff'd, 14 N.Y.S.2d 147 (1939) ("so long as the trustee does not step beyond the provisions of the indenture itself, its liability is measured, not by the ordinary relationship of the trustee and cestuique, but by the expressed agreement between the trustee and the obligor of the trust mortgage. Where the terms of the indenture are clear, no obligations or duties in conflict with them will be implied."); *Nobel* v. *European Mortgage & Investment Corp.*, 165 A. 157 (Del. Ch. 1933) (the indenture is "quite clear in reserving to the bondholders complete liberty of action to enforce all payments due them whether for principal or coupons so long as the procedure they adopt is not under the indenture"); see also American Bar Foundation, *Commentaries on Indentures* (1971), at 2 ("the debt security-holder can do nothing to protect himself against actions of the borrower which jeopardize its ability to pay the debt unless he takes a mortgage or other collateral or establishes his rights through contractual provisions set forth in the debt agreement or indenture").

641 For a discussion of earlier regulation proposals, see Barbara Franklin, "SEC Considers Stiffer Rules for Tender Offers," *New York Law Journal* (1990), May 24, at 5.

642 In 1990, FMR Corp., the parent corporation of Fidelity Management and Research Company, and The Prudential Insurance Company of America petitioned the SEC to initiate a rule-making project to revise Rule 14e-1 under the Securities Exchange Act. The petitioners argued that a tender offer conditioned on the prior receipt of exit consents is impermissibly coercive since a bondholder who does not know whether the consent solicitation will be successful will be effectively forced to tender and consent. On that basis, the petitioners argued that the result of the consent solicitation was material information relating to the value of the security which should be disclosed to the holders at least ten days prior to the expiration date for the tender offer and, therefore, the withholding of that information in a concurrent consent solicitation and tender offer should be considered to be a deceptive and manipulative practice within the meaning of Section 14(e) of the Securities Exchange Act. On that basis, the petitioners proposed a new subsection (e) to Rule 14e-1 under the Securities Exchange Act which would provide that, during the course of a tender offer, the issuer shall not solicit the holders of the subject securities for any consent, proxy, or otherwise effect a material change in the terms of the relevant security. See references to this petition in Royce De R. Barondes, fn 633 above.

5.3 Payments for consent

Within a few months from the delivery of the *Katz* opinion, Chancellor Allen had a second opportunity to consider the issue of coercion in corporate liability management transactions in the case of *Kass* v. *Eastern Airlines* (hereinafter, "*Kass*").[643] In *Kass*, the issuer of the debt securities (i.e., Eastern Airlines) solicited existing holders for amendments to its outstanding bonds in order to permit the issuer to pay a cash dividend to its shareholders following a proposed merger. The indenture precluded the payment of dividends because the issuer was at that time not in compliance with the applicable financial ratios specified in the indentures. The issuer agreed to pay a specified cash payment (or, alternatively, Eastern Airlines ticket vouchers) to those holders consenting to the amendments.

In the lawsuit that followed, the plaintiff complained that the payment for consent was "vote buying," violated public policy, and constituted a breach of the issuer's implied duty to deal fairly and in good faith with the holders of its debt securities. Chancellor Allen disagreed with both arguments and dismissed the complaint. He found that: (i) there is nothing wrong with vote-buying in the context of corporate debt securities on the part of an issuer of corporate bonds, as long as the offer is made on equal terms to all bondholders; and (ii) as far as the good faith and fair dealing argument is concerned, Chancellor Allen's opinion in *Katz* was still good law. Chancellor Allen's opinion confirmed that payments for consents, within the limits described in the opinion, were permissible.[644]

5.4 Exit consents and the Trust Indenture Act

The ability of the issuer to induce the completion of a restructuring exchange offer through the coercive effects of simultaneous exit consents appears to be dilutive of the bondholder protections of the Trust Indenture Act, especially Section 316(b).

While the holders of the majority of the principal amount of the outstanding debt securities cannot vote certain fundamental amendments to the terms of the securities, such as a reduction of principal amount or

[643] Del. Ch., Civil Action Nos. 8700, 8701, 8711, Allen C. (November 14, 1986).

[644] See also *Pisik* v. *BCI Holdings Corp.*, No. 14593/87, slip op. at 3 (N.Y. Sup. Ct. June 21, 1987) (reaching the same conclusion under New York law on essentially the same facts as *Kass*); see also an English case reaching the same conclusion, *Azavedo* v. *IMCOPA*, 12 WL 1933371, Queen's Bench Division (Commercial Court).

interest or an extension of the stated maturity date,[645] the same restructuring effect can be achieved indirectly through the exchange of the debt securities with newly issued securities, boosted by a simultaneous exit consent that is designed to eliminate all the non-core protective covenants of the indenture. What cannot be achieved directly (through the consents of the holders of the majority outstanding principal amount of securities) can be induced indirectly (through the combination of a restructuring exchange offer and an exit consent solicitation).[646] The devaluation of the existing securities through the consensual elimination of protective covenants could be seen as an indirect impairment of the right of holders to receive the agreed principal amount and/or interest, especially if the end result in a combined exit consent and exchange offer is indeed the exchange of the securities for newly issued securities with fundamental economic terms that could not have been voted on by the majority due to the protective provisions of Section 316(b) of the Trust Indenture Act. To date, US courts have not read Section 316(b) in this broad manner.

5.5 *Exit consents in English law*

The technique of exit consents for international debt restructurings has attracted renewed practical and academic interest following the *Assenagon Asset Management*,[647] a 2012 decision of the English High Court of Justice, Chancery Division.

In *Irish Bank*, the claimant had acquired subordinated debt securities issued by Anglo Irish Bank Corporation Ltd (the "issuer"). The securities were redeemable at par, on maturity, or prior thereto. The instrument governing the securities, a trust deed governed by English law, permitted the holders of the securities, by extraordinary resolution, to assent to any modification of the provisions contained in the trust deed which shall be proposed by the issuer or the trustee. An extraordinary resolution could only pass if it was accepted by 75 percent of persons voting at a holders' meeting in which there was a two-thirds quorum. When the issuer became insolvent in the 2008 financial crisis, the Irish government rescued it by guaranteeing certain liabilities that included some of the relevant securities. Following the issuer's nationalization, the Irish government announced that the issuer's subordinated liabilities (including

[645] See section 2.3 above. [646] See generally Roe, fn 568 above.
[647] See fn 634 above.

the securities) would share in the issuer's losses, either through a voluntary restructuring of the issuer's liabilities or through legislation. To effect the restructuring, the issuer announced an exchange offer in which holders of the securities were invited to exchange their securities for new senior notes (having 20 percent of the face value of the securities offered for exchange). As a condition to the exchange, consenting holders were asked to vote in favor of a resolution to amend the terms of the securities to grant a call option on unexchanged securities for a nominal cash payment. The claimant in *Irish Bank* chose not to participate in the exchange offer (which was accepted with a comfortable majority) and sought a declaration that the exchange offer was invalid for three reasons: (i) the resolution that conferred power on the bank to expropriate the securities for nominal consideration constituted an *ultra vires* act; (ii) majority holders who voted in favor of the exchange offer held their notes beneficially for and on account of the issuer, and therefore, those votes should have been disregarded pursuant to the terms of the trust deed; and (iii) the resolution was oppressive and unfair, because the exercise of power by the majority holders was not in good faith and conferred no benefit to the holders as a class.

The opinion of the court was based on the

> well recognised constraint upon the exercise of [power to bind the minority] by a majority, namely that it must be exercised *bona fide* in the best interests of the class of bondholders as a class, and not in a manner which is oppressive or otherwise unfair to the minority sought to be bound.[648]

The court rejected the claimant's first argument, pointing out a simple truth: in light of the provisions of the trust deed as a whole, the holders must be deemed to have assented to the exercise of a power in the majority to bind the minority both to a cancellation of the principal payable on the securities and to a cancellation of the minimum interest payable thereon.

The court, however, accepted the claimant's second argument. The securities offered and accepted for exchange were actually held for the benefit of the issuer by the time of the holders' meeting under contracts for sale between the relevant holders and the issuer, thus conferring a beneficial interest in the securities on the issuer from the moment of the issuer's acceptance of the exchange on the day before the meeting. Thus, the securities at that time were caught by the prohibition in the trust

648 Ibid.

deed of voting the securities in the interests of the issuer rather than in the interests of the holders as a class.

The court also considered the claimant's third argument and held that the question of abuse of power raised a question of wide importance for the bond market. The court held that there was not a single holder who can be said to have accepted the exchange offer unaffected by the coercive effect of the exit consent. Using strong words, the court accepted that the exchange offer was no more than a negative inducement to deter holders from refusing the proffered exchange; the majority holders, rather than the issuer, wielded the negative inducement; and the offer was designed in substance to destroy rather than to enhance the value of the securities and had, on its own, no conceivable benefit to the holders as a class.[649] On that basis, the court held that it was not lawful for the majority to lend its aid to the coercion of the minority by voting for a resolution which expropriates the minority's rights under their bonds for a nominal consideration.

Although the facts in *Irish Bank* were particularly harsh and unusual (the amendments resulted in the effective expropriation of holdout securities for a nominal consideration), it is difficult to see how the case will not have pervasive effects on the use of exit consents in corporate debt restructurings for securities governed by English law. On the other hand, the decision may not necessarily preclude debt exchanges conferring real market value to non-consenting holders (for example, when securities held by minority holders are exchanged for new securities or cash payment at a premium over current market values). The importance of the decision should not be underestimated. Exit consents were tested for legality under English law for the first time and the case will clearly set the benchmark for future cases. The court also recognized that its holding was contrary to decisions under US law in which exit consents have survived judicial scrutiny in the face of challenge by minority holders alleging a coercive exchange offer.

[649] Ibid.

INDEX

Lightning Source UK Ltd.
Milton Keynes UK
UKOW06f1117190416

272538UK00014B/494/P